VMware vRealize Orchestrator Cookbook

Second Edition

Over 90 recipes to satisfy all your automation needs and leverage vRealize Orchestrator 7.1 for your projects

Daniel Langenhan

BIRMINGHAM - MUMBAI

VMware vRealize Orchestrator Cookbook

Second Edition

First published: January 2015

Second edition: October 2016

Production reference: 1241016

Published by Packt Publishing Ltd.
Livery Place
35 Livery Street
Birmingham
B3 2PB, UK.

ISBN 978-1-78646-278-7

www.packtpub.com

Credits

Author

Daniel Langenhan

Reviewers

Burke Azbill
Christophe Decanini
Spas Kaloferov

Commissioning Editor

Pratik Shah

Acquisition Editor

Divya Poojari

Content Development Editor

Parshva Sheth

Technical Editor

Murtaza Tinwala

Copy Editor

Safis Editing

Project Coordinator

Sheejal Shah

Proofreader

Safis Editing

Indexer

Tejal Daruwale Soni

Production Coordinator

Aparna Bhagat

Cover Work

Aparna Bhagat

About the Author

Daniel Langenhan is a Virtualisation expert with formidable skills in Architecture, Design and Implementation for large multi-tier systems. His experience and knowledge of process management, enterprise-level storage, Linux and Windows operation systems has made him and his business a highly sought after international consultancy in the Asia-Pacific and European regions for multinational clientele in the areas of Finance, Communication, Education and Government. Daniel has been working with VMware products since 2002 and is directly associated with VMWare since 2008. His proven track record of successful integrations of Virtualisation into different business areas while minimizing cost and maximizing reliability and effectiveness of the solution for his clients.

Currently, Daniel is operating in the Europe and Asia-Pacific region with his company vLeet GmbH and Melbourne Business Boosters Pty Ltd.

Daniel's expertise and practical approach to VMWare has resulted in the publication of the following books:

- *Instant VMware vCloud Starter*, Packt Publishing
- *VMware View Security Essentials*, Packt Publishing
- *VMware vCloud Director Cookbook*, Packt Publishing
- *VMware vRealize Orchestrator Cookbook*, Packt Publishing
- *VMware vRealize Orchestrator Essentials*, Packt Publishing

He has also lent his expertise to many other publishing projects as a Technical Editor.

This book would not have been possible without my understanding and loving wife. She not only endured a "tunnel-vision" writer but actively contributed as Editor number 1.

I would also acknowledge Pooja Nair, who helped me out with valuable editing and checking.

About the Reviewers

Burke Azbill has been a technology professional since 1996 and has held certifications from Cisco, Citrix, ITIL, Linux Professional Institute, Microsoft, Novell, and VMware. He joined VMware in 2007 as part of the acquisition of Dunes Technologies from Lausanne, Switzerland where he began his work with Orchestrator. Burke is a founder and contributor of the blog http://www.vcoteam.info as well as a leading contributor to the VMTN Communities for Orchestrator. During his tenure at VMware, Burke has trained hundreds of employees on Orchestrator, built many integrations for customers and partners, and has worked various roles in the VMworld Hands On Labs. Publications include contributing author for *VMware vCloud Architecture Toolkit (vCAT)*, VMware Press 2013 and technical resource for *Automating vSphere with VMware vCenter Orchestrator*, VMware Press 2012) and *VMware vSphere for Dummies*, For Dummies 2011.

Christophe Decanini is a Consulting Architect at VMware, Inc., where he started in 2007; currently, he is the technical lead for Orchestration. Based in Gland, Switzerland, Christophe is a global resource supporting customers in their orchestration and automation needs. He has presented orchestration solutions at conferences such as VMworld and is the main contributor of the www.vcoteam.info blog and in the official VMware Orchestrator community. Christophe has reviewed and contributed to books covering vCenter Orchestrator including *VMware vCloud Architecture Toolkit*. Christophe was awarded the vExpert designation for several years given to the top VMware evangelists in the industry. He has 19 years of experience in IT automation and holds a bachelor's degree in computer science.

Spas Kaloferov has been a technology professional since 2004 and holds over 30 industry certifications. He studied in Germany and is now living back in Sofia, Bulgaria, where he joined the VMWare family in 2014. While working with many VMware products, his work remains mainly focused on Orchestrator. He has been an Orchestrator contributor not only internally, but also via the VMTN communities and his personal blog: http://kaloferov.com/blog.

www.PacktPub.com

For support files and downloads related to your book, please visit www.PacktPub.com.

Did you know that Packt offers eBook versions of every book published, with PDF and ePub files available? You can upgrade to the eBook version at www.PacktPub.com and as a print book customer, you are entitled to a discount on the eBook copy. Get in touch with us at service@packtpub.com for more details.

At www.PacktPub.com, you can also read a collection of free technical articles, sign up for a range of free newsletters and receive exclusive discounts and offers on Packt books and eBooks.

https://www.packtpub.com/mapt

Get the most in-demand software skills with Mapt. Mapt gives you full access to all Packt books and video courses, as well as industry-leading tools to help you plan your personal development and advance your career.

Why subscribe?

- Fully searchable across every book published by Packt
- Copy and paste, print, and bookmark content
- On demand and accessible via a web browser

Table of Contents

Preface

1

Chapter 1: Installing and Configuring Orchestrator

11

Introduction   11

Licensing   12

vRealize Orchestrator 7 changes   12

Orchestrator appliance basics   13

Orchestrator and vRealize Automation (vRA)   14

Deploying the Orchestrator appliance   15

Getting ready   15

How to do it…   15

Download   15

Deploy   16

Log in to the Orchestrator Client   18

Log into Control Center   19

How it works…   20

There's more…   21

See also   22

Important Orchestrator settings   22

Getting ready   22

How to do it…   22

Starting, stopping, and restarting the Orchestrator service   22

Licensing   23

Package Signing Certificate   24

Trusted SSL certificates   25

Force plugins reinstall   25

How it works…   25

See also   26

Configuring an external database   26

Getting ready   26

How to do it…   26

How it works…   28

Sizing   28

Database roles   29

Exporting and importing a database   29

Purging the Database   30

There's more…   30

Microsoft SQL   30

Oracle   31
Internal PostgreSQL   31
See also   31

Configuring external authentication   31
Getting ready   31
How to do it…   32
vSphere (PSC) and vRealize Automation (vRA)   32
SSO (legacy)   33
LDAP   35
How it works…   37
vRealize Automation and vSphere Authentication   37
Test login   38
Internal LDAP   38
There's more…   39
See also   39

Connecting to vCenter   40
Getting ready   40
How to do it…   40
Well, there is that…   42
How it works…   43
Access, rights, and logging   43
Technical user   43
vRA, Orchestrator, and vCenter   44
See also   44

Installing plugins   44
Getting ready   44
How to do it…   45
How it works…   46
Plugin log level   46
Updating plugins   47
Disabling and uninstalling plugins   47
See also   47

Updating Orchestrator   47
Getting ready   48
How to do it…   48
Using an ISO file   48
Using the VMware repository   49
Applying the update   49
How it works…   49
There's more…   50
See also   51

Moving from Windows to appliance   51
Getting ready   51

How to do it...   51
    Migration tool   52
    External database   53
    Package transfer   54
How it works...   54
There's more...   55
Orchestrator Client and 4K display scaling   57
Getting ready   57
How to do it...   57
How it works...   58
There's more...   58

Chapter 2: Optimizing Orchestrator Configuration   59

Introduction   59
Tuning the appliance   60
Getting ready   60
How to do it...   60
    Virtual Hardware   61
    Changing the IP and hostname   61
    Setting the time (NTP)   61
    Turning SSH access to Orchestrator on and off   62
    Switching off unneeded services   62
    Root account expires   63
How it works...   63
See also   64
Tuning Java   64
Getting ready   64
How to do it...   64
How it works...   64
    JVM metrics in Control Center   65
See also   66
Configuring the Kerberos authentication   66
Getting ready   66
How to do it...   67
How it works...   67
See also   68
Configuring access to the local filesystem   68
Getting ready   68
How to do it...   68
    Fast and easy   68
    Configuring access   68
How it works...   69

There's more…   69
See also   70
Configuring the Orchestrator service SSL certificate   70
Getting ready   70
How to do it…   70
Self-signed certificates   70
Using VMCA generated certificates   71
CA-signed certificate   72
How it works…   73
Default, self-signed, or CA-signed?   73
VMCA   74
PEM encoded files   74
There's more…   74
Getting the SSL store password   75
Backing up the default certificates   75
Creating certificates and requests   75
Generating certificates with alternative names (SAN certificate)   76
Signing and importing certificates   76
See also   77
Orchestrator log files   77
Getting ready   77
How to do it…   77
Server log in Control Center   77
Configuring the server log with the Control Center   78
Accessing the log files via SSH   79
Changing log file behavior   80
How it works…   81
See also   82
Redirecting Orchestrator logs to an external server   82
Getting ready   82
vRealize Log Insight   82
How to do it…   83
Syslog with Log4J   83
Log Insight Agent   84
How it works…   85
Configuring the Orchestrator Log Insight Agent to forward to Syslog   86
There's more…   87
See also   87
Backup and recovery   87
Getting ready   87
How to do it…   87
Backing up Orchestrator configuration   88
Backing up an internal database   89

Restore	89
How it works…	91
External database	91
There's more…	91
Cron job	91
vRO policy	91
vRO Control Center API	92
See also	92
Control Center titbits	92
Getting ready	92
How to do it…	92
Inspecting workflows	92
System properties	94
Changing the Control Center user name	95
File System Browser	96
How it works…	97
Control Center API	98
System properties	98
There's more…	99
See also	100
Chapter 3: Distributed Design	101
Introduction	101
Cluster design	102
Distributed design	103
Geographically Distributed	104
Logically Distributed	104
Scaling out	105
Central management	105
Building an Orchestrator cluster	106
Getting ready	106
How to do it…	106
Preparation work	106
Configuring the first node of the cluster	107
Configure cluster settings	108
Join a node to the cluster	109
Configuring an Orchestrator cluster in vSphere	110
Playing with the cluster	111
Push configuration	112
How it works…	113
SSL Certificates in vRO7.1.0	114
Cluster and Orchestrator Client	114
Changing cluster content	114
Changing cluster settings	114

Removing a node from the cluster 115
There's more… 115
Logs 115
Another method of load-balancing 115
Example workflow – cluster test 116
See also 116
Load-balancing Orchestrator 116
Getting ready 117
How to do it… 117
Creating a new NSX Edge 117
Configuring the load-balancer 119
Dealing with SSL certificates 119
Monitors – health checks 120
Configure pools 120
Virtual server 121
Done 122
How it works… 123
SSL certificates and load-balancing 124
SSL passthrough 124
SSL SAN (SSL passthrough) 124
SSL offload 124
Load-balanced Orchestrator cluster with vSphere Web Client 125
See also 126
Upgrading a cluster 127
Getting ready 127
How to do it… 127
Minor upgrades 127
Major upgrades 127
How it works… 128
See also 128
Managing remote Orchestrators 128
Getting ready 128
How to do it… 128
Adding an Orchestrator server 129
Creating proxy workflows 130
Managing packets on the remote Orchestrator 131
How it works… 132
See also 134
Synchronizing Orchestrator elements between Orchestrator servers 134
Getting ready 134
How to do it… 134
How it works… 135
See also 136

Chapter 4: Programming Skills | 137

Introduction | 137
    The Orchestrator icons | 137
    Gotcha | 139
    Auto-setup of parameters | 140

Version control | 141
  Getting ready | 142
  How to do it... | 142
    Showing differences between versions | 143
    Reverting to an older version | 144
  How it works... | 144
  See also | 145

Changing elements in a workflow | 145
  Getting ready | 145
  How to do it... | 145
    Changing the parameters of workflows and actions | 145
    Renaming and moving actions | 146
    Finding related elements | 147
  How it works... | 148
  See also | 149

Importing and exporting Orchestrator elements | 149
  Getting ready | 149
  How to do it... | 149
    Exporting an object | 149
    Importing an element | 150
  How it works... | 150
  See also | 151

Working with packages | 151
  Getting ready | 152
  How to do it... | 152
    Create a new package | 153
    Export a package | 153
    Import a package | 154
    Deleting a package | 156
    Import from remote | 157
  How it works... | 158
    Export and import options | 159
  There's more... | 160
  See also | 162

Workflow auto documentation | 162
  Getting ready | 163
  How to do it... | 163

How it works… 163

Resuming failed workflows 164

Getting ready 164

How to do it… 164

How it works… 166

There's more… 166

See also 167

Using the workflow debugging function 167

Getting ready 167

How to do it… 167

How it works… 168

There's more… 169

See also 169

Undelete workflows and actions 170

Getting ready 170

How to do it… 170

How it works… 171

Scheduling workflows 171

Getting ready 171

How to do it… 171

How it works… 173

There's more… 174

See also 174

Sync presentation settings 175

Getting ready 175

How to do it… 175

How it works… 176

Locking elements 176

Getting ready 176

How to do it… 176

Locking workflows 176

Unlocking workflows 177

How it works… 177

See also 177

Chapter 5: Visual Programming 179

Introduction 179

Variables (general, inputs, and outputs) 179

Variables in the general section 180

Variables in the input section 180

Variables in the output section 181

Variable types	181
Working with a schema	182
Presentation	183
Scripting with logs	183
Getting ready	183
How to do it…	183
Creating logs	184
Checking log files	185
How it works…	186
Log file location	187
Altering log elements	187
See also	187
Scripting with decisions	188
Getting ready	188
How to do it…	188
Basic decision	189
Custom decisions	190
Decision activity	191
The Switch element	191
How it works…	192
JavaScript – if and else	194
JavaScript – Switch	195
See also	195
Error handling in workflows	195
Getting ready	196
How to do it…	196
Default error handler	197
How it works…	197
Ignoring errors	198
The handle error element	199
See also	199
Scripting with loops	200
Getting ready	200
How to do it…	200
The decision loop	200
The Foreach loop	202
How it works…	203
Types of decision loops	204
Foreach and arrays	204
JavaScript	205
There's more…	206
See also	206
Workflow presentations	206

Getting ready   207
How to do it…   207
Preparation   207
Description   207
In-parameter properties   208
Steps and groups   209
Hiding input values   210
Basic linking   211
How it works…   211
General properties   212
Plugin-specific properties   213
select value as   214
show in inventory   214
Specify a root object to be shown in the chooser   214
Authorized only   214
There's more…   215
See also   215
Linking actions in presentations   216
Getting ready   216
How to do it…   216
How it works…   217
See also   218
Changing credentials during runtime   218
Getting ready   218
How to do it…   219
How it works…   220
See also   220

Chapter 6: Advanced Programming   221

Introduction   221
Cool stuff in the scripting tasks   222
A – show all objects   222
B – find stuff   222
C – line and character   222
JavaScript (the very basics)   223
JavaScript tricks and tips   223
Is a string part of another string? (indexOf)   223
Case sensitivity (toUpperCase)   224
Getting rid of extra space (trim)   224
String replacement with regular expressions (replace)   225
Check a variable for type (instanceof)   225
Working with dates   226
Add minutes to a date   227
JavaScript complex variables   227

Getting ready 227
How to do it... 227
   Arrays 227
   Properties 228
   Objects 229
How it works... 230
   Array methods 230
   Properties within properties 231
   Array of properties 231
See also 232
Working with JSON 232
Getting ready 232
How to do it... 232
   Parsing JSON REST returns 233
   Creating a JSON object 233
   Change JSON object 234
How it works... 234
See also 235
JavaScript special statements 235
Getting ready 235
How to do it... 236
   The try, catch, and finally statement 236
   The function statement 237
How it works... 237
See also 237
Turning strings into objects 238
Getting ready 238
How to do it... 238
How it works... 238
There's more... 239
See also 240
Working with the API 240
Getting ready 240
How to do it... 240
   Searching for items in the API 240
   Programming help from the API 241
How it works... 244
See also 245
Creating actions 245
Getting ready 245
How to do it... 245
   Creating a new action 246

Implementing an action into a workflow 247

How it works… 248

See also 249

Waiting tasks 249

Getting ready 249

How to do it… 249

Creating a help task 249

Using the Sleep task 250

Waiting for a date 250

How it works… 251

There's more… 251

See also 252

Sending and waiting for custom events 252

Getting ready 252

How to do it… 252

Receiving a custom event 252

Sending a custom event 253

Trying it out 254

How it works… 254

External events 254

See also 255

Using asynchronous workflows 255

Getting ready 255

How to do it… 255

The first example 256

The second example 257

How it works… 258

See also 259

Scripting with workflow tokens 259

Getting ready 259

How to do it… 259

How it works… 260

See also 262

Working with user interactions 262

Getting ready 262

How to do it… 262

Creating the workflow 263

Answering the user interaction 265

How it works… 266

There's more… 267

Answering using vRealize Automation 268

See also 268

Chapter 7: Interacting with Orchestrator 269

Introduction 269
User management 270
  Getting ready 270
  How to do it… 271
    Giving non-administrative users access to Orchestrator 271
    Configuring access to Orchestrator elements 272
  How it works… 273
    Same user – two groups 273
    Edit user rights 273
    Right inheritance 273
    Rights for sub-elements 274
    Visibility 274
    Access right 275
  There's more… 275
    The login format 275
    Typical error messages 275
    Disabling non-administrative access to Orchestrator 276
User preferences 276
  Getting ready 276
  How to do it… 277
  How it works… 277
    General 278
    Workflow 278
    Inventory 279
    Script editor 280
Using Orchestrator though the vSphere Web Client 280
  Getting ready 280
  How to do it… 281
    Configure workflows for the vSphere Web Client 281
    Run workflows 283
    Writing workflows for web integration 284
    Passing information along 284
  How it works… 285
    Orchestrator presentation properties in vSphere Web Client 285
  There's more… 285
  See also 286
Accessing Orchestrator REST API 286
  Getting ready 286
  How to do it… 286
    Accessing the API documentation and enable "play mode" 287
    Try it out! 287
    Interactive REST request 288

How it works…	291
There's more…	292
See also	292
Accessing the Control Center via the REST plugin	292
Getting ready	292
How to do it…	293
Explore the Control Center API	293
Adding start and stop calls	294
Usage	295
How it works…	295
See also	295
Running Orchestrator workflows using PowerShell	296
Getting ready	296
How to do it…	296
Run a workflow	296
Run a script with input	298
Getting the output of a workflow	298
How it works…	299
Variables	299
JSON return	299
There's more…	300
See also	300
Using PHP to access the REST API	300
Getting ready	300
How to do it…	301
How it works…	302
There's more…	302
See also	302
Chapter 8: Better Workflows and Optimized Working	303
Introduction	303
Working with resources	304
Getting ready	305
How to do it…	305
Adding resources manually	305
Using resources in workflows	305
Creating a new resource element	306
Create a resource by uploading a file	307
Updating a resource	307
How it works…	308
There's more…	308
Accessing resources directly	309

Deleting a resource	309
See also	309
Working with configurations	310
Getting ready	310
How to do it…	310
Creating a configuration	310
Using a configuration in a workflow	311
How it works…	312
There's more…	313
See also	314
Working with Orchestrator tags	314
Getting ready	314
How to do it…	314
Tagging an element (manual)	314
Tagging a workflow (workflow)	315
Viewing all tags in a workflow	316
Finding workflows by tag	317
How it works…	317
There's more…	318
See also	318
Using the Locking System	318
Getting ready	319
How to do it…	319
Create a lock	319
Check for lock	319
Unlock	320
How it works…	321
See also	321
Language packs (localization)	322
Getting ready	322
How to do it…	322
How it works…	323
Working with policies	323
Getting ready	324
How to do it…	324
How it works…	327
Policy templates	328
Triggers	328
The event variable	330
See also	330
Chapter 9: Essential Plugins	331

Introduction   331
Working with e-mail   332
  Getting ready   332
  How to do it...   332
    Configuring the e-mail connection   332
    Sending e-mails   333
    Receiving e-mails   335
  How it works...   336
    Working with attachments   337
  There's more...   338
  See also   339
File operations   339
  Getting ready   339
  How to do it...   340
    Writing a file   340
    Reading a file   341
    Getting information on files   342
    Creating, renaming, and deleting a file or directory   342
  How it works...   343
    Executing scripts   344
    Shared directories   344
  There's more...   344
    CSV files   344
    Doing things as root   345
  See also   345
Working with SSH   346
  Getting ready   346
  How to do it...   346
    Using SSH   346
    Using SSL key authentication   347
    Using SCP   348
  How it works...   349
  See also   349
Working with REST   350
  Getting ready   350
  How to do it...   350
    Connecting to a REST host   350
    Using GET   351
    Using POST   352
    Creating a workflow from a REST operation   353
    Phrasing the return value   354
    Using the Swagger spec URL   354
  How it works...   354

Authentications	355
Working with the results of a REST request	356
Default content type	356
See also	356

Chapter 10: Built-in Plugins | 359

Introduction	359
Dealing with return values	360
Shared or Per User Session	360
Working with XML	361
Getting ready	361
How to do it…	361
Creating an XML document	361
Parsing XML structures	364
How it works…	365
There's more…	365
See also	366
Working with SQL (JDBC)	367
Getting ready	367
How to do it…	367
Creating a JDBC connection URL	367
Connecting to and disconnecting from a database using JDBC	369
Executing an SQL statement using JDBC	369
SQL queries using JDBC	370
How it works…	371
The difference between the prepare and create statements	372
Creating a new database in the appliance's PostgreSQL	372
See also	373
Working with SQL (SQL plugin)	373
Getting ready	373
How to do it…	374
Add an SQL DB to Orchestrator	374
Run SQL statement	375
Run an SQL query	375
How it works…	376
See also	376
Working with PowerShell	376
Getting ready	376
How to do it…	377
Preparing the Windows host with WinRM	377
Adding a PowerShell host	378
Using Kerberos authentication	379
Executing a script	379

There's more…   432
    Using vCloud Air for recovery   432
    Integration into vSphere Web Client   433
See also   433
SRM (Site Recovery Manager) integration   434
Getting ready   434
How to do it…   434
    Preparation   434
    Configuration   434
    Working with the plugin   435
How it works…   436
There's more…   437
    vSphere Web Client integration   437
    vRealize Automation integration   437
See also   437
vROps (vRealize Operations Manager) integration   437
Getting ready   438
How to do it…   438
    Deploy   438
    Working with the plugin   440
How it works…   442
There's more…   442

Chapter 12: Working with vSphere   443
Introduction   443
vSphere automation   443
    The vCenter MoRef   444
    The vim3WaitTaskEnd action   445
    Other vCenter wait actions   446
Things to try…   447
    vAPI   447
    Linked Cloning   447
    vSAN   447
Working with the vCenter API (to change a VM's HA settings)   448
Getting ready   448
How to do it…   448
How it works…   453
There's more…   453
See also   454
Standard vSwitch and Distributed Switch ports   454
Getting ready   455
How to do it…   455
    Creating an action   455

Creating the workflow	457
Making it work with presentation	458
How it works…	458
See also	460
Getting started with vAPI	460
Getting ready	460
How to do it…	460
Configuring vCenter endpoint and metadata	460
Exploring the content	461
How it works…	462
See also	463
Custom Attributes and Tags (vAPI)	463
Getting ready	463
How to do it…	463
Custom Attributes	464
vSphere Tags	465
The Notes field	467
How it works…	467
Custom Attributes	468
vAPI tagging	468
See also	469
Executing a program inside a VM	469
Getting ready	469
How to do it…	469
Creating a waiting workflow	469
Creating an installation workflow	472
An example run	475
How it works…	476
There's more…	476
See also	476
An approval process for VM provisioning	476
Getting ready	476
How to do it…	477
Using User interaction	477
Using e-mail	478
Using a web page	478
How it works…	479
Chapter 13: Working with vRealize Automation	481
Introduction	481
How the integration of vRA and Orchestrator works	482
Installation	484

Read more...   484
Working with the vRA-integrated Orchestrator   484
Getting ready   485
How to do it...   485
   Accessing the vRA-integrated Orchestrator Client   485
   Starting the vRA-integrated Orchestrator Control Center   485
   Tuning vRA   485
How it works...   486
   Users   486
   Database   486
Automating a vRA instance in Orchestrator   487
Getting ready   487
How to do it...   487
   Preparation   487
   Example   488
How it works...   489
Configuring an external Orchestrator in vRA   490
Getting ready   490
How to do it...   490
   Building and configuring an external Orchestrator   490
   Configuring a general default external Orchestrator   491
   Configuring an external Orchestrator for each Tenant   491
   Connecting the external Orchestrator   491
How it works...   492
   Authentication   492
There's more...   493
Adding Orchestrator as an infrastructure endpoint   493
Getting ready   493
How to do it...   493
How it works...   494
There's more...   495
Adding an Orchestrator endpoint   495
Getting ready   495
How to do it...   495
How it works...   496
Integrating Orchestrator workflows as XaaS Blueprints   497
Getting ready   497
How to do it...   497
   Activating the XaaS tab   498
   Adding a XaaS Blueprint   498
   Publishing and adding the workflow to the catalog   499
How it works...   501

Orchestrator presentation properties in vRA   501

Managing AD users with vRA   502

Getting ready   502

How to do it…   502

Creating a custom resource   502

Creating the service Blueprint   503

Creating a resource action   504

Conducting a test run   505

How it works…   506

Using the Event Manager to start workflows   506

Getting ready   506

How to do it…   506

Create a workflow   507

Seting up the Blueprint   507

Subscribing to an event   508

Try it out   509

How it works…   510

There's more…   511

Index   513

Preface

Several things have happened since the first edition of this book. The most important thing is that vRealize Orchestrator 7.1 (vRO) was released and changed a lot with the Control Center; I can see that the next thing would be Orchestrator being used more, last but not least, I released the *vRealize Orchestrator Essentials* book. It allowed me to remove a lot of beginner stuff from this book and have a greater focus on the more interesting stuff. The release of vRealize Automation 7.1 (vRA) bought about a lot of changes too, as Orchestrator is now even more integrated into vRA than before.

 If you're completely new to Orchestrator I would suggest that you start your journey with the *vRealize Orchestrator Essentials* book.

To do so go to `http://bit.ly/1KVVara`.

Changes in this edition

The following are the changes from the First edition:

- We have restructured all chapters and recipes
- We have focused on the new Control Center
- We now have complete chapter on Clusters, distributed design, and loadbalancing
- We have reworked on all recipes to fit vRO7.1 and vRA7.1
- We focus on REST and JSON
- We have included an chapter on how to use PowerShell, REST, PHP and other methods to interact with Orchestrator workflows
- We have included the NSX, Horizon, Replication, SRM, and VROPS plugins
- We will introduce you to the new vAPI
- We have a complete chapter on vRA7.1 integration including Event Broker

Chapter 6, *Advanced Programming*, dives into more advanced operations such complex Java objects, JSON and other items that will add value to your workflows.

Chapter 7, *Interacting with Orchestrator*, focuses on how to interact with Orchestrator. We will use PowerShell, REST, and PHP to interact with workflows.

Chapter 8, *Better Workflows and Optimized Working*, dives into resources, configurations, packages, and more for optimizing your workflows.

Chapter 9, *Essential Plugins*, deals with the most plugins used, such as e-mail, files, SSH and REST.

Chapter 10, *Built-in Plugins*, dives into all the other plugins that are preinstalled in Orchestrator.

Chapter 11, *Additional Plugins*, takes a look at NSX, Horizon, Replication, SRM and vROPS plugins.

Chapter 12, *Working with vSphere*, is a full chapter dedicated to all things vSphere (vCenter).

Chapter 13, *Working with vRealize Automation*, dives into how to use Orchestrator in vRealize Automation.

What you need for this book

This book covers a lot of ground and discusses the interactions with a lot of other infrastructure services such as Active Directory (AD), e-mail, the vSphere infrastructure, and vRealize Automation.

You can use this book with Orchestrator versions 5.0, 5.1, and 5.5 and with the renamed version, vRealize Orchestrator (5.5.2.x, 6.x, 7.x, and newer).

The requirements differ from chapter to chapter. For Chapter 1, *Installing and Configuring Orchestrator*, and Chapter 2, *Optimizing Orchestrator Configuration*, you just require some space on your virtual infrastructure to deploy Orchestrator and maybe a working vCenter. Chapter 3, *Distributed Design*, requires more space and a loadbalancer or NSX. For Chapter 7, *Interacting with Orchestrator*, you may need a web server. Chapter 9, *Essential Plugins*, requires SSH, e-mail and a REST host; however, in the examples we will use easily accessible methods. Chapter 10, *Build-in Plugins*, is about SQL, PowerShell (Windows host), Active Directory SNMP, and AMQP, so there is some requirement for these services; again, I will provide some easy ways to handle this. Chapter 11, *Additional Plugins*, deals with NSX, Horizon, Replication, SRM, and vROPS. I will provide links that will help you set them up, but you will need to provide the infrastructure. Chapter 12, *Working with vSphere*, is about vCenter, and you should have that already. The last Chapter 13, *Working with vRealize Automation*, is about vRealize Automation. You will need to install and configure it in order to use it. This is much easier and straightforward in vRA7 than in all the other versions.

Some readers might not have all the resources or infrastructure to rebuild or play with some of the recipes; however, I sometimes have been in the same boat. I used the following little mini lab.

My mini lab is a Shuttle XPC-SZ170R8 with an i7 4 GHz and 64 GB using 1 TB SSD and 3 TB HHD.

My base VMs in my domain Mylab.local look like this:

Name	Content	Virtual hardware
Central	AD, DNS, DHCP, MS-SQL 2k14R2, HMail, NFS, SMB, CA, NTP, RabbitMQ	Windows 2 K12R2, 2 vCPU, 8 GB, 40 GB
vCenter	vCenter Appliance	Appliance, 2 vCPU, 8 GB, ~15 GB
vRO	vRealize Orchestrator Appliance	Appliance, 2 vCPU, 6 GB, 12 GB
vRA	vRA Appliance	Appliance, 4 vCPU, 18 GB, 65 GB
IaaS	IaaS server for vRA	Windows 2 K12R2, 2 vCPU, 8GB, 40 GB
NSX	NSX Manager	Appliance, 2 vCPU,16 GB, 60 GB
vROPS	vROPS Appliance	Appliance, 4 vCPU, 16 GB, 270 GB
vLI	vRealize Loginsight	Appliance, 4 vCPU, 8 GB, 530 GB

For the vSphere Replication, SRM, and Horizon recipes I used extra setups.

The trick is to choose the minimum number of VMs to power on at the same time.

Who this book is for

This book addresses intermediate and advanced VMware enthusiast. You should have some know-how about Orchestrator. An absolute beginner should take a look at the *vRealize Orchestrator Essentials* book.

Example workflows

All workflows, actions, and so on that you can find in this book are also available for download. The example package that contains more than 140 workflows and actions is available for download. Simply follow these instructions:

Navigate to `https://www.packtpub.com/virtualization-and-cloud/vmware-vrealize-orchestrator-cookbook-second-edition`.

Click on **Code Files** and download the example package.

Follow the recipe, *Working with packages*, in `Chapter 4`, *Programming Skills*, to upload the example package into your Orchestrator.

All example workflows can be found in the `Orchestrator Cookbook 2ndEdition` folder and the actions can be found in the `com.packtpub.Orchestrator-Cookbook2ndEditor` modules.

I have also packed some extras in. Check out the workflow folder `Daniels Toolsbox`.

Conventions

In this book, you will find a number of styles of text that distinguish between different kinds of information. Here are some examples of these styles, and an explanation of their meaning.

Code words in text, database table names, folder names, filenames, file extensions, pathnames, dummy URLs, user input, and Twitter handles are shown as follows: All example workflows can be found in the folder `Orchestrator Cookbook 2ndEdition`.

A block of code is set as follows:

```
var current = new Date();
return current
```

When we wish to draw your attention to a particular part of a code block, the relevant lines or items are set in bold:

```
configurationElement.setAttributeWithKey(Key, Value);
```

New terms and **important words** are shown in bold. Words that you see on the screen, for example, in menus or dialog boxes, appear in the text like this: "After selecting **Create project**, you'll be brought to the **Editor** Window"

> Warnings or important notes appear in a box like this.

> Tips and tricks appear like this.

Reader feedback

Feedback from our readers is always welcome. Let us know what you think about this book—what you liked or disliked. Reader feedback is important for us as it helps us develop titles that you will really get the most out of.

To send us general feedback, simply e-mail feedback@packtpub.com, and mention the book's title in the subject of your message.

If there is a topic that you have expertise in and you are interested in either writing or contributing to a book, see our author guide at www.packtpub.com/authors.

Customer support

Now that you are the proud owner of a Packt book, we have a number of things to help you to get the most from your purchase.

Downloading the example code

You can download the example code files for this book from your account at http://www.p acktpub.com. If you purchased this book elsewhere, you can visit http://www.packtpub.c om/support and register to have the files e-mailed directly to you.

You can download the code files by following these steps:

1. Log in or register to our website using your e-mail address and password.
2. Hover the mouse pointer on the **SUPPORT** tab at the top.
3. Click on **Code Downloads & Errata**.
4. Enter the name of the book in the **Search** box.
5. Select the book for which you're looking to download the code files.
6. Choose from the drop-down menu where you purchased this book from.
7. Click on **Code Download**.

You can also download the code files by clicking on the **Code Files** button on the book's webpage at the Packt Publishing website. This page can be accessed by entering the book's name in the **Search** box. Please note that you need to be logged in to your Packt account.

Once the file is downloaded, please make sure that you unzip or extract the folder using the latest version of:

- WinRAR / 7-Zip for Windows
- Zipeg / iZip / UnRarX for Mac
- 7-Zip / PeaZip for Linux

The code bundle for the book is also hosted on GitHub at https://github.com/PacktPubl ishing/VMware-vRealize-Orchestrator-Cookbook-Second-Edition. We also have other code bundles from our rich catalog of books and videos available at https://github.com/P acktPublishing/. Check them out!

Downloading the color images of this book

We also provide you with a PDF file that has color images of the screenshots/diagrams used in this book. The color images will help you better understand the changes in the output. You can download this file from https://www.packtpub.com/sites/default/files/down loads/VMwarevRealizeOrchestratorCookbookSecondEdition_ColorImages.pdf.

Errata

Although we have taken every care to ensure the accuracy of our content, mistakes do happen. If you find a mistake in one of our books—maybe a mistake in the text or the code—we would be grateful if you could report this to us. By doing so, you can save other readers from frustration and help us improve subsequent versions of this book. If you find any errata, please report them by visiting http://www.packtpub.com/submit-errata, selecting your book, clicking on the **Errata Submission Form** link, and entering the details of your errata. Once your errata are verified, your submission will be accepted and the errata will be uploaded to our website or added to any list of existing errata under the Errata section of that title.

To view the previously submitted errata, go to https://www.packtpub.com/books/content/support and enter the name of the book in the search field. The required information will appear under the **Errata** section.

Piracy

Piracy of copyrighted material on the Internet is an ongoing problem across all media. At Packt, we take the protection of our copyright and licenses very seriously. If you come across any illegal copies of our works in any form on the Internet, please provide us with the location address or website name immediately so that we can pursue a remedy.

Please contact us at copyright@packtpub.com with a link to the suspected pirated material.

We appreciate your help in protecting our authors and our ability to bring you valuable content.

Questions

If you have a problem with any aspect of this book, you can contact us at questions@packtpub.com, and we will do our best to address the problem.

1
Installing and Configuring Orchestrator

In this chapter, we explore how to install and configure Orchestrator. We will be looking at the following recipes:

- Deploying the Orchestrator appliance
- Important Orchestrator settings
- Configuring an external database
- Configuring external authentication
- Connecting to vCenter
- Installing plugins
- Updating Orchestrator
- Moving from Windows to appliance
- Orchestrator Client and 4K display scaling

Introduction

This chapter is dedicated to the configuration of Orchestrator and discusses how to set the tone for your Orchestrator deployment.

Until vRO 7, there were three different Orchestrator versions that one could use. The Windows-based installation (that was also automatically installed along with vCenter), the appliance, and the vRealize Automation integrated one. In **vRO7**, only the appliance and the **vRealize Automation** (**vRA**) integrated Orchestrator versions are left. All other versions have been discontinued.

If you still have a Windows version, you need to think about moving it to the appliance. Check out the recipe *Moving from Windows to appliance* in this chapter. You can currently still download and use the vRO 6.0.4 appliance or Windows version, however, you should consider updating.

Before the vRO appliance came along, the configuration of Orchestrator wasn't easy; therefore, not many people really used it. Now, the initial configuration is already done out of the box and people can start using Orchestrator directly without too much fuss. However, if one plans to use Orchestrator in a production environment, it is important to know how to configure it properly.

Licensing

One of the questions that I constantly hear from customers is about licensing of Orchestrator.

Orchestrator is licensed with vCenter or with vRealize Automation, if you own one of them, you own Orchestrator.

With vSphere, you need at least a **vSphere Standard** license to use Orchestrator. For vRO7, this means you either need vSphere 6 or vRA 7 license numbers. Although Orchestrator is available with the Essentials or Essentials Plus licensing, it operates in Player mode only. This limits your usage to executing existing workflows and prevents you from editing or creating them.

If you want to test Orchestrator you just need to get a vSphere trial license, which you can acquire over the VMware webpage.

vRealize Orchestrator 7 changes

There are huge differences between vRO versions 5.x, 6.x, and 7.x. The first and foremost is that in vRO7 the Configurator has been fully replaced by the new Control Center. The Control Center is an easy tool to use that does all the work of the Configurator and more. Trust me you are going to love it.

The other important thing is that LDAP as an authentication source for Orchestrator is now scheduled to be removed. It's still working with vRO7, but if you are currently using LDAP you need to start thinking about a change.

Speaking of authentication, vRO7 fully supports the vSphere Platform Services Controller architecture and the new vIDM that has been introduced with vSphere 6 and vRealize Automation 7.

The other important changes are in the network section:

- HTTP 8280 now forwards to HTTPS 8281
- HTTPS 8283 is now used for the Orchestrator Control Center

Orchestrator appliance basics

The vRO 7.1 appliance requires the following virtual resources:

CPU	2 vCPU with at least 2.0 GHz
Memory	6 GB
Disk Space	17 GB (1.5 GB thin)
Network	1 x NIC 1 x IP (DHCP possible)
vHardware	Version 7

The only change from the previous Orchestrator versions is that the memory has increased from 3 GB to 4 GB. Please note that this is the base appliance configuration, we will see how to change and improve the performance in the recipe *Tuning the appliance* that is in Chapter 2, *Optimizing Orchestrator Configuration*.

The same is true for the following table of Orchestrator limits. These limits are not hard limits and can be changed, we will discuss this in the recipe *Control Center titbits* in Chapter 2, *Optimizing Orchestrator Configuration*.

Maximal concurrent connected vCenters	20
Maximal concurrent connected ESXi hosts	1280
Maximal concurrent connected VM	35,000
Maximal concurrent running workflows	300

Last but not least, we have to discuss network security in detail and all the ports that need to be opened for Orchestrator to function. We will expand the list of ports when we start working with plugins, but these are the ones most commonly used:

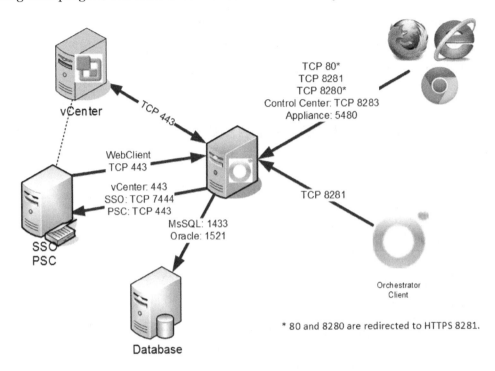

Orchestrator and vRealize Automation (vRA)

The vRealize Automation (formerly vCloud Automation Center or vCAC) appliance is shipped with a preinstalled and preconfigured vRO. Orchestrator installed on vRA is already configured and works the way the normal Orchestrator appliance does.

The vRA integrated vRO is normally only used for small environments or test environments. If you are deploying vRA for a production, large, or even worldwide role, you should consider using a vRO cluster and/or a distributed Orchestrator design. We will discuss distributed design in more detail in Chapter 3, *Distributed Design*. We also discuss the vRA integrated appliance in more detail in *Working with the vRA integrated Orchestrator* in Chapter 13, *Working with vRealize Automation*.

Deploying the Orchestrator appliance

We will now deploy the Orchestrator appliance based on Linux. If you are using the vRA integrated Orchestrator, see the introduction to Chapter 13, *Working with vRealize Automation*.

Getting ready

We can deploy the Orchestrator appliance on either a vSphere environment or on a VMware workstation (or Fusion if you are a MAC user).

Have a quick look at the requirements in the introduction of this chapter.

How to do it...

In this recipe, we will learn how to download and deploy Orchestrator. We will configure it in a later recipe.

Download

1. Navigate to http://vmware.com and select**Downloads**.
2. Click on **Download Product** next to **VMware vSphere** or **vRealize Automation**.
3. Look for VMware **vRealize Orchestrator Appliance 7.1** and click on **Go to Downloads**.
4. Look for the OVA file and click on **Download Now**.

Deploy

1. Log into vCenter using the vSphere Web Client.
2. Right-click on the cluster or ESXi server and select **Deploy OVF Template…**.
3. The **Deploy OVF Template** wizard starts. Select the OVA file you have downloaded and click **Next**.
4. Accept the EULA and click **Next**.
5. Select a name (or accept the default) as well as the vCenter folder for the Orchestrator appliance and click **Next**.
6. Select the cluster or ESXi server or a resource pool for the Orchestrator appliance and click **Next**.
7. Select the datastore you would like to deploy the Orchestrator appliance on and click **Next**.
8. Select a network for the Orchestrator appliance and click **Next**.
9. In the **Customize template** section, set a password for the root user.
10. Enable SSH if you wish. This can be done later too. See the recipe *Tuning the appliance* in the next chapter.
11. If you like, tick to join the **Customer Experience Improvement program**.
12. Set a **Hostname** for the Orchestrator appliance.
13. If you want to use a fixed IP, expand the **Network Properties** section, enter all IP related entries, and then click **Next**. If you want to use DHCP, just click on **Next**.

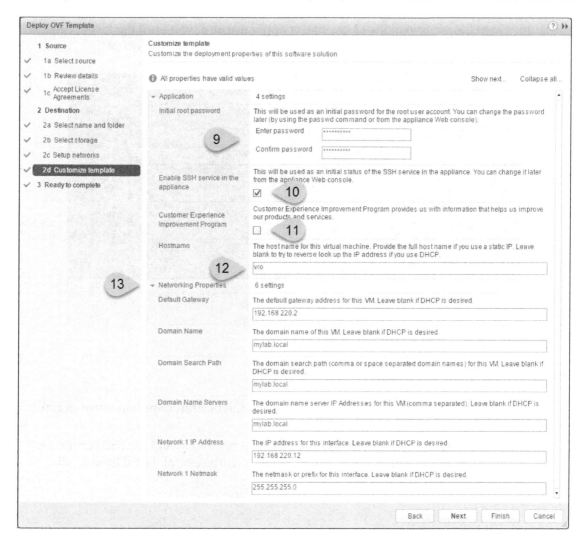

14. Select to power on the VM after deployment and click on **Finish**.
15. Wait until the VM has finished deploying and is powered on.

16. Open the console of the Orchestrator appliance and wait until the install process has completed and the VM console shows the following screenshot:

```
VMware vRealize Orchestrator Appliance - 7.1.0.19044 Build 4276164

To manage your appliance browse to http://192.168.220.12/

Welcome to VMware vRealize Orchestrator Appliance

Quickstart Guide: Use the following URLs to use the appliance:
    1 - http://192.168.220.12          - Orchestrator Appliance Home Page
    2 - https://192.168.220.12:8283/vco-controlcenter - Orchestrator Control Cent
er
    3 - https://192.168.220.12:8281/vco - Orchestrator Server
    4 - https://192.168.220.12:5480 - Appliance Configuration




►Login
 Set Timezone (Current:UTC)                   Use Arrow Keys to navigate
                                              and <ENTER> to select your choice.
```

Log in to the Orchestrator Client

1. Open a browser and browse to the IP of the Orchestrator appliance (for example, `http://192.168.220.12`).

2. Depending on your environment, you might need to accept the SSL certificate. You are now on the Orchestrator home page with several useful links to all important Orchestrator topics:

VMware vRealize™ Orchestrator™

Getting Started with vRealize Orchestrator

To create and modify workflows, or to perform administrative tasks, start the Orchestrator client by using Java Web Start:

- Start Orchestrator Client

To use the Orchestrator client on your local machine, install the Orchestrator client. After you complete the installation, start the Orchestrator client and connect to the Orchestrator server.

- Download Orchestrator Client Installable

Configure the Orchestrator Server

To make additional configuration changes to the Orchestrator server, use the Orchestrator configuration interface:

- Orchestrator Control Center

vRealize Orchestrator Resources

- Product Information
- Orchestrator Blog
- Community
- Support
- Plug-ins

VMware Quick Links

- VMware Communities
- VMware Forums
- VMware Site

3. To open up the Orchestrator Client, click on **Start Orchestrator Client**.
4. Enter `vcoadmin` as user and `vcoadmin` as the password.

You are now logged into the Orchestrator Client.

Log into Control Center

Some of the next recipes need us to log into Control Center, here is how to do that:

1. On the **Orchestrator Home** page click on **Orchestrator Control Center**.

2. Enter the user `root` and the password you assigned during deployment.

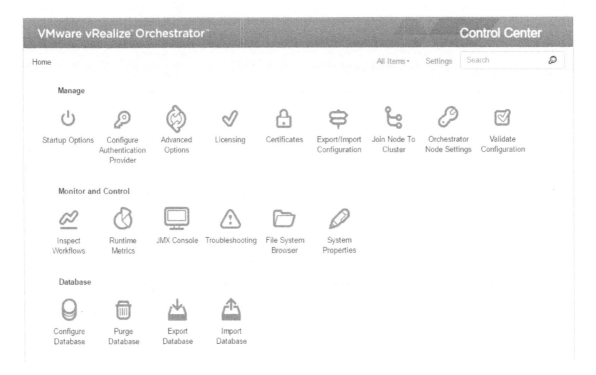

How it works...

The Orchestrator appliance is a preconfigured Orchestrator installation that uses the following software:

- SUSE Linux Enterprise Server (SLES) 11 Patch level 3
- VMware-Postgres 9.4.5.0
- ApacheDS LDAP 2.4.42

Everything is ready to run; however, no integration with vCenter or any external service is configured. The Orchestrator appliance comes with a 90-day evaluation license installed.

There's more…

If you want to deploy the Orchestrator appliance on VMware Workstation, the process of deploying the Orchestrator appliance differs from the one described in this recipe. Follow these steps instead:

1. Use Windows Explorer to navigate to the downloaded `.ova` file.
2. Double-click on the OVA file. VMware workstation opens up.
3. Select a name and a path for the new VM and click on **Import**.
4. Accept the EULA and wait until the VM is deployed.
5. You might need to select a different network (for example, **Host-Only**) depending on your lab environment.
6. Power on the VM and wait until the install pauses at the line indicated in this screenshot:

```
Successfully removed /var/adm/autoinstall
+ RES=0
+ log '/etc/bootstrap/firstboot.d/04-cleanup-autoinstall-logs done, status: 0'
++ date '+%Y-%m-%d %H:%M:%S'
+ echo '2016-03-20 10:23:46 /etc/bootstrap/firstboot.d/04-cleanup-autoinstall-lo
gs done, status: 0'
2016-03-20 10:23:46 /etc/bootstrap/firstboot.d/04-cleanup-autoinstall-logs done,
 status: 0
+ for script in '"${BOOTSTRAP_DIR}"/*'
+ echo

+ '[' '!' -e /etc/bootstrap/firstboot.d/05-init-password ']'
+ '[' '!' -x /etc/bootstrap/firstboot.d/05-init-password ']'
+ log '/etc/bootstrap/firstboot.d/05-init-password starting'
++ date '+%Y-%m-%d %H:%M:%S'
+ echo '2016-03-20 10:23:46 /etc/bootstrap/firstboot.d/05-init-password starting
'
2016-03-20 10:23:46 /etc/bootstrap/firstboot.d/05-init-password starting
+ /etc/bootstrap/firstboot.d/05-init-password
Unable to find the ovf environment.
SET INITIAL PASSWORD: Enter an initial password for the root user. You can chang
e the password later by using the passwd command or from the appliance Web conso
le.
New password:
Retype new password: _
```

7. Enter and confirm a new password for the root account.
8. The installation will now continue. Wait until it has finished.

The appliance will start with a DHCP address from the workstation. To set a static IP, you will have to access the admin interface of the appliance.

See also

See the recipe *Tuning the appliance* in Chapter 2, *Optimizing Orchestrator Configuration*.

Important Orchestrator settings

The following is a small collection of things that one should do or at least know how to do. It includes licensing, certificates, and virtual hardware.

Getting ready

We just need a working Orchestrator as well as access to the Control Center.

How to do it...

There are several things you should do or at least know how to do.

Starting, stopping, and restarting the Orchestrator service

These are operations that have to be done quite often, so it's best to know how to do them:

1. Open Control Center and click on **Startup Options**.
2. You can see the current status of the Orchestrator service.
3. Click on one of the action buttons.
4. After choosing an action, wait until the status has changed.

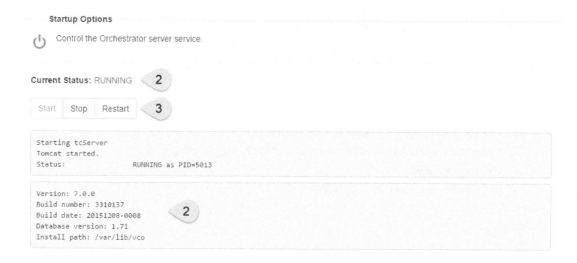

Licensing

You can either enter a license key manually or connect to the vCenter Server or vRealize Automation to acquire the license.

> If you are planning to use vSphere or vRealize Automation as an external authentication, you can skip this step as the licensing will be configured automatically.

If you change the database, you will need to redo the licensing:

1. Open Control Center and click on **Licensing**.
2. If you have an authentication provider configured (vSphere or VRA) then you can select **vSphere License**.
3. If you used SSO or LDAP, you need to use **Manual License**. With vRO7 you will need to enter a vSphere 6 vCenter or vRealize Automation 7 License number.
4. Click on **Save**.

Package Signing Certificate

The Packaging Signing Certificate signs all packages or exports. One is automatically generated with the Orchestrator's VMs Hostname. We will now show how to create a custom one:

1. Open Control Center and click on **Certificates**.
2. Click on **Packaging Signing Certificate** and then on **Generate**.
3. Enter either personal information or information of the VM.
4. Click on **Generate**.
5. Restart the Orchestrator service.

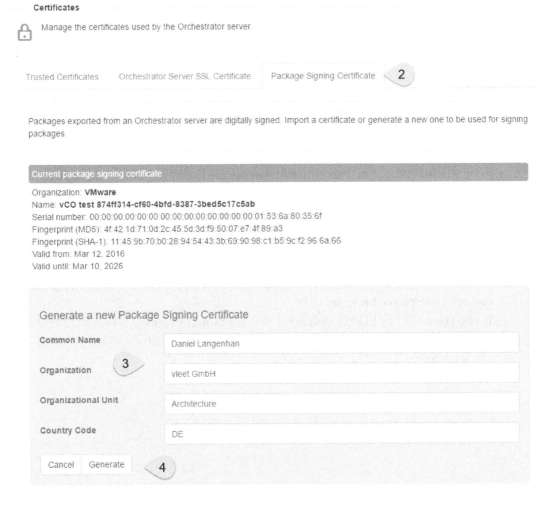

Certificates

Manage the certificates used by the Orchestrator server.

Trusted Certificates   Orchestrator Server SSL Certificate   Package Signing Certificate   2

Packages exported from an Orchestrator server are digitally signed. Import a certificate or generate a new one to be used for signing packages.

Current package signing certificate

Organization: **VMware**
Name: **vCO test 874ff314-cf60-4bfd-8387-3bed5c17c5ab**
Serial number: 00:00:00:00:00:00:00:00:00:00:00:00:00:01:53:6a:80:35:6f
Fingerprint (MD5): 4f:42:1d:71:0d:2c:45:5d:3d:f9:50:07:e7:4f:89:a3
Fingerprint (SHA-1): 11:45:9b:70:b0:28:94:54:43:3b:69:90:98:c1:b5:9c:f2:96:6a:66
Valid from: Mar 12, 2016
Valid until: Mar 10, 2026

Generate a new Package Signing Certificate

Common Name   Daniel Langenhan

Organization   3   vleet GmbH

Organizational Unit   Architecture

Country Code   DE

Cancel   Generate   4

Trusted SSL certificates

If your database or LDAP is secured with SSL, which by the way isn't such a bad idea, you will need to import the certificate into Orchestrator first. To do this, follow these steps:

1. Open Control Center and click on **Certificates**.
2. In the **Trusted Certificates** section click on **Import**.
3. In **Import from URL**, enter `https://Central.mylab.local`.
4. Click on **Import**.

For almost all VMware infrastructure the import of their certificate is integrated into the workflows and doesn't need to be done by hand anymore.

Force plugins reinstall

If you have changed the database, you will need to do this step in order for you to use all the workflows that come with the plugins.

1. Open Control Center and stop the Orchestrator service.
2. Return to the main Control Center page and click on **Troubleshooting**.
3. At the end of the screen click on **Force plug-ins reinstall**.
4. Wait until you see the green **Operation started successfully**.
5. Start the Orchestrator service again.

When Orchestrator restarts, it installs all new plugins that exist, but as the plugins haven't changed in the versions before this, updating the database leads to this little problem.

How it works...

The settings we have just applied are important and need to be done in order to make Orchestrator production-ready.

The package signing, as well as the licensing, needs to be done only once, except if you intend to change the database.

Importing an SSL certificate is an action that we will encounter more often. Every time we want to establish a secure connection (SSL) between Orchestrator and another server, we first have to import this server's SSL certificate. However, most workflows in the current version of Orchestrator include an automatic import (most of the time).

See also

Have a look at the recipe *Backup and recovery* in `Chapter 2`, *Optimizing Orchestrator Configuration*, to learn how to export and import the configuration.

Configuring an external database

In this recipe, we will attach Orchestrator to an external database. The internal Orchestrator PostgreSQL is production-ready, however for certain designs, such as Orchestrator Cluster and large deployments we still require one.

Getting ready

We will need a database; the following databases are supported with vRO7:

- Oracle 11g all editions – 64 bit
- Oracle 12g/c all editions – 64 bit
- SQL Server 2008 R1/R2 all editions – 64 bit
- SQL Server 2012 R1/R2 all editions – 64 bit
- PostgreSQL

You will need to create an empty database for Orchestrator, and you should also create a dedicated user account for Orchestrator to access the database.

If your database requires SSL, you will need to import the SSL certificate first; for this, see the *How it works...* section of this recipe.

> When you replace the database, you will have to reconfigure the following items: Licensing and Packaging Signing Certificate.

How to do it...

In this example, we have added an MS-SQL database to Orchestrator. The other databases are not that much different.

The following information is needed for each type of database:

Database type	Oracle	SQL Server	PostgreSQL
Login	required	required	required
SSL	optional	optional	optional
Hostname	required	required	required
Port	1521 or custom	1433 or custom	5432 or custom
Database name	–	required	required
Instance	required	optional	–
Domain	–	optional	–
Use NTLMv2	–	optional	–

To configure a database, follow these steps:

My MS-SQL database is stored on the VM called `Central.mylab.local`.

1. Open **Control Center**.
2. Click on **Configure Database**.
3. Select **SQL Server** for Microsoft SQL server.
4. Fill in the required information. You only need to fill in the domain if you are using Windows authentication.
5. Click on **Save Changes**.
6. You are now asked to **Update database**.
7. After updating, the screen returns to the following one. You have configured the external database. You may need to configure the licensing and Package Signing Certificate as they were stored in an internal PostgreSQL database. Additionally, you may need to force the re-installation of plugins:

Configure Database

Database is one of the most important dependencies of the Orchestrator server. Reliable access to the database is crucial for the efficient and predictable operation of the Orchestrator server. Provide the database configuration properties.

Database type	**3**	SQL Server ▾
Server address		addnsdb.mylab.local : 1433
Use SSL		☐
Database name		vroprime
User name	**4**	vrouser
Password		(Required)
Instance (if any)		
Domain		
Use Windows authentication (NTLMv2)		☐

Cancel   Save changes   **5**

How it works...

The Orchestrator database contains the entire configuration, workflows, workflow runs, events, runtime information, actions, and a lot more.

If you want to use your existing co-operation, backup, and restore procedures of your database or a database cluster for more security, an external database is a good idea.

Orchestrator comes with an embedded PostgreSQL database, which is rated for production for small and medium deployments by VMware and can be easily backed up using the Control Center or a **cron** script on the Linux console of the appliance. However, we still require a shared database for clustering; see the recipe *Building an Orchestrator cluster* in Chapter 3, *Distributed Design*.

Using the vCenter Server database for Orchestrator is not really a pretty solution. IT best practices dictate the usage of dedicated resources for production environments.

Sizing

Sizing is hard to predict. Each Workflow run consumes around 4 KB, and most objects (for example, vCenter Server object) require around 50 KB each. VMware recommends 1 GB for a production database. The good thing is that Orchestrator regularly runs clean-up jobs to reduce the database content. Also have a look at the recipe *User preferences* in Chapter 7, *Interacting with Orchestrator*, where we discuss certain properties that influence how much information is kept in the database.

Database roles

For the initial setup (and for updates), you should give the dedicated Orchestrator user the db_owner rights of the Orchestrator database.

For normal usage scenarios the Orchestrator user only requires db_dataread and db_datawrite rights.

Exporting and importing a database

If you are using the internal PostgreSQL or an external PostgreSQL database, you can use the Control Center to export as well as import the database content.

The export can include information on the last workflow runs as well as the logs.

See also the recipe *Backup and recovery* in Chapter 2, *Optimizing Orchestrator Configuration*.

Purging the Database

This sounds much harsher than it is. Purging means getting rid of stuff you may not need anymore and making the database a bit smaller.

Home

Purge Database

Logs, events, and workflow runs compile the majority of the Orchestrator content and can sometimes be deleted safely. Perform purge only when the server is stopped, otherwise the behavior is undefined.

Purge all scheduled tasks ⚠

Purge server logs, events, and messages ⚠

Purge workflow runs ⚠

Purge database

Purging the database from time to time isn't such a bad idea, however, you can't be sure whether or not you will throw away stuff you might need. For example, workflow runs and logs can take up a lot of space after some time, but they may also be important. (for example, SOX compliance).

There's more...

Here are some things you might find useful.

Microsoft SQL

Giving the database the settings, ALLOW_SNAPSHOT_ISOLATION and READ_COMMITTED_SNAPSHOT, will reduce the possibility of deadlocks and is also a prerequisite for Orchestrator clusters. This can be done by running the following script on the SQL cluster:

```
ALTER DATABASE [vRO DB Name] SET ALLOW_SNAPSHOT_ISOLATION ON; GO; ALTER
DATABASE [vRO DB Name] SET READ_COMMITTED_SNAPSHOT ON; GO;
```

Oracle

The database should have `NLS_CHARACTER_SET` = `AL32UTF8` set before you start allowing Orchestrator to build its tables.

To avoid an `ORA-01450` error, it is important that you have the database block size configured in correspondence with your database index.

Internal PostgreSQL

To access the local DB (for example, for backups), you need the following information:

Database name	vmware
User	vmware
Password	vmware

The PostgreSQL install is protected to only allow local access to it. You'll find the installation in `/var/lib/pgsql`.

See also

The recipe *Backup and recovery* in `Chapter 2`, *Optimizing Orchestrator Configuration*.

Configuring external authentication

To use Orchestrator to its fullest possibilities we should configure it with an external authentication.

Getting ready

We need an up and running Orchestrator and access to the Control Center (root account). Also see, the recipe *Deploying the Orchestrator appliance* in this chapter.

You should have an AD/LDAP group for your Orchestrator Administrators with at least one user in it. I will use the AD group `vroAdmins` with its member `vroAdmin` and my domain is called `mylab.local`. My PSC/SSO is on `vcenter.mylab.local`.

If you are using AD/LDAP, then you need only to know the LDAP path to your vroAdmin user and group.

If you are using SSO or vSphere(PSC), you should either have configured SSO to use AD or created a local SSO group and user.

How to do it...

We are splitting the recipe into multiple parts, one for each authentication method.

vSphere (PSC) and vRealize Automation (vRA)

For both vSphere 6 and vRA7, the entry forms look alike and follow the same pattern. However, there are some really important considerations to take into account for both. Please see the *How it works...* section of this recipe.

To set either vSphere (PSC) or vRealize Automation (vIDM), follow these steps:

1. Open the Control Center and click on **Configure Authentication Provider**.
2. Choose **vSphere** or **vRealize Automation**.
3. Enter the host name of your vSphere PSC or vRA.
4. After clicking on **Connect**, you may need to accept the SSL certificate.
5. You are now asked to enter the **User name** and **Password** of an SSO administrator.
6. Clicking on **Configure licenses** will automatically configure Orchestrator licensing with the vCenter license.
7. Enter the default tenant of your SSO and click on **Register**:

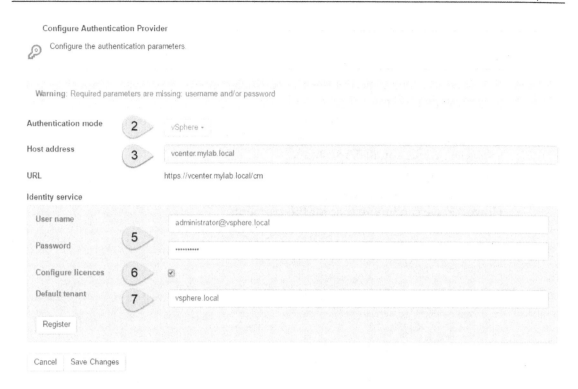

8. After the registration, you are asked for the admin group. Enter the name of your admin group (or the first letters, such as `vro`) and click on **Search.**

9. Select your admin group from the drop-down menu, such as **mylab.local\vroAdmins**. In vRA, there is a preconfigured group called **vsphere.local\vcoAdminis**.

10. Click on **Save Changes** and restart the Orchestrator service.

SSO (legacy)

If you are using vRO7 with vSphere 5.5 (minimum update 2) you need to use the SSO configuration:

1. Open the Control Center and click on **Configure Authentication Provider**.

2. Choose **SSO (legacy)**.

3. Enter the following for Admin URL:
   `https://vcenter.mylab.local:7444/sso-adminserver/sdk/vsphere.lo cal`.

4. Enter the following for STS URL:
   `https://vcenter.mylab.local:7444/sts/STSService/vsphere.local`.

5. Click on **Save Changes**.

6. You will now need to accept the SSL certificate of your SSO server (not shown in the following picture).

7. After you have accepted the certificate you will be asked to enter an SSO admin account and its password, followed by the **Default tenant**, which is `vsphere.local` for all 5.5 systems.

8. Click on **Register**.

9. If everything is fine you will now be asked to restart the Orchestrator service. However, we can ignore that for the moment:

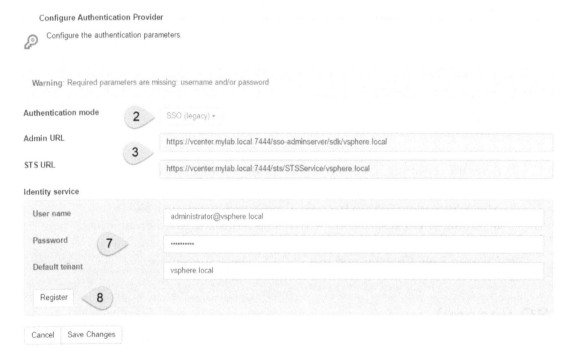

10. Now you need to choose admin group. Enter the name of your admin group (or the first letters, such as `vro`) and click on **Search**.

11. Select your admin group from the drop-down menu, such as `mylab.local\vroAdmins`. SSO 5.5 has a preconfigured Orchestrator group called `vcoAdministrators@vsphere.local`.

12. Click on **Save Changes** and restart the Orchestrator service again.

LDAP

Please note LDAP will be discontinued in further Orchestrator releases and should not be used anymore. Furthermore, using LDAP won't allow Orchestrator to use all its awesome features.

If you are using LDAP, you can choose from the **In-process LDAP (ApacheDS)**, the built-in LDAP, **Active Directory,** or **OpenLDAP**.

Please note that LDAP entries are case sensitive. To configure Orchestrator with **Active Directory**, follow these steps:

1. Open the Control Center and click on **Configure Authentication Provider**.
2. Choose **LDAP** and then **Active Directory**.
3. Enter the domain name of your AD and set the port to 389.
4. As root, enter your domain in LDAP dc=mylab,dc=local.
5. Enter the username in LDAP and then the password. Be mindful that in AD, the folder Users is not an OU but a CN,
   cn=vroAdmin,cn=Users,dc=mylab,dc=local.
6. It is easiest to set the user and group lookup base to the root of your domain, for example, dc=mylab,dc=local. However, if your AD or LDAP is large, it might be better performance-wise to choose a different root.
7. Enter the Orchestrator admin group in LDAP,
   cn=vroAdmins,cn=Users,dc=mylab,dc=local.
8. Click on **Save Changes**.

9. If everything is fine you will be asked to restart the Orchestrator service.

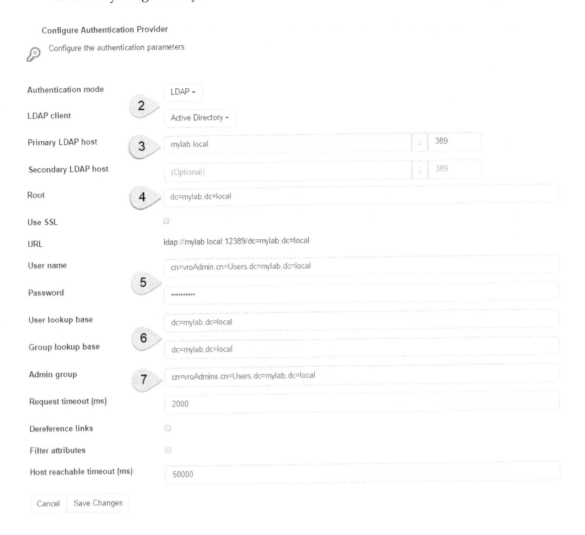

How it works...

Configuring Orchestrator to work with an external authentication enables AD users to log in to the Orchestrator Client. The alternative would be to either have only one user using it or adding users to the embedded LDAP. However, for a production Orchestrator, the embedded LDAP solution is not viable.

PSC/vIDM/SSO is a highly integrated part of vSphere, it can proxy multiple AD and/or LDAP domains and lets you integrate Orchestrator directly into vCenter as well as other corner pieces of VMware software offerings.

If you are using vSphere or vRealize Automation authentication, you have the additional benefit of having Orchestrator automatically licensed. If you are using LDAP or SSO you have to assign a license to Orchestrator.

When using SSO or vSphere, Orchestrator will register in SSO as a Solution User with the prefix vCO.

vRealize Automation and vSphere Authentication

The entry masks look the same, however, they are not. vSphere uses SSO and vRA 7 uses vIDM and those are very different beasts indeed.

When you register Orchestrator with vRealize Automation or you use the vRA embedded Orchestrator you will not be able to use a per-user session with vCenter as the SSO token and the vIDM token are incompatible at this time. I have been informed that the ability to configure the vRA embedded Orchestrator version will not be able to use PSC configuration anymore. The best way to solve this is to use a secondary Orchestrator.

Test login

With the test login, you can test if you can log on to Orchestrator using the Control Center:

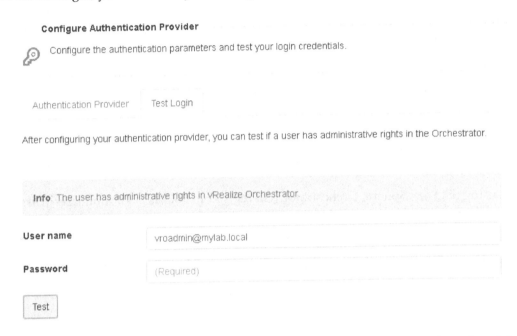

If you get a reply in yellow saying **Warning: The user does not have administrative rights in vRealize Orchestrator. Login to the Orchestrator client depends on the user view permissions**, it means that the user has been found by Orchestrator but he is not a member of the Orchestrator admin group. See also, the recipe *User management* in `Chapter 7, Interacting with Orchestrator`.

Internal LDAP

The internal LDAP has the following preconfigured entries:

Username	Password	Group membership
vcoadmin	vcoadmin	vcoadmins
vcouser	vcouser	vcousers

The LDAP installation is protected to only allow local access to it. Using the internal LDAP is not recommended at all.

There's more...

Changing the **Authentication Provider** is quite easy. If you choose LDAP and now want to change it to something else, just select the new provider.

If you chose vSphere SSO or vRealize Automation you need to first unregister the existing **Authentication Provider**. To do this, follow these steps:

1. Open the Control Center and click on **Configure Authentication Provider**.
2. Click on **Unregister** and then enter the SSO admin's password and click **Unregister**.
3. Now you can select another **Authentication mode**.

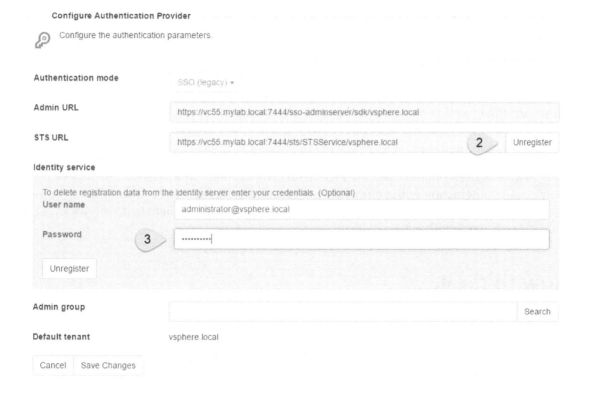

See also

Recipes in Chapter 11, *Additional Plugins*, depict which authentication is the most preferable for the plugins discussed there.

Connecting to vCenter

In this recipe, we connect Orchestrator to vCenter. This will allow Orchestrator to access vCenter objects as well as **vSphere Web Client** users to access Orchestrator workflows. For an Orchestrator used with vRA, you need to use the endpoint configuration, see the *How it works...* section.

Getting ready

We need a running Orchestrator that needs to be registered with vSphere (SSO or vRA works as well).

 If you are planning to use a customer SSL certificate for your Orchestrator, then exchange the certificate before you continue here. See the recipe *Configuring the Orchestrator service SSL certificate* in `Chapter 2`, *Optimizing Orchestrator Configuration*.

You should consider having a technical user that is able to log into vCenter as a vCenter administrator as well as being a member of the Orchestrator admin group. Using a dedicated user will go in the right direction for automation, see the *How it works...* section. I will use my dedicated user, `srv_vro@mylab.local`.

 Check out the VMware Product Interoperability Matrixes for the interaction with your vRO version and the vSphere Web Client. For example, vRO 7 will only work with vSphere Web Client 6, it will not work with 5.5.

How to do it...

To configure the vCenter connection we need to follow these steps:

1. Open the Orchestrator Client with an Orchestrator Administrator.
2. Start the workflow **Library** | **vCenter** | **Configuration** | **Add a vCenter Server instance**.
3. Enter your vCenter FQDN.
4. Select that you would like to orchestrate this instance as well and that you would like to accept SSL certificates even if they are self-signed.

Orchestrating a vCenter means that the content of the vCenter will show up in the Orchestrator **Inventory** and you can select and use it.

5. Click on **Next**.
6. Select **No**, meaning that you will use a technical user for the connection between Orchestrator and vCenter. This is also the recommended setting if you are using the vRA integrated Orchestrator.
7. Enter a vCenter server administrative user or a technical user you specified, such as srv_vro@mylab.local and the password of that user.
8. Click on **Submit**.

9. Wait until the workflow is successfully finished.
10. Start the workflow **Library | vCenter | Configuration | Register vCenter Orchestrator as a vCenter Server Extension**.
11. Select your vCenter from the Orchestrator Library.
12. If you have a load balancer or NAT between Orchestrator and vCenter, enter the external Orchestrator address here.

13. Click on **Submit**.

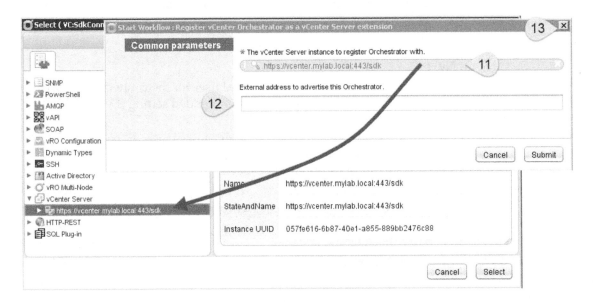

14. Now log in to the vSphere Web Client as a technical user.
15. Navigate to **vRealize Orchestrator | vRO Home | Summary**. Your Orchestrator should be registered there.

For more information and usage, see the recipe *Using Orchestrator through the vSphere Web Client* in Chapter 7, *Interacting with Orchestrator*.

Well, there is that...

Sometimes the vSphere Web Client – Orchestrator integration doesn't work out-of-the-box after you have set it up. Here are some things to do in that case:

- Check the VMware Product Interoperability Matrixes for interaction with your vRO version and the vSphere Web Client.
- Use the same versions of vRO and vCenter. For example, vRO7.0.1 (or newer) doesn't integrate into vCenter 6.0U2 (or earlier) due to an SSL problem, it works fine with vCenter 6.0U3 (and newer). This is due to a change in encryption.
- Have some patience. It may take some 15 minutes until the Web Client gets it (in a slow lab). The Web Client will continue to show the following error message: **Error occurred while processing request. Check vSphere Web Client logs for details**.

- Restart the vSphere Web Client.
- Check your vCenter logs. When you register an extension, a plugin is downloaded. In Orchestrator's case, the URL is:`https://[Orchestrator IP]:8281/vco/vsphere-web-client/vco-plugin.zip`.
- Make sure that the vCenter user has access rights on Orchestrator (see the recipes *User management* and *Using Orchestrator through the vSphere Web Client* in `Chapter 7`, *Interacting with Orchestrator*).
- Unregister all Orchestrator extensions using the MOB and then try again. See `kb.vmware.com/kb/1025360`.
- If you use a cluster, you need to use the external address. The register workflow registers the Orchestrator extension with its IP: `https://[Loadbalancer_Address]:8281`. Also see the recipe *Load-balancing Orchestrator* in `Chapter 3`, *Distributed Design*.

How it works...

Since vCenter Server 5.1, vSphere Web Client is (or better, should be) the main method to access vCenter. Orchestrator completely integrates with vSphere Web Client, making it possible for Orchestrator workflows to be executed directly from vSphere Web Client.

Access, rights, and logging

The access from Orchestrator to vCenter works with the technical user we used to make the connection.

When a workflow is started from Orchestrator, vCenter will log the user who started the workflow but the execution of the workflow will be logged with the technical user.

For a vSphere Web Client user to be able to start a workflow they need to have access to Orchestrator. Either they need to be a member of the Orchestrator admin group or they need non-administrative access.

Technical user

The idea of a technical user is to use a dedicated user that connects between Orchestrator and vCenter. This technical user would be a full vCenter admin. The alternative is to use a per-user base, which means that each user uses his/her vCenter rights to run workflows. The difference is that we either need to set rights and roles throughout vCenter for different users/groups or we create good workflows and security in Orchestrator.

vRA, Orchestrator, and vCenter

As we already discussed in the recipe *Configuring external authentication* in this chapter, the difference between vSphere and vRealize Automation authentication, namely SSO or vIDM. When you configure an Orchestrator, especially for vRA, you should not configure the vCenter plugin but use the endpoints, as we show in the recipe *Adding Orchestrator*, as an infrastructure endpoint in the final chapter.

See also

To learn more about the Orchestrator user management, see the recipe *User management* in Chapter 7, *Interacting with Orchestrator*.

To configure the Orchestrator workflows in vSphere Web Client, see the recipe *Using Orchestrator through the vSphere Web Client* in Chapter 7, *Interacting with Orchestrator*.

Installing plugins

In this recipe, we will learn how to install plugins for Orchestrator. Configuration and programming-related topics are discussed in Chapter 9, *Essential Plugins*, Chapter 10, *Built-in Plugins*, and Chapter 11, *Additional Plugins*.

Getting ready

We need an Orchestrator server installed and running, as well as access to the Orchestrator Control Center.

Please see the introduction to Chapter 11, *Additional Plugins*, for information on where to obtain plugins.

Please note that when you download a plugin, your download should contain a .vmoapp or .dar file. A ZIP file needs to be unpacked/unzipped first.

How to do it...

We will now install a new plugin. I will use the **Autodeploy** plugin:

1. Open the Orchestrator Control Center.
2. Click on **Manage Plug-Ins**.
3. Click on **Browse** and select the .vmoapp file you downloaded, then click **Install**:

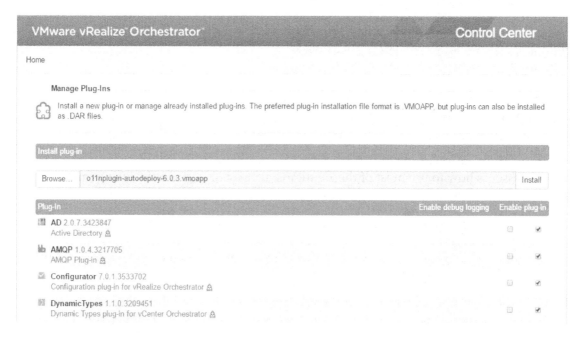

4. **Accept EULA** and click on **Install**.
5. Restart the Orchestrator service.

How it works...

Orchestrator becomes more exciting with additional plugins, such as plugins from VMware and other vendors. The current version of vRO (7.1) comes with quite a few plugins already installed, such as the following:

AD 3.0.2 4209033	SOAP 2.0.0.4147531
AMQP 1.0.4.3217705	SQL 1.1.4.4009493
Configurator 7.0.1.3533702	SSH 7.0.1.3430925
DynamicTypes 1.2.0.426821	VAPI 7.1.04262825
Enums 7.0.1. .3767915	VC 6.5.0.4132889
Library 7.0.1.3767915	VCO 7.1.0.4262825
Mail 7.0.1. 3767915	Workflow documentation 7.1.3767915
Net 7.0.1. 3767915	XML 7.0.1.3767915
PowerShell 1.0.9.3895915	vCAC 7.1.0.4147052
REST 2.0.1.4157277	vCACCafe 7.1.0.4176993
SNMP 1.0.3.3767921	

We will discuss how to use most of these plugins in `Chapter 9`, *Essential Plugins* and `Chapter 10`, *Built-in Plugins*.

Plugins make Orchestrator the great product that it is and create a variety of possibilities. If there isn't a plugin for a system, think outside the box. For instance, you can connect Orchestrator to Microsoft **System Center Virtual Machine Manager** (**SCVMM**) via SOAP, to Red Hat Satellite using REST, or to your Docker using SSH.

Last but not least, you can create your own plugins. There is an Orchestrator plugin SDK guide that is dedicated to the creation of plugins. See the developer documentation for Orchestrator.

Plugin log level

With vRO7.1, you are now able to define a log level for each plugin. The log level ranges from **DEFAULT** to **OFF**:

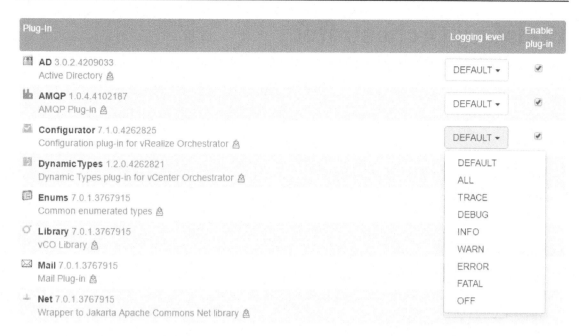

Updating plugins

To update a plugin, just download the new version and deploy it as shown in this recipe. The plugin will be updated.

Disabling and uninstalling plugins

You can switch off plugins by de-selecting the **Enable plug-in** check box. Uninstalling plugins isn't that straightforward and should only be done if you have no other choice, there is a KB that shows how:

```
kb.vmware.com/kb/2064575.
```

See also

The introduction of Chapter 11, *Additional Plugins* gives information where you can find plugins and show how to use some of these.

Updating Orchestrator

Here we will describe the update process for the Orchestrator appliance as well as the best way to get from 5.x or 6.x to 7. As a Windows install isn't supported in 7 anymore, please see the recipe *Moving from Windows to appliance* in this chapter. If you are updating a cluster, please see the recipe *Upgrading a cluster* in `Chapter 3`, *Distributed Design* first.

Getting ready

We need an older version of Orchestrator as well as access to a VMWare webpage.

How to do it...

There are two methods for updating the appliance. First there is updating via an ISO file and second, directly accessing the update repository.

Before you start updating
Make sure you have a backup or at least a snapshot of the Orchestrator VM. If you are using an external database, make a backup of the DB as well.

Using an ISO file

Follow these steps if you wish to use the ISO file.

1. Open `vmware.com` in your web browser and then click on **Download** and **vSphere**.
2. Look for **VMware vRealize Orchestrator Appliance** and click on **Go to Downloads**.
3. At the very end of the download, you should find the **.iso Update Repository Archive**. Click on **Download now**.
4. After the download has finished, go to your vCenter and mount the image to the Orchestrator appliance.
5. Browse to the Orchestrator backend: `https://[Orchestrator]:5480`
6. Navigate to **Update | Settings**.
7. Continue with **Apply the Update**.

Using the VMware repository

Follow these steps if you wish to use the VMware repository. Your Orchestrator needs a HTTPS connection to the VMware website (`vmware.com`)

1. Open a web browser and browse to the Orchestrator backend:
   `https://[Orchestrator]:5480`.
2. Navigate to **Update | Settings**.
3. Continue with **Apply the Update**.

Applying the update

After we have the update source in place, we can finally update the appliance.

1. From where we left off, click on **Check Updates**.
2. You should now see the version you'd like to upgrade to if that's not the case check the source of the update (for example, ISO file or iNET connection).
3. Click on **Install Updates**:

4. Accept the EULA and acknowledge you would like to update with **OK**.
5. The update process will take some time. Wait until Orchestrator tells you: **System reboot is required to complete the update**.
6. Reboot the Orchestrator appliance.
7. After the reboot, access the Control Center and check that everything is fine.

How it works...

The update process of Orchestrator is pretty simple and straightforward. All versions have the default repository configured and with Internet access, you can use it directly.

Before you update, you should always read the release notes of the newest Orchestrator release to see if there are any problems you might encounter. The update from 5.5 or 6.x to 7 is pretty easy and just requires the newest 7 ISO.

> If you are upgrading from 5.5 or 6 to 7 you might want to change the authentication to **vsphere** to make use of the vSphere 6 features.

In the **Update** | **settings**, there is also the ability to automatically check for updates as well as to automatically check and install updates. I personally wouldn't use the feature in any production setting; an update should always be a controlled process.

> After an upgrade, you need to check your workflows. I have had several cases where a method, a standard library workflow, or a plugin wasn't working the same anymore. If you find something like that please report it to VMware so they can fix it in the next release.

There's more...

If your Orchestrator has no Internet connection but you would still like to use the repository feature and you have a web server (for example IIS), you can do the following:

1. Download the `.zip` Update Repository Archive from `vmware.com`.
2. Unpack the ZIP file. After unpacking, copy the contents of the following directory into the web server so that it can be accessed using `http(s)\build\mts\release\bora-3571217\publish\exports\Update_Rep o`.
3. The web server should now contain two folders; `manifest` and `package-pool`. Make sure that the folders are browseable and that they are accessible. In IIS you might need to add the `.sig` and `.sha265` file type as a `text/scriptlet` MIME type.
4. Open a web browser and browse to the Orchestrator backend: `https://[Orchestrator]:5480`.
5. Navigate to **Update** | **Settings**.

6. Select **Use Specified Repository** and enter your web server URL into **Repository URL** and, if needed, the subdirectory where the patch files are located.

7. Now just follow the recipe to update from the repository.

Update Repository

○ Use Default Repository

RepositoryURL   **https://vapp-updates.vmware.com/vai-catalog/valm/vmw/00642c69-abe2-4b0c-a9e3-77a6e54bffd9/7.0.1.17606.latest**

○ Use CDROM Updates

⦿ Use Specified Repository

Repository URL   `http://192.168.220.5/vro`   6

Username (Optional)

Password (Optional)

See also

The recipe *Upgrading a Cluster* in `Chapter 3`, *Distributed Design*.

Moving from Windows to appliance

With vRO 7, the Windows install of Orchestrator doesn't exist anymore. This recipe discusses how to move an existing Windows Orchestrator installation to the appliance.

Getting ready

We need an Orchestrator installed on Windows.

Download the *same version* of the Orchestrator appliance as you have installed in the Windows version. If needed, upgrade the Windows version to the latest possible one.

How to do it...

There are three ways; using the migration tool, repointing to an external database, or exporting/importing the packages.

Migration tool

There is a migration tool that comes with vRO7 that allows you to pack up your vRO5.5 or 6.x install and deploy it into a vRO7. The migration tool works on Windows and Linux. It collects the configuration, the plugins, as well as their configuration certificates, and licensing into a file. Follow these steps to use the migration tool:

1. Deploy a new vRO7 appliance.
2. Log in to your Windows Orchestrator OS.
3. Stop the **VMware vCenter Orchestrator Service** (Windows services).
4. Open a web browser and log into your new vRO7 – Control Center and then go to **Export/Import Configuration**.
5. Select **Migrate Configuration** and click on the **here** link. The link points to: `https://[vRO7]:8283/vco-controlcenter/api/server/migration-tool`.
6. Stop the vRO7 Orchestrator service.
7. Unzip the **migration-tool.zip** and copy the subfolder called `migration-cli` into the Orchestrator director, for example, `C:\Program Files\VMware\Infrastructure\Orchestrator\migration-cli\bin\`.
8. Open a command prompt.
9. If you have Java installed, make sure your path points to it. Try `java -version`. If that works, continue, if not, do the following:
10. Set the PATH environment variable to the Java install that comes with Orchestrator, `set PATH=%PATH%;C:\Program Files\VMware\Infrastructure\Orchestrator\Uninstall_vCenter Orchestrator\uninstall-jre\bin`
11. `CD` to the directory `..\Orchestrator\migration-cli\bin`.
12. Execute the command; `vro-migrate.bat export`. There may be errors showing about **SLF4J**; you can ignore those.
13. In the main directory (`..\Orchestrator`) you should now find an `orchestrator-config-export-VC55-[date].zip` file.
14. Go back to the web browser and upload the ZIP file into **Migration Configuration** by clicking on **Browse** and selecting the file.

15. Click on **Import**. You can now see what can be imported. You can unselect the items you don't wish to migrate. Click **Finish Migration**.

16. Restart the Orchestrator service.

17. Check the settings.

Export/Import Configuration

Export, Import and Migrate Orchestrator server configurations.

Export Configuration   Import Configuration   Migrate Configuration

Import a configuration created by the Orchestrator server migration tool. The Orchestrator server migration tool can be downloaded from here. You can find instructions on the usage of the tool in the readme.txt file, located in the downloaded archive. The supported Orchestrator versions from the Orchestrator server migration tool are between 5.5.x and 6.0.x.
Before migrating the configuration you must stop the source and destination Orchestrator servers. After the migration is successful start the destination Orchestrator server from the Startup Options page.
If you exported the configuration with a password, use the same password when importing.

Configuration snapshot information:

Exported from: VC55
Version/build: 5.5.2/1946710
Database version: 1.63
Exported on: Mar 29, 2016

Migrate Options

Migrate Database configuration   ☑

Migrate Plugins   ☑

Migrate Plugin configurations (filesystem) ☑

Migrate Server certificate   ☑

Migrate trusted certificates   ☑

Cancel   Finish Migration

External database

If you have an external database, things are pretty easy. For using the initial internal database, please see the additional steps in the *There's more...* section of this recipe.

1. Backup the external database.
2. Connect to the Windows Orchestrator Configurator.

3. Write down all the plugins you have installed as well as their version.

4. Shut down the Windows version and deploy the appliance, this way you can use the same IP and Hostname if you want.

5. Log into the appliance version's Configurator.

6. Stop the Orchestrator service

7. Install all plugins you had in the Windows version.

8. Attach the external database.

9. Make sure that all trusted SSL certificates are still there, such as vCenter and SSO.

10. Check if the authentication is still working. Use the test login.

11. Check your licensing.

12. Force a plugin reinstall (**Troubleshooting | Reinstall the plug-ins when the server starts**).

13. Start the Orchestrator service and try to log in.

14. Make a complete sanity check.

Package transfer

This is the method that will only pull your packages across. This the only easy method to use when you are transitioning between different databases, such as between MS SQL and PostgreSQL:

1. Connect to your Windows version

2. Create a package of all the workflows, actions, and other items you need.

3. Shut down Windows and deploy the appliance.

4. Configure the appliance with DB, authentication, and all the plugins you previously had.

5. Import the package.

How it works...

Moving from the Windows version of Orchestrator to the appliance version isn't such a big thing. The worst-case scenario is using the packaging transfer. The only really important thing is to use the same version of the Windows Orchestrator as the appliance version. You can download a lot of old versions, including 5.5, from www.vmware.com. If you can't find the same version, upgrade your existing vCenter Orchestrator to one you can download.

After you have transferred the data to the appliance, you need to make sure that everything works correctly, and then you can upgrade to vRO7.

There's more...

When you just run Orchestrator from your Windows vCenter installation and don't configure an external database, then Orchestrator uses the vCenter database and mixes the Orchestrator tables with the vCenter tables. In order to only export the Orchestrator ones, we will use the MS SQL Server Management Studio (free download from www.microsoft.com called **Microsoft SQL Server RTM**).

To transfer only the Orchestrator database tables from the vCenter MS-SQL to an external SQL, do the following:

1. Stop the **VMware vCenter Orchestrator Service** (Windows Services) on your Windows Orchestrator.
2. Start the **SQL Server Management Studio** on your external SQL server.
3. Connect to the vCenter DB. For SQL Express, use `[vcenter]\VIM_SQLEXP` with Windows Authentication.
4. Right-click on your vCenter Database (SQL Express: `VIM_VCDB`) and select **Tasks | Export Data**.
5. In the wizard, select your source, which should be the correct one already, and click **Next**.
6. Choose **SQL Server Native Client 10.0** and enter the name of your new SQL server. Click on **New** to create a new database on that SQL server (or use an empty one you created already). Click **Next**.
7. Select **Copy data from one or more tables or views** and click **Next**.

8. Now select every database which starts with **VMO_** and then click **Next**.

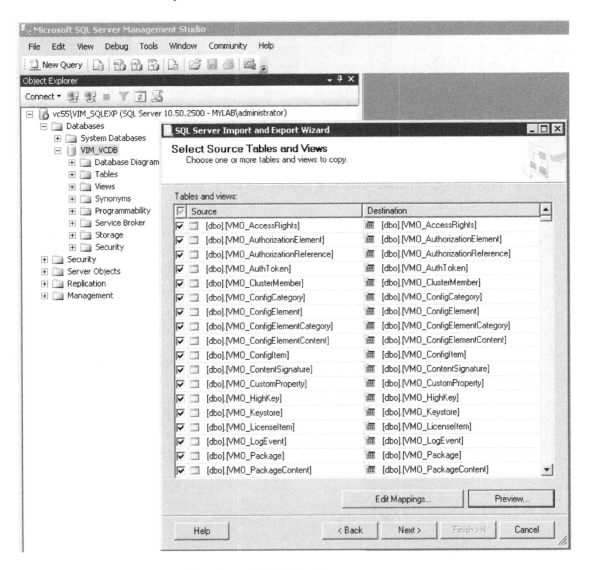

9. Select **Run immediately** and click **Finish**.

Now you have the Orchestrator database extracted as an external database. You still need to configure a user and rights. Then proceed with the *External database* section in this recipe.

Orchestrator Client and 4K display scaling

This recipe shows a hack to make the Orchestrator Client scale on 4K displays.

Getting ready

We need to download the program Resource Tuner (`http://www.restuner.com/`). The trial version will work, however, consider buying it if it works for you.

You need to know the path to your Java installation, it should be something like this:

```
C:\Program Files (x86)\Java\jre1.x.xx\bin\.
```

How to do it...

Before you start....

> Please be careful as this impacts your whole Java environment. This worked very well for me with Java 1.8.0_91-b14.

1. Download and install **Resource Tuner**.
2. Run Resource Tuner as administrator.
3. Open the file `javaws.exe` in your Java directory.
4. Expand `manifest` and then click on the first entry (the name can change due to localization).
5. Look for the line `<dpiAware>true</dpiAware>`.
6. Exchange the `true` for a `false`
7. **Save** and exit.
8. Repeat the same for all the other `java*.exe` in the same directory as well as `j2launcher.exe`.

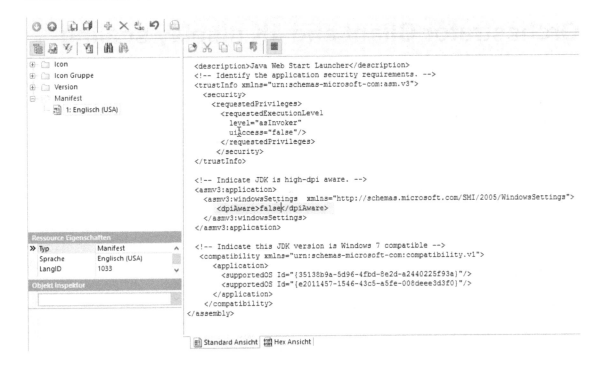

9. Start the `Client.jnlp` (the file that downloads when you start the web application).

How it works...

In Windows 10 you can set the scaling of applications when you are using high definition monitors (4K displays).

What you are doing is telling Java that it is not DPI aware, meaning that it will use the Windows 10 default scaler, instead of an internal scaler.

There's more...

For any other application, such as Snagit or Photoshop, I found that this solution works quite well:

http://www.danantonielli.com/adobe-app-scaling-on-high-dp.

2
Optimizing Orchestrator Configuration

In this chapter, we will explore how to optimize the Orchestrator installation and look at the following recipes:

- Tuning the appliance
- Tuning Java
- Configuring the Kerberos authentication
- Configuring access to the local filesystem
- Configuring the Orchestrator service SSL certificate
- Orchestrator log files
- Redirecting Orchestrator logs to an external server
- Backup and recovery
- Control Center titbits

Please also note that in the workflow package that comes with this book, there are several workflows that will configure Orchestrator.

Introduction

As in all production environments, you should consider using dedicated service accounts for connections between different services. For Orchestrator, there are several connections that we should have a look at.

The connection between Orchestrator and PSC/SSO will only be set up once with an SSO administrative user, after that Orchestrator will use the solution user.

The connection between Orchestrator and vCenter depends on how you would like to handle the role and rights management between them. You can either use one administrative connection between Orchestrator and vCenter, or choose to limit access by the role and rights of the logged-in Orchestrator user. We have already discussed this a bit in the recipe *Connecting to vCenter* in Chapter 1, *Installing and Configuring Orchestrator* and we will discuss it a bit more in the recipe *User management* in Chapter 7, *Interacting with Orchestrator*.

The connection between clients (desktops and application servers) and Orchestrator is regulated by the membership of the Orchestrator Administration group and by non-administrative users in Orchestrator. We will discuss how to add non-administrative users to Orchestrator in the *User management* recipe in Chapter 7, *Interacting with Orchestrator*.

In general, one should follow the IT base rule: *Dedicated Services, Dedicated Users*.

Please note that the vRA integrated Orchestrator is described in more detail in the recipe *Working with the integrated vRA Orchestrator* in Chapter 13, *Working with vRealize Automation*.

Tuning the appliance

In this recipe, we will learn how to tune an Orchestrator appliance. This includes changing IP settings as well as switching off unused services to get more performance out of the appliance.

Getting ready

We need a configured and running Orchestrator appliance as well as a web browser and an SSH tool (such as PuTTY).

How to do it...

There is a lot that could be done to tune the Orchestrator appliance.

Virtual Hardware

When you deployed the Orchestrator appliance, it came in Virtual Hardware Version 7. The best thing to do is to upgrade the Virtual Hardware of the appliance to the most current version. To do this, follow these steps:

1. Open the vCenter vSphere Web Client and find the Orchestrator VM.
2. Right-click the VM and select **Compatibility**.
3. If your VM is running, use **Schedule VM Compatibility Upgrade**, if the VM is powered off, choose **Upgrade VM Compatibility**.
4. Acknowledge the upgrade and select the compatibility you wish to use. Use the highest Virtual Hardware setting.
5. If your VM was running, restart it.

Changing the IP and hostname

The IP and hostname should normally be assigned when the appliance is deployed; however, some aftercare has to be performed when using a DHCP or VMware workstation. Follow these steps to change the IP and hostname:

1. Open the **virtual appliance management interface** (**VAMI**) area on port 5480.
2. Click on **Network** and select **Address**.
3. Change all settings as required.
4. Click on **Save Settings**.
5. Reconnect the browser to the new IP.

You also should consider giving your appliance a new SSL certificate. See the *Configuring the Orchestrator service SSL certificate* recipe in this chapter.

Setting the time (NTP)

This is especially important when using encrypted services such as Kerberos and Orchestrator clusters. Follow these steps to set the time:

1. Open the VAMI area on port 5480.
2. Click on **System** and then on **Time Zone**.
3. Set the correct time zone and click on **Save settings**.
4. Click on **Admin** and then select **Time Settings**.
5. Set **Time Sync. Mode** to **Use Time Server**.

6. Enter NTP servers in **Time Server** fields and click on **Save Settings**.

It is very important to have the same time settings in the Orchestrator server and vCenter PSC/SSO, as well as the Orchestrator Client. If the drift is too high, some updates, such as the workflow system logs, might not be updated properly. The worst case scenario could be that you lose connectivity between the components.

Turning SSH access to Orchestrator on and off

SSH access to the Orchestrator appliance is by default switched on. If your environment requires stricter security policies, here is how you can switch SSH off:

1. Open the VAMI area on port 5480.
2. Click on **Admin** and then select **Admin**.
3. You can switch on general SSH connectivity as well as root access separately:

Switching off unneeded services

If you are using external authentication and a database, you might as well switch off the database and LDAP services to gain more resources for Orchestrator. If you switch a service off, the service will not start on the next reboot:

1. Using SSH, log in to your Orchestrator appliance.
2. To see the status of a service, type chkconfig [Linux service name].
3. To switch off a service, type chkconfig [Linux service name] off.

4. To switch the service back on, type `chkconfig [Linux service name] on`.
5. To stop, start, or restart the service immediately, use the `service [Linux service name] {start|stop|restart}` command.

Here is the list of all Linux service names that are relevant for Orchestrator appliances:

Service	Linux service name
Orchestrator server	`vco-server`
Orchestrator Configurator Tool	`vco-configurator`
Embedded Database	`vpostgres`
Embedded LDAP	`ldap`

Root account expires

By default, the root account expires after 365 days. To change this setting, follow these steps:

1. Using SSH, log in to your Orchestrator appliance as root.
2. Use the `passwd -x 99999 root` command.

Your root password will now never expire, as `99999` (in some 273 years) is the highest value that can be entered.

How it works...

The Orchestrator appliance comes with a fully working Linux operating system, and therefore, it is highly adaptable to your needs.

If you are into Linux, you also can edit the configuration files. Please note that the SLES licensing used for the appliance might not cover additional packages. Also, installing additional software on the Orchestrator appliance might not be supported by VMware.

The appliance's `iptables` firewall is not configured. So, if you want to configure the firewalls, you have to use the `iptables` commands.

See also

The example workflow `02.01 Tuning the Appliance`.

Tuning Java

This recipe shows how to increase the Java heap size so that Orchestrator performs better by making better use of the allocated memory resources.

Getting ready

First of all, we need more virtual memory allocated to the VM on which Orchestrator is running.

You also need SSH access to the appliance.

How to do it...

This how-to is for vCO 5.5 and higher, for versions 5.1 and lower please see `kb.vmware.com/kb/2007423`:

1. Log in to the Linux operating system of your Orchestrator.
2. Stop the Orchestrator service with `service vco-server stop`.
3. Make a backup of the file with `cp /usr/lib/vco/app-server/bin/setenv.sh /usr/lib/vco/app-server/bin/setenv.sh.bak`.
4. Type `vi /usr/lib/vco/app-server/bin/setenv.sh`.
5. The `vi` command opens up and displays the contents of the file.
6. Move the cursor to the line that starts with `MEM_OPTS="-Xmx2048m`.
7. Press *I* and remove `2048`. Enter your desired heap size in MB.
8. Press *Esc* and then type `:qw` to exit and save. If you want to exit `vi` without saving, enter `:q!` instead.
9. Start the Orchestrator service with `service vco-server start`.

How it works...

If you are increasing the virtual memory assigned to the VM, you will also need to increase the Java heap size, as it doesn't automatically adjust itself.

The Orchestrator service (vco-server) is a Java process that is set by default to a heap size set to 2 GB. Before going ahead and increasing the Java heap size, it's probably a good idea to check how many resources the Java process actually takes.

You need to balance the amount of memory that you give to the Orchestrator Java process with the rest of the memory usage of the system. This is especially important if you are running Orchestrator together with vRealize Automation. You can easily end up with programs competing for memory, which will slow the whole system down. Don't forget that the Linux system needs some memory too.

JVM metrics in Control Center

The new Control Center now contains a collection of Java metrics. To access them, click on **Runtime Metrics** and then on **Generic**. These metrics are also stored every five minutes in `/var/log/vco/app-server/metrics.log`.

In regards to the Java heap size, you can find a lot of answers here.

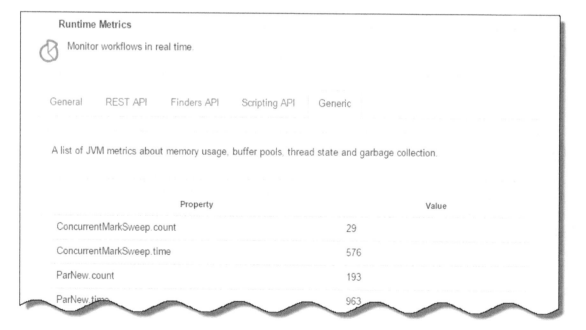

The most important metrics in regards to the Java Heap are:

JVM metric	Value in	Explanation
`ConcurrentMarkSweep.count`	Number	The number of times the Concurrent Mark-Sweep garbage collector has run.
`ConcurrentMarkSweep.time`	Number	The amount of time the Concurrent Mark-Sweep garbage collector has run.
`heap.max`	KB	The current amount of system memory allocated to the JVM.
`heap.used`	KB	The amount of allocated heap memory currently in use.
`non-heap.*`	KB	The current amount of system memory allocated to non-heap storage. This memory is used by Java to store loaded classes and other meta-data.

See also

The recipe *Working with the vRA integrated Orchestrator* in `Chapter 13`, *Working with vRealize Automation*.

Configuring the Kerberos authentication

This recipe shows how to configure the Kerberos authentication with Orchestrator. The Kerberos configuration is only needed for special plugins, such as **PowerShell**.

Getting ready

We just need administrative access to the Orchestrator operating system. You need to make sure that the clocks are in sync between Orchestrator and the KDC. See the *Tuning the appliance* recipe in this chapter. The domain in this example is called `mylab.local` and the AD server (KDC) is called `central.mylab.local`.

How to do it...

1. Log in to the Orchestrator operating system with root.
2. Edit the `/usr/java/jre-vmware/lib/security/krb5.conf` file. You might have to create this file.
3. Add the following lines to the file. In the following example, replace `mylab.local` with your domain settings. Make sure that you use the same case as in the example:

```
[libdefaults]
    default_realm = MYLAB.LOCAL
    udp_preference_limit = 1
[realms]
    MYLAB.LOCAL = {
        kdc = central.mylab.local
        default_domain = mylab.local
    }
[domain_realm]
.mylab.local= LAB.LOCAL
mylab.local= MYLAB.LOCAL
```

4. Make sure that the file is owned by root:root and has the rights `644`. Execute the `chmod 644 /usr/java/jre-vmware/lib/security/krb5.conf` command.
5. Save the file and then restart the Orchestrator service using either the Control Center or the Linux `service vco-server restart` command.

How it works...

Kerberos is an authentication protocol that uses tickets that allow systems to securely talk to each other.

Let's see how Kerberos works with a simple example. A client (Orchestrator) wants to communicate with a server (Windows host) securely. The client will communicate with a **Key Distribution Center (KDC)** to acquire a ticket. In Windows, the KDC is your AD controller, who then authenticates the login as a valid user and grants access. The KDC will then issue a ticket. This ticket is then used to login to the Windows server.

Configuration of the `krb5.conf` file is needed for Orchestrator in any version, as the connecting service is really the Java process and not the operating system underneath.

Since Windows 2000, Microsoft uses Kerberos as its main method for authentication. It is a secure method that uses encrypted communication and therefore the best choice for any production environment.

See also

This recipe is especially important for the *Working with PowerShell* recipe in Chapter 10, *Built in Plugins*. The example workflow 02.03 Configure Kerberos.

Configuring access to the local filesystem

Here, you will learn how to set permissions for Orchestrator to access its local filesystem and make an external filesystem accessible to Orchestrator.

Getting ready

We need administrative access to the operating system of Orchestrator.

How to do it…

There are two ways to give Orchestrator access to its local filesystem.

Fast and easy

Orchestrator already has full access to the folder /var/run/vco and can read and write from it. You can place files there via SCP for Orchestrator to use or have Orchestrator write files into that directory.

Configuring access

If you need to access additional folders on the appliance then follow these steps:

1. Connect to the Orchestrator appliance via SSH and root.
2. Make sure that the directory you would like to use with Orchestrator is accessible for the Orchestrator user. The user or group should be vco.
3. Edit the following file /etc/vco/app-server/js-io-rights.conf.

4. To give Orchestrator access to a directory, simply add the directory path and the rights such as +rwx (see the *How it works...* section of this recipe).

5. Save and close the file.

6. Restart the Orchestrator service.

How it works...

Access for Orchestrator to its local filesystem is needed for quite a lot of things, such as using SCP and uploading and downloading files. The access for Orchestrator is regulated by the entries in the js-io-rights.conf file. The following snippet shows the default settings in the file:

```
-rwx /
+rwx /var/run/vco/
-rwx /etc/vco/app-server/security/
+rx /etc/vco/
+rx /var/log/vco/
```

The available rights for Orchestrator are as follows:

Allow	Deny	Read	Write	Access
+	−	r	w	x

As you can see, Orchestrator has full access preconfigured for the /var/run/vco directory.

The x operator means that Orchestrator has the right to access the directory, for example, to list the content or to execute a file.

> In a clustered Orchestrator environment, where storing local files isn't a good solution, you should use NFS or SMB.

There's more...

You can use the file writer to write to a shared directory. This follows the same principle as normal file writing. The only thing is that the methods differ between Orchestrator OS versions:

1. Login as root.

2. Create a new directory and make sure it has the correct permissions.

3. Make sure Orchestrator has rights to access this directory.
4. Mount the Windows directory `mount -t cifs //host/share /mnt -o username=user,password=password`. If you have any special characters in the password, you need to escape them with `password`.
5. Access the `/mnt/` directory as you have learned.

Naturally, you can also mount NFS directories using the following code:

```
mount -t nfs host:/share /mnt -o nolock
```

See also

See the *Working with SSH* and *File operations* recipes in `Chapter 9`, *Essential Plugins*. The example workflow `02.04 Add Folder to Orchestrator access`.

Configuring the Orchestrator service SSL certificate

In this recipe, we will have a closer look at the SSL certificate of the Orchestrator server.

Getting ready

You need a running Orchestrator server.

If you are intending to use an SSL certificate signed by a **Certificate Authority (CA)**, you need to be able to sign a certificate request. You also need the CA root certificate, as well as any intermediate certificate, so that you can import it into the Orchestrator SSL store.

If you are creating a clustered vRO, please see the recipe *Load-balancing Orchestrator* in `Chapter 3`, *Distributed Design* first.

How to do it...

There are basically two kinds of certificates we can use, self-signed or CA-signed.

Self-signed certificates

When you installed vRO, a self-signed certificate has been created, but you are free to create a new one containing your details:

1. Open the Orchestrator Control Center.
2. Click on **Certificates** and select **Orchestrator Server SSL Certificate**.
3. You will then see the current certificate.
4. Click on **Generate** to generate a new self-signed certificate.
5. As the **First and last names**, you have to enter the FQDN of the server name. The **Country code** is a two-letter code: DE = Germany, AU=Australia.
6. Click again on **Generate** and then reboot the appliance.

After the reboot, your Orchestrator should show the new certificate when connecting.

Using VMCA generated certificates

This creates a PEM file using the **VMCA (VMware Certificate Authority)** that is part of the **PSC (Platform Controller Service)**. Consider to create a snapshot of Orchestrator before trying this out:

1. Open an SSH connection to your PSC (or to vCenter if your PSC is installed with vCenter).
2. Create a configuration file, /tmp/vro.conf, with content similar to this:

```
Country = DE
Name= vro
Organization = vLeet GmbH
OrgUnit = Consulting
State = Bayern
Locality = Munich
IPAddress = 192.168.220.12
Email = daniel.langenhan@vleet.de
Hostname = vro.mylab.local
```

If you want to create **subject alternate names (SAN)** names just add the additional hostnames onto the Hostname. This is especially needed if you want to use CNAMEs. For example:

```
Hostname =vro.mylab.local,orchestrator.mylab.local
```

3. Run the following commands to generate a certificate using VMCA:

```
cd /usr/lib/vmware-vmca/bin/

./certool --genkey --privkey=/tmp/vro.prikey --pubkey=/tmp/vro.pubkey

./certool --gencert --privkey=/tmp/vro.prikey --cert=/tmp/vro.cert
--config /tmp/vro.conf
```

4. Download the VMCA root certificate:

```
cd /tmp

wget https://127.0.0.1/certs/download --no-check-certificate
-O /tmp/vmca.zip

unzip  vmca.zip
```

5. Select the correct VMCA root certificate. If your vCenter is not a CA sub authority, the correct file is 6bc2e122.0, or else it should be the second one with the .0 ending. Copy the file to /tmp:

```
cp certs/6bc2e122.0 vmcaroot.cert
```

6. Build the .pem file:

```
awk 1 vro.prikey vro.cert vmcaroot.cert >vro.pem
```

7. Use SCP to download the .pem file and then use the next section to import the .pem file.

CA-signed certificate

A CA-signed certificate can be imported using a PEM encoded file, see the *How it works...* section.

1. Open the Orchestrator Control Center, click on **Certificates** and select **Orchestrator Server SSL Certificate**.
2. You will then see the current certificate.
3. Click on **Import** and select the .pem file to import. If you secured the file with a password, enter it also.
4. Click on **Import** again and then reboot the appliance.

After the reboot, your Orchestrator should show the new certificate when connecting.

How it works...

Orchestrator uses an Apache web server that is installed along with Orchestrator. The SSL certificate is stored within the Java environment of the Orchestrator installation. The SSL certificate we discuss here is the certificate that Orchestrator uses to communicate with other instances, such as the Orchestrator Client or other programs.

vRO 7 made some changes to its certificates encryption. MD2 and RSA must have a minimum length of 1024 bit. In vRO7.1, an additional change was introduced:

- In Cluster mode, the nodes exchange certificate information, which leads to the fact that all nodes share the same certificate. This requires you to use SAN certificates in the Cluster mode. Also, see the recipe *Building an Orchestrator cluster* in `Chapter 3`, *Distributed Design*.
- Plugins now need to use the plug-in SDK to retrieve a certificate.

For rounded information about all the Orchestrator certificates that exist, see Spas's post:

`http://kaloferov.com/blog/orchestrator-certificates-explained/`

Default, self-signed, or CA-signed?

The question now is which certificate should we use, the default SSL certificate, a self-signed certificate, or a CA-signed certificate?

The main difference between the default and the self-signed certificates is that the self-signed certificate is issued with the correct FQDN of the Orchestrator server, and therefore, is more secure than the default certificate.

A CA-signed certificate has the advantage as it is automatically accepted by all hosts that trust the CA. This makes large deployments easier to manage as well as comply with the security demands of your company.

VMCA

The VMCA is an integrated part of vSphere 6 and creates a CA that signs and publishes all ESXi and solution user certificates. The cool thing is that if you have used your own enterprise CA to make the VMCA a Subordinate Certificate Authority (kb.vmware.com/kb/2111219) then your CA trusts your VMCA and VMCA trusts vRO.

If you don't have a CA, you can export the VMCA root certificate and import it into your trusted root certificates on your computer, which automatically results that the certificates for vCenter and all ESXi server URLS are trusted. (see http://blogs.vmware.com/vsphere/2015/03/vmware-certificate-authority-overview-using-vmca-root-certificates-browser.html).

PEM encoded files

PEM encoded files are a one-stop shop and the new way forward in regards to certificates. They combine not only a signed certificate, but also the certificate's private key, the root certificate, and any intermediate certificates. Orchestrator, as well as vRealize Operations Manager, now uses this method. The structure is as follows:

```
-----BEGIN PRIVATE KEY-----
(Your Primary SSL certificate: PrivateKey.key)
-----END PRIVATE KEY-----
-----BEGIN CERTIFICATE-----
(Your Primary SSL certificate: Server.crt)
-----END CERTIFICATE-----
-----BEGIN CERTIFICATE-----
(Your Intermediate certificate: Intermediate.crt)
-----END CERTIFICATE-----
-----BEGIN CERTIFICATE-----
(Your Root certificate: TrustedRoot.crt)
-----END CERTIFICATE-----
```

The – – – –, as well as the headers are important and should not be changed. Also, make sure that you copy the header and footer notes of the certificate.

There's more...

Next to using the PEM integration of the Control Center you can also use the *old* method shown here.

Getting the SSL store password

Security has *improved* as the password of the SSL keystore isn't `dunesdunes` anymore. It is now generated when you start the appliance and is stored in `/var/lib/vco/keystore.password`. As we need that password, let's save it into a bash variable and also create one for the SSL store:

```
STOREPASS=`cat /var/lib/vco/keystore.password`
STORE="/etc/vco/app-server/security/jssecacerts"
```

Backing up the default certificates

First of all, we need to back up the default certificate that comes with Orchestrator:

1. Log in to the Orchestrator appliance via SSH as `root`.
2. Stop the Orchestrator service.
3. Make a copy of the existing SSL store:

```
cp $STORE $STORE.bak
```

Creating certificates and requests

We will now create the new self-signed certificate and then create a request from it to get it signed by the CA making it a CA-signed certificate. After this we will import the signed certificate. The alias for the Orchestrator certificates is still `dunes` and refers to the original name of the company that created Orchestrator before it was bought by VMware. Follow these steps to create a certificate and request:

1. First, we need to delete the existing certificate:

```
keytool -keystore $STORE -storepass $STOREPASS -alias dunes -delete
```

2. We will now create the certificate:

```
keytool -keystore $STORE -storepass $STOREPASS -alias dunes -keypass
$STOREPASS -keyalg RSA -sigalg SHA512withRSA -keysize 2048 -genkey
```

3. As the **First and last names**, you have to enter the FQDN of the server name. The **Country code** is a two-letter code: `DE` = Germany, `AU`=Australia.

4. Fill in the rest of the required information. When asked for a password, just press *Enter*.

5. Generate a new certificate-signing request (CSR) with the following command:

```
keytool -keystore $STORE -storepass $STOREPASS -alias dunes -keypass
$STOREPASS -certreq -sigalg SHA512withRSA -file /tmp/cert.csr
```

Generating certificates with alternative names (SAN certificate)

This is an alternative method to the preceding one, and you can use it for an Orchestrator cluster and if you are using not only FQDNS but IPs (only in Labs please). For more details, see the recipe *Load-balancing Orchestrator* in `Chapter 3`, *Distributed Design*.

Replace the content of `dname` and `SAN` with your DNS names and/or IPs:

```
keytool -keystore $STORE -storepass $STOREPASS -alias dunes -keypass
$STOREPASS -genkey -keyalg RSA -sigalg SHA512withRSA -keysize 2048 -dname
"CN=vro1.mylab.local, OU=consulting, O=vLeet GmbH, L=Munich, ST=Bayern,
C=DE" -ext SAN="ip:192.168.220.20,dns:vro2.mylab.local,ip:192.168.220.21"
```

Signing and importing certificates

1. Have the certificate request signed by your CA. Export the CA root as well as any intermediate certificates.

2. Import the CA's root certificate into the keystore:

```
keytool -keystore $STORE -storepass $STOREPASS -alias root   -import
-file [root file certificate]
```

3. Import the CA-signed certificate into the keystore:

```
keytool -keystore $STORE -storepass $STOREPASS -alias dunes  -import
-keypass $STOREPASS -sigalg SHA256withRSA -file [file name].crt
```

4. Reboot the appliance.

Your CA-signed certificate is now imported into Orchestrator.

See also

Create a Microsoft CA VMware template:

```
http://blogs.vmware.com/vsphere/2015/06/creating-a-microsoft-certificate-aut
hority-template-for-ssl-certificate-creation-in-vsphere-6-0.html
```

Orchestrator log files

In this recipe, we will have a closer look at the Orchestrator log file. Where they are and how to configure them.

Getting ready

You need access to the Orchestrator Control Center.

You also need SSH root access to the Orchestrator appliance. See the recipe *Tuning the appliance* in this chapter.

How to do it...

As log files are a bigger theme, this section is split up into multiple parts.

Server log in Control Center

The server log can be directly shown in the Control Center:

1. Login to Control Center.
2. Click on **Live Log Stream**. The server log is then shown.
3. Entering a search string into the **Search** window will trigger a highlighting function.
4. Click on **Filter (grep)** to only show entries that contain the search string.

5. Use **View full screen** to show the log in full-screen mode.

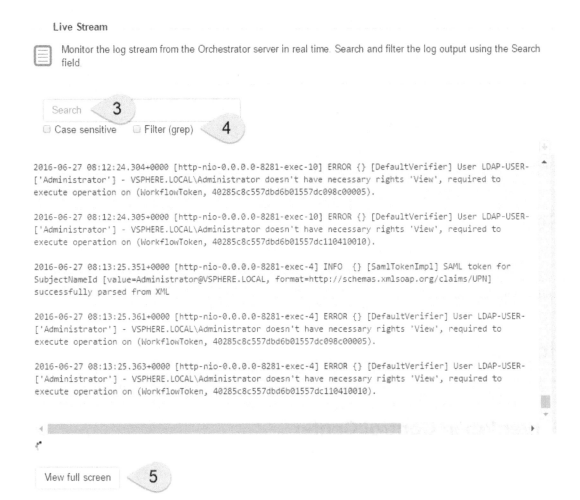

Configuring the server log with the Control Center

We will now configure the server log behavior:

1. Login to Control Center.
2. Click on **Configure Logs**.
3. The **Log level** defines the log level threshold. You select which log events will be included in the server logs.

4. The **Max file count** defines how many log files are stored.

5. The **Max file size** defines how big one of these files can maximally grow. When a file grows bigger, a new file will be created.

6. **Require disk space** shows how much space the configuring will take up. It is *[Max file count] * [Max file size]*.

7. Click on **Save**. No restart is needed:

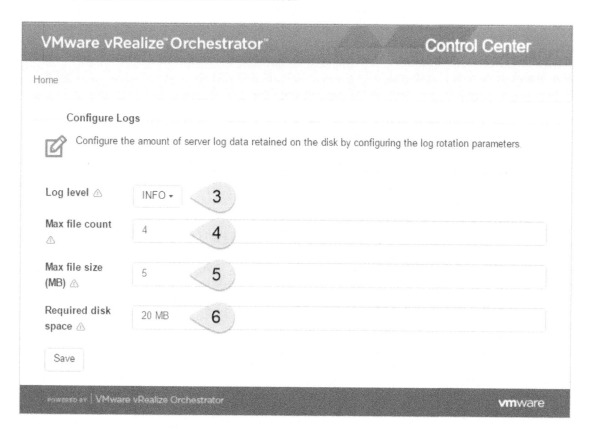

Accessing the log files via SSH

We will now access the log files using the Orchestrator OS:

1. Login to Orchestrator using SSH and root.

2. All log files are located in /var/log/vco/, see the *How it works...* sections for more detail about them.

3. To view the logs, use `less server.log`. You can then use the cursor keys to browse the log and q to exit the command. You can search by pressing / and then enter (case sensitive) what you're looking for. Use G to go to the end of the log and g to go back to the beginning.

4. To watch a log file, use the command `tail -f server.log`, this will continue displaying the log file and show each new entry into it. Exit with *Ctrl + C*.

Changing log file behavior

This shows how you can change all log file behavior, not just the `server.log`. Check the *How it works...* sections for more details about the different log files:

1. Login to Orchestrator using SSH and root.

2. Use the following lines to create a backup:

```
cd /etc/vco/app-server/
cp log4j.xml log4j.xml.bak
```

3. To change the settings, use `vi log4j.xml`.

4. Look for the comment `<!---` tags. Leave all sections with `used by Log Insight Agent` alone:

```
<!-- ================================= -->
<!-- Server log                        -->
<!-- ================================= -->
<appender class="org.apache.log4j.RollingFileAppender" name="FILE">
    <param name="File" value="${catalina.base}/logs/server.log"/>
    <param name="Append" value="true"/>
    <param name="Encoding" value="UTF-8"/>
    <!-- Rollover at 5MB and allow 4 rollover files -->
    <param name="MaxFileSize" value="8MB"/>
    <param name="MaxBackupIndex" value="4"/>
    <layout class="org.apache.log4j.PatternLayout">
        <!-- The default pattern: Date Priority [Category] Message\n -->
        <param name="ConversionPattern" value="%d{yyyy-MM-dd
        HH:mm:ss.SSSZ}
        [%t] %-5p {%X{full}} [%c{1}] %m%n"/>
    </layout>
</appender>
```

5. To change the maximum file size, alter the parameter: `<param name="MaxFileSize" value="8MB"/>`

6. To change the amount of log files that are created, change the parameter: `<param name="MaxBackupIndex" value="4"/>`

7. To change the priority, scroll down to the `<category` tags and change the parameter: `<priority value="INFO"/>`.

8. No reboot or restart is needed.

How it works...

The log files that Orchestrator creates are the following in `/var/log/vco/app-server/`:

LogFiles	Usage
`server.log`	Contains all Orchestrator login information. This is the main log.
`scripting.log`	Contains all logs in regards to workflows, their execution, and users. The same information is also shown in `server.log`.
`metrics.log`	Contains all matrixes that are collected for Orchestrator every five minutes. These are the values shown in the Control Center under **Runtime Metrics**.
`localhost_access.log`	Contains all HTTP requests that the Orchestrator service is getting.
`integration-scripting` `integration-server`	All these logs are for usage with VMware Log Insight and are just copies (see `log4j.xml`).
`warning.log`	Contains all server logs that are the type warning or higher.

The log files that Orchestrator creates are in `/var/log/vco/configuration/`, they are as follows:

LogFiles	Usage
`catalina.out`	Contains detailed information about the Tomcat server instance running Orchestrator.
`controlcenter.log`	Contains all logs in regards to the Control Center.
`vco_database.log`	Contains information about the database upgrades.

See also

The recipe *Redirecting Orchestrator logs to an external server* in this chapter, and the recipe *Scripting with logs* in `Chapter 5`, *Visual Programming*.

Redirecting Orchestrator logs to an external server

In this recipe, we will configure the Orchestrator server to send all logs to a centralized Syslog server. This is especially important when using Orchestrator clusters.

Getting ready

You need a Syslog server or a vRealize Log Insight Server as a target.

You may also need access to the Orchestrator appliance OS (SSH).

vRealize Log Insight

When you buy vSphere, you also get licensing for Log Insight for 25 hosts.

If you are using vRealize Log Insight then you should also consider downloading the vRO7 package. You can find some details here:

`http://blogs.vmware.com/management/2016/04/vrealize-orchestrator-7-0-content-pack-log-insight.html`.

We are now configuring Log Insight to access Orchestrator:

1. Log into the vRealize Log Insight website.
2. Click in the upper right corner and select **Content Packs**.
3. Select the **VMware – Orchestrator** content pack:

4. Tick the install tickbox and then on **Install**.

How to do it...

The redirection of Syslog became much easier in vRO7 as everything is more or less done in the Control Center:

1. Login to the Orchestrator Control Center.
2. Go to **Logging Integration**.
3. Tick the box next to **Enable logging to a remote log server** to configure Syslog.

Syslog with Log4J

Sadly, Log4J is deprecated at this stage. However, you can and should use the Log Insight Agent to send Syslog messages:

1. From where we left off, select **Use Log4j Syslog Appender**.
2. Enter your FQDN or IP of the Syslog host as well as the port, if it's not 514.
3. Select the **Facility**. The facility is a kind of folder where the log files should be stored. You can choose between **User** and **Local0** to **Local7**.
4. The **Threshold** is setting from what level you want to forward Syslog messages. I would not recommend anything lower than **INFO**, but that depends on the purpose for forwarding.

5. The **Network Protocol** can be either **UDP** or **TCP**. Normally **UDP** is the way to go.

6. Click on **Save** and then **Test connection**. If that works, check your Syslog server for incoming messages:

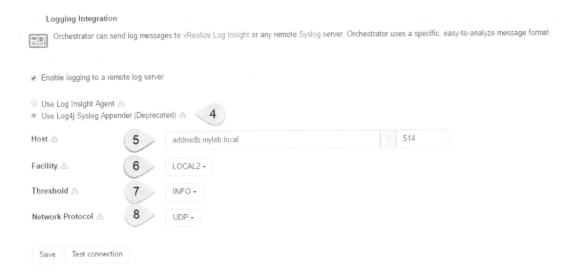

Log Insight Agent

Orchestrator has been fitted with an agent for VMware vRealize Log Insight. Here is how to configure it from where we left off:

1. Select **Use Log Insight Agent**.

2. Enter your FQDN or IP of your vRealize Log Insight Server as well as the port, which is default `9000`. If you want to send Syslog messages to a Syslog server, choose the Syslog hostname or IP and then select port **514**.

3. Select the **Protocol**. Use **cfapi** with Log Insight and **Syslog** for the usage with a Syslog server.

4. Click on **Save**.

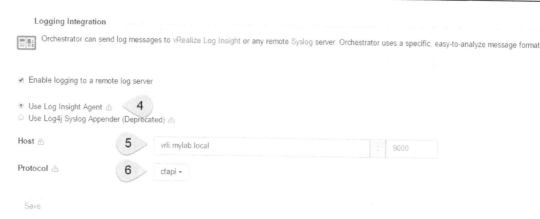

5. We now need to configure the Log Insight Agent to send logs across. For this, see the *There's more...* section.

How it works...

Redirecting Syslog files to a central logging facility can be quite a useful thing. Not only does the Orchestrator Syslog contain the normal Orchestrator Syslog entries, but also information on by whom and when was the workflow run. See the *Scripting with logs* recipe in `Chapter 5`, *Visual Programming*, for more information.

A Syslog server is normally used to analyze and/or monitor the behavior of a given system. Typical actions are to make sure problems are captured early as well as to track the performance of a system. A lot of companies also use Syslog to keep a record of what workflow has been run by whom and when.

You can download and test vRealize Log Insight for free, just go to the `vmware.com` webpage and join the trial.

For working with the Orchestrator log files, have a look at the recipe *Orchestrator log files* in this chapter.

Configuring the Orchestrator Log Insight Agent to forward to Syslog

If you want to use a classic external Syslog server (such as Splunk), but you like to use the Log Insight Agent on Orchestrator, to forward the logs you need to do some configuration. To do this, follow these steps:

1. Configure the logging integration to use **Log Insight Agent**.
2. Enter the Syslog host IP or FQDN and then choose port 514.
3. Set **Protocol** to **syslog**.
4. Connect to Orchestrator via SSH.
5. Edit the file /var/lib/loginsight-agent/liagent.ini.
6. Add the following entries at the end:

```
[filelog|scripting]
directory=/var/log/vco/app-server
include= scripting.log; scripting.log.*

[filelog|server]
directory=/var/log/vco/app-server
include=server.log;server.log.*
```

7. Restart the log insight agent with the service liagentd restart command.
8. Check the log files for errors:

```
/var/log/loginsight-agent/liagent_[date].log
```

This should now forward all the servers and scripting log files to your Syslog server. Also, see the recipe *Orchestrator log files* in this chapter.

 The Log Insight Linux Agent sends the logs via TCP, not UDP so you may need to adjust your Syslog server.

The configuration of the Log insight Linux Agent is documented in the VMware vRealize Log Insight 3 Agent Administration Guide (http://tinyurl.com/VMwareLI30Admin)

There's more...

There are tons of Syslog software tools for Windows and for Linux. Here is a short list of the most common ones for Windows:

- `http://www.kiwisyslog.com/`
- `http://www.splunk.com`
- `http://www.balabit.com/network-security/syslog-ng`

All Linux servers come with a Syslog service installed and can be used as well. However, in general, they do not have a comfortable web or GUI frontend.

See also

The *Scripting with logs* recipe in `Chapter 5`, *Visual Programming*.

All Orchestrator log files can be found at `kb.vmware.com/kb/1010956`. The example workflow `02.06 Configure Syslog for LoginSight`.

Backup and recovery

In this recipe, we look into backing up and restoring Orchestrator. To back up and restore single packages or workflows, please see the *Importing and exporting Orchestrator elements* and *Working with packages* recipes in `Chapter 4`, *Programming Skills*.

Getting ready

We need an installed and running Orchestrator server.

How to do it...

There are several things that should be backed up; we will have a look at all of them.

A snapshot is not a backup.

Backing up Orchestrator configuration

This is a one off job. You only need to do it when you change the Orchestrator configuration:

1. Open the Orchestrator Control Center.
2. Click on **Export/Import Configuration** and then on **Export Configuration**.
3. Select all the checkboxes.
4. Depending on your security needs, assign a **Password** to the export.
5. Click on **Export**.
6. Place the file in a secure location where you can easily retrieve it in the case of a restore.

Export/Import Configuration

Export, Import and Migrate Orchestrator server configurations.

Export Configuration   Import Configuration   Migrate Configuration

2

Export the current Orchestrator server configuration.

Export server configuration	☑	Export configuration files, certificates, encryption key, etc.
Export license	☑	Export license.
Bundle plug-ins	☑ *3*	
Export plug-in configurations	☑	

Protect the exported file with a password as it contains sensitive information (certificates, passwords, encryption keys, etc.). Use the same password when importing the configuration.

Password ⚠   *4*   (Optional)

Export   *5*

Backing up an internal database

The backup of an external database is done with the normal enterprise methods. The internal Orchestrator PostgreSQL DB is a different thing:

1. Connect to your Orchestrator OS via SSH.
2. Run the following command to backup the Orchestrator DB:

```
pg_dump vmware -U vmware -Fp -c | gzip -c > vRO-DB.gz
```

3. Save the dump in a place where you can find it again. Please also see the *There's more...* section of this recipe.

The Control Center database export uses the same method and both files are compatible.

Restore

Assuming that your Orchestrator installation died and you need to restore it, follow these steps:

1. Deploy a fresh Orchestrator appliance of the *same* version you lost.
2. Open the Orchestrator Control Center.
3. Stop the Orchestrator service.
4. Click on **Export/Import Configuration** and then on **Import Configuration**.
5. Browse to the Orchestrator backup file.
6. You may need to enter a **Password**.
7. Click on **Import**.

If you are using an external DB, that's it, you're done, just start the Orchestrator service again. If you are using the internal database, continue below.

8. Click on **Home** and then go to **Import Database**.
9. Browse to the exported database file.

10. Click **Import database**.

11. Select the item you want to import (for a full restore, tick everything).

Export Configuration   Import Configuration   Migrate Configuration

Import an Orchestrator server configuration created by the Orchestrator Control Center. If you exported the configuration with a password, use the same password when importing.

Configuration snapshot information:

Exported from: 192.168.220.12
Version/build: 7.0.1/3533702
Database version: 1.71
Exported on: Apr 14, 2016

Import Options

Server Configuration

Import server configuration properties files	☑
Change "localhost" in DB connection string to	(Optional) Use exported hostname
Import custom properties (vmo-managed.properties)	☑
Import trusted certificates	☑
Import server certificate	☑

License

Import License	☑

Plugins

Import plug-ins	☑
Force import plug-ins	☑

Plugin Configurations

Import plug-in configurations (database)	☑
Import plug-in configurations (filesystem)	☑

Cancel   Finish Import

12. Click on **Finish Import**.

13. Start the Orchestrator service.

How it works...

The Control Center configuration export helps quite a bit with preserving your Orchestrator configurations; however, it's not perfect. The best protection against any loss is solid documentation, where you write down the Orchestrator configurations, as well as why an item is configured the way it is.

External database

Using an external database for Orchestrator has the immense advantage that this database can be backed up using the already-existing methods of your business. The Orchestrator database contains most parts of the configuration, but more importantly, it contains all workflows and workflow executions. Having a regular database backup is important.

If one restores the database, it's important to *stop* the Orchestrator server first.

There's more...

The continued backup of the internal Orchestrator PostgreSQL database can be done with quite a lot of methods. Here we will discuss some of them.

Cron job

The idea is to use the internal Linux scheduler (called CRON) to facilitate the backup. You need access to the Orchestrator OS as well as to a shared drive. There is a nice article that goes into this in more detail:

```
https://communities.vmware.com/docs/DOC-24026
```

vRO policy

Using Orchestrator Policies, it is possible to create re-occurring tasks. We can use this to create a workflow that will back up the Orchestrator database either to a shared drive or send the export via a mail attachment.

See the recipe *Working with policies* in `Chapter 8`, *Better Workflows and Optimized Working* and the recipes *Working with mails* and *File operations* in `Chapter 9`, *Essential Plugins*.

vRO Control Center API

The Control Center has an API that is REST and can be accessed. We have a short look at it in the recipe *Control Center titbits* in this chapter and a more detailed look in the recipe *Accessing the Control Center via REST plugin* in `Chapter 7`, *Interacting with Orchestrator*. You could use the REST to connect to the Control Center and then export the database this way.

See also

The recipe *Working with packages* in `Chapter 4`, *Programming Skills,* shows you how to back up elements in Orchestrator.

Control Center titbits

This recipe contains a lot of small little bits and pieces around the Orchestrator Control Center.

Getting ready

We need access to the Control Center.

How to do it...

This is a collection of little bits and pieces...

Inspecting workflows

This enables you to check what workflows are running, to cancel running workflows and to inspect them:

1. In the Orchestrator Control Center, go to **Inspect Workflow**.
2. You now see all the currently running workflows. You can use the example workflow `06.04.01 Sleep` for testing.
3. To cancel the workflow, tick it and then select **Cancel all selected**.

4. Click on **Refresh Grid** to show the changes.

 Inspect Worklfows

Browse a list of currently running or already finished workflow runs.

Running Workflows   Finished Workflows

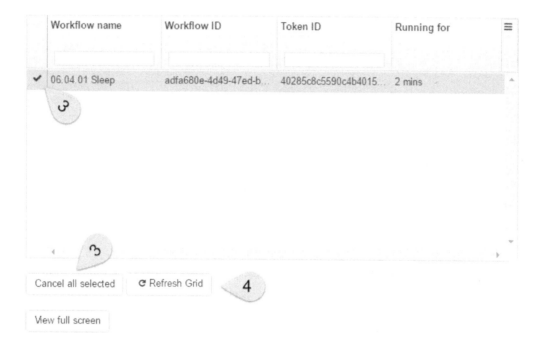

Workflow name	Workflow ID	Token ID	Running for	≡
✔ 06.04.01 Sleep	adfa680e-4d49-47ed-b...	40285c8c5590c4b4015...	2 mins	

Cancel all selected   ↻ Refresh Grid

View full screen

5. Click on **Finished Workflows**.
6. You can now select for either failed, completed, and/or canceled workflows.
7. You can also narrow down the timeframe of the search.

8. As well as search by the **Workflow name**, its **Workflow ID**, or its **Token ID**.
9. By clicking on one of the blue links, you can get additional information of the workflow, such as its logs and schema.

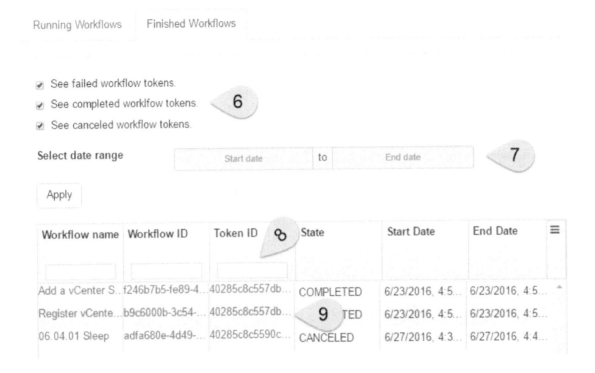

System properties

You can configure several system properties that will change the way Orchestrator behaves:

1. In the Orchestrator Control Center, go to **System Properties**.
2. Click on the plus sign.
3. Enter the **Key** you would like to change as well as the **Value** it should now have. A **Description** helps quite a lot at this stage.

4. Click on **Add** and then restart the Orchestrator service.

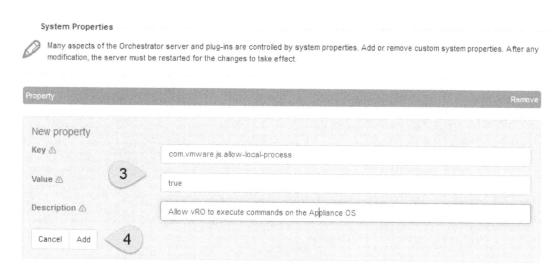

In the *How it works...* section is a list of common system properties to set.

Changing the Control Center user name

You can change the login name for the Control Center in order to increase security:

1. In the Orchestrator Control Center, click on **Settings** (top right).
2. Click on the **Change Credentials**.
3. Enter the **Old password**.
4. Now enter a **New user name** for the Control Center user. The default is `root`.

5. Enter the **New password** and click on **Change Credentials**:

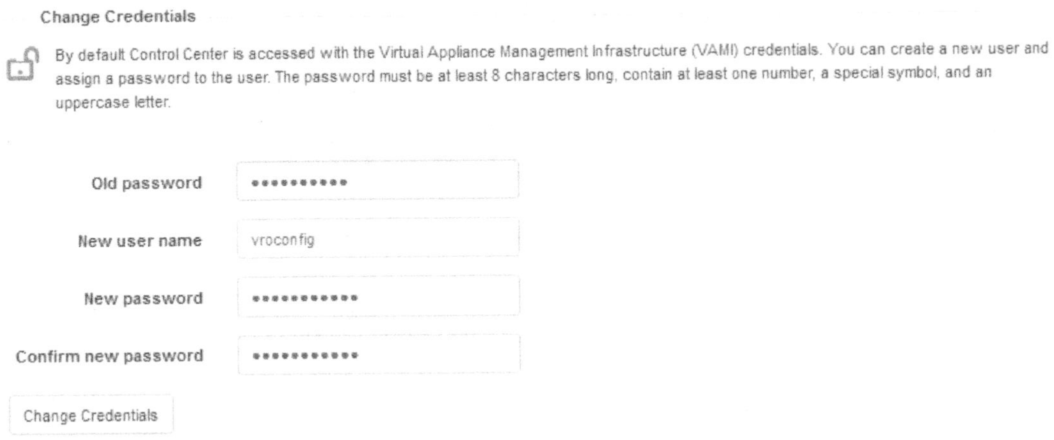

Change Credentials

By default Control Center is accessed with the Virtual Appliance Management Infrastructure (VAMI) credentials. You can create a new user and assign a password to the user. The password must be at least 8 characters long, contain at least one number, a special symbol, and an uppercase letter.

Old password	••••••••••
New user name	vroconfig
New password	••••••••••••
Confirm new password	••••••••••••

Change Credentials

File System Browser

The Control Center also includes a file browser, which is also able to download you some files:

1. In the Orchestrator Control Center, go to **File System Browser**.
2. You are presented with four different folders that you can access (see the following screenshot).
3. Click on one of the folders to see its content.

4. Select the blue icon on the right of the file to download it:

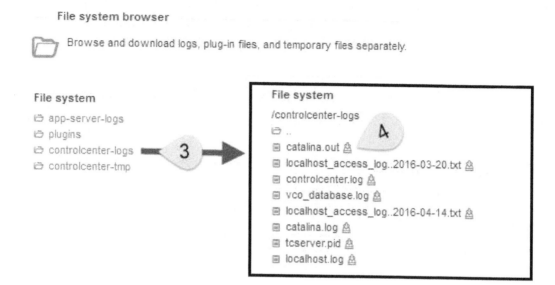

How it works...

The Control Center has quite a lot of features and turns out to be much more interesting than the old Configurator. The ability to use a REST interface pushes automated configurations and deployments further and further. One could create in Orchestrator a workflow that deploys two Orchestrators, and then by using the Control Center API, configure them as clusters.

Control Center API

The Control Center comes with its own REST API. This allows you to configure Orchestrator via REST and so automate the configuration. The whole thing comes with a bit of documentation to have a look at:

```
https://[Orchestror FQDN]:8283/vco-controlcenter/docs
```

We will have a much closer look at it in the recipe *Accessing the Control Center via REST plugin* in `Chapter 7`, *Interacting with Orchestrator*.

System properties

Here we have a selection of system properties:

Property	Value	Description
`com.vmware.js.allow-local-process`	true	Allows orchestrator to execute commands on the appliance OS.
`com.vmware.o11n.smart-client-disabled`	true	Disables any non-admin access to the Orchestrator Client.
`com.vmware.scripting.rhino-class-shutter-file`	[file location]	Integrates new Java classes in Orchestrator.
`com.vmware.vmo.plugin.vi4.waitUpdatesTimeout`	[ms]	vCenter time out. Default 20,000 ms.

There's more...

The advanced options let you re-define some of the limitations of Orchestrator. In the Orchestrator Control Center, go to **Advanced Options**.

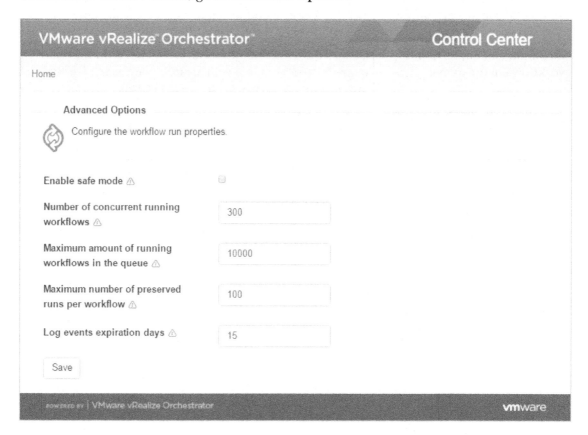

Advanced Options	Usage
Enable safe mode	This option cancels all running workflows without restarting them after an Orchestrator restart.
Number of concurrent running workflows	The number of workflows that run at the same time.
Maximum amount of running workflows in the queue	Defines the length of the workflow queue. Workflow requests are stored in the queue until they are run. If the queue is full, no new workflows can be run.
Maximum number of preserved runs per workflow	How many workflow executions should be kept before the oldest get deleted?
Log events expiration days	The number of days log events are kept in the database before being purged.

Before changing these settings to higher values, consider scaling out your Orchestrator deployment, see the *Introduction* to `Chapter 3`, *Distributed Design*.

See also

The recipe *Accessing the Control Center via REST plugin* in `Chapter 7`, *Interacting with Orchestrator*.

3

Distributed Design

This chapter is dedicated to discussing how a distributed design of Orchestrators looks and can be designed. We will be discussing the following recipes:

- Building an Orchestrator cluster
- Load-balancing Orchestrator
- Upgrading a cluster
- Managing remote Orchestrator
- Synchronizing Orchestrator elements between Orchestrator servers

Introduction

Why a full chapter dedicated to multiple Orchestrators? Well… since Orchestrator became the central turning stone for vRealize automation, there are more and more customers that distribute and protect their Orchestrator infrastructure.

We differentiate between different goals and scenarios, such as **high availability (HA)**, workload spreading, scaling out, and bandwidth optimization and localization. In the following sections I break this down into the three most common forms: cluster, distributed, and scale out designs.

Please note that the **vRealize automation** (**vRA**) internal Orchestrator should not be clustered as described here. If you scale out vRA, you should consider using an external Orchestrator cluster, not the built-in vRA Orchestrator. See `Chapter 13`, *Working with vRealize Automation* for more information.

Cluster design

As Orchestrator becomes more and more production-critical for companies, it is a solid idea to cluster Orchestrator to guarantee that it's up and working. An Orchestrator cluster is most powerful when combined with a load-balancer. However, if you are only using Orchestrator to run workflows without any other input (headless), then you can use an Orchestrator cluster without a load-balancer and use the steps outlined in this chapter to make sure that workflows are started or logs are checked using a central Orchestrator controlling all other installations.

A typical situation where a clustered Orchestrator (with a load-balancer) is a very good idea is when the Orchestrator acts as a **domain manager**. What is meant by that is that Orchestrator is responsible for automating the VMware domain (all things vSphere) and another automation tool (such as Ansible, Chef, or something else) uses the Orchestrator workflows. The domain manager concept is another solution to the automation problem. Instead of using one tool (such as Orchestrator or vRA) to automate everything, you use tools specialized for their domain. Examples of domains are VMware, Microsoft, Red Hat, EMC or NetApp storage, and Cisco networking. In each of these domains, a tool exists that is specialized to deal with the automation of its domain. For Red Hat there is Satellite, for Microsoft there is SMS or SCOM, and so on. Each of these tools has a SOAP or REST interface that can be accessed by a general management tool. Orchestrator would be a domain manager for VMware.

The following pictures show how an Orchestrator cluster can look and how it can be accessed. Please note that the use of the vSphere client isn't supported in cluster mode.

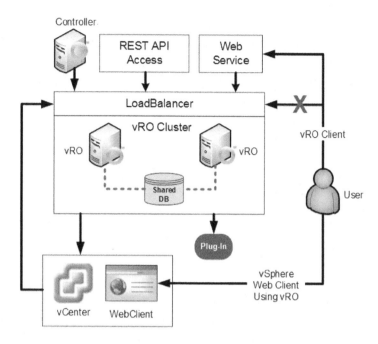

Distributed design

When we talk about distributed, we mean that you have multiple Orchestrator installations that are not in the same place or not looking after the same things. For example, your main corporate data center sits in Europe and you have others in North America, Asia, and Oceania. If you have one Orchestrator sitting in Europe that manages all other centers, the result would be massive problems from various sources, such as bandwidth, time zones, workflow distribution, and versioning.

But that's not the only example. One can generally differentiate Orchestrator deployments into **Geographically Distributed** and **Logically Distributed** ones:

Geographically Distributed

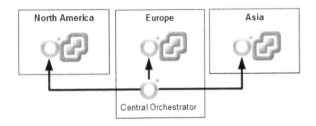

Logically Distributed

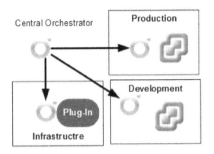

Geographically Distributed

The use of geographically dispersed Orchestrators is common in large companies. Here, a central Orchestrator instance executes workflows on remote environments. The amount of bandwidth used to execute a workflow remotely (using the multi-node plugin) is much less than the amount that would be needed to run the workflows directly. This is especially true when a lot of input variables have to be collected to run the workflow.

Logically Distributed

Logically Distributed means that your Orchestrators are located in different environments, such as production, development, and so on. In this case, you may have an Orchestrator infrastructure that creates and manages your different infrastructure, or is used for deployments or automation. Central management is then also quite important.

Please note that the remote Orchestrator doesn't necessarily have to be paired with a vCenter. A remote Orchestrator could be used to handle your server, storage, or any other add-on infrastructure services or hardware.

Scaling out

The last design deals with scaling out and discusses how to distribute workloads and how to deal with Orchestrator's limitations. There are cases where the maximum number of concurrent workflows running (300) is too small. One way to deal with this is to increase the limit (see the recipe *Control Center titbits* in Chapter 2, *Optimizing Orchestrator Configuration*), but the better way is to scale your deployment.

There are two ways to do this. You either use a distributed design or use a cluster design, as seen in the following figure:

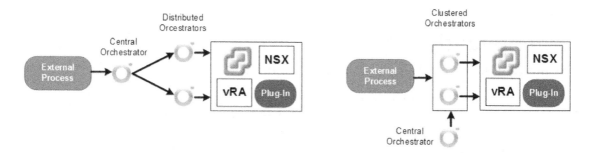

The central Orchestrator in both approaches is responsible for syncing workflows and settings between the actual working Orchestrators.

Central management

A central Orchestrator instance can be used to keep control of all the distributed installations.

A central Orchestrator server would be connected to all sub-Orchestrators using the multi-node plugin (also known as the VCO plugin). This will allow you to develop and then distribute your workflows centrally.

Using proxy workflows, you can run workflows on geographically remote sites without running into bandwidth or timing problems. You can also schedule the execution of workflows in remote locations to suit time zone differences.

Using the Orchestrator Control Center REST API, you can control the remote/distributed/clustered Orchestrators tidily and even automate their behavior.

In theory, it would be a quite a lot of work, but it's possible to create a workflow that deploys multiple Orchestrator instances using the vSphere plugin, then configure and cluster them using the Control Center API, and then create a load-balancer using the NSX plugin.

Building an Orchestrator cluster

In this recipe, we are building an Orchestrator cluster and configuring it for HA. Load-balancing is discussed in a separate recipe in this chapter.

Getting ready

The prerequisites for a cluster are not that hard, but they are important:

- **Shared DB**: Please have a look at the recipe *Configuring an external database* in `Chapter 1`, *Installing and Configuring Orchestrator*. Also, check that you have set the required extras as stated in the *There's more...* section of the recipe *Configuring an external database*. This is especially important if you are using an MS SQL DB. Also note that if you're serious about HA, you may want to use a DB cluster.
- You need two Orchestrator installations. It's best to use fresh ones, each with fixed IPs.
- Make sure NTP is configured and the time is synced.
- You should be familiar with the content of the recipe *Important Orchestrator settings* in `Chapter 1`, *Installing and Configuring Orchestrator*, as well as with the recipe *Configuring the Orchestrator service SSL certificate* in `Chapter 2`, *Optimizing Orchestrator Configuration*.

How to do it...

In this recipe, I will deploy and configure two fresh Orchestrator installations and configure them into a cluster.

 We will discuss SSL certificates and clusters in the recipe *Load-balancing Orchestrator* in this chapter. If you want to use load-balancing or CA signed certificates with your cluster, please read the *How it works...* section of that recipe first before continuing.

Preparation work

Before we come to the main event, we need to prepare some things:

- Create an external DB with dedicated user (the third rule of IT: *Dedicated Services = Dedicated Users*) and configure the DB according to *Configuring an external database* in `Chapter 1`, *Installing and Configuring Orchestrator*
- Deploy two Orchestrator installations, as shown in the recipe *Deploying the Orchestrator appliance* in `Chapter 1`, *Installing and Configuring Orchestrator*

Configuring the first node of the cluster

We now prepare the first node of the cluster:

1. Connect the Orchestrator to an authentication source, as shown in the recipe *Configuring external authentication* in `Chapter 1`, *Installing and Configuring Orchestrator*.
2. Connect the Orchestrator to an external DB as shown in the recipe *Configuring an external database* in `Chapter 1`, *Installing and Configuring Orchestrator*.
3. If you want to use CA signed server certificates or the SSL SAM variant, then you need to configure them now. See the recipe *Configuring the Orchestrator service SSL certificate* in `Chapter 2`, *Optimizing Orchestrator Configuration*, and *Load-balancing Orchestrator* in this chapter.
4. Configure licensing and a package signing as shown in the recipe *Important Orchestrator settings* in `Chapter 1`, *Installing and Configuring Orchestrator*.
5. You may need to force plugins reinstall, as shown in the recipe *Important Orchestrator settings* in `Chapter 1`, *Installing and Configuring Orchestrator*.
6. Configure the vCenter connection, as shown in the recipe *Connecting to vCenter* in `Chapter 1`, *Installing and Configuring Orchestrator*.
7. Add and configure any other plugins you need, as shown in the recipe *Installing plugins* in `Chapter 1`, *Installing and Configuring Orchestrator*.
8. Upload any package you need. Basically, make this Orchestrator installation production-ready.

Configure cluster settings

We are now configuring the cluster settings:

1. In the Orchestrator Control Center, click on **Orchestrator Cluster Management**.
2. For this example, set the **Heartbeats** to 1 and the **Failover Heartbeats** to 5. This setting will make sure that the Orchestrator server fails over after 5 seconds. More about the settings in the *How it works...* section.
3. Click on **Save** and restart the Orchestrator service:

Orchestrator Cluster Management

Orchestrator Cluster Management

Orchestrator Node Settings   Join Node To Cluster

Configure the settings of an Orchestrator node. The configured settings apply to all Orchestrator nodes, that are joined together in a cluster

The configuration synchronization states of the cluster nodes are evaluated from the view point of the local node.

Number of active nodes ⚠	1
Heartbeat interval (in seconds) ⚠	1
Number of failover heartbeats ⚠	5

Save   Set Defaults   Cancel

Nodes	Local Node	Configuration Synchronization State
Hostname: vro.mylab.local Node Id: f3a4b0a1-d478-4cad-8a56-aa21eb7885af Instance Id: a614bf88-956f-4aa6-9259-74fe0b4fd333 Host IP Addresses: 192.168.220.12 State: RUNNING Active Configuration Fingerprint: 2f360396a34e22ea4ebc63464b8dbb004c Pending Configuration Fingerprint: 2f360396a34e22ea4ebc63464b8dbb004c	✓	Synchronized

Refresh

Join a node to the cluster

Now we are joining an additional Orchestrator to the cluster; with 7.1 this becomes extremely easy:

1. Log in to the second Orchestrator's Control Center.
2. In Control Center, click **Orchestrator Cluster Management | Join Node To Cluster**.
3. Enter the FQDN or IP of the first Orchestrator node.
4. Enter the credentials of the root user and click on **Join**:

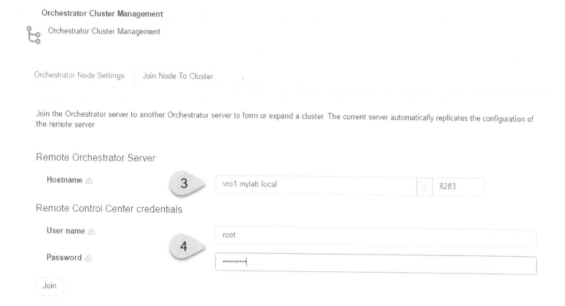

5. Restart the Orchestrator service.
6. Click on **Orchestrator Cluster Management**. The current status of the cluster is displayed at the bottom. It may take some time for the second node to show up:

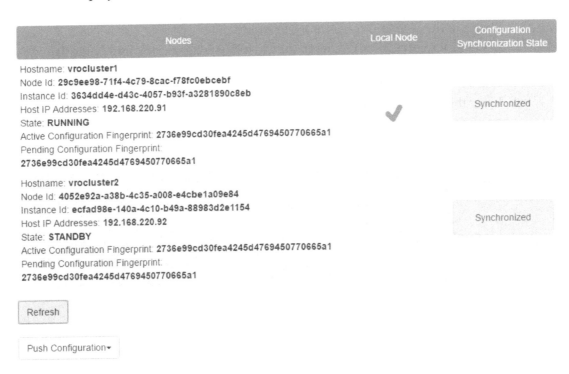

Nodes	Local Node	Configuration Synchronization State
Hostname: **vrocluster1** Node Id: **29c9ee98-71f4-4c79-8cac-f78fc0ebcebf** Instance Id: **3634dd4e-d43c-4057-b93f-a3281890c8eb** Host IP Addresses: **192.168.220.91** State: **RUNNING** Active Configuration Fingerprint: **2736e99cd30fea4245d4769450770665a1** Pending Configuration Fingerprint: **2736e99cd30fea4245d4769450770665a1**	✓	Synchronized
Hostname: **vrocluster2** Node Id: **4052e92a-a38b-4c35-a008-e4cbe1a09e84** Instance Id: **ecfad98e-140a-4c10-b49a-88983d2e1154** Host IP Addresses: **192.168.220.92** State: **STANDBY** Active Configuration Fingerprint: **2736e99cd30fea4245d4769450770665a1** Pending Configuration Fingerprint: **2736e99cd30fea4245d4769450770665a1**		Synchronized

Refresh

Push Configuration▾

You can see which Orchestrator is the active node by looking at the state. The local node is the node you are currently connected to.

Please note that the SSL certificate of the primary node has also been pushed out to the new node. Please also see the *How it works...* section of this recipe.

Configuring an Orchestrator cluster in vSphere

When you want your Orchestrator cluster to work properly, you also need to configure the Orchestrator VMs to be properly configured in vSphere:

1. Log in to vCenter and navigate to the cluster where your Orchestrator VMs are.
2. Click on **Manage**, then on **VM Overrides**, then on **Add**.

3. Add both Orchestrator VMs and set **Automation Level** to **Disabled** to make sure that the failed Orchestrator VM doesn't restart. This could cause a very unstable configuration. Click on **OK**.

4. Click on **VM/Host Rules** and then on **Add**.

5. Give the new rule a name, such as `SeparateOrchestrator`.

6. Select **Separate Virtual Machines** and then **Add** the two Orchestrator VMs. This will make sure that if an ESXi hosts fails, only one Orchestrator node is affected.

7. Click **OK** when you are finished.

Playing with the cluster

We will now simulate cluster failover:

1. Log in to vCenter.

2. Power off the active Orchestrator node; that should be at this stage the first node.

3. You will have to wait 5 seconds for the failover (see the settings in step 2 of the *Configure cluster settings* section).

4. Log in to the second node and check **Orchestrator Cluster Management**. You should see that the second node is now running and the first one is down (not responding):

Nodes

Hostname: **vro2**
Host IP Addresses: **192.168.220.21**
Instance Id: 340647e9-a5e8-4370-baac-9fcee1943b8e
State: **RUNNING**

Hostname: **vro1**
Host IP Addresses: **192.168.220.20**
Instance Id: 3cd5caa7-82b9-4f15-bf89-1be2ffa1b397
State: **NOT RESPONDING**

5. In vCenter, power on the first node again.

6. After a while, you should now see that the first node is in standby mode.

Push configuration

The push configuration is a new feature in vRO 7.1 and makes the synchronization of clusters much easier. Let's have a look at this:

1. Log in to the active node of your cluster.
2. Add an additional plugin, as shown in the recipe *Installing plugins* in `Chapter 1,` *Installing and Configuring Orchestrator*.
3. Check **Orchestrator Cluster Management**. You should see that the second node is not in sync:

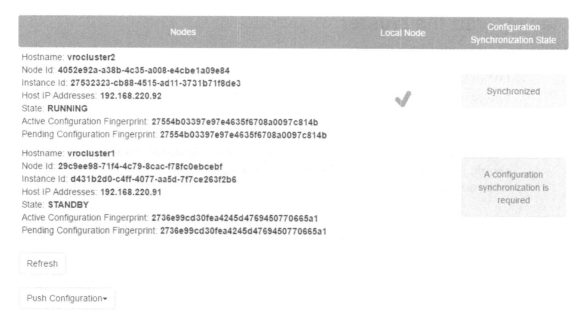

Nodes	Local Node	Configuration Synchronization State
Hostname: **vrocluster2** Node Id: **4052e92a-a38b-4c35-a008-e4cbe1a09e84** Instance Id: **27532323-cb88-4515-ad11-3731b71f8de3** Host IP Addresses: **192.168.220.92** State: **RUNNING** Active Configuration Fingerprint: **27554b03397e97e4635f6708a0097c814b** Pending Configuration Fingerprint: **27554b03397e97e4635f6708a0097c814b**	✓	Synchronized
Hostname: **vrocluster1** Node Id: **29c9ee98-71f4-4c79-8cac-f78fc0ebcebf** Instance Id: **d431b2d0-c4ff-4077-aa5d-7f7ce263f2b6** Host IP Addresses: **192.168.220.91** State: **STANDBY** Active Configuration Fingerprint: **2736e99cd30fea4245d4769450770665a1** Pending Configuration Fingerprint: **2736e99cd30fea4245d4769450770665a1**		A configuration synchronization is required

Refresh

Push Configuration▾

4. Click on **Push Configuration**, and wait until you see the notification saying that the node configuration was pushed successfully.
5. Click on **Refresh**. You should see that the second node requires a rest. You can now either restart the second node via the Control Center or click on **Push Configuration and reset node**.
6. Wait a little and then click **Refresh**.

Please note that a push configuration will also push the SSL certificate to all the nodes. Please also see the *How it works...* section of this recipe.

How it works...

Since vRO7.1, the configuration of Orchestrator clusters has become a lot easier. The function that an additional node will automatically be synced to the configuration of the cluster is a massive improvement and makes things a lot easier. The other function that was added is the ability to actively push a configuration to all the nodes, making it easier to change clusters.

 Please note that with vRO7.1, the certificates are shared between the nodes when you join a cluster. This results in the fact that you will need to use SAN certificates for the Orchestrator cluster. Please also see the *How it works...* section of this recipe.

The Orchestrator cluster can function in two ways. The first and easiest is HA mode. This means that we have at least two Orchestrator installations, and if one fails, the other will continue running. When a workflow is running, Orchestrator will save the state of the workflow to the database, before executing a workflow element. This is the same behavior that lets us resume failed workflows or do debugging (see the recipe *Resuming failed workflows* in `Chapter 4`, *Programming Skills*).

What is happening when one server fails is that the last state of the workflow execution will be picked up by the new active node and continued. For a purely HA function, you set the **Number of active nodes** to one.

The difference between HA and load-balanced is that in the load-balanced versions multiple Orchestrators can execute workflows at the same time, meaning that each Orchestrator instance is doing less work. For load-balancing, you need to set the **Number of active nodes** to more than one and you should configure a load-balancer to **Round-Robin**.

Clearly, you can use both modes at the same time. For example, if you have four Orchestrator nodes and you have configured **Number of active nodes** to two, two of the Orchestrators are running and two are in standby. If one of the active nodes fails, then one of the standby nodes will be brought to active mode. If the failed node is available again, it becomes a standby node.

The **Heartbeat interval (in seconds)** gives the interval in which an Orchestrator node sends keep alive signals to all other nodes of the cluster.

The **Number of failover heartbeats** defines how many keep alive signals can be missed before a node is declared *dead* by the other members of the cluster.

You determine the failover time by multiplying the **Heartbeat interval (in seconds)** by the **Number of failover heartbeats**.

If you want to use *local* files in a clustered Orchestrator environment you should use NFS or SMB shares. See the recipe *Configuring access to the local filesystem* in `Chapter 2`, *Optimizing Orchestrator Configuration*.

SSL Certificates in vRO7.1.0

At the time of writing (vRO 7.1.0), when a node joins a cluster it will automatically take the certificate of the primary host. If you reconfigure a node for a different certificate, the cluster will be out of sync. If your security isn't allowing for SAN certificates, you can run with an unsynced cluster. It's not nice, but it works.

VMware has promised to make sure that in the next release the certificates will not be pushed out automatically, allowing you to create a separate machine account for each node.

Cluster and Orchestrator Client

When you have more than one active Orchestrator, you need to have a think about the Orchestrator Client usage. Officially, the usage is not supported but, works anyhow. The idea behind it is that it would be possible for two users (one on each of the Orchestrators) to modify the same resource (for example, a workflow). This can be worked around by not giving the users edit or administrator rights (see the recipe *User management* in `Chapter 7`, *Interacting with Orchestrator*) or by using locks (see the recipe *Using the Locking System* in `Chapter 8`, *Better Workflows and Optimized Working*).

The supported and best practice, however, is to test a change on a separate Orchestrator installation and then transfer it to the cluster when only one Orchestrator node is running and the workflow that is to be changed is not in use.

Changing cluster content

When you want to change content, such as workflows, that are stored on the cluster, you must shut down all but one Orchestrator services, then change the content on one server and restart all the other Orchestrator services.

If you are adding a new plugin, you will need to install this plugin on all nodes before restarting the Orchestrator services.

Changing cluster settings

When you would like to change the Orchestrator server settings, it's best to stop all but one Orchestrator nodes, change the settings, and then restart the others. If you don't do that, you will end up with an unstable cluster, meaning that the cluster fails over from one node to the other all the time. Try it out...

Removing a node from the cluster

This is easier than you think; just delete the node or reconfigure it to use a different database (such as the built-in PostgreSQL).

There's more...

There are several more interesting things.

Logs

When you are writing to logs in your workflow while using clusters, you should use the `Server` log, not the `System` log, as the `System` will be written to the localhost while the `Server` is written to the database. Check out the example workflow for this recipe.

Please remember that excessive logging will impact DB growth.

Another method of load-balancing

If you are looking for pure load-balancing, as in trying to run a process on several Orchestrators in parallel, you could also consider using the AMQP plugin. Have a look at the recipe *Working with AMQP* in `Chapter 10`, *Built-in Plugins*.

Example workflow – cluster test

In the example package, there is a workflow called `03.01 Cluster Test`. For it to work, follow these steps:

1. Connect with the Orchestrator Client to the active node.
2. Start the workflow and wait until the first counts show in the logs.
3. Power off the active node.
4. Connect with the Orchestrator Client to the new active node (you need to wait a few seconds).
5. Check the workflow logs and then the events of the workflow.

You will see that the logs show only the entries that have been made after workflow execution was switched to the new host (`System.log`). The events tab will show all the log entries (`Server.log`).

See also

The recipe *Working with AMQP* in `Chapter 10`, *Built-in Plugins,*for alternative workload balancing.

The recipe *Configuring the Orchestrator service SSL certificate* in `Chapter 2`, *Optimizing Orchestrator Configuration*, for creating SSL certificates.

The recipe *Load-balancing Orchestrator* in this chapter to understand and set up load-balancing.

Load-balancing Orchestrator

In this recipe, we will build a load-balancer and discuss the situation with certificates as well.

Getting ready

Here, we will be using VMware NSX, but the same methods apply to all load-balancers. So, for this recipe you need VMware NSX. If you don't have a license for NSX, check out F5 Networks, who have a trial program, or the Apache load-balancer. Alternatively, you could also use Nginx; see `https://kb.vmware.com/kb/2058674`.

The NSX appliance needs to be deployed along with the controllers. If you need some help with that, check out these YouTube videos:

- `https://www.youtube.com/watch?v=CATcY254pP8`
- `https://www.youtube.com/watch?v=tum3eBIC-_c`

No VXLANs or any fancy configuration is needed.

How to do it...

I split this recipe into several parts for easier reading; execute them in sequence.

Creating a new NSX Edge

If you don't have an NSX Edge yet, let's get one running:

1. Log in to vCenter and click on **Network Security** and then on **NSX Edges**.
2. Click on the green plus sign to create a new NSX Edge.
3. We can run with the defaults mostly, just change the settings I point out. Give the NSX Edge a name such as `vROCluster` and click **Next**.
4. Set a new password and click **Next**.
5. Click on the green plus sign to add some settings for the new Edge. You need to define the cluster, the datastore, the host, and the VM folder that the new Edge VM should live in. Click **Next**.

6. Click on the green plus sign to create a new interface, basically the IP that the load-balancer will be working on. Specify the load-balancer IP and the network you want to connect to. Make sure it's an **Uplink**. Click on **OK**:

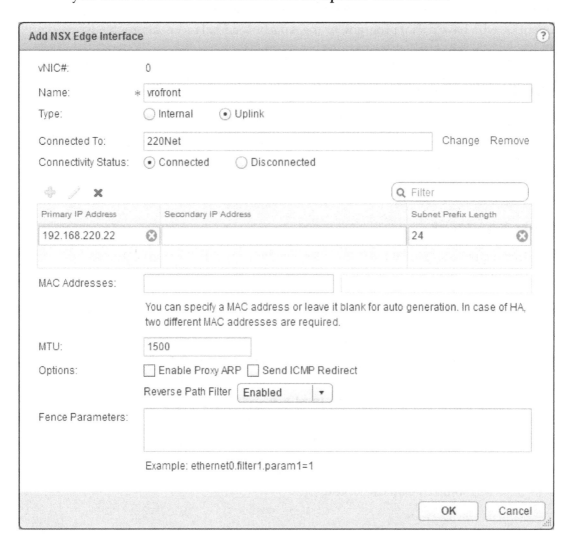

7. You can untick the **Configure Default Gateway** option and click **Next**.
8. Tick **Configure Firewall default policy** and switch it to **Accept**. Click **Next**.
9. Finish the wizard and wait until the Edge is deployed.

Configuring the load-balancer

This enables the basic load-balancing functionality:

1. From where we have left off, double-click on the new Edge. You are now redirected to the Edge and can configure it.
2. Click on **Load Balancer** and then on **Global Configuration**.
3. Click on **Edit** (on the right side) and tick **Enable Load Balancer**. Click **OK**.

Dealing with SSL certificates

Set how you want to deal with the certificates (see the *How it works...* section for more information). We will be setting up SSL passthrough in this example:

1. Now select **Application Profiles** and click on the green plus sign.
2. Give the policy a name and set it to **HTTPS**.
3. Ticking **Enable SSL Passthrough** will be okay for this example; depending on what you would like to do, you can also untick it and go with SSL offload. Leave the rest as the defaults. Click **OK**.

Monitors – health checks

Create a new health check for the Orchestrator services. The health of a node is captured in `https://[VRO FQDN]:8281/vco/api/healthstatus`:

1. Select **Service Monitoring** and click on the green plus sign. (previous screenshot **A**).
2. Enter a name for the check. VMware's recommended settings are captured in the previous screenshot and in the table in the *How it works...* section.

Configure pools

This configures what VMs belong to the load balancing setup:

1. Select **Pools** and click on the green plus sign.
2. Enter a name for the new pool and select the monitor that you created in step 2 of the *Monitors – health checks* section.
3. Click on the green plus sign to add the first member of our pool.
4. Give the pool member a name (best to give it the VM name) and then fill in its IP and port 8281 for both **Port** and **Monitor Port**. Click on **OK** and then add the next member. Click on **OK** when finished:

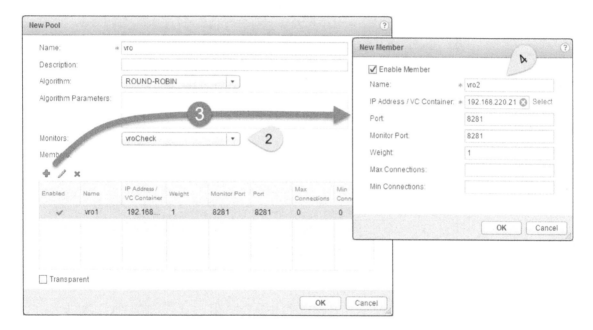

Virtual server

This is the interface that a client will connect to:

1. Select **Virtual Servers** and click on the green plus sign.
2. Enter a new name for the service and give it the IP of the frontend you selected in step 6 of the *Creating a new NSX Edge* section.

3. Set the **Protocol** to **HTTPS** and enter 8281 as **Port**.

4. Assign this virtual server to use the pool you created in step 2 of the *Configure pools* section and click **OK**:

Done

You have finished configuring the NSX load-balancer. You should now be able to connect to it using the frontend IP you assigned in step 6 of the *Creating a new NSX Edge* section: https://192.168.220.22:8281/vco/.

How it works...

Load-balancing is a method by which a central unit (the load-balancer) is contacted by the user instead of one of the Orchestrator installations. The load-balancer has two functions. The first is to check the availability of the underlying Orchestrators for that, the load-balancer is checking each Orchestrator's health status by contacting `https://[vro]:8281/vco/api/healthstatus`. If the Orchestrator service is alive then it will respond with the following:

```
<node-status xmlns="http://www.vmware.com/vco">
<state>RUNNING</state>
<health-status state="OK" time="1463231814183"/>
<instance-id>9d40b766-e278-4f6c-8fa1-ab143d5b73e7</instance-id>
```

The other function of a load-balancer is to forward the connection request to one of the active Orchestrator nodes. The method we should use for this with Orchestrator is called Round-Robin, which will give a connection to the next available Orchestrator node. For example, if there are three active Orchestrators (vro1, vro2, and vro3) then the first request will be given to vro1, the next one to vro2, then to vro3, and then again to vro1, and so on.

The following settings are usable for all load-balancers. The settings may be called something slightly different, but they all function in the same way:

Setting	Value
Health check protocol	HTTPS
Health check link	GET/vco/api/healthstatus
Health check return	RUNNING
Health check interval	3 sec
Health check timeout	9 sec
Health check max retries	3
Load-balancing mechanism	Round-Robin
Load-balancing port	8281
SSL certificate	Offload or passthrough
SSL persistency	None

SSL certificates and load-balancing

All connections to Orchestrator use HTTPS and SSL certificates, so we need to discuss this. The problem is as follows: when the load-balancer forwards the connection to one of the Orchestrators, the client will be connecting to a different certificate.

There are basically three methods to deal with this.

SSL passthrough

This is the default for most load-balancers. The certificate of the underlying Orchestrator is passed to the connecting user. If the certificate is CA signed and trusted by the connecting computer, then this works quite well. If you are using self-signed certificates that are not trusted by the connecting computer, the connection must be approved each time, which can lead to a lot of problems.

If you use a VMCA-signed certificate, this can work very well. (See the *Use VMCA generated certificate* section in the recipe *Configuring the Orchestrator service SSL certificate* in Chapter 2, *Optimizing Orchestrator Configuration*.

SSL SAN (SSL passthrough)

You can create a SSL certificate with alternative names, so-called **SAN (Subject Alternative Name)**. The certificate contains not only one FDQN and/or IP, but multiple ones. The load-balancer is configured for passthrough and the connecting server gets a certificate that is valid for not only one Orchestrator node but multiple ones.

See the *There's more...* section of the recipe *Configuring the Orchestrator service SSL certificate* in Chapter 2, *Optimizing Orchestrator Configuration*.

SSL offload

This mode is not supported by all load-balancers. Offloading means that the load-balancer will trust each Orchestrator certificate but will present its own certificate to the connecting computer. Using this method, you can use self-signed untrusted certificates on the Orchestrator and use one single trusted CA certificate on the load-balancer:

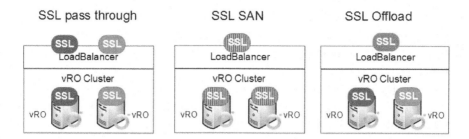

Load-balanced Orchestrator cluster with vSphere Web Client

One of the very cool features of the vSphere Web Client is that you can execute Orchestrator workflows directly from it. When you are using a load-balanced Orchestrator cluster, you will need to register the load-balanced address instead of any single Orchestrator:

1. Execute the recipe *Connecting to vCenter* in `Chapter 1`, *Installing and Configuring Orchestrator*, for both Orchestrator servers. Make sure you enter the FQDN or IP of your Orchestrator cluster you created in step 6 of the *Creating a new NSX Edge* section as the external address (see the following screenshot):

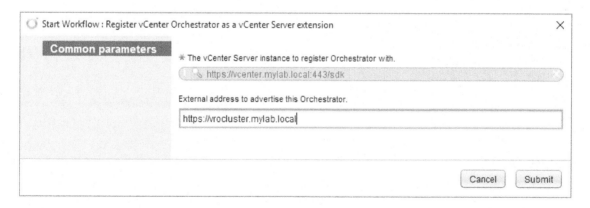

2. Log in to vCenter with an administrator account.
3. Go to **vRealize Orchestrator**. In **vRO Home**, click on **Manage**, and under **Server**, select your vCenter. Your Orchestrator cluster should already be set up here. If not, continue this recipe.

4. Click on **Edit Configuration** and enter the FQDN or IP of the Orchestrator Cluster you created in step 6 of *Creating a new NSX Edge* section.

5. Click on **Test Connection** to check weather the connection is working, then click **OK**.

6. Click on the workflows in the inventory list to see whether the inventory is loading; if that is not the case you need to check your SSO registration of your Orchestrator. See the recipe *Connecting to vCenter* in `Chapter 1`, *Installing and Configuring Orchestrator*.

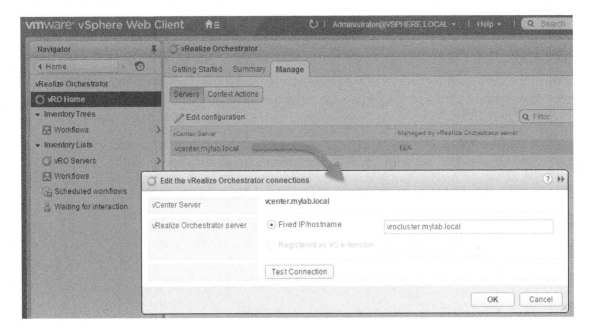

See also

Load balancing Orchestrator with F5: `kb.vmware.com/kb/2118472`.

F5 trial license: `https://www.f5.com/trial`.

VMware NSX product overview and **Hands on Lab**:
`http://www.vmware.com/products/nsx/`.

Upgrading a cluster

In this recipe, we are looking to upgrade a cluster. This recipe works for updates as well as upgrades.

Getting ready

We need a cluster that consists of at least two nodes and is ready to be upgraded.

How to do it...

This is a simple process that I will split in 3 parts. First execute the following steps and then continue with either *Minor upgrades* or *Major upgrades*:

1. Shut down all the Orchestrator servers in the cluster.
2. Upgrade the Orchestrator servers, as seen in the recipe *Updating Orchestrator* in `Chapter 1`, *Installing and Configuring Orchestrator*.
3. After finishing the upgrade, you need to log in to the Control Center.
4. Make sure all the node settings are correct.
5. Continue with either *Minor upgrades* or *Major upgrades*.

Minor upgrades

If you are upgrading between minor versions, such as 7.0 and 7.0.1, where no hardware change was made, then follow this step:

Upgrade the next Orchestrator server until you have upgraded the whole cluster.

Major upgrades

If you are upgrading between major versions, such as 5.x, 6.x, or 7.0 and 7.1, where hardware changes have been made, you should follow these steps:

1. Deploy a new instance of the appliance and push the configuration out to it.
2. Continue until you replace the whole cluster.
3. Then replace the first Orchestrator you upgraded with a new instance.

How it works...

As clustering changed between vRO 5, 6, 7, and 7.1, you need to be a bit more careful with the upgrade. That's why you need to bring down the whole cluster. This is especially true when the hardware has been changed:

Version	5.5 and 6	7.0	7.1
Memory	3 GB	4 GB	6 GB
vCPU	2	2	2
Hard disk	7 + 5 GB	7 + 5 GB	7 + 10 GB

If you are just updating a minor version, such as 7.0.1 to 7.0.2, you can try to upgrade the cluster hot. However, this could be problematic and should be tested for each minor upgrade before doing it in production.

See also

Updating Orchestrator in `Chapter 1`, *Installing and Configuring Orchestrator*.

Managing remote Orchestrators

This recipe centers on using the multi-node plugin (formerly known as the VCO plugin). This plugin will allow us to manage other Orchestrators.

Getting ready

We need at least two Orchestrator installations.

It is also quite important that both Orchestrator instances are compatible with each other, meaning they should preferable be of the same version and build.

How to do it...

This recipe will call the first Orchestrator installation the *local Orchestrator*, and the one we add will be called the *remote Orchestrator*. The remote Orchestrator can be a cluster.

Adding an Orchestrator server

1. Log in to your local Orchestrator.
2. Start the workflow: **Library** | **Orchestrator** | **Server Management** | **Add an Orchestrator server**.
3. Enter the FQDN or IP of your remote Orchestrator and specify port `8281`.
4. It helps if you accept the certificate silently as it creates less work for you.
5. You may not want to create proxy workflows at this stage as this will create proxy workflows for every existing workflow (including all the library ones).
6. Click on **Next**. The following page will ask you about the timeouts (in seconds) for the connection to the remote Orchestrator. You should align this according to your bandwidth and or cluster settings.
7. The **Retry timeout (minutes)** is the time the local Orchestrator will wait for a response form the remote Orchestrator.
8. Select **Yes** if you want to share the connection, meaning that the user you specify will be used to execute workflows on the remote Orchestrator. If you select **No**, the user executing a proxy workflow will be the one that will execute the remote workflow. This requires both the local and the remote Orchestrator to be registered on the same SSO:

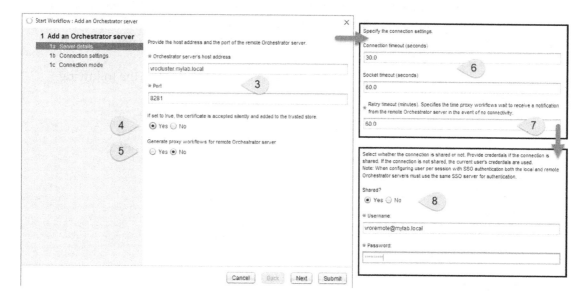

9. Click on Next. The following page will ask you about the timeouts (in seconds) for the connection to the remote Orchestrator. You should align this according to your bandwidth and or cluster settings. The Retry timeout (minutes) is the time the local Orchestrator will wait for a response form the remote Orchestrator. Select Yes if you want to share the connection, meaning that the user you specify will be used to execute workflows on the remote Orchestrator. If you select No, the user executing a proxy workflow will be the one that will execute the remote workflow. This requires both the local and the remote Orchestrator to be registered on the same SSO: After the workflow has finished, go to the inventory and have a look under the vRO multi-node plugin. There, you will find all the items that exist in the remote Orchestrator.

Creating proxy workflows

We declined in the previous section to create proxy workflows because we will do it here:

1. Using the local Orchestrator Client, start the workflow by navigating to **Library | Orchestrator | Remote Executions | Create a proxy workflow**.

2. Select the remote workflow you would like to use. Click on **Next**.

3. Choose to create proxy workflows that are executed synchronously (**Yes**) or asynchronously (**No**). Synchronous means that Orchestrator will wait until the workflow is executed completely (use the default, which is **Yes**).

4. Wait until the workflow has finished. Then, check whether the new folder has been created in the workflow tree called VCO@[IP or FQDN Orchestrator]:8281, as well as the workflows under it. See the following collage:

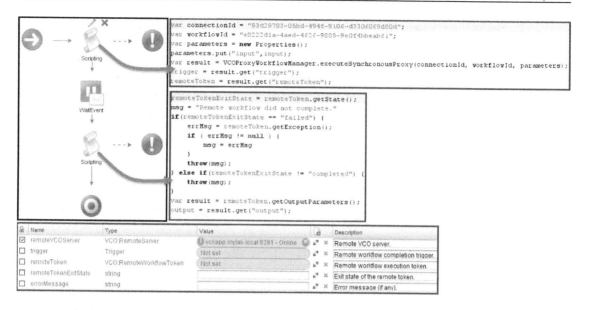

```
var connectionId = "93d29783-05bd-494f-91D6-d330f0f9d80d";
var workflowId = "e0222d1a-4aed-4f2f-9885-9e0f4bbeab81";
var parameters = new Properties();
parameters.put("input", input);
var result = VCOProxyWorkflowManager.executeSynchronousProxy(connectionId, workflowId, parameters);
trigger = result.get("trigger");
remoteToken = result.get("remoteToken");
```

```
remoteTokenExitState = remoteToken.getState();
msg = "Remote workflow did not complete."
if(remoteTokenExitState == "failed") {
    errMsg = remoteToken.getException();
    if ( errMsg != null ) {
        msg = errMsg
    }
    throw(msg);
} else if(remoteTokenExitState != "completed") {
    throw(msg);
}
var result = remoteToken.getOutputParameters();
output = result.get("output");
```

Name	Type	Value		Description
☑ remoteVCOServer	VCO:RemoteServer	vcoapp.mylab.local:8281 - Online	✕	Remote VCO server.
☐ trigger	Trigger	Not set	✕	Remote workflow completion trigger.
☐ remoteToken	VCO:RemoteWorkflowToken	Not set	✕	Remote workflow execution token.
☐ remoteTokenExitState	string		✕	Exit state of the remote token.
☐ errorMessage	string		✕	Error message (if any).

5. Now, execute one of the proxy workflows. When finished, check on both Orchestrators; you will find that the proxy workflow will have executed on both sides. However, log messages and variable tracking will only be in place on the remote server.

6. It's a good idea to go and check what happened on the remote Orchestrator. Look at the execution and the logs.

Instead of just creating one proxy workflow, you can create proxies of all the workflows of the remote Orchestrator by navigating to **Library** | **Orchestrator** | **Remote Executions** | **Server Proxies** | **Create proxy workflows for an Orchestrator Server**, or a workflow folder, **Library** | **Orchestrator** | **Remote Executions** | **Create proxy workflows from a folder**.

Also, note that you can refresh the proxy workflows. This will make sure that changes in the input or output variable are synced to the proxy workflows.

Managing packets on the remote Orchestrator

Another useful function is the ability to deploy packages to remote servers. Perform the following steps:

1. Using the local Orchestrator Client, start the workflow by navigating to **Library** | **Orchestrator** | **Remote Management** | **Packages** | **Deploy a package from a local server**.

2. Select the package you would like to deploy from the local Orchestrator to the remote Orchestrator.

3. When selecting the remote server, you are actually able to choose multiple remote Orchestrators. An array window will open; select **Insert Value**. An additional popup will show up here; select the remote Orchestrator and click on **Add**.

4. The chosen package is now installed on the remote Orchestrator.

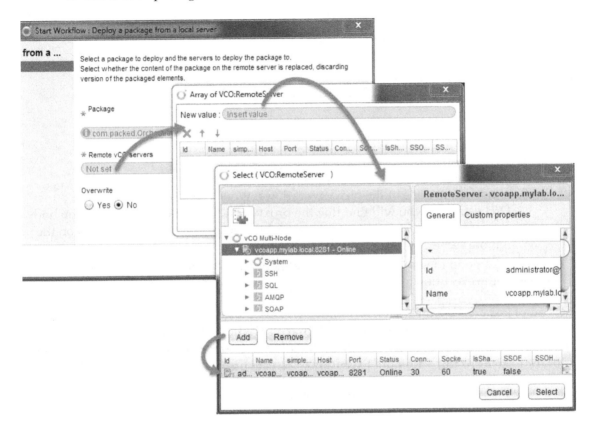

How it works...

The multi-node plugin can be used in quite a lot of situations. The first and foremost is to manage remote servers that are in a cluster; see the recipe *Building an Orchestrator Cluster* in this chapter. Using the **Multi-Node Plugin**, we can now manage the Orchestrator clusters workflows and packages as shown in the following image:

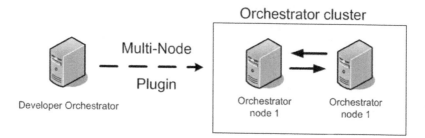

Another good idea is to make sure that workflows, or basically any other Orchestrator element (by building a specific workflow), are replicated between Orchestrator installations. For example, for load-balancing or audit reasons, you have multiple Orchestrator servers and you need to make sure that elements are the same on all of them.

A very common use of the multi-node plugin is for maintenance work, such as cleaning out all finished workflows from remote Orchestrators.

Last but not least, you can execute workflows from a different Orchestrator. For example, you can write a workflow that automatically configures a new Orchestrator installation.

Please note that you can create a task from a workflow (see the recipe *Scheduling workflows* in Chapter 4, *Programming Skills*) and thus create an automated push or pull update from a cluster.

Explore the workflows that come with the VCO plugin, as there is quite a lot you can do. The following are examples:

Type	Description
Proxy workflows	Server: Create, delete, refresh; create one proxy workflow, create from folder, create multi-proxy action.
Packages	Delete, delete by name, deploy from local, deploy from remote, deploy packages from local.
Workflows	Delete all finished, delete remote, deploy from local, deploy from remote. Refresh stale workflow runs in waiting state. Start in series, start in parallel.
Server	Add, update, delete.
Tasks	Create, create recurring.

As a last note, when you delete an Orchestrator server using the workflow by navigating to **Library** | **Orchestrator** | **Server Configuration** | **Delete a vCO Server**, all the proxy workflows of the remote Orchestrator will also be deleted from the local Orchestrator.

See also

- See the recipe *Building an Orchestrator cluster* in this chapter

- See *Distributed Deployment* in the introduction to this chapter

Synchronizing Orchestrator elements between Orchestrator servers

This recipe will show how to use synchronization to update Orchestrator objects between two Orchestrator servers.

Getting ready

We will need at least one workflow, action, or other Orchestrator object that can be synced.

Additionally, we also need two Orchestrator servers; they should not be in a cluster. For test purposes, you can deploy an Orchestrator appliance without any additional configuration.

How to do it...

We will use a workflow in this example. The same method applies to all other Orchestrator elements that can be synchronized:

1. Right-click on a workflow (or a folder) and select **Synchronize**.
2. You will now be asked to enter the IP or FQDN of the other Orchestrator server as well as some credentials for the connection. Click on **Login**.

3. You will now see a summary of all workflows you have selected for synchronization on both Orchestrator servers:

- **A**: Here, the version number of a given workflow is shown
- **B**: You have four options that we will discuss in the *How it works...* section of this recipe
- **C**: Clicking on the magnifying glass icon will produce a split screen that shows you the difference between the versions (see the recipe *Version control* in `Chapter 4`, *Programming Skills*)

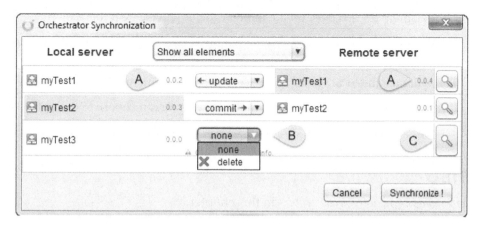

4. Click on **Synchronize !** to synchronize the workflows.

How it works...

Synchronizing Orchestrator objects is one of the easiest ways to make sure that two servers have the same elements. This doesn't work for clusters as both Orchestrators in a cluster share the same database (same workflow IDs). A good example here is a sync between a development environment and a production environment.

The Orchestrator objects that can use synchronization are workflows, actions, resources, configurations, packages, policy templates, and WebViews.

When synchronizing a local element that doesn't exist on the remote server, Orchestrator will not only create the element but also the folder structure for it. This will make sure that the same structure exists on both servers. Also, the ID of the Orchestrator object will be kept the same when synchronizing.

Please note that depending on which direction you sync, the options you see might be different:

Action	Description
None	*This is not what you expect.* This will update the remote version with the local version. If the element doesn't exist on the remote side, it will create it there.
Update	Update will take the version from the remote server and will overwrite the local version.
Commit	This will take the local version and overwrite the remote version.
Delete	If an element doesn't exist on the remote server, you can choose to delete the local version.

See also

The recipe *Managing remote Orchestrators* in this chapter.

The recipe *Working with REST* in Chapter 9, *Essential Plugins*.

4
Programming Skills

This chapter deals with the skills that an Orchestrator user needs on a more or less daily basis. We will be looking at the following recipes:

- Version control
- Changing elements in a workflow
- Importing and exporting Orchestrator elements
- Working with packages
- Workflow auto documentation
- Resuming failed workflows
- Using the workflow debugging function
- Undelete workflows and actions
- Scheduling workflows
- Sync presentation settings
- Locking elements

Introduction

In this chapter, we will focus on using the Orchestrator Client and what one should know about it. The Orchestrator Client is a Java-based client that can be launched via the Orchestrator home page or can be locally installed. The Orchestrator Client is mainly used to create new workflows as well as to configure plugins. However, you also can use it for executing workflows. In this case, it is a good idea to configure non-administrative access to Orchestrator as shown in the *User management* recipe in `Chapter 7`, *Interacting with Orchestrator*.

The Orchestrator icons

The Orchestrator Client has three modes: **Run**, **Design**, and **Administer**. The setting can be changed by selecting the value from the top drop-down menu. You will use the Orchestrator Client mostly in the **Design** mode when you program. If you are a user, you probably will use the **Run** mode.

Let's have a quick look at all the icons of Orchestrator Client:

Icon	Used in recipe/chapter	What is covered?
My Orchestrator	*User management* recipe in `Chapter 7`, *Interacting with Orchestrator*.	Overview and non-admin access.
Scheduler	*Scheduling workflows* recipe in this chapter.	Management of scheduled workflows.
Policies	*Working with policies* recipe in `Chapter 8`, *Better Workflows and Optimized Working*.	A policy is basically an event trigger.
Workflows	`Chapter 5`, *Visual Programming* and most of the other chapters too.	Manage everything that has to do with workflows.
Inventory	Recipes in `Chapter 9`, *Essential Plugins*, `Chapter 10`, *Built-in Plugins*, and `Chapter 11`, *Additional Plugins*, as well as `Chapter 12`, *Working with vSphere*.	Shows all the objects that each plugin has access to.
Actions	*Creating actions* recipe in `Chapter 6`, *Advanced Programming*.	Manage everything that has to do with actions.
Resources	*Working with resources* recipe in `Chapter 8`, *Better Workflows and Optimized Working*.	A resource is a file that can be used from workflows.

Configurations	*Working with configurations* recipe in `Chapter 8, Better Workflows and Optimized Working.`	Configurations are centrally defined attributes that are available to all workflows.
Packages	*Working with packages* recipe in this chapter.	A package contains workflows, actions, as well as all other elements to export and import Orchestrator solutions.
Policy templates	*Working with resources* recipe in `Chapter 8, Better Workflows and Optimized Working.`	Templates for policies.
Authorizations	–	Left over and not used today anymore (deprecated).

Gotcha

One of the things you need to know is that when Orchestrator asks you for something (for example, workflows) you might end up with an empty window such as this:

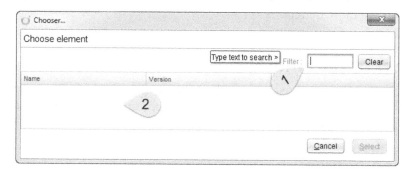

You need to enter something into **Filter** (**1**) and then press *Enter* (or just press *Enter*). The area below (**2**) will then fill up with the available options you can choose from.

Since vRO7, the search window has been introduced, which looks as follows:

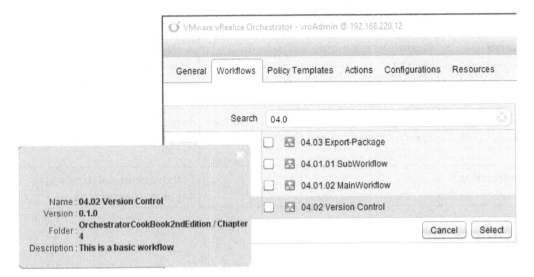

You start typing in parts of the name you are looking for and if you hold the mouse on one selection you can see more details.

Auto-setup of parameters

When you add a workflow to the schema you can make it easier for you to assign all the parameters. Just click on **Setup...** and then assign the parameter either as an **Input** parameter, give it a **Value**, or **Skip** it to set it up later:

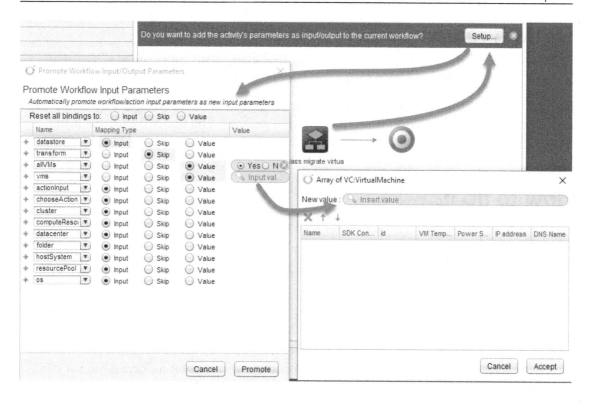

Version control

In this recipe, we will look at how to use the Orchestrator version control and use it to control your software development. Version control is part of almost all elements.

Getting ready

A working Orchestrator is required, and you will need the rights to create new workflows and run them. We will work with the Orchestrator Client.

We need an existing workflow that we can play around with. In this recipe, we will use the `00.00 BasicWorkflow` workflow of the example package. The finished example is the `04.02 VersionControl` example workflow.

How to do it...

We will use a workflow for this example; however, it works for other elements too:

1. Make a duplicate of the `00.00 BasicWorkflow` workflow.
2. Click on **General** and have a look at the current version (see the following screenshot).
3. Open the workflow for editing by right-clicking on it and selecting **Edit**.
4. Drag a system log element from the log section into the schema.
5. Bind the text in-parameter to an existing string variable.
6. Click on **General** and then on the second version counter to increase the version of the workflow to `0.1.0` (see the following screenshot).
7. You can now enter a comment to the new version. This is a good place to record changes that have been made. When finished click on **OK**.
8. The version counter in the **General** section should now be increased.
9. Click on **Show version history** to see an overview of all existing versions:

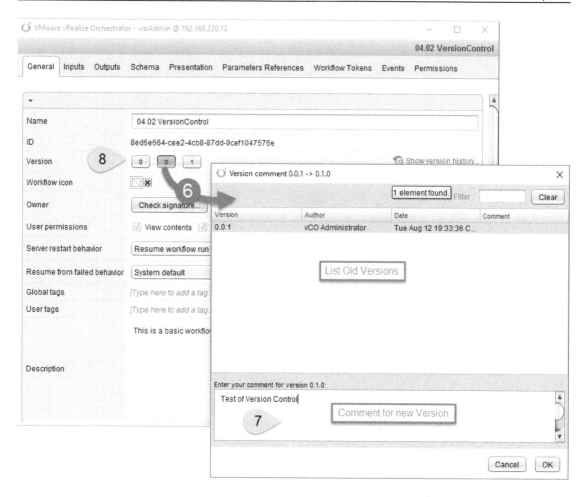

10. Now click on **Save and Close**. If you now select **Increase version**, you will create version 0.1.1, so you should select **Continue anyway**.

Showing differences between versions

You use this function to compare the differences between versions of a workflow:

1. On the workflow's **General** tab, click on **Show version history**.
2. Select the version you would like to compare the present one against and click on **Diff Against Current**.
3. A window will pop up and show both versions next to each other. Resize the window as required.

4. When you are finished, click on **Close**:

Reverting to an older version

1. Click on **Show version history**.
2. Select the version you would like to revert to and click on **Revert**.

Your workflow is now of an earlier version, but the newer version is still available. You can also *revert* to a newer version if you wish.

How it works...

Version control is a very important tool in software development. It not only helps you keep track of your code development, but also helps you in other ways. For instance, when you import a workflow or a package, you can directly see whether the import is newer or older than the existing one. The other thing is that you can check versions against each other, as well as revert to different versions. You can use the revert function to make duplicates of older versions.

Version control is available for **Workflows**, **Actions**, **Configurations**, **Resources**, and **Policy Templates**.

See also

The example workflow 04.02 Version Control.

Changing elements in a workflow

In this recipe, we will have a closer look at the challenges that change the workflow elements in a schema pose. Changing the in- and out-parameters, as well as moving or renaming actions will be discussed. You will learn how to make these changes as well as what to avoid.

Getting ready

We need a workflow that has an additional workflow as well as an action in its schema.

You can use the 04.01.02 MainWorkFlow and 04.01.01 SubWorkflow example workflows as well as the reNameMe action, which is part of the example package.

How to do it...

There are only two major tasks: changing the parameters and renaming/moving the actions.

Changing the parameters of workflows and actions

If you change a subworkflow's in/out-parameters, you will need to synchronize its parameters by following these steps:

1. Make sure that you have a workflow that has a workflow as an element in its schema. You can use the 04.01.02 MainWorkFlow and 04.01.01 SubWorkflow example workflows.
2. In the subworkflow, change the name of an out-parameter and add another in-parameter. Then save and exit the subworkflow as a new version (making it easier to repeat the lesson).
3. In the main workflow, go to the schema and edit the subworkflow element.
4. Click on **Info** and then on **Synchronize parameters**.

5. Now, check the in- and out-parameters of the element. You will find a second in-parameter and that the out-parameter isn't bound anymore:

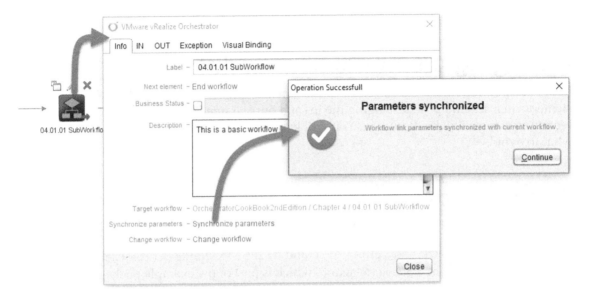

The same method also works for actions. Try the following:

- Renaming the subworkflow
- Moving the subworkflow to another folder

Renaming and moving actions

Actions are tied into a workflow using their module name and the action name. So, if an action is moved to a different module or renamed, you will have to do the following:

1. Make sure that you have a workflow that calls an action either as a scripting task or schema element. You can use the `04.01.02 MainWorkFlow` example workflow and the `reNameMe` action.
2. Change the name of the action or move it to another module.
3. In the main workflow, go to the schema and edit the action element.

4. You will see that you can't change the scripting that points to the action, so the only thing you can do is delete the action element and insert it again:

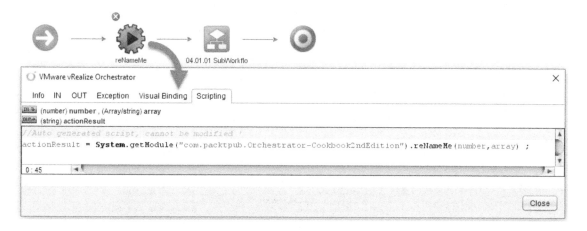

5. If you called the action in a **Scriptable task**, you can change the name or module.

Therefore it's important to know which element is used where. See the next section on how to do that.

Finding related elements

We will now see how we can find out what action is used by what other elements:

1. Go to the actions and into the `com.packtpub.Orchestartor-cookbook2ndEdition.helpers` module.

2. Now right-click on the **getNow** action and select **Find elements that use this element** from the menu.

3. A new window will pop up displaying all the Orchestrator elements that use this action.

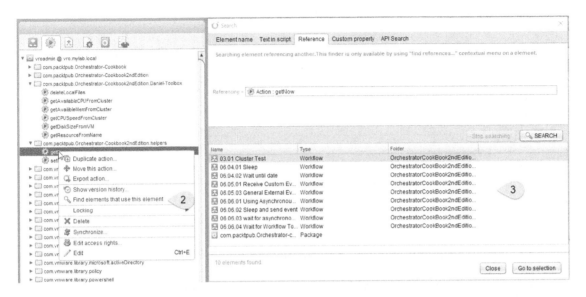

This also works for Resource and Configuration elements.

How it works...

Workflows are tied in with each other via their ID (which can't be changed and is unique) and not their name. So, renaming or moving a workflow has no impact.

If you add or remove an in/out-parameter from a workflow or action, you can simply synchronize the parameter. When you change the name of an in/out-parameter in a workflow or action and then synchronize, you will have to redefine the binding of that parameter.

An action is always called in the following way:

```
System.getModule([module name]).[action name]([in-parameter],)
```

When you move or rename an action, you will need to adjust this call by either changing the `module name` (move) or the `action name` (rename).

If you rename a configuration element or parameter, you will have to bind it again in the workflow. The setting will point to the old configuration element that doesn't exist anymore.

See also

The example workflows `04.01.02 MainWorkFlow` and `04.01.01 SubWorkflow` as well as the `reNameMe` action.

Importing and exporting Orchestrator elements

In this recipe, we will learn how to import and export elements from one Orchestrator to another using Orchestrator Client.

Getting ready

We need at least one workflow, action, or other element that we can export, delete, and import. If you have two Orchestrator servers, you can export the element on one and import into the other.

How to do it...

In this example, we will use a workflow to import and export an object. However, the same methods apply to all Orchestrator elements.

Exporting an object

We will use the `00.00 BasicWorkflow` workflow of the example package in this example. Exporting also works for other elements:

1. To export a workflow, right-click on it and select **Export workflow**.
2. A window will pop up that shows you your local drives from the computer you are running Orchestrator Client on.
3. Select a directory and a name for the workflow (the default name is the name of the workflow). The default file extension is `.workflow`.
4. You can define a name to encrypt the export with, basically an encryption string. This will make it possible for other importers to import the file, but not to edit it. The name is not a password and Orchestrator will not ask for it; encrypting with the name will just create an encrypted file.

5. Click on **Save**.

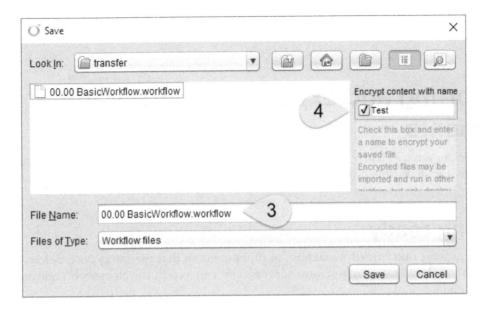

Importing an element

To import a workflow:

1. Right-click on a folder and select **Import workflow**.
2. A window will pop up that shows you your local drives from the computer you are running the Orchestrator Client on.
3. Select a directory and a name for the workflow you would like to import.

Orchestrator will not ask you to confirm the SSL certificate, nor will it import any dependencies that this workflow might have.

4. If the workflow already exists, a warning will be displayed. You can either select **Cancel** or continue the import.
5. The workflow will now be imported into the folder you right-clicked on in step 1.

How it works...

You can import and export single Orchestrator objects. This will only import and export the element and not its sub-elements or elements the workflow (or action) depends on. You can use a package (see the *Working with packages* recipe in this chapter) to export multiple workflows as well as their dependent elements. As workflows are identified by their IDs and actions by their name and module, it is important to realize that a single workflow export/import might not result in a working configuration. You can try this with the 04.03 Export-Package workflow.

When you export an object, then it will be exported along with the SSL certificate of the Orchestrator installation (the one we created in the *Package Signing Certificate* section of the *Important Orchestrator configurations* recipe in Chapter 1, *Installing and Configuring Orchestrator*).

> The elements that can be imported and exported are **Workflow**, **Action**, **Resource**, **Configuration**, and **Policy Template**.

In addition to this, the element will keep its ID when exported and imported. As all IDs are unique (even across Orchestrator installations), this is an important point.

See also

Have a look at the *Working with packages* recipe in this chapter and the *Managing Remote Orchestrator* recipe in Chapter 3, *Distributed Design*.

Working with packages

In this recipe, you will learn how to create, export, and generally work with packages. Packages are great for shipping complete Orchestrator solutions between Orchestrators to customers or for backup.

Getting ready

We need at least one workflow or action to work with in this recipe. Optimally, you have workflows and actions that depend on each other. You can test with the 04.03 Export-Package example workflow; it contains an action and another workflow.

How to do it...

This recipe has several sections. As an overview, the following screenshot shows all the icons and their usages. To get to the correct section, follow these instructions:

1. Using Orchestrator Client, make sure that you are in **Design** mode.
2. Click on packages (the yellow box with a white circle icon):

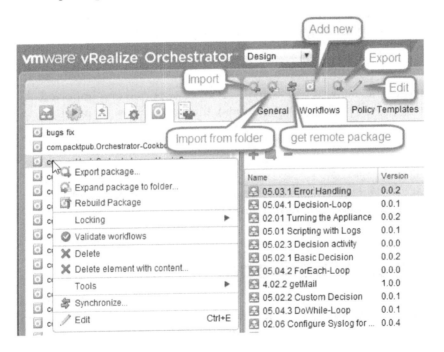

Create a new package

1. Either right-click on the white space below the displayed packages and select **Add package**, or select the icon from the right-hand side (the yellow box with a white circle icon).
2. Select a new name for the package; the default is **org.company.mypackage**. A good naming convention is useful.
3. The new package is created; now click on the package and either right-click and select **Edit** or select **Edit** from the right-hand side (the pencil icon).

4. Click on **Workflows**.
5. To add a workflow, you can either select single workflows using **Insert workflow (List search)** (the green plus icon) to select a single workflow or **Insert workflows (Tree browsing)** (the folder icon) to insert all workflows of a specific folder. Remember that when Orchestrator shows you an empty selection window, you need to use the **Filter** option (see the introduction to this chapter).
6. Choose one option and click on **Select** to add the workflow(s). If your workflow depends on other elements, such as **Actions, Configurations, Resources**, and so on, these elements will be automatically imported into the package as well.
7. Click on **Save and close** and finish the packaging process.

Export a package

1. Before we export a package, we should make sure that its content is current. To do so, we right-click on the package and select **Rebuild package**. The content of the package will now be updated with the latest versions (and their dependencies) of all elements in the package.
2. After the rebuild has finished, we now export the package by right-clicking on the package and selecting **Export package**, or from the menu, as shown in the beginning of this recipe.

3. The export window opens up. Choose an appropriate directory and filename. You also see that there are several options on the right-hand side; we will discuss them in detail in the *How it works...* section of this recipe:

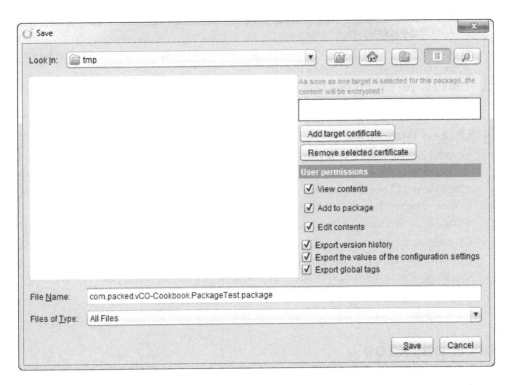

4. Click on **Save**. Your package has now been exported.

Import a package

1. Either right-click on the white space below the displayed packages and select**Import package** or select from the menu, as shown at the beginning of this recipe.
2. Browse to the appropriate directory and select the package you would like to import and click on **Open**.

3. You might now be presented with a request to accept the user certificate of this Orchestrator server (also see the *Important Orchestrator settings* recipe in `Chapter 1`, *Installing and Configuring Orchestrator*). You can choose to import just the package (**Import once**) or import the package and add the SSL certificate of this user to your trusted certificates (**Import and trust provider**). We will work with these certificates more in the *There's more...* section of this recipe:

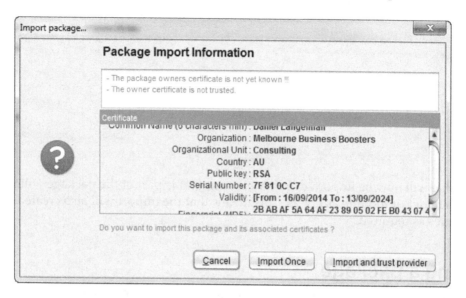

4. Orchestrator will now check the content of your package against what is already installed. The following window will be displayed. Here, you can choose whether an element should be imported or not. You see on the left-hand side the version and name of the element in the package and on the right-hand side the same information for the Orchestrator server (if that element already exists). You can use the magnifying glass icon on the far right to check the version log of your Orchestrator server-based element. You can force an import by just ticking the box of the element. Please note that we will discuss the **Import the values of the configuration settings** option in detail in the *How it works...* section of this recipe:

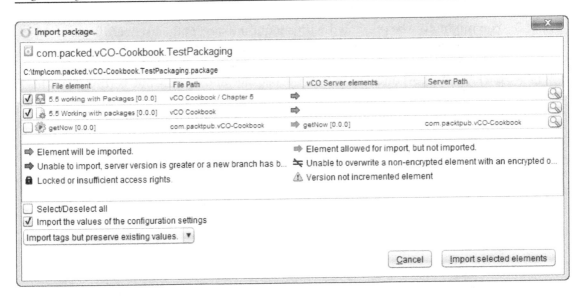

The package will now be imported. Every element that is part of the package will be placed back in its folder or module as it was. This means that the import will also create folders and modules as required.

Deleting a package

When right-clicking on a package, you will see there are two delete options:

Option	Description
Delete	This will delete the package only but no content (workflows, actions, and so on) will be deleted.
Delete element with content	This not only deletes the package but also its content (workflows, actions, and so on) from Orchestrator.

In this example, we will delete the package as well as the content:

1. Right-click on the package and select **Delete element with content**.
2. If you used the example package or have elements in this package that are used by other elements, then you will see the following warning message:

3. If you are not sure, you can **Keep shared** elements or **DELETE ALL!**.
4. Your package and its elements will now be deleted.

Import from remote

This option lets you import a package that is stored on another Orchestrator installation:

1. Go to packages and click on **get remote package**.
2. Enter the URL (including the port, 8281) of the remote Orchestrator, followed by a user ID and password.
3. You now see all the additional packages (not the basic ones).
4. Select a package and click on **Import....**.

5. You are now presented with a window similar to the one we saw when importing a workflow that shows the difference between the versions of the elements between **Remote server** and **Local server**. Click on **Synchronize!**:

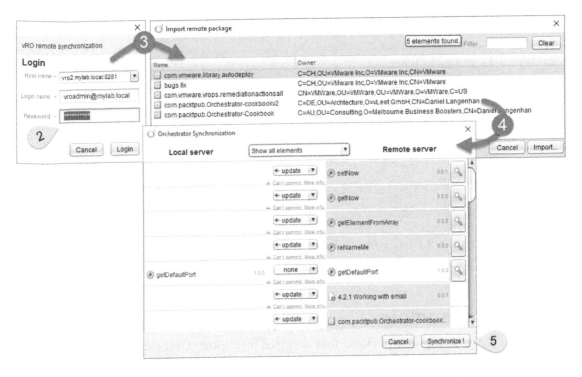

6. The package is now imported. If you change the content on the **Remote server**, you can right-click on the package and select **Synchronize** to actualize the content on the **Local server**.

How it works...

Building packages makes it very easy to transport or publish Orchestrator solutions that have been developed. A package contains all the important elements such as **Workflows**, **Actions**, **Policy Templates**, **Web Views**, **Configurations**, **Resources**, and **Plugins** used.

Another typical usage for packages is to create a backup.

When your package contains workflows or actions from a plugin, such as vCenter, vCloud Director or such like, the plugins and their versions are displayed in the **Used plugin** tab of the package. Orchestrator doesn't display any warnings or messages when you import a package that depends on a certain plugin. It will just import all the elements of this plugin that are part of the package. However, because of the dependencies, you will not be able to execute workflows that depend on this plugin.

Please note that when you export a package that contains AMQP, SNMP, or other Orchestrator plugins, the resource element that contains the server configuration is exported as well. Before delivering this package to a customer, you might want to delete these elements.

The package that is created is zipped and contains all the files. When you export to a folder, the content of the package is more exposed, but it's not the same format as when extracting the package.

Export and import options

When exporting a package, you have several options that you can choose from. When you deselect an option, all elements in this package will inherit the settings:

Option	Description
Add target certificate	We shall discuss this in the *There's more...* section of this recipe.
View Contents	This is not really as restrictive as one would expect. When you deselect this option, you can still see all the normal tabs in the workflow. The only thing that won't work is that you can go to an element by double-clicking on it. For example, if the workflow contains an action, double-clicking on it won't open the action element. However, the action can be accessed normally and you can see the scripting content.
Add to package	Deselecting this option will make it impossible for users to export a package that contains elements from this package. You can still create packages with elements that don't have the **Add to package** flag; however, you will get an error message when trying to export the package.
Edit content	Without this flag, users that import this package will not be able to edit the workflow. This flag is mostly set for all packages that are part of a plugin or to make sure that for support reasons changes are not possible.

Export version history	Deselecting this option will not export the full version history of each element. Instead, the element will be displayed in the latest version with the remark **imported content from package**.
Export values of the configuration settings	Deselecting this section will export the configuration and its attributes; however, it will not export their values.
Export global tags	This will export the global tag of the objects in the package. See the *Working with Orchestrator tags* recipe in `Chapter 8`, *Better Workflows and Optimized Working*.

When importing a package, you can deselect the **Import the values of the configuration settings** option. This will import the configuration and its attributes, but not its values.

The function to switch off editing is extremely important when delivering an Orchestrator solution to a customer. You will want to lock down the customer's ability to edit workflows or actions in order to make it possible to support the solution.

The target server function comes in handy if you want to make sure that Orchestrator packages do not get into the wrong hands. Typical things to mention here are configuration items in Orchestrator that contain sensitive information.

There's more...

Each package that is created is encrypted with this user certificate. You may have seen that when you imported the package onto a different Orchestrator installation. The certificate is the one we created in the *Important Orchestrator settings* recipe in `Chapter 1`, *Installing and Configuring Orchestrator*.

When you import a package, you can choose to trust this certificate. If you do so, it will be stored in the certificate store. You can manage the certificate store by clicking on **Tools** (this is in the top-right corner of Orchestrator Client) and then selecting **Certificate manager...**:

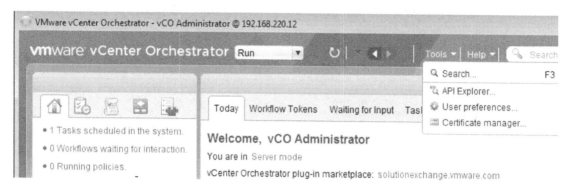

A popup will appear in which the upper part shows your user certificate and the lower part shows all known certificates (you might need to adjust the length of the window). See the following screenshot.

You are able to export your own certificate and also import others or remove others from the certificate store.

When you export a package, you can select the **Add target certificate** option to make sure that the package can only be read by a certain Orchestrator server. When you add a certificate to the package that is contained in your certificate store, you can make sure that only the Orchestrator server that is the owner of this certificate can import the package. If you try to import a package that is not intended for you, you will get an error message that says this package is not intended for you.

In the example package that comes with this book, I have placed a certificate in `resources` that you can use to test this:

See also

See the example workflow `04.03 Export-Package`. Also, see the recipe *Important Orchestrator settings* in `Chapter 1`, *Installing and Configuring Orchestrator*, and the recipe *Managing Remote Orchestrator* in `Chapter 3`, *Distributed Design*.

Workflow auto documentation

This recipe will showcase the automatic documentation ability of Orchestrator. We will learn what Orchestrator documents and how it documents workflows.

Getting ready

We need at least one workflow for this recipe that we can document. A good example workflow would be one that contains other workflows, actions, and scriptable tasks.

How to do it...

1. Right-click on a workflow or a folder and select **Generate Documentation**.
2. Select a directory and give the file a name.

A PDF with the documentation is now created.

How it works...

The documentation that is created isn't that flashy, but it is quite useful. The created PDF document contains the following sections:

Section	Description
Versions	This is a summary of all existing versions this workflow has, including the create date, create user, and any comments you have made regarding this version.
Inputs	This contains a list of all the in-parameters of the workflow as well as their type and description.
Outputs	This contains a list of all out-parameters of the workflow as well as their type and description.
Attributes	This contains a list of all attributes of the workflow as well as their type and description. It does not contain any values.
Parameter presentation	This shows all properties of all in-parameters that are defined in the presentation of this workflow.
Workflow schema	This is a picture of the workflow that shows the elements of the schema.
Workflow items	This is a tabular overview of all existing elements in the workflow schema.
Source code for the used actions	This lists every script that was used in an action, scriptable task, log element, and so on.

If you are running the documentation feature from a folder, each workflow in this folder will be documented.

Resuming failed workflows

This recipe looks at the ability to resume a failed workflow. It allows you to resume a workflow when an error has occurred.

Getting ready

We just need a working Orchestrator, and you will need the rights to create new workflows and run them. We will work with the Orchestrator Client.

To make it easier, we reuse the workflow we will create in the *Error handling in workflows* recipe in Chapter 5, *Visual Programming* (the `05.03.01 Error Handling` example workflow). If you don't have it, please create it as described or use the example package that is supplied with this book.

How to do it...

The following steps showcase the functionality:

1. Create a new workflow.
2. Drag **Workflow element** onto the schema and select the workflow we created in the *Error handling in workflows* recipe in Chapter 5, *Visual Programming*.
3. Assign the in-parameter of the **Error Handling** workflow to the in-parameter of the workflow you added in step 2.
4. Drop two additional **System log** instances before and after the workflow element and have it write something, such as `Before` and `After` onto the log.
5. Drop a **Throw exception** element directly onto the workflow from step 2.
6. Click on **General** in the main workflow and then select **Enable** for **Resume from failed behavior**:

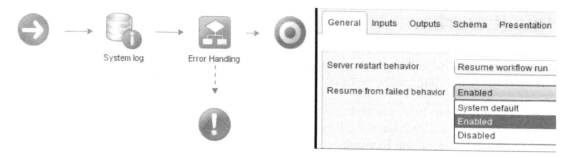

7. Click on **Save and Close**.
8. Run the workflow and enter 5 (this will result in an error). A window will now pop up and ask whether you would like to **Cancel** or **Resume** the workflow:

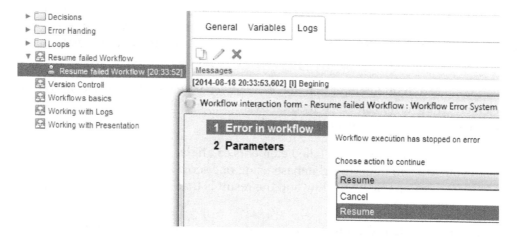

9. Choose **Resume**. You can now change *all* the variables of the workflow. Enter 2 and click on **Submit**.
10. The script now runs through as if nothing has happened. Check the **Logs**.

Notice that the first log messages and the log message from the **Error Handling** workflow was only written once, so the resume process would just rerun the scriptable task and not the whole workflow from the beginning.

How it works...

The ability to resume a workflow is quite a powerful tool. Instead of rerunning failed workflows again, and in some cases, roll back the previous operations, you are now able to resume at the same element the error occurred in.

Please note that in our little example we used a workflow inside a workflow, and the workflow that failed didn't have the **Resume** action assigned to it. What this means is that you don't have to assign the **Resume** action to all workflows, but just to the main one that calls all the others. Also, you see that only the failed element is allowed to be rerun, which in our case is the scriptable task inside the **Error Handling** workflow, not the whole workflow of error handling.

For example, you have a workflow that creates a VM, adds a virtual disk, and powers it on. If the workflow fails because you are out of disk space on the datastore, you will have to rerun the workflow again. This is especially true if some other application triggers the workflow via the Orchestrator API. Now, you can simply add the required disk space to the datastore and resume the workflow, or just use a different datastore.

However, you need to understand that you can only change variables or rerun the same failed element. If the error can't be remedied by a change of the variable content or by rerunning later, the `resume` function will not help you.

In addition to this, rerunning some failed elements can have very undesirable results. For example, if you add two items to a database using one scriptable task, the insertion of the second fails. You resume the workflow and the result is that you have added the first item twice. So be careful.

The secret to the resume feature lies in the way that Orchestrator works. When a workflow is executed, Orchestrator writes checkpoints in its database. One checkpoint before a step in the workflow is executed. These checkpoints consist of all variable values. This is why when you resume a workflow, you are presented with all the variables that exist in the workflow.

There's more...

The `resume` function is, by default, switched off system-wide. You can switch it on system-wide using the `com.vmware.vco.engine.execute.resume-from-failed` system property and setting it to `true`. See the *Control Center titbits* recipe in Chapter 2, *Optimizing Orchestrator Configuration*.

If you consider using the `resume` function, it is a good idea to define the timeout. The timeout defines how long a workflow waits in resume mode before failing. This feature can be used to make sure that workflows don't stay in resume mode indefinitely and that a human interaction can take place in a certain time frame.

> I personally would urge caution with switching on the resume feature system-wide, because as mentioned, not every workflow can or should be recoverable. Instead of switching on the resume feature system-wide, consider writing a good error response and making a general decision if you want to roll back or push forward.

See also

The example workflow `04.04 Resume Workflow`.

Using the workflow debugging function

This recipe showcases how to use the debug feature to find and resolve errors in a workflow. The debug function was introduced in version 5.5.

Getting ready

We just need a working Orchestrator, and you will need the rights to create new workflows and run them. We will work with the Orchestrator Client.

We need a new workflow, and to make things easier we reuse some old workflows, such as `00.00 BasicWorkflow` and `05.03.01 Error Handling` from the example package.

How to do it...

1. Create a new workflow and add the `00.00 BasicWorkflow` and `05.03.01 Error Handling` workflows (as shown in the following screenshot).
2. Bind all variables as required.
3. Right-click on the first element of your workflow and select **Toggle breakpoint**. A blue ball appears on the left next to the element.

4. You can debug a workflow either while still in edit mode or when you exit it. Choose one and click on **Debug** (the bug icon) to start the debug process.

5. The debug process starts the workflow and will stop the execution on the first breakpoint. It will not execute the step the breakpoint is located on, but stops before it. Please note that you have access to all variables and logs during the debug process:

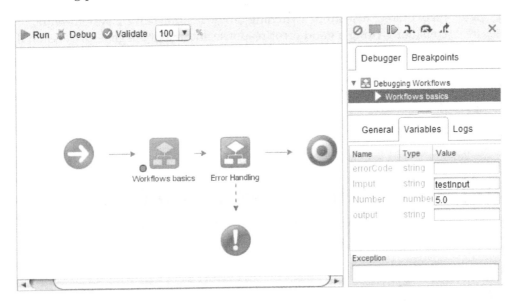

6. While debugging a workflow, you have choices such as **Cancel, Answer, Resume** (*F8*), **Step into** (*F5*), **Step over** (*F6*), and **Step return** (*F7*). You can use the icons or the function keys to perform the said processing. See the *How it works...* section for more details.

7. Use **Step into** to work through the workflow.

How it works...

The debugging feature was introduced in vCO 5.5. Before this feature existed, debugging Orchestrator was quite a bit more complicated and mostly involved using logs to write checkpoints and display variable content. With the debugging feature, things are now fairly easy. The debugging feature ties in with the checkpoints that Orchestrator uses when it executes a workflow. Orchestrator writes all variable content to its database before it executes one step. These checkpoint variables are displayed in the debug process.

You can set multiple **breakpoints** in each script and advance to them directly using **Resume** (*F8*).

The following table shows all the actions you can take during debugging:

Action	Description
Cancel	This stops the workflow execution.
Answer	This answers an interaction that the workflow has issued.
Resume	This resumes the workflow until the next breakpoint.
Step into	This steps into an element and starts debugging inside the element. This can also be used to go to the next element.
Step over	This will step over an element. The debugging will not enter the element.
Step return	This steps out of an element. The debugging will continue with the main element.

There's more...

When you use complex variables such as arrays or objects (for example, a VM), the content can be rather vast and won't be displayed in the **Values** section. In this case, have a closer look at the **Variables** screen. You will notice a small **i** icon before the variable value. Clicking on it will show you the content of the variable in a separate window. However, this doesn't work for all variable types. Properties and complex variables such as PowerShell output will not show up.

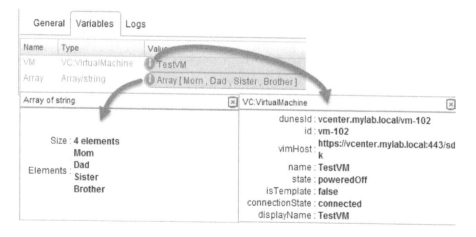

See also

The example workflow `04.05 Debugging Workflows`.

Undelete workflows and actions

This recipe shows how to undelete deleted workflows and actions, as this comes in handy when one deletes something that one shouldn't have.

Getting ready

To undelete a workflow, we need a deleted workflow or action first.

How to do it…

We will use a workflow in this example, as the undelete function for actions works exactly the same:

1. Right-click on a folder (or the root element 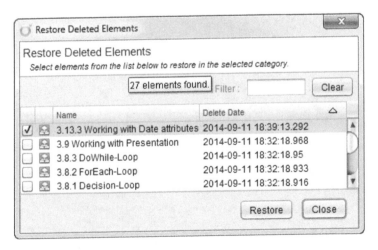) and select **Restore deleted workflows**.
2. A popup will display all the workflows or actions that can be restored. Tick all the workflows you would like to restore and click on **Restore**:

The workflows or actions will now be restored.

How it works...

All workflows and actions are stored in the Orchestrator database and as such, they can be restored. However, you cannot restore a workflow with the same ID that already exists; names of workflows are of no importance in Orchestrator.

Scheduling workflows

In this recipe, you will learn how to schedule workflows. Scheduled workflows will automatically run at given times and intervals.

Getting ready

We need at least one workflow we can schedule. The workflow should not contain a user interaction.

How to do it...

1. Right-click on the workflow you would like to schedule and choose **Schedule workflow**.
2. Select **Task name**. By default, the task name is set to be the workflow name. A good naming standard comes in handy here, especially if you schedule recurring tasks.
3. Set a start date and time.
4. If this task has been scheduled in the past, you can still run the workflow. This setting is useful if a task had been scheduled but during the planned execution time, Orchestrator server was not available (for example, powered off). The task will then start as soon as Orchestrator server is available again.
5. You can create a recurring task. You have the base setting for every minute, hour, day, week, and month. Except for the week setting, you can schedule multiple executions by clicking on the green plus sign. So, you can, for example, set a task that runs every day at 9 AM and 9 PM.
6. Last but not least, you can set a stop date and time at which the recurring task will stop.
7. Click on **Next** to get to the in-parameters for this workflow. Fill them out as required and when finished, click on **Submit**.

8. Orchestrator will now automatically jump into the **Run | Scheduler** view and show you the scheduled task:

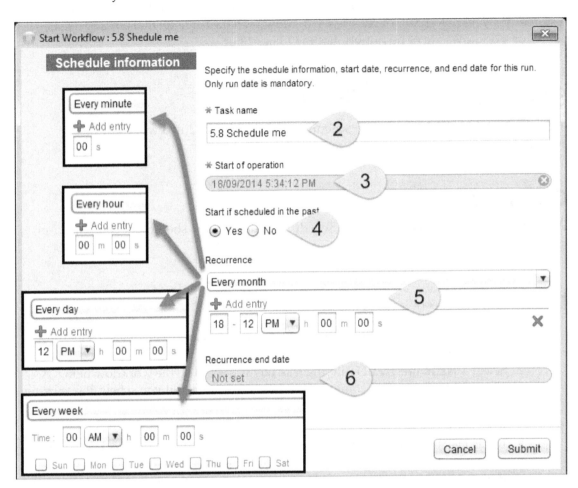

How it works...

Using the Orchestrator scheduler allows you to make sure certain tasks are running at a specific time. There are multiple examples. There is a maintenance task that is scheduled to run every evening to disconnect all CD-ROM drives from VMs or a provisioning/decommissioning task that you want to enact at a certain time. However, you could also use a policy for this, see the *Working with policies* recipe in `Chapter 8`, *Better Workflows and Optimized Working*.

You can manage all scheduled tasks from the **Run | Scheduler** view. Here, you can review all the relevant information for all the scheduled tasks. The information provided includes what workflow it is currently running when the last run was made, and when it will run next; you also see the in-parameters (**Parameters**) you have supplied to the workflow. By right-clicking on the task, you can suspend and resume it as well as cancel/delete and edit it. When editing the task, you can change all settings with regard to the scheduling; however, you cannot change the workflow you have scheduled or the in-parameters you entered when you scheduled the task:

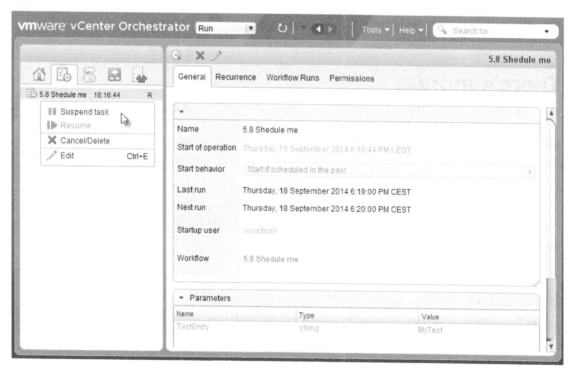

If you click on the **Workflow Runs** tab, you can see all the information for each run. You see the start and end time as well as the workflow state (waiting, failed, completed, canceled, running). If the workflow is currently running, you can see which element of the workflow is currently running (**Current item**) as well as its business state:

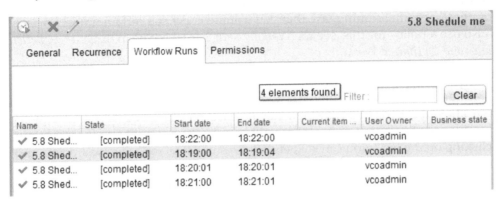

In addition to this, you can also schedule and monitor a scheduled task from vCenter. In the vCenter Web Client, click on **vCenter Orchestrator** and then on **Scheduled workflows**.

There's more...

You can interactively schedule a workflow using a workflow. A typical example for this is a workflow that requests a VM but then schedules the actual provisioning at a later date and time. To do this, just use the **Schedule workflow** schema element that you find in the **Generic** section. This element only schedules tasks once; it doesn't allow recurring tasks.

You can schedule workflows using JavaScript. By using the two `Workflow.schedule()` and `Workflow.scheduleRecurrently()` methods, you can now schedule this workflow. Have a closer look at the **Schedule workflow** schema element; the `Workflow.schedule()` method is used there.

See also

See the example workflow `5.8.1 Schedule me!` and `5.8.2. Automatic schedule.`

Sync presentation settings

In this recipe, we will make it easier for you to reuse presentation settings from embedded workflows.

Getting ready

We need a workflow with a presentation assigned to it; you can use the 05.05 Workflow Presentation example workflow.

How to do it...

1. Log into the Orchestrator Client and create a new workflow.
2. Drag the workflow with the presentation onto the schema. You can use the 05.05 Workflow Presentation example workflow.
3. Right-click the workflow and select **Synchronize** | **Synchronize presentation**.
4. Confirm that you want to sync.
5. Check the presentation of your new workflow.

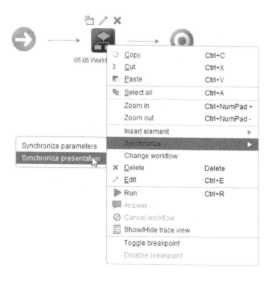

How it works...

This is one of the functions that has been around for some time but people don't know about. It not only syncs the presentation but also links up all the workflow elements inputs as INPUTs.

Locking elements

We will have a quick look at the locking mechanism of Orchestrator.

Getting ready

For locking workflows, we need a workflow that we can use to lock, primarily, a workflow that calls other actions or workflows. If you don't have one in hand, use the 06.06.01 Using Asynchronous Workflows example workflow.

How to do it...

There are only two options in the locking system.

Locking workflows

To lock a workflow, action, or package, follow these steps:

1. Right-click on a workflow, action, or package.
2. Navigate to **Locking** | **Lock** or **Locking** | **Lock with dependencies**. The **Lock with dependencies** option will lock all subworkflows and subactions that are used in this workflow.

Notice that the little lock icon on the item you have locked; you will not be able to edit this workflow anymore. However, you are still able to run it.

Unlocking workflows

Unlocking should be obvious now. However, note that there is no unlock with dependencies option, which means that you have to unlock each element by itself:

1. Right-click on a locked workflow, action, or package.
2. Navigate to **Locking | Unlock**.

How it works...

Locking locks the edit mode of a workflow, which marks it as not accessible. Anyone with **Admin** rights can place or lift a lock.

A lock disables **Edit**, **Delete**, **Synchronize**, and **Move**. Locks cannot be exported.

Workflow locking actually has nothing to do with the locking system (see the *Using the locking system* recipe in Chapter 8, *Better Workflows and Optimized Working*). Workflow locking locks workflows and actions, whereas the locking system locks resources.

Locks can be useful in a production environment where one wants to make sure that an important production workflow can't be altered.

See also

The *Using the Locking System* recipe in Chapter 8, *Better Workflows and Optimized Working*.

5
Visual Programming

This chapter looks into the basic visual programming tools we can use. We will have a look at the following recipes:

- Scripting with logs
- Scripting with decisions
- Error handling in workflows
- Scripting with loops
- Workflow presentations
- Linking actions in presentations
- Changing credentials during runtime

Introduction

As this chapter focuses on basic visual programming tools, it is a good place to have a quick look at how the programming of workflows works.

A workflow is made up of several sections. This chapter's focus will be on the creation of new workflows. We will work with the general, inputs, outputs, schemas, and presentation.

Variables (general, inputs, and outputs)

Each workflow can have **variables** in three different areas. Variables are called attributes or parameters depending on where they are.

In JavaScript, the naming convention for variables is to start with lowercase and use uppercase when a new word starts, for example, `myFirstAttribute`, `currentVM`, and so on. This is what programmers call a **camelCase** convention. We should use the same convention when programming in Orchestrator.

Variables in the general section

A variable in the **General** section is called an **attribute**. An attribute is accessible throughout the whole workflow, but, not outside it. An attribute can have an initial value (at the start of a workflow), but it can also be changed at any stage.

Attributes are mostly used for two things: as a constant (defined once and not changing) or as a way to exchange a value between two workflow elements. You can lock an attribute (see the following screenshot) to make sure that the initial value can't be changed.

You can move an attribute to become an input or output parameter if you have created it in the wrong spot. Just right-click on the variable and choose the **Move as...** option:

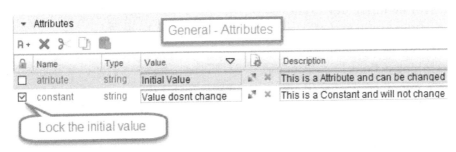

Variables in the input section

A variable in the input section is called an **in-parameter**. The content of an input variable is defined at runtime and entered by the user. Input variables cannot be changed during workflow execution directly, as you cannot assign an in-parameter as the output of a workflow element. You can move an input parameter to become an attribute:

Variables in the output section

A variable in the output section is called an **out-parameter**. The content of an output variable can be defined within the workflow and is available to other elements when the workflow has finished. You can move an output parameter to become an attribute:

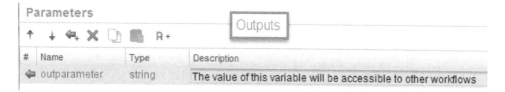

Variable types

There are many variable types that are already implemented in Orchestrator out-of-the-box, but the basic variable types are as follows:

Variable type	Description
Any	This can contain *any* content. It is used to carry variables to other elements that are not defined in the Orchestrator GUI, such as XML. Note that Any should only be used if nothing else will do, as it has been known to mishandle some content such as complex variables.
boolean	This has only two values, either true or false. However, Orchestrator uses **Yes** and **No** in the GUI.
Credential	This contains a username and password. The password is encrypted.
Date	This is used to store the date or time in the JavaScript format.
number	This contains only numbers, which can be integers or real numbers. Everything is stored as floats in Orchestrator.
SecureString	When entering values, ***s** will be shown instead of characters. The value is plain text and visible to the workflow developer, but encrypted when the workflow runtime information is stored in the database.
EncryptedString	This is like**secure string**; however, the value is always encrypted.
string	This can contain any characters.
NULL	This is not really a type, but defining a variable as NULL means that anything that is put into it will be discarded.

In addition to the base types, each plugin will install its own type. These types are identified by their prefixes. For example, types that come with the vCenter plugin have the **VC:** prefix and types from the SSH plugin have the **SSH:** prefix:

Working with a schema

Any Orchestrator workflow programming is done in the **schema**; each element in the schema is connected by either a blue (**normal**), green (**True**), or dotted red (**Error/False**) line between a start point and an endpoint. You can have more than one endpoint, but only one start point:

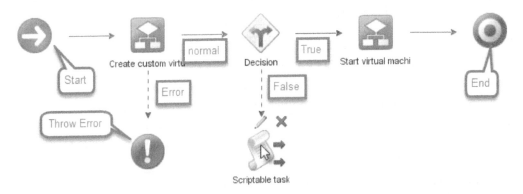

Dropping an element on a line will insert it into the flow. You can delete elements or lines by right-clicking on them and selecting **Delete** (you can also use the *Delete* key).

To create a new line, hover the mouse above an element (see **Scriptable task** in the previous figure) and then drag one of the arrows to the destination element.

You can rename any element by just double-clicking on it and entering a new name.

Presentation

In presentation, we define how the workflow input masks look and behave. You can define the order of the input fields, a default value, whether a given field should be mandatory and link it to other fields and values.

The presentation is quite handy for workflow execution used with the Orchestrator Client and the vSphere Web Client. For websites, and especially for workflows used in vRA, it's not that important. vRA itself has an interface that determines all the things above. See more about workflow presentations in vRA in the recipe *Workflow presentation* in Chapter 5, *Visual Programming*.

Scripting with logs

In this recipe, we will look into how logging works in scripting. You will learn how to create log entries and where they are stored.

Getting ready

We just need a working Orchestrator, and you will need the rights to create new workflows and run them. We will work with the Orchestrator Client.

Additionally, we need administrative (root) access to the Orchestrator's operating system.

How to do it...

We will split this recipe into two sections, *Creating logs* and *Checking the log files*.

Creating logs

We will now create log entries during a workflow:

1. Create a new workflow.
2. Drag all log elements from the **Log** section into the workflow and arrange them as shown here:

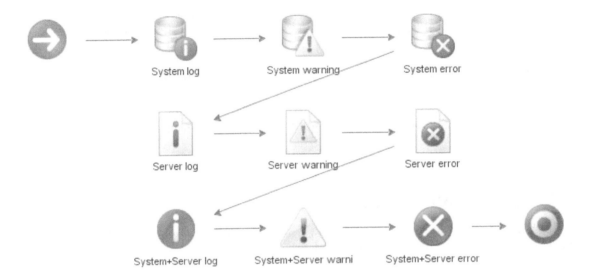

3. Create the following variables:

Name	Type	Section	Binds with
logText	String	IN	Transports error text
logObject	String	IN	Transports object text

4. Bind each log element with the required in-parameter.
5. Save and exit the workflow.
6. Run the workflow and enter two different phrases, such as **LogText** and **LogObject**.

Checking log files

We will now check the logs:

1. Go to the workflow execution.
2. Check the **Events** tab.

Description	Type	Time	User	Origin
Workflow '05.01 Working with Logs' has started	ⓘ Info	23:38:03	Administrator	439711601
LogText	ⓘ Info	23:38:04	Administrator	439711601
LogText	⚠ Warning	23:38:04	Administrator	439711601
LogText	✕ Error	23:38:04	Administrator	439711601
LogText	ⓘ Info	23:38:04	Administrator	439711601
LogText	⚠ Warning	23:38:04	Administrator	439711601
LogText	✕ Error	23:38:04	Administrator	439711601
Workflow '05.01 Working with Logs' has completed	ⓘ Info	23:38:04	Administrator	439711601

3. Click on the **Schema** tab and then on **Logs**:

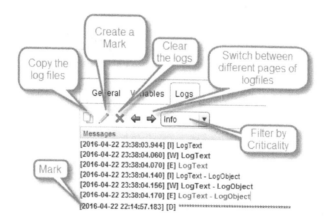

How it works...

Logs are an important tool for programmers and for system administrators. Log files help programmers understand where a program went wrong or show them the values of variables during runtime. For system administrators, log files help them keep track of who ran what workflow, and when.

In logs generated by the execution of a workflow, you can copy the content (the copy icon), insert a *** line (the pencil icon), or delete the whole log (the red **X** icon) and filter by criticality, and even switch between pages.

The main difference between server and system logs is that server logs are stored in the Orchestrator database and system logs are stored in the system's log files. This is especially important if you work with Orchestrator clusters; see the recipe *Building an Orchestrator cluster* recipe in Chapter 3, *Distributed Design*.

The server log files get rolled as specified in the recipe *Orchestrator log files* in Chapter 2, *Optimizing Orchestrator Configuration*. Server logs are stored with the workflow execution until purged depending on user settings (see the recipe *User preferences* in Chapter 7, *Interacting with Orchestrator*). Server logs are persistent as they are stored in log files on the Orchestrator server.

A log event can have four categories:

Syslog value	Debug	Info	Warn	Error
Workflow element	–	Log	Warning	Error
Logs	[D]	[I]	[W]	[E]
JavaScript	System.debug (text)	System.log (text)	System.warn (text)	System.error (text)
	Server.debug (text, object)	Server.log (text, object)	Server.warn (text, object)	Server.error (text, object)

Each of the four categories can be chosen at will. Any information that would be critical to troubleshoot a workflow several hours/days after it's run should be logged using the server.

Sending excessive logs to the server will dramatically increase the size of the Orchestrator database and slow down the orchestration engine performance, so it must be used wisely.

In JavaScript, using logs is quite a good way to fix bugs. A typical thing to do is to write out variables that exist only inside a script element, for example, `System.log("Mark")`, `System.log("Log: "+variable)`.

Log file location

There are multiple ways to check the *physical* log files. The most common one is to check the log files on the Orchestrator OS. The one we are interested in is: `/var/log/vco/app-server/scripting.log`.

This directory also contains other log files that are discussed in the recipe *Orchestrator log files* in `Chapter 2`, *Optimizing Orchestrator Configuration*.

This directory contains all information about running scripts. When we look at it, we should see the following entry for our example workflow:

```
2016-04-22 23:38:04.140+0200 INFO
{Administrator@mylab.local:40285c8c543d802d01543fe885a40127}
[SCRIPTING_LOG] [05.01 Working with Logs (4/22/16 23:38:03)] LogText -
LogObject
```

There is quite a lot of information, for example, what workflow (`05.01 Scripting with Logs`) was executed and also the Orchestrator user (`Administrator@mylab.local`) who executed it.

Alternatively, instead of logging into the appliance, you can use the Control Center to access logs in two ways:

- You can download the `scripting.log` from the Control Center file browser in the `/app-server-logs` folder
- You can inspect a workflow and check the logs there

For the last two methods, please see the recipe *Control Center titbits* in `Chapter 2`, *Optimizing Orchestrator Configuration*.

Altering log elements

You can easily use log elements to delete the input variable out of it and then use scripting to fill in whatever you like.

See also

The example workflow, `05.01 Scripting with Logs`.

The recipe, *Redirecting Orchestrator logs to an external server* in `Chapter 2`, *Optimizing Orchestrator Configuration*.

The recipe, *Orchestrator log files* in `Chapter 2`, *Optimizing Orchestrator Configuration*.

There is a nice example in the recipe, *Building an Orchestrator cluster* in `Chapter 3`, *Distributed Design* to show the difference between server and system logs.

Scripting with decisions

In this workflow, we will see how decisions can be implemented into scripts. You will learn how to create basic and custom decisions.

Getting ready

We just need a working Orchestrator, and you will need the rights to create new workflows and run them. We will work with the Orchestrator Client.

We need a new workflow where we can add a decision. You also should know how to work with logs.

For the **Decision activity** element, we will be using the example workflow `00.00 BasicWorkflow`, which is stored in the `Basic Helper` folder.

How to do it...

There are three decisions that can be used in Orchestrator; we will discuss them in the following sections.

Basic decision

The Basic decision lets you check a single variable against a condition. A condition is always something that is either true or false. For example, the condition $5 > 3$ is true, whereas the condition *Team* contains *i* is false.

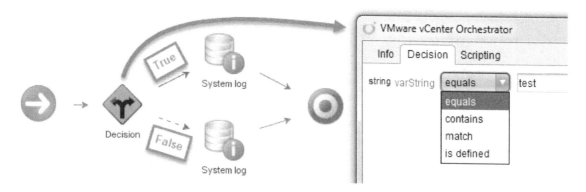

1. Create a new workflow and define an in-parameter of the String type.
2. Assemble the structure as seen in the previous figure. You will need to rearrange the lines of the workflow.
3. Have the **System log** element write something such as **True** (green line) or **False** (red dashed line) into the logs.
4. Edit the **Decision** element and click on **Decision**.
5. Choose a condition and set a value as seen in the previous figure. When done, click on **Ok**.
6. Save and run the workflow.

What happens is that the workflow will check whether the value entered fulfills the condition you have specified and then will fork to either the true or false path.

Try this out for several other variable types. Each variable type has other conditions with it. For example, the VC:VirtualMachine type has not only the name of a VM, but also its state (power).

Custom decisions

A **Custom decision** enables you to check a single variable or multiple variables against complex conditions using JavaScript code.

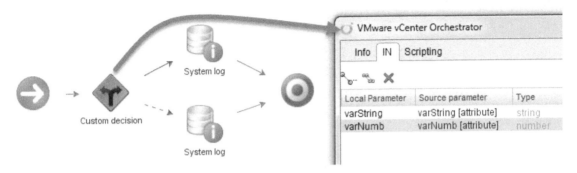

1. Create a new workflow (or reuse the last one) and define two in-parameters:

Name	Type	Section	Use
varString	String	IN	This contains a word
varNumber	Number	IN	This contains the length of the word

2. Assemble the structure as seen in the previous screenshot.
3. Have the **System log** element write something such as true (green line) or false (red dashed line) into the logs.
4. Edit the **Custom decision** element and bind both in-parameter to **IN**.
5. Click on **Scripting** and enter the following script (also see the *How it works...* section of this recipe):

```
if (varString.length == varNumber)  {
     return true;
} else {
     return false;
}
```

6. Save and run the workflow.

When the workflow executes the **Custom decision**, it will compare the entered string's length with the entered number and then will fork to either the true or false path.

Please note that you have to use the JavaScript `return` command with either `true` or `false` to make this decision element work.

Decision activity

A **Decision activity** lets you check the output of a workflow against a basic condition.

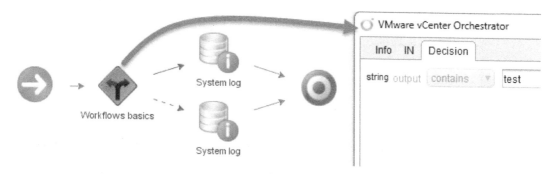

1. Create a new workflow (or reuse the last one) and define an in-parameter of the type `String`.
2. Assemble the structure as seen in the previous screenshot. When you add the **Decision activity** element, you will be asked what workflow you want to use with it. For simplicity, we will use the `00.00 BasicWorkflow` workflow, which is stored in the `Basic Helper` folder.
3. Click on **IN**. You will now see all the in-parameters of the workflow you have selected. Bind the workflow input to the in-parameter you defined in step 1.
4. Click on **Decision**, choose one of the output variables of the workflow you selected, and then choose a basic condition you would like to test the output against. Click on **OK** when finished.
5. Have the **System log** element write something like true (green line) or false (red dashed line) into the logs.
6. Save and run the workflow.

When you run the workflow, the in-parameter you defined will be forwarded to the basic workflow and then the output of the workflow will be checked against the condition you have defined.

The Switch element

This element introduces multiple choices. Just drag a blue arrow from the **Switch** element to the case element and then enter a basic condition:

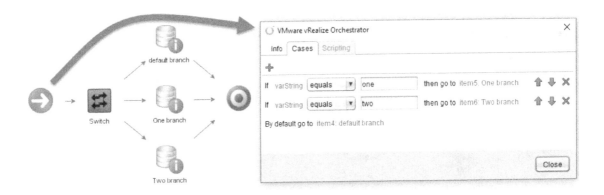

1. Create a new workflow (or reuse the last one) and define an in-parameter of the type `String`.
2. Drag the **Switch** element onto the schema and edit the element.
3. Click the green plus sign twice, each time a new end element will be created.
4. Assign the in-parameter to the new branches and define a Basic decision, as seen previously.
5. Have the **System log** elements write something such as `one`, `two` into the logs.
6. Save and run the workflow.

How it works...

Decisions are a commonly-used tool in programming. Each of the three decision types lets you fork your workflow into different areas.

A **Basic decision** is in itself easy to use and powerful, as it doesn't require you to use any JavaScript. The previous example showed you which conditions are possible for the type `String`, but each variable type comes with its own pool of conditions.

A **Custom decision** is useful if your decision depends on things that the Basic decision doesn't cover or more than one variable is needed to make a decision. It requires you to use JavaScript, but you also gain a lot more agility.

A **Decision activity** checks one output of a workflow against a basic condition. It is commonly used to check whether a workflow produced a certain result. A **Decision activity** can be substituted by the following schema:

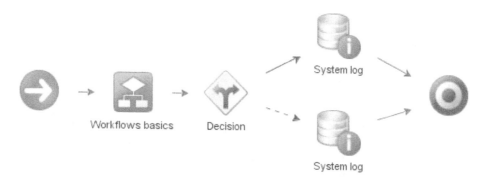

The major difference is that you won't have to use an attribute to *park* the output of the workflow and then use this attribute in the Basic decision. However, a **Decision activity** is good only for a single variable and a basic condition. If you need a more complex condition or multiple variables, you would need to build the preceding schema and use a **Custom decision** element.

The **Switch** element allows you to reduce complex code and use multiple decision trees. Not only can you use the **Switch** element like the Java version, but you can actually use different variables for each decision. In this respect, it behaves more like an `if-else if` structure.

> The Switch element and **Decision activity** have been added in vRO6 and should not be imported into older versions of Orchestrator.

JavaScript – if and else

As we already saw in the *Custom decisions* section, the JavaScript code for an `if` statement isn't that difficult. It is made up of operators and the `If` clause itself. The form looks like this:

Statement	Example

`if (condition) {`
`    code block`
`} else if (condition) {`
`    code block`
`} else {`
`    code block`
`}`
	`if (varString == "test") {`
	`    return true;`
	`} else {`
	`    return false;`
	`}`

The condition is made up of a statement that is either true or false. This statement is built using operators. The operators that JavaScript knows are the following:

and	or	not	Equal	Not equal	Smaller	Bigger
`&&`	`||`	`!`	`==`	`!=`	`< <=`	`>= >`

As an example, if you want to know whether the number that is stored in variable `A` is bigger than 5, the conditional statement will be `(A > 5)`. If you want to know whether the string stored in the variable `Text` equals *Hello*, the statement will be `(Text == "Hello")`.

You can glue conditions together with the `&&` (and) and `||` (or) operators and normal breaks (). For example, if `A` is bigger than 5 and `Text` is *Hello*, the conditional statement will look like this: `((A>5) && (Text == "Hello"))`.

JavaScript – Switch

The Switch statement in JavaScript looks like this:

Statement	Example

Switch (expression) {
 case condition:
 code block
 break;
 default:
 default code block
 }
	Switch (GuestOS) {
	 case "RedHat":
	 SCSI="LSi Logic";
	 break;
	 case "Win2008":
	 SCSI="Paravirtual";
	 break;
	 default:
	 throw "Unknown OS";
	 }

In expression, you fill in the variable you would like to check, and in the case condition: part, you fill in the condition you want to check against. Please note that you can only check the equals (==) condition with the Switch statement. The default: part is used if all other tests fail.

See also

Also, see the example workflows:

- 05.02.1 Basic Decision
- 05.02.2 Custom decision
- 05.02.3 Decision activity
- 05.02.4 Switch

Error handling in workflows

This recipe is dedicated to showing how to handle errors in workflows. We will learn how to catch errors and redirect them.

Getting ready

We just need a working Orchestrator, and you will need the rights to create new workflows and run them. We will work with the Orchestrator Client.

How to do it...

1. Create a new workflow. We will reuse this workflow in the recipe, *Resuming failed workflows* in Chapter 4, *Programming Skills*.
2. Add the following variables:

Name	Type	Section	Use
number	Number	IN	Used to create an intentional error

3. Assemble the workflow (as seen in the following screenshot) by dragging a **Scriptable task** into the workflow and then a **Throw exception** element from the generic section *onto* the **Scriptable task**. Add the two log elements to the workflow by just dropping them onto the lines:

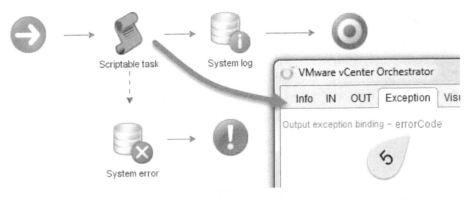

4. Bind the in-parameter to the scriptable task and add the following script, which will throw an error when the value 5 is entered:

```
if (number==5) {
    throw "Intentional Error";
}
```

5. In the **Scriptable task**, click on **Exception**. You will find that Orchestrator has automatically created a new workflow attribute called **errorCode** of the String type and bound it to the **Output exception**.

6. Use the log elements to indicate in the logs which path has been taken. You can do this by removing the in-parameter Text in the log element. In the scripting part of the log element, replace the variable Text with something such as Normal Path and Error Path.

7. Save and close the workflow.

8. Run the workflow. If you enter 5, the workflow will exit with an error. Check the workflow logs.

Default error handler

The default error handler is used to catch all errors regardless of where they originated and pushes them into one error-handling routine. This cleans up the workflow and makes them easier to follow.

> The default error handler has been added in vRO6 and should not be imported into older versions of Orchestrator.

1. Copy the workflow you have created in the last section or copy the example workflow, 05.03.01 Error Handling.

2. Delete the error path including the exception.

3. Drag the default error handler onto the schema (anywhere).

4. Insert a new log element and test the workflow.

Scriptable task   System log

System error

How it works...

Error handling is defined as a reaction to an error (an **exception**) when it occurs.

In automation, there are generally two types of handling errors: push through and rollback. What this means is that you can either decide that you push on and try to resolve the error in the code, or you roll back any change that you made to the system. It mostly depends on the task you are performing and exceptions you have.

In our little example, we intentionally created an error using the JavaScript command `throw`, as errors normally only occur when one doesn't need or want them.

Each Orchestrator element has an **Exception** section in which you can define an attribute of the type `String`, which will carry the error message that occurred in this element. In addition to this, each Orchestrator element has a blue line (normal execution) and red dashed line (exception).

We connected the red (exception) line to the **Throw exception** element to stop further execution of the workflow, but we used a log element in between. Have a closer look at the workflow. You will notice that there is a red line from the scriptable task to the error log, but there is a blue line between it and the **Throw exception** element. What this means is that, if an error occurs in the scripting, we fork the program into a new path. Instead of stopping the workflow in a *failed* state, we could have used other programming elements to resolve the error.

For example, if you have a workflow that creates a VM and the workflow fails with the error **Not enough space**, you can then use Orchestrator to attach an additional data store and then rerun the created VM workflow.

Ignoring errors

It is also possible to ignore errors in a workflow. To do so, you just drag the red line to the same element that the blue line already points to. The result is a red and blue dashed line. This basically means that the workflow continues with or without an error to the next element. If you don't need the error message that will be generated, bind the exception to **Null**.

A typical example of this configuration is deleting a VM. If you want to delete a VM, it has to be stopped. The workflow, **Power off virtual machine and wait**, will give an error if the VM is already switched off. To solve this, you can connect the blue and the red path of the **Power Off** workflow to the **Delete VM** workflow. This will make sure that a VM is powered off; if not, then the error will just be ignored.

The handle error element

There is an element called handle error that helps you with your error paths. Just drag the element onto a workflow element and then you can choose from several options. Depending on the option, a new error path will be created.

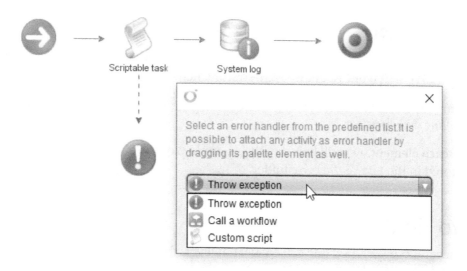

See also

The example workflows:

- 05.03.1 Error Handling
- 05.03.2 Ignore Errors
- 05.03.3 Default Error handler

Scripting with loops

Here, we will explore how to create loops in scripts. You will learn how to build loops and use them.

Getting ready

We just need a working Orchestrator, and you will need the rights to create new workflows and run them. We will work with the Orchestrator Client.

You need to understand how decisions are used in Orchestrator; this was explained in the recipe *Scripting with decisions*.

For the **Foreach** element, we will be using the example workflow `00.00 BasicWorkflow`, which is stored in the `Basic Helper` folder.

How to do it...

There are several types of loop one can create; however, they can all be reduced to the following two basic types.

The decision loop

This basic kind of loop runs until a certain condition is met. We will build a so-called `for` loop in this example. A discussion about the different types of decision loops (`for`, `do-while`, and `while-do`) can be found in the *How it works...* section of this recipe.

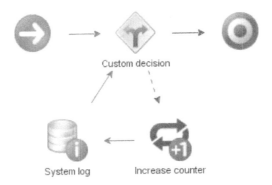

1. Create a new workflow and build the preceding schema.
2. Add the following variables:

Name	Type	Section	Use
number	Number	IN	This is used to stop the loop
counter	Number	Attribute	This has the value 0 and count loop iterations

3. Assign the **counter** attribute the initial value, 0.
4. Bind the **counter** attribute to the **IN** and **OUT** sections of the **Increase counter** element.
5. Bind the text in-parameter of **System log** to the counter. This will write the current count into the logs.
6. In the **Custom decision** element, bind the counter and the in-parameter to the **IN** section.
7. In the **Scripting** section, enter the following script:

```
if (number == counter) {
    return true;
} else {
    return false;
}
```

8. Save and run the workflow.
9. The workflow will run as many times as the value entered.

What happens is that the decision will check whether the attribute counter is equal to the value entered; if it is not, the loop will run and increase the counter by one.

The Foreach loop

A `Foreach` loop will repeat one workflow with different inputs. For the input, you must select an array.

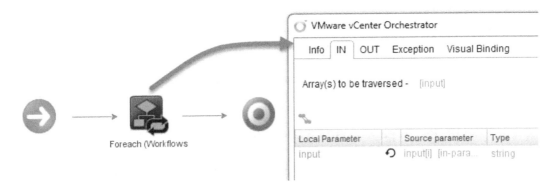

1. Create a new workflow and create the following variables:

Name	Type	Section	Use
input	Array of string	IN	This is an array of input variables
output	Array of string	OUT	This is an array of output variables

2. Drag the **Foreach** element onto the schema. You will be asked what workflow you want to use with it. For simplicity, we will use the workflow `00.00` `BasicWorkflow`, which is stored in the folder, `Basic Helper`.
3. Open the **Foreach** element in the **IN** section. You will see that the input is already bound. If in another workflow, you want to choose another iterator, click on **Array(s) to be traversed**, choose another array, and bind the variable.
4. Bind the output variable.
5. Save and run the workflow.

When the workflow runs, you will be prompted to enter values into an array. The basic workflow will run for each element you have entered into the array. The result of each run will be stored in the array.

Foreach workflows are run synchronously, meaning that if one fails the whole element will fail.

Have a look at the *There's more...* section to find out how to deal with exceptions in the
Foreach element.

How it works...

Loops are a very common tool in programming. They enable programs to go through
repetitions. The two basic types we have introduced are different in the way they work.
Decision loops use a condition to terminate, whereas the `Foreach` loop terminates when all
elements of the input have been processed.

There is a major difference between looping in JavaScript (such as inside a **Scriptable task**)
and using the workflow schema. Control! When we loop in the schema we can control error
handling, exceptions, attribute handling, and get a better grip on troubleshooting.

An example of a decision loop is a loop that checks for e-mails with a certain subject every
minute. The loop in this example is actually a combination of a `do-while` loop and a `for`
loop at the same time. The double loop is done to make sure the loop doesn't run forever.
After 10 runs, the loop will terminate.

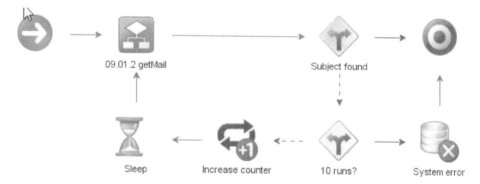

The classic example for a `Foreach` loop is renaming multiple VMs. You define in one array
the VMs you want to rename and in the other the new names.

Types of decision loops

There are three types of decision loops:

Loop type	Description
for	A counting variable is used to count the number of runs. The loop terminates when the count has reached a predefined value.
do-while	An action is performed and, after that, the result of the action is checked against a condition. As in the previous e-mail example, we check whether the e-mail has arrived. This loop will run at least once.
while-do	This is the same as the do-while loop, except the check is performed before any action is taken. If the check is true, the loop will not be run.

Foreach and arrays

The **Foreach** element needs arrays for input and for output. However, if you create a normal (non-array) variable in **General** or **Input**, you can add it as an input parameter for the **Foreach** element, meaning that this would be a static value for all runs of the **Foreach** element. Please note that you still need at least *one* array as input.

An example for this discussion is the creation of 10 VMs that all have the same attributes except their name. You would use a **Foreach** loop on the Create VM workflow, the VM name would be an array, and all the others would be normal attributes.

If you want to add an attribute array to a **Foreach** element, then you need to follow these steps:

1. Add the arrays to **Array(s) to be traversed**.
2. Your arrays are now selectable when setting them:

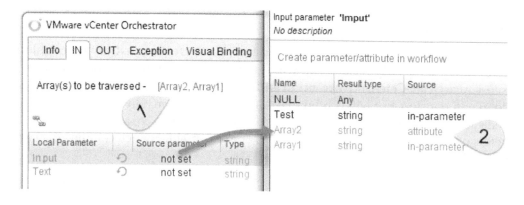

JavaScript

JavaScript has the following loops:

	Statement	**Example**
for	```for (start,``` ```condition,``` ```increase) {``` ```code block;``` ```}```	```for (i = 0; i < 5; i++) {``` ```System.log(i);``` ```}```
while	```while (condition) {``` ```code block;``` ```}``` ```do {``` ```code block;``` ```}``` ```while (condition);```	```Var i = 0;``` ```while (i < 10) {``` ```System.log(i);``` ```i++;``` ```}```
for each	```for each (variable in array) {``` ```code block;``` ```}```	```for each (day in week) {``` ```System.log(day);``` ```}```

This is straightforward. `condition` is like any other condition we explained in the recipe *Scripting with decisions* in this chapter. `code block` is any JavaScript code you would like to implement. The only thing that might need a bit of explanation is `for each`. The `(variable in array)` part defines a new `variable` that is filled each time with a new element from the `array`. For example, if we have an array that contains the days of the week, each time the loop is run the `day` variable will be filled with another day.

There's more...

When handling exceptions with the for each loop, there are some extras you might find useful. Just adding the output exception will stop the for each loop as soon as an error occurs. If you activate **Catch any exception and continue with the next iteration**, the for each loop will not stop, but will continue. Additionally, you can add code that will be executed each time an exception happens in the loop. You have access to all the in-parameters of the for each loop, but also the $index variable, which contains the current iteration of the loop:

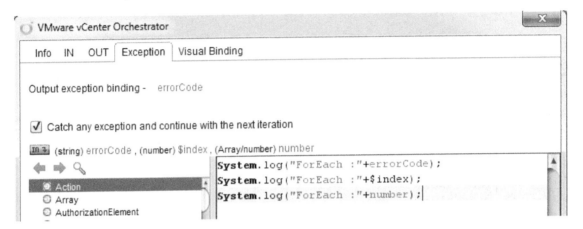

See also

The example workflows:

- 05.04.1 Decision-Loop
- 05.04.2 ForEach-Loop
- 05.04.3 DoWhile-Loop
- 05.04.4 ForEach-Exceptions

Workflow presentations

In this recipe, you will learn how to configure the input window (the presentation) and make it not only more user-friendly, but also reduce the amount of errors a user can enter. You will learn how to link values, hide inputs on conditions, and use predefined answers.

Getting ready

We just need a working Orchestrator, and you will need the rights to create new workflows and run them. We will work with the Orchestrator Client.

How to do it...

We will split this recipe into several sections. We will only create a presentation, not a *working* workflow.

Preparation

This preparation is just so that we can see some results:

1. Create a new workflow using the following variables:

Name	Type	Section	Use
number	Number	IN	This is used for presentations
string	String	IN	This is used for presentations
boolYesNo	Boolean	IN	This is used for presentations
input	Array of Strings	IN	This is used for presentations
text	String	IN	This is used for presentations
selection	Array of String	Attribute	This fills this array with strings in the order: first, second, third…
length	Number	Attribute	This sets the value to 8

2. Drag a log task onto the schema and assign all the variables to it. This is just so that the validation of the workflow will work.

Description

1. Switch to **Presentation** and click on the first variable you see.
2. Click on **General** and enter some text into **Description**.

Each element (including Steps and Groups) in the presentation has a **General** tab with a **Description** field. In this tab, you can enter text that will be displayed when the workflow runs. Each in-parameter automatically gets the name of the respective in-parameter in **Description**. You can, and probably should, change this to rather more meaningful description.

The description is interpreted as HTML, but not all tags work; however, `<br>`, `<u>`, `<b>`, `<i>`, `<l>`, and `<a href>` work quite well.

There is a way to include the content of a simple variable in **Description** of a variable. Just add the variable in the `${variableName}` form.

In-parameter properties

You can add to each in-parameter a list of different properties to change the presentation. We cannot discuss all the properties in this recipe, just the basic ones (also see the recipe *Linking actions in presentations* in this chapter):

1. Click on **Presentation** and then on one of the in-parameters.
2. Click on **Properties** and then on **Add property** (the blue triangle icon).

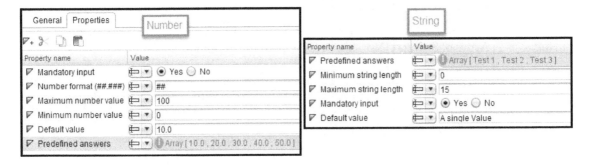

3. You can now add various properties, which can differ for each variable. Go and try them out. A full table of properties can be found in the *How it works...* section of this recipe.
4. Make some settings and run the workflow to see the results. I really recommend that you play with the properties.

Steps and groups

Steps and groups let you sort inputs by themes, such as one page for general parameters and one for advanced inputs:

1. In **Presentation**, click on the root element presentation.
2. Click on **Create new Step** (the paper icon).
3. A new step is added to the end of the presentation tree. Give it a new name by double-clicking on the step, typing a new name into the textbox, and pressing *Enter*.
4. Now, click on the boolean value and drag it under the new step. Move at least three more variables underneath this step.
5. Create a second step and drag all the rest of the variables underneath it.
6. Now, we add a group. Click on the first step you have created and then on **Create Display Group** (the yellow bar icon).
7. A new group has been added; you can rename the group as required and press *Enter*.
8. Now, drag variables under the group.
9. Create another group and drag some other variables underneath it.
10. Run the workflow. I would also recommend experimenting with this feature.

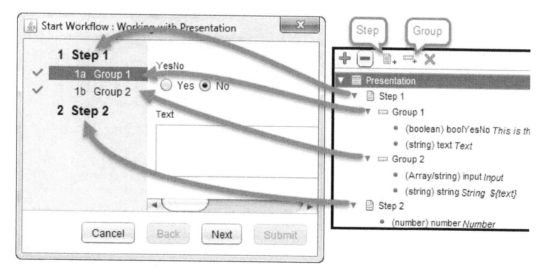

Hiding input values

To make the input window even more user-friendly, it's sometimes better to hide some inputs, steps, or groups if they are not used. For example, a step that contains advanced parameters can be hidden:

1. In **Presentation**, make sure that the boolean in-parameter is the first one in the presentation tree.
2. Add the **Default value** property to it and set it to `True`.

3. Click on the second step you created and add the **Hide parameter input** property.
4. Click on the pencil icon on the right of the hide property. A popup will appear; select the boolean variable and click on **Accept**. Note that the variable is now shown in the `#[variableName]` format. You can also enter directly the value as `True` or `False`. You can also always put an `!` before the `#` of the variable in order to use a `NOT`.

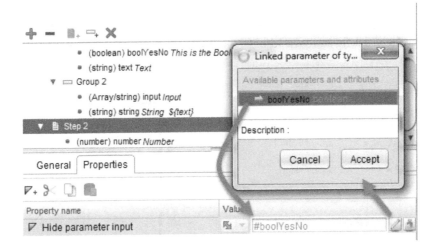

5. Repeat these steps to link a hide property to a group and to an in-parameter variable.
6. Run the workflow. Change the boolean value to `false` and watch the results. All elements that have the hide-property will respond to the value change in the boolean value.

Basic linking

We actually have already used linking in the instruction to hide inputs; now we will explore it in more detail. Linking can help you create drop-down boxes or define default values:

1. Click on **Presentation** and then select one of the string in-parameters.
2. If you have not already done so, assign it the **Maximum string length** property.
3. Now, click on the drop-down menu in front of **Value** and select the yellow arrows (**dynamic binding**). The box icon represents the **static binding**.

4. You will see that the **Value** field changes. Click on the pencil icon (Help editing OGNL), and in the pop-up window, you will see all the variables (attributes and in-parameters) that can be used in this field. Select the **number** attribute and click on **Accept**.
5. Select a string in-parameter in **Presentation**, assign it the **Predefined answers** property, and link it to the array of strings attributes.
6. Run the workflow and test out the results.

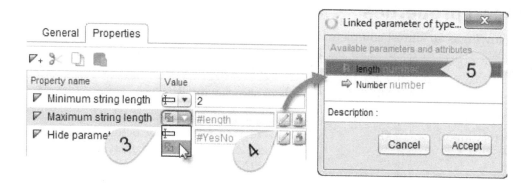

How it works...

The presentation section of a workflow allows us to change the general layout of the input window that a user encounters when they start the workflow. With the different properties that can be defined, it is easy to create a presentation that helps the user interact with the workflow and make sure that they enter the correct (or expected) values. This can dramatically reduce the number of errors a user is able to cause by making incorrect entries. A typical example of this is to provide the user with a list of predefined answers they can choose from, making sure that only the correct values are entered.

It is important to understand that the presentation is **WYSIWYG** only in the Orchestrator Client. The presentation may not work the same for Orchestrator Client, vCenter, vRA, or REST. For example, vRA will not be able to use **Show root element**, or the list view doesn't show properties in vSphere Web Client. One should develop workflows for a given consumer.

Please note that presentations that are configured with the workflow work fine within the vSphere Web Client and in vRA integration, but not in REST calls that launch a workflow. You can test the behavior with the example workflow, `07.05.1 Presentations test`.

In the previous example, we linked several properties to different variables. If you have a look at the value field, you will notice that Orchestrator will use the # symbol to mark a variable. In the example workflow, we used a Boolean named `boolYesNo`, which shows up in the hide-property as `#boolYesNo`. The entries that we can make in these value fields follow **OGNL (Object-Graph Navigation Language)**. We will have a closer look at OGNL in the recipe *Linking actions in presentations* in this chapter.

General properties

The following is an almost complete list of common properties:

Property	Type	Explanation
Show/hide parameter input	All	Hide or show an input
Mandatory input	All	The user has to enter a value before the workflow can be started. An error will be displayed if this variable is empty (NULL).
Default value	All	This value is displayed when the input window is displayed.
Data binding	All	Binds data
Predefined answers Predefined list of elements	All	This is a list of elements that you can select from. A drop-down list will be displayed. Answers let you define an array of string; Elements let you link an array of strings
Custom validation	All	This property allows for the use of OGNL to perform your own validation on an input. (see the *There's more...* section in the recipe *Linking actions in presentations* in this chapter).

Minimum (string length)	Number, String, Path	This is the minimum length/value. You will receive an error message if you exceed the maximum.
Maximum (string length)	Number, String, Path	This is the maximum length/value. You will receive an error message if you are under the minimum.
Number format	Number	This defines a format in which numbers are displayed. #
Matching regular expression	String	This uses a regular expression to check the content. An error is displayed if the content isn't part of the regular expression.
Multi-lines text input	String	This displays a larger text window instead of one line, where more text can be entered.
Valid internet address	String	Validates an input if it's a host or IP address (v4 or v6)
Allow same values	Array	Allow only unique elements in Array
Input date before	Date	Last possible date
Input date after	Date	First possible date

Plugin-specific properties

Certain plugin objects (such as the vCenter plugin) come with additional properties that can be extremely useful. We will now have a look at the most commonly-used properties that come with the base plugins.

select value as

The `select value as` property has three choices: **Tree**, **List**, and **Dropdown**. This property makes it easier to manage what the input of an object looks like:

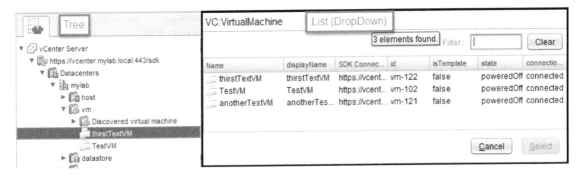

show in inventory

The `show in inventory` property is quite a powerful property. When you start a workflow from vSphere Web Client, the object you started the workflow on will be passed to the workflow as an in-parameter. We will discuss this in more detail in the recipe *Using Orchestrator through the vSphere Web Client* in `Chapter 7`, *Interacting with Orchestrator*.

This property also makes the workflow accessible from the Orchestrator inventory. This means that you can right-click on an object in the inventory and then select a workflow to be executed onto it.

Specify a root object to be shown in the chooser

This setting lets you define a certain start point for your searches. For example, if you choose an ESXi cluster as the root element, then a user can only select objects under this cluster. To use the root element, you need to link an action or a variable to this property. The following is an example:

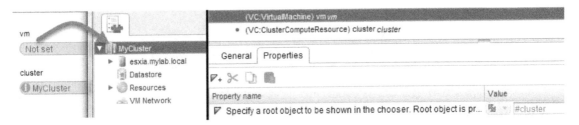

Authorized only

Adding this property to an in-parameter will make sure that only an authorized user can access this in-parameter.

There's more...

Custom validation can be used to check a value against a more complex set of rules. For an example, let's create a custom validation that checks if a given VM name already exists in vCenter:

1. Create an action called checkExistingVMName.
2. The action has a string as return value and an in-parameter of vmName:

```
allVMs=System.getModule("com.vmware.library.vc.vm").getAllVMs();
for each (vm in allVMs) {
   System.log(vm.name);
   if (vm.name.toUpperCase() == vmName.toUpperCase()) {
        return "A VM with the name "+vm.name+" allready exists";
        break;
   }
}
return null;
```

3. Create a new workflow with an in-parameter.
4. Add the presentation parameter **Custom validation**, and link the action you just created to it.

Also see the example workflow, 05.06.02 Custom validation.

See also

Learn regular expressions at the following links:

- http://regexone.com/
- http://regex.learncodethehardway.org/book/

The example workflow, 05.05 Workflow Presentations and 05.06.02 Custom validation, and the checkExistingVMName action.

The recipe *Integrating Orchestrator workflows as XaaS Blueprints* in Chapter 13, *Working with vRealize Automation.*

Linking actions in presentations

This recipe will show how to further improve and automate presentations in workflows by linking actions into them. This is done to present to the user only a specific list of options derived on runtime.

Getting ready

We will create a new workflow and reuse the action `getElementFromArray`, which we created in the recipe *Creating actions* in Chapter 6, *Advanced Programming* (see the `com.packtpub.Orchestrator-Cookbook2ndEdition` module in the example pack).

You should be familiar with the topics we introduced in the recipe *Workflow presentations* in this chapter.

How to do it...

1. Using the Orchestrator Client, create a new workflow.
2. Create the following variables:

Name	Type	Section	Use
string	String	IN	This is a placeholder for the linked action
number	Number	IN	This is used to select a value from an array
array	Array of string	Attribute	This can take values such as Mon, Tue, Wed, Thu, Fri, Sat, Sun

3. Create a log element and bind all variables so that the workflow validation will succeed.
4. Click on **Presentation** and then select the string in-parameter.
5. Add the **Data binding** property to the string in-parameter.
6. On the **Data binding** property, click on **Link action** (the purple puzzle piece icon).
7. In the pop-up window, in the filter enter the name of the action you want to use. We will use `getElementFromArray`.

8. Click on the action; underneath it, you will see the in-parameters that this action requires. You might also notice that each in-parameter can take either a **Static** value (the white rectangle icon) or an OGNL-linked parameter (the yellow arrow icon).

9. Bind the number and the array in-parameter to the action and click on **Apply**:

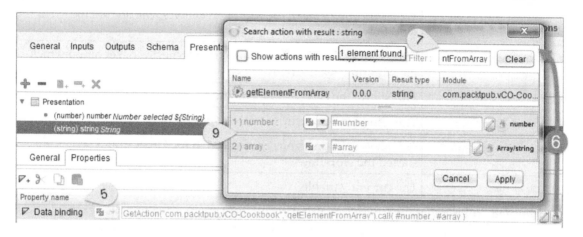

10. Save and run the workflow.

11. Enter a value between 0 and 6 into the **Number** field and see how the value of the string fields changes.

How it works...

Basically, Orchestrator uses OGNL to create the interaction with an action. OGNL is used most commonly with the Apache web server to enhance presentations; however, VMware has deprecated the full use of OGNL in Orchestrator from version 4.1 onwards; the only remains are variables and the ability to call actions. Variables are identified with a leading # symbol and the action call is GetAction([Module],[Action]).call([in-parameters]). You can use action linking for a lot of things. A typical example is that you use an action such as getAllVMsOfVApps to display a **Predefined list of elements** for a user to select a VM from.

The in-parameter property, **Data binding**, makes sure that values in the presentation are updated as soon as the value that it is bound to changes. If you use other properties, such as **Default value**, the value might not be updated instantaneously in the presentation.

There are a couple of predefined OGNL variables that Orchestrator recognizes and can become useful:

Variable name	Description
#__username	This is the username of the user who started the workflow.
#__userdisplayname	This is the full name of the user (if available) who started the workflow.
#__serverurl	This is either the IP or the name of the Orchestrator server on which the workflow was started.
#__datetime	This shows the current date and time.
#__date	This shows the date current date at midnight.
#__timezone	This shows the time zone configured in the Orchestrator server that started the workflow.
#__current	The current variable.

In addition to linking variables, you can also directly insert values using #. For example, instead of referencing a Boolean in **Hide parameter input**, you can also just add the value directly. Just enter the value as true or false.

See also

The example workflows 05.06.01 Linking actions in Presentations.

Changing credentials during runtime

This recipe will show you how to use the **Change credential** element to change the user who is currently executing the workflow.

Getting ready

We need to create a new workflow.

For this recipe, you will need to have more than one AD/LDAP group configured to have access to Orchestrator. Remember that you can use the Orchestrator internal LDAP to test this. To facilitate this, please follow the *User management* recipe in Chapter 7, *Interacting with Orchestrator.*

How to do it...

1. Create a new workflow with the following variable:

Name	Type	Section	Use
newCredential	Credential	IN	The user name and password of the new user

2. Drag a **Change credential** element onto the schema.
3. Bind the `newCredential` in-parameter to the **Change credential** element.
4. Now, drag one **System log** element before and one after the **Change credential** element.
5. Edit the **System log** elements. Remove the text input and change the log to `workflow.runningUserName`. This will log the username that is currently running the workflow.
6. Save and run the workflow.
7. When asked, enter new credentials (for example, `vcouser`). When the workflow is finished, have a look at the logs. You should see that the name of the user who executed the workflow has changed (see the following screenshot):

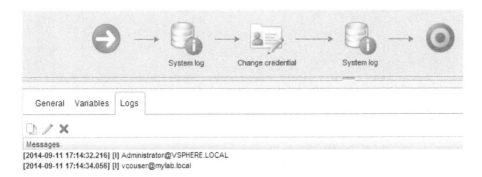

How it works...

The usage is simple; you define the user who executes the workflow from the **Change Credential** element onward.

A typical usage is that you have a workflow started by a user who has no rights to create a VM on vCenter. So, what you need to do is switch credentials before the VM is created and switch them back for the rest of the workflow. The best practice (please note that this is only true when you use the vCenter plugin with a session for each user) for this is to put the elevated credentials that are used into a configuration (see the recipe *Working with configurations* in Chapter 8, *Better Workflows and Optimized Working*).

See also

The example workflow 05.07 Change Credentials.

6

Advanced Programming

In this chapter, we are aiming at improving your programming skills. We will look at the following recipes:

- JavaScript complex variables
- Working with JSON
- JavaScript special statements
- Turning strings into objects
- Working with the API
- Creating actions
- Waiting tasks
- Sending and waiting for custom events
- Using asynchronous workflows
- Scripting with workflow tokens
- Working with user interactions

Introduction

JavaScript is the scripting language that Orchestrator is based on. Learning JavaScript makes for a much-improved workflow build. JavaScript is especially useful in the creation of actions.

The JavaScript of Orchestrator doesn't have the same modules and functions you may find in other JavaScript implementations.

Cool stuff in the scripting tasks

There are some nice little things that help you a bit if you know about them.

A – show all objects

When you are in a scriptable task, start typing something such as `Server.` or define a variable of type `VC:VirtualMachine` (`vmObject`) and then type `vmObject`. Then press *Ctrl* and the spacebar. You will see a window that shows you all the properties and methods that go along with this object.

You can now start typing the attribute or method you want and see the list shrinking.

B – find stuff

Just press *Ctrl* + *F* and then enter what you are looking for.

C – line and character

Have a look at the lower left corner of the editor field. The line number, as well as the character, is displayed there. Some error message will state the line number where the error in the script is:

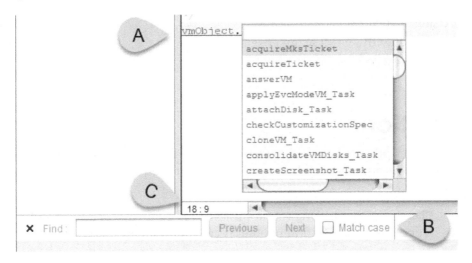

JavaScript (the very basics)

The following is a very short and quick reference for JavaScript. It is aimed at people who already know a programming language and just need to adapt to the syntax of JavaScript.

To learn JavaScript, you can have a look at `http://www.w3schools.com/js/`.

Here is a list that shows the very basic things one needs to know about JavaScript:

- Every line ends with a semicolon (`;`).
- Single-line comments are done with `//`.
- Multiline comments begin with `/*` and end with `*/`.
- Everything in JavaScript is case sensitive.
- Variables are just text (for example, `myTest5`) and must start with a letter.
- Math operations are performed using symbols such as +, –, *, and /.
- Strings are combined using the + operator, for example, `"a" + "b"` or `stringVariable + " text to append"`.
- JavaScript is not Java; make sure you always search for JavaScript on the Web.
- Have a look at `http://javascript.crockford.com/code.html` to understand how JavaScript should be formatted.

- Variables don't have to be declared when auto casting is working. To declare a variable, use `var variable name = new variable_type;` for example, `var myString = new String();`.

Check `Chapter 5`, *Visual Programming*, for JavaScript on decisions, loops, and logs and `Chapter 9`, *Essential Plugins*, and `Chapter 10`, *Built-in Plugins*, for more examples.

JavaScript tricks and tips

This is a small collection of some tricks and tips that are quite handy to know.

Is a string part of another string? (indexOf)

A typical situation that you may come across is this: you have a parameter that contains a string and you would like to know if this string contains another string.

For example, you have a parameter, `myVM` that contains the string `testVM.mylab.local`. You want to know if this VM is in the `mylab` domain, and if the `myLab` string is part of it. You can use the `indexOf()` method of the type `string`. The index functions return the position of the first occurrence. If the string is not part of the other string, the return value will be -1. Here's an example:

```
Var myVM = "testVM.mylab.local";
If ( myVM.indexOf("myLab") > 0) {
   //is part of mylab
} else {
   //is NOT part of mylab
}
```

Case sensitivity (toUpperCase)

Another common problem is that a user might enter `MyLab`, `myLab`, or `MYLAB` instead of the `myLab` you are expecting and checking for. Here is a simple way to solve this one. You just make everything capital and then check. So instead of the following code:

```
var myEntry = "MyLab";
var myTest = "myLab":
if ( myEntry == myTest ) {
   // both are the same
}
```

use the `.toUpperCase()` method of the type `string`:

```
If ( myEntry.toUpperCase() == myTest.toUpperCase() ) {
   // both are the same
}
```

The same method applies, for example, to the hostnames or VM names. VM names or hostnames are mostly held in lowercase. Use the `.toLowerCase()` method to do this.

Getting rid of extra space (trim)

It can happen that users enter "`myLab `" or "` myLab`" by mistake (an extra space at the beginning or end) and you can imagine how this can play havoc with an `if` clause. Use the `.trim()` method to solve this:

```
var dirtyString = "   Hello World!   ";
var cleanString = dirtyString.trim();
```

String replacement with regular expressions (replace)

You can use regular expressions with strings, which goes a long way, for example, with HTML mails.

Create an HTML mail body, such as a table that contain some places that you later want to exchange. Such a table could look like this:

```
<table border=1> <tr> <td>VM Name</td><td>{VM}</td> </tr><tr>
<td>vCPU</td><td>{CPU}</td> </tr></table >
```

You then can store this as an attribute (or even better, as a resource) and when you need it, you replace it with the following:

```
mailContent=mailContent.replace(new RegExp("\{VM\}","g"),vmName);
mailContent=mailContent.replace(new RegExp("\{CPU\}","g"),vCPU);
```

The result is a nice e-mail that is easily formatted. Please not, that we have to escape the { in the regex.

Check a variable for type (instanceof)

`instanceof` is used to determine if a variable is of a given type. This example shows how to use it. Also see the example action, `getAvailableCPUFromCluster`.

If we have a vSphere cluster with HA configuration, it can be either configured as *n+1* or with %. The exact mode is stored as follows:

```
HApolicy = clusterObject.configuration.dasConfig.admissionControlPolicy
```

Using an `if` statement, we can determine which it is:

```
if (HApolicy instanceof VcClusterFailoverResourcesAdmissionControlPolicy)
if (HApolicy instanceof VcClusterFailoverLevelAdmissionControlPolicy)
```

Working with dates

Just a few words on working with the `Date` type in JavaScript. Working with `Date` is easy if you understand how it works. Basically, it counts the milliseconds since January 1, 1970 (in 1970, UNIX was released). If you want to read or set the time, it's best to use the methods that are encapsulated with the type.

	Values	Read	Write
Day of the week	0-6	`getDay`	`setDay`
Day of the month	1-31	`getDate`	`setDate`
Number of month	0-11	`getMonth`	`setMonth`
Year	Four digit year: for example, 1970	`getFullYear`	`setFullYear`
Milliseconds since 01.01.1970	–	`getTime`	`setTime`
Seconds	0-59	`getSeconds`	`setSeconds`
Minutes	0-59	`getMinutes`	`setMinutes`
Hours	0-23	`getHours`	`setHours`

Have a look at the full list of attributes on w3Schools: `http://www.w3schools.com/jsref/jsref_obj_date.asp`

It is also important to know that if you set a workflow attribute of the `Date` type, it is null (it doesn't contain the current time or the time you started the workflow); however, if you set a date as a workflow in-parameter, you will automatically see the current date and time when you try to define it.

To initialize a `Date` attribute, you can bind it to an action to do it for you. Create an action with an out-parameter of the `Date` type and the following script:

```
var current = new Date();
return current;
```

This action will set an existing attribute to the current time when the action is invoked. Also see the example workflow, `06.04.03 Working with date attributes`, and the example action, `setNow`.

To display the date, there isn't a nice way implemented in Orchestrator, so you have to go the long way:

```
date.getDate()+"."+date.getMonth()+"."+date.getFullYear()
```

Add minutes to a date

This is a typical problem in workflows. You have a wait task or a user interaction that requires a timeout as `Date` type. You can define the new end date with the following:

```
var endDate = new Date();
endDate.setMinutes(endDate.getMinutes() + minutes);
```

This will create a new `endDate` that is `minutes` in the future. The same can be done with all the gets and sets from the previous table. To add days, use 24 hours.

JavaScript complex variables

In this recipe, we will have a look at JavaScript complex variables, such as arrays, objects, and properties. All these are needed to deal with plugin return codes such as from REST calls.

Getting ready

We need a new workflow and a scriptable task inside it to try it out.

The example workflow `06.01 JavaScript complex variables` contains all the examples that follow.

How to do it...

We will look into several different JavaScript complex variable type pieces.

Arrays

Arrays are pretty useful for storing multiple elements of the same type:

1. To define a new empty array in JavaScript, use either one of the following codes:
    - `var family = new Array();`
    - `var myArray = [];`

2. You can define a new filled array by using either of the following examples:
    - `var family = new Array("Father","Mother","Daughter","Son");`

- `var myArray = ["Father","Mother","Daughter","Son"];`

3. While accessing the element (numbering starts at zero), `System.log(family[2]);` will show `Daughter`.

4. You can add element(s) with `push`. You can add multiple ones using a ", ":
   - `family.push("baby");`

5. The amount of elements in an array can be found with `length`:
   - `System.log(family.length);`

6. As seen in the recipe *Scripting with loops* in `Chapter 5`, *Visual Programming*, you can loop through an array with a `for each` loop:

```
for each (element in family) {
  system.log(element)
}
```

These are the basic functions; there are additional ones discussed in the *How it works...* section of this recipe.

Properties

The `properties` variable type can be extremely useful to transport complex content. A property can be seen as a hash table, which means that you can assign multiple pairs of keys with their values.

Define a new property using the following code:

```
var relatives= new Properties();
```

Note that even if you define a property in Orchestrator (attributes or out-parameters), you still need to initialize it (see step 1) before you can fill it.

2. Add a key (`Uncle`) and a value (`David`) to the property:

```
relatives.put("Uncle","David");
```

Please note that all Property and Object keys are case sensitive.

3. You read elements by referring to its key (Uncle). The value will be shown as follows:

```
System.log(relatives.get("Uncle"));
```

4. Show all keys in a property (as an array):

```
System.log(relatives.keys);
```

5. Loop through properties:

```
for each (key in relatives.keys) {
    System.log(key+" : "+ relatives.get(key));
}
```

6. Remove an element from a property:

```
relatives.remove("Aunt");
```

Objects

Objects are a bit like properties, although not as well defined and user-friendly.

1. Declare a new object:

```
var pets = new  Object();
```

2. Create a property named Dog with the value Fido for the object. Use either one of the following:
   - `pets["Dog"]="Fido";`
   - `pets.Dog="Fido";`

3. Read out an object. It will return Fido as a string. Use either one of the following:
   - `System.log(pets["Dog"]);`
   - `System.log(pets.Dog);`

4. To create an array inside an object, use the following form:

```
var pet.mice=["mouse1"," mouse2"," mouse3"," mouse4"]
```

5. To read this array, use the following:

```
System.log(pets.mice.length);
System.log(pets.mice[2]);
```

A good usage for objects is to use them together to form JSON objects.

We will take look at JSON in the recipe *Working with JSON* in this chapter.

How it works...

Complex variables are used quite often in Orchestrator, especially when we are using plugins such as PowerShell.

Array methods

The following table shows all the methods that are associated with arrays:

Function	Explanation
array3=array1.**concat**(array2)	Joins two arrays and returns the new one.
string=array.**join**(separator)	Makes a string out of the array using the separator between elements.
any=array.**pop**()	Removes the last element and returns it.
number=array.**push**(Any)	Adds a new element to the end of the array and returns a new length.
array.**reverse**()	Reverses the order of the elements in the array.
any=array.**shift**()	Removes the first element and displays it.
newArray=array.**slice**(n,m)	Slices an array from n to m out of an array.
array.**sort**()	Sorts an array alphanumerically.
array.**splice**(n,m,any)	Inserts (and/or removes) elements.
number=array.**unshift**(any)	Inserts an element at the beginning of the array and returns a new length.
number=array.**indexOf**(any)	Returns the index of the element you are looking for.

Properties within properties

Sometimes, you have properties inside properties. This is harder than it sounds. Just have a look at the example here:

```
var mailProperties= new Properties();
mailProperties.put("mailTo","info@langenhan.info");
mailProperties.put("mailCC","info@langenhan.info");
mailProperties.put("subject","Test email");
var mailReplacements= new Properties();
mailReplacements.put("vm.name","myVM");
mailReplacements.put("vm.ip","192.168.220.10");
mailReplacements.put("vm.mac"," 0A:0B:0C:0D:0E:0F");
mailProperties.put("mailReplacements",mailReplacements);
```

To read, use this example:

```
mailTo=mailProperties.get("mailTo");
keys=mailProperties.keys
if (keys.indexOf("mailCC")>=0){
    mailCC=mailProperties.get("mailCC");
}
mailSubject=mailProperties.get("subject");
mailReplacements=mailProperties.get("mailReplacements");
for each (key in mailReplacements.keys){
    System.log(key+" : "+mailReplacements.get(key));
}
```

Array of properties

An array of properties can be even more useful, as JavaScript doesn't really do multidimensional arrays. An array of properties is more or less a two-dimensional array. To create an array of properties, use the following steps:

```
Var myArray = new Array();
var myProp = new Properties() ;
myProp.put("myKey","Key Value") ;
myArray.push(myProp);
```

Here's an example of an array of properties:

```
Var mails = new Array();
var mail = new Properties() ;
mail.put("subject","Test Email 1") ;
mails.push(mail);
var mail = new Properties() ;
mail.put("subject","Test Email 2") ;
mails.push(mail);
```

We will use properties in the recipe *Working with mail* in Chapter 9, *Essential Plugins*.

See also

See the example workflow 06.01 JavaScript complex variables.

Working with JSON

Some REST clients use XML and some use JSON to exchange data. In this recipe, we will look at how to parse and construct JSON objects in Orchestrator.

Getting ready

You should be comfortable with the recipe *JavaScript complex variables* in this chapter before starting this recipe.

How to do it...

We will divide this recipe into multiple sections, each of which will deal with the different aspects of JSON.

Parsing JSON REST returns

The (undocumented) `JSON.parse` function makes an object out of a JSON string. This is typically used with JSON REST returns.

In this example, we look at the REST return from the Control Center GET call: `api/server/status`.

The method `response.contentAsString` returns the following string:

```
{"id":null,"error":null,"warning":null,"requestedStatus":null,"initialStatu
s":"RUNNING","currentStatus":"RUNNING","progress":"Status-ing
tcServer\nInstance name:          app-server\nRuntime version:
8.0.30.C.RELEASE\ntc Runtime Base:        /var/lib/vco/app-server\nStatus:
RUNNING as PID=24470\n","finished":true}
```

We are only interested in `currentStatus`. We can access that part in the following ways:

```
var jsonObj = JSON.parse(response.contentAsString);
System.log ("Serverstate = "+ jsonObj.currentStatus);
```

Or:

```
System.log ("Serverstate = "+ jsonObj['currentStatus']);
```

Creating a JSON object

When working with REST and JSON, you not only need to know how to parse JSON, but also how to create a JSON object. There is a very good article that shows all the methods: `http://www.vcoteam.info/articles/learn-vco/305-creating-json-objects-in-orchest rator.html`.

I will quickly show how to do it. You want to create a basic JSON object that looks like this:

```
{
"private":"mobile number",
    "business":"landline number"
}
```

First, we need to build a property with this content:

```
var propList=new Properties();
propList.put("private","mobile number");
propList.put("business"," landline number");
Then we have to convert it to JSON
var jsonObj = new Object();
for each (key in propList.keys){
    jsonObj[key]=propList.get(key);
}
Content= JSON.stringify(jsonObj);
```

This will create the JSON object string we can use in a REST call. If you need to create more complex JSON with arrays, the same method applies. You construct an array of properties and then `stringify` it.

Change JSON object

We also have the ability to alter JSON objects quite easily. A typical example is that you have a REST GET that results in a JSON and you like to PUT the same back with some slide changes. Here is how that works:

```
getContent= REST.getContentAsMimeAttachment();
jsonObj = JSON.parse(getContent.content);
jsonObj['private'] = "another number";
putContent= JSON.stringify(jsonObj);
```

How it works...

Orchestrator uses the JSON data interchange standard to exchange information via the REST API. Some other REST APIs (such as vCloud Director) use XML. JSON stands for **JavaScript Object Notation** and is a standard for exchanging information.

JSO knows the following elements:

> N knows the following elements: String: It is enclosed by " " and can contain alphanumeric characters as well as escapes

- **Number**: A simple number with the English separation of a dot between full numbers and fractions
- **Value**: A value can be a string, number, object, array, true, false, and null

We can also create more complex types, such as objects and arrays.

A JSON object is constructed as follows:

Format	`{ string : value } or {string1:value1, string2:value2}`
Example	`{"version":"7.0.1", "Build Number":3232}`

An array in JSON is represented as follows:

Format	`[value1,value2]`
Example	`["Mother","Father"] or [{"Mother":"Mary", "Father":"Adam"}]`

JSON is quite simple when you get the hang of it. If you need to construct JSON you are mostly working with objects, properties, and arrays. All these are explained in the recipe *JavaScript complex variables* in this chapter.

See also

See the example workflow `07.04.1 Orchestrator Service Status`.

More information on JSON can be found here:
`http://www.json.org/`

JavaScript special statements

This recipe introduces three usages that are rather advantageous and important, try, catch, and finally functions.

Getting ready

We need a new workflow and a scriptable task inside it to try these out.

The example workflow, `06.02 JavaScript special statements`, contain all the following examples.

How to do it...

There are two sections in this recipe.

The try, catch, and finally statement

When writing any code, you want to make sure that when the code produces an error, you are still able to execute some critical operations, such as closing an open connection:

1. Create a scriptable task and enter the following code:

```
try {
  //Main code;
    System.log("Start Main");
    if (error) {
        throw("Create Error");
    }
    System.log("End Main");
}
catch( ex ) {
  // error handling
    System.log("Error: "+ex);
} finally {
  //Final Part
    System.log("Finally");
}
```

2. Create an input-parameter of the type Boolean (error) and bind it to the scriptable task.

3. When executing, you can create an error (`throw` statements create an intentional error). Without an error, the main code (`try`) would be executed and then the `finally` code. When an error is thrown in the main code, the execution (`try`) will be stopped before "End Main" and then will execute the `catch` code followed by the `finally` code.

The function statement

The `function` command enables us to repeat a program code. A function needs to be defined before it is used, which means that it is placed at the beginning of a program:

1. Create a scriptable task and enter the following code:

```
function functionName (parameter1, parameter2) {
    // program example
    parameter3 = parameter1 + parameter2
    return parameter3
}
```

2. You now can call the function in the same scriptable task by using:

```
result = functionName(2,3);
```

The call will put the value 2 into `parameter1` and the value 3 into `parameter2` of the `functionName` function. The `result` variable will contain the return value of the function.

How it works...

A typical example where `try/catch/finally` is used; is to make sure an open connection to a database is closed if an error occurs. Open connections can cause servers to perform slower, rendering them more vulnerable to intrusion or even corrupt data. You would open the connection in the `try` section and write the close function in the `finally` section.

If `try`, `catch`, and `finally` are used, you would place the function before the `try` command. A function is similar to the way an action works. We discussed actions in the recipe *Creating actions* in this chapter.

See also

See the example workflow `06.02 JavaScript special statements`.

Turning strings into objects

In this recipe, we will take a quick look at how to turn a string into an Orchestrator object (such as VC:VirtualMachine). This technique is rather important when you use REST to start workflows.

Getting ready

We only need the Orchestrator Client with the right to create a workflow.

How to do it...

In this example, we turn a string into VC:VirtualMachine:

1. Create a workflow with a string input (vmString) and a VC:VirtualMachine output (vmObject).
2. Add a scriptable task and connect the in- and output parameter.
3. In the script, enter the following code:

```
query = "xpath:name='" + vmString + "'";
vms=Server.findAllForType("VC:VirtualMachine", query);
vmObject=vms[0];
```

4. Run the workflow and enter a Virtual Machine name.
5. Check the output and logs.

How it works...

The find function looks for all elements of a given type and can be limited using a search function. It's very important to write the correct type and the search string.

The next important thing is to make sure your naming of objects is unique, meaning if you have two VMs in vCenter that have the same name, the search will return two elements. You could use other search arguments, such as ID (vSphere MoRef), but mostly you will use a name.

A typical example for all this is follows.

You used the recipe *Using PHP to access the REST API* in Chapter 7, *Interacting with Orchestrator*, to create a website. In that website, you show a dropdown list of all VMs that the user can use. For this, you would create a workflow that returns an array of strings, which you can then put into your dropdown.

When you select one of the dropdowns and press a button, you send a Virtual Machine name as a string back to Orchestrator. To make use of that, you need to transfer the string into an object as previously described.

Here is a list of the common types you might be looking for:

vCenter Virtual Machine	VC:VirtualMachine
ESXi host	VC:HostSystem
Datastore	VC:Datastore
Network	vc:network
VM folder	vc:vmfolder
Resource pool	vc:resourcepool
vRA Virtual Machine	vCAC:VirtualMachine
vRA server	vCACCAFE:VCACHost
IaaS server	vCAC:vCACHost

There's more...

Booleans are a bit special. You could easily use an if...else statement to do this, as follows:

```
if ((typeString.toLowerCase() =="true") || (typeString.toLowerCase()
=="yes")){
    typeBoolean=true;
}
if ((typeString.toLowerCase()=="false") || (typeString.toLowerCase()
=="no")) {
    typeBoolean=false;
}
```

However, if you know what value comes back and in what case you can make your life easier by using:

```
typeBoolean=(typeString == "true");
```

or

```
typeBoolean=(typeString == "yes");
```

See also

See the example workflows `06.09.1 String to Object` and `06.09.2 String to Boolean`.

Working with the API

To be efficient in programming using Orchestrator plugins, one needs to know how to work with the Orchestrator API. In this recipe, we showcase how to access and get information from the Orchestrator API.

Getting ready

We only need the Orchestrator Client with rights to edit a workflow.

How to do it...

We will split this recipe into several sections.

Searching for items in the API

The first step is to have a look at the API. To access the API, follow these steps:

1. Open the Orchestrator Client.
2. Navigate to **Tools | API Explorer**:

10. In the API tree, scroll down to and click on `connect()` method. In the detail area underneath, you will see details for this command, such as what inputs are needed and of what type. The method needs a host, a port, a username, and a password.

11. Now, copy and paste the `connect()` method as you did in steps 8 and 9 into a new line in the scripting area. Orchestrator automatically fills in some parts, and the new line will look like this:

```
connect(?String_host , ?number_port , ?String_username ,
?String_password)
```

12. To make this line work, we will need to put an object before it; in this case, it's the `MailClient` object we created in step 9. Just add `myMailClient` before `connect` with a period between them. This will enact the method `connect` on the `MailClient` instance. The result will look like this:

```
myMailClient.connect(?String_host , ?number_port , ?String_username ,
? String_password).
```

13. The next step is to substitute each of the placeholders (the `?names`) with either Orchestrator variables or values. Replace the first placeholder, `?String_host`, with a mail host address, such as `mail.mylab.local`.

14. As we want to showcase the API a bit more, we will get the value for the `?number_port` placeholder a bit differently. Insert a new line above the connect line.

15. Use the API search to search for `getDefaultPort`. You will see that it is an action in the module called `com.vmware.libary.mail` and needs the input of a type `string` (a protocol name). Its return value is a `number` (the port). If you like, take a look at the action itself and its script. This will help you understand how it works and what input it requires.

16. Now, copy and paste the action from the API tree to the scripting area, as done previously. You will see that additional code is created and looks like this:

```
System.getModule("com.vmware.library.mail").getDefaultPort(protocol)
```

17. We want the output of the action to be put into a local variable, so insert `var port = ` before `System.getModule`.

18. Now, we need to tell the action what protocol we want, so replace `protocol` with `imap`. This will save the default port for IMAP into the variable `port`.

19. Next, replace the `?number_port` placeholder in the connect line with the `port` variable.

20. Last but not least, let's add an Orchestrator variable to the connect line. In the scriptable task, create an in-parameter of a type `string` called `userName`.

21. Replace the `?String_username` placeholder with `userName`. Notice the color change of `userName` when it matches the in-parameter.

At this stage, we leave the showcase, as we have explored the interesting parts. Your little script should look something like this:

```
var myMailClient = new MailClient();
var port =
System.getModule("com.vmware.library.mail").getDefaultPort("imap");
myMailClient.connect("192.168.220.4" , port , userName, ?String_password);
```

The full working script can be found in the recipe *Working with mails* in `Chapter 9, Essential Plugins`.

How it works...

The Orchestrator API contains all types, methods, attributes, objects, and so on that can be used for programming. All the content comes from Orchestrator or its plugins and gives the Orchestrator programmer a wide range of tools to use.

As you can see in the preceding showcase, the items in the API are color-coded; the following table shows you all the item colors along with a short description of their meaning:

Icon	Name	Usage
Gray bullet	Type	Types are complex variables.
Purple bullet	Function set	A set of functions that centers on certain topics, for instance, the `System` function set that contains the `.log` and `.warn` methods.
Blue bullet	Primitive	A primitive is a basic variable type. These are array, function, number, object, secure string, string, Boolean, and char. String and array contain methods.
Green bullet	Object	Objects contain attributes, constructors, and methods.
Gray and blue gear	Module	Modules contain actions. We worked with actions and modules in the recipe *Creating actions* in this chapter.

Color icons	SDKModule	SDKModule is part of the plugins and contains types and objects.
C-shaped icon	Constructor	A constructor creates a new entity of a given type. Sometimes, there is no constructor; in this case, you can try to copy and paste the parent object.
Empty square	Attribute	An attribute is a property of an object; it can be either read-only or read-write.
Filled square	Method	The function (action) that is implemented with the object and acts on the object.

See also

In the recipe *Working with the vCenter API (to change a VM's HA settings)* in `Chapter 12`, *Working with Vsphere*, we will explore the vCenter API integration in Orchestrator.

Creating actions

In this recipe, we will take a look at actions and their differences to workflows as well as their creation and usage.

Getting ready

We just need a working Orchestrator and you will need the rights to create new workflows and actions as well as the right to run workflows. We will work with the Orchestrator Client.

JavaScript arrays will be used, so you should read the introduction to this chapter.

How to do it...

We will split this recipe into two sections, the creation and the implementation of an action.

Creating a new action

1. In the Orchestrator Client, click on **Actions** (the gray gear icon).
2. Right-click on the top-level (the orange icon) and select **New module**.
3. Give the module a name that is based on either your URL or the type of work you intend to do with it. For example, I chose `com.packtpub.Orchestrator-Cookbook`.
4. Right-click on the module you have created and select **Add-action**.
5. The name should be descriptive and tell a user directly what it does. For this example, I chose the name `getElementFromArray`.
6. Click on **Add Parameter** (the yellow right arrow icon) and add the following variables:

Name	Type	Values
`number`	Number	This is the index number of the array that should be returned. The first element in an array has index 0.
`array`	Array	This is the array that contains all elements

7. Now, click on **void** directly to the right of **Return type** and select `String`.
8. In the scripting field, enter the following code:

```
return array[number];
```

9. Click on **Save and Close**.

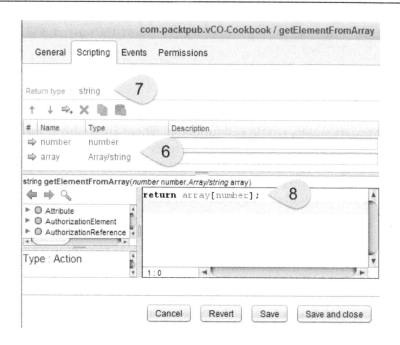

Implementing an action into a workflow

1. Using the Orchestrator Client, create a new workflow.
2. Drag **Action element** (out of **Generic**) onto the schema. In the **Choose Action Dialog** field, enter the beginning of the name of the action you have just created. As you type, you will see the list of objects to choose from decreases. Alternatively, you can also use the **All Actions** section and browse through the existing actions.
3. Add the getElementFromArray action to the schema.
4. Create and assign the following variables to the action:

Name	Type	Variable type
number	IN	This is a number.
weekDays	Attribute	This is an array of string values such as Mon, Tue, Wed, Thu, Fri, Sat, Sun.
output	Out	This is a string value.

5. Click on **Save and Close** to save and close the workflow and run the workflow.

When you now enter a number during workflow execution, the output will be one of the days of the week.

How it works...

Actions are what programmers would call functions. There are multiple differences between a workflow and an action; the main difference is that an action can only return *one* variable, whereas a workflow can return multiple variables. Another is that actions are purely JavaScript-based and do not contain any visual programming. Actions can still call other actions; however, you will need the JavaScript command `System.getModule([Module]).[Action]([in-parameter])` to call them. As you can see, an action is called using its module name, while a workflow is called (for example, via the API) using its ID. This is a rather important difference, as renaming an action is hard because its name, and maybe the module name, must be changed everywhere.

In an action, in-parameters are defined the same way as in a workflow; however, the return type is a bit different. The return code is always one variable and its value is assigned using the JavaScript `return` command. If you don't want or need any return code, define the return code as `void`.

Binding an action into a workflow can be done just as you would integrate any workflow, by dragging the **Action element** onto the schema. When binding the out-parameter of an action, you will notice that the name that is displayed in the **Action element** is `ActionResult`. Your attribute or out-parameter that is bound to the return value of the **Action element** should be named something more meaningful.

Another thing that is important for good programming is the name of the action and the module you place it in. Browse through the existing action modules to explore how other programmers have done it.

A good recommendation is to start the name with a verb, such as get, set, create, delete, and so forth. Then, describe what the action is doing. A good way to make the name more readable is to capitalize each word (except the first). Examples of good naming are `startVM`, `removeAllSnapshots`, and `getAllVMsOfVApps`. If you need more information on this, check the JavaScript style guide at `http://javascript.crockford.com/code.html`.

Exploring the existing action library, you will find a lot of useful actions that are pre-created and can be used in your own workflows.

See also

See the example workflow `06.03 Creating actions` and the `getElementFromArray` action.

See *Changing elements in a workflow* in `Chapter 4`, *Programming Skills*.

Waiting tasks

This is a recipe that will make you wait for it...

Getting ready

We need a new workflow and time!

How to do it...

There are two different kinds of wait tasks, tasks that wait for a duration and tasks that wait for a specific date and time until they proceed.

Creating a help task

We need to create an action to help us track time. It will just log the current date and time. The action already exists in the `action` folder `com.packtpub.Orchestrator-Cookbook2ndEdition.helpers`:

1. Create a new action and call it `getNow`. There is no need to define any in- or out-parameters.
2. In the script section, place the following script:

```
var current = new Date();
System.log(current);
```

Using the Sleep task

1. Create a new workflow.
2. Drag a **Sleep** task onto the schema and create the `sleepTime` in-parameter as input for the workflow.
3. Add the `getNow` action we have just created before and after the **Sleep** task.
4. When running the workflow, check the log. You will notice how the workflow will wait for the allocated seconds.

Waiting for a date

1. Create a new workflow.
2. Drag a **Wait until date** task onto the schema and create the `waitDate` in-parameter as input for the workflow.
3. Add the `getNow` action we have just created before and after the **Wait until date** task.
4. When running the workflow, check out the log. You will notice how the workflow will wait until the allocated date and time:

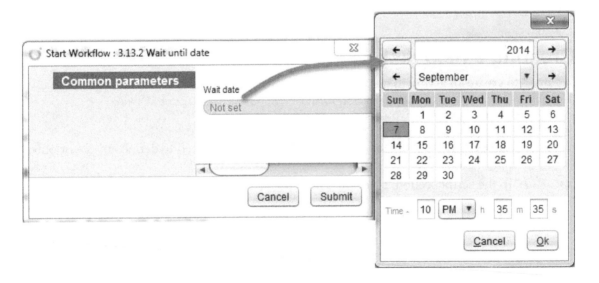

How it works...

A wait task will pause the workflow execution for a certain amount of time. The main difference between a **Sleep** task and a **Wait until** task is the amount of system resources that are used for waiting.

The **Sleep** task will just wait; however, it will still require memory and one thread per sleep task. The **Wait until** task is more specific in how it saves system resources. When the **Wait until** task starts, the workflow is saved to the Orchestrator database and is woken up again on the specified date and time. Orchestrator uses a single thread to deal with the all the workflows that are set to wait until a certain date/time. This preserves quite a bit of resources.

This leads us directly to the most important usage for wait tasks, long-running workflows. If a workflow is running for a long time, such as polling for new e-mails or waiting for a user interaction, a wait task can reduce the amount of system resources consumed during the wait period.

There are actually two waits for date tasks, one in **Generic** called **Waiting timer** and the other in **Basic** called **Wait until date**. Both are essentially the same.

There's more...

The JavaScript commands for waiting are `System.sleep([milliseconds])` and `System.waitUntil([Date],[Number of milliseconds])`.

Please note that the `sleep` command works with milliseconds, whereas the **Sleep** schema element works with seconds.

The `waituntil` command has two inputs: the date and the number of milliseconds. The milliseconds define the delay time between two checks to see whether a certain date has been reached. Also, the command returns a Boolean value that is `true` when the wait has finished.

 No JavaScript wait tasks will save any system resources, as the schema tasks do.

See also

See the example workflows:

- 06.04.01 Sleep
- 06.04.02 Wait until date
- 06.04.03 Working with date attributes

See the example actions: getNow and setNow.

Sending and waiting for custom events

This recipe will showcase how to send interactions between workflows. This is mostly used together with asynchronous workflows, which we will explain in the recipe *Using asynchronous workflows* in this chapter.

Getting ready

We need to be able to create two workflows.

We will reuse the getNow action that we created in the recipe *Waiting tasks* in this chapter (see the com.packtpub.Orchestrator-Cookbook2ndEdition.helpers module in the example pack).

How to do it...

This recipe requires us to create two workflows and then use them together.

Receiving a custom event

First, we create the receiving part:

1. Create a new workflow using the setup shown in the following figure:

2. Create the following variables:

Name	Type	Section	Use
isExternalEvent	Number	Attribute Value: false	This is a setting to indicate where Orchestrator has to listen to for the event.
eventName	String	IN	This is a string that contains the event identifier.
endDate	Date	IN	The date/time until Orchestrator should listen for the event.
Success	Boolean	Attribute	This returns a value from the wait element. true indicates that the event was received.

3. Bind all the variables to the **Wait for customer event** task; only success will be bound to the output.
4. Bind the **Decision** task to the success attribute.
5. Add some meaningful text to the system log tasks, such as Success and Failure.
6. **Save and close**, but don't run this workflow yet. Proceed to the next section.

Sending a custom event

We now create the workflow that sends the custom event:

1. Create a new workflow with the following variable:

Name	Type	Section	Use
eventName	String	IN	This is a string that contains the event identifier

2. Just drag a **Send Custom event** task onto the schema and bind the `eventName` in-parameter to it.

3. **Save and close** the workflow. Don't run this workflow yet. Proceed to the next section.

Trying it out

As we have now created all the moving parts, let's give it a spin:

1. Start the receive workflow and enter an event name such as `getThis` as well as a date/time that is in the future (10 minutes or so).

2. Now, start the send workflow and enter the same event name you entered in the receive workflow. Watch the result and the logs.

Start both workflows again, but this time, let the time expire and watch the result.

How it works...

Custom events are Orchestrator internal events that help exchange states between workflows. A typical example is that you have a workflow that needs to wait for another workflow to finish. Another example is that a workflow should not proceed before a certain event has taken place. In the recipe *Using asynchronous workflows* in this chapter, we will have a closer look at how this works. Another possibility is to use an event as a crude approval mechanism.

Check the introduction to this chapter on how to work with dates.

External events

External events enable workflows to wait for an input from outside of Orchestrator. This input is received using the SOAP interface. As the SOAP interface is gone, external events don't work anymore.

The custom event URL that is used, looked like `http://[server IP]:8280/vmware-vmo-webcontrol/SendCustomEvent?EventName=[event name]`.

This leaves only REST, e-mail, and SNMP as input methods. You could send an e-mail to an e-mail account that is monitored by Orchestrator (see the recipe *Working with mails* in `Chapter 9`, *Essential Plugins*) or you could use PHP (see the recipe *Using PHP to access the REST API* in `Chapter 7`, *Interacting with Orchestrator*) in a website to send an (internal) event or answer a user interaction (see the recipe *Working with user interactions* in this chapter). SNMP traps are discussed in the *Working with SNMP* in `Chapter 10`, *Built-in Plugins*.

See also

See the example workflows:

- `06.05.01 Receive Custom event`
- `06.05.02 Sending Custom event`
- `06.05.03 Generate External Event`
- `06.05.04 Receive External Event`

See the recipe *An approval process for VM provisioning* in `Chapter 12`, *Working with vSphere*.

Using asynchronous workflows

A workflow executes its elements along its path one after another. Using asynchronous workflow execution, we can change this behavior and actually execute workflows in parallel.

Getting ready

We will need to build a new workflow.

For the first example, we will reuse the sleep workflow as well as the `getNow` action we created in the recipe *Waiting tasks* in this chapter. (`06.04.01 Sleep` and the `com.packtpub.Orchestrator-Cookbook2ndEdition.helpers` module in the example pack).

How to do it...

We will see two examples to demonstrate the asynchronous feature.

The first example

Here are some basics:

1. Create a new workflow and create the following variables:

Name	Type	Section	Use
sleepTime	Number	IN	It defines the time the workflow should sleep
wfToken	WorkflowToken	Attribute	The workflow token of the asynchronous workflow

2. Drag an **Asynchronous workflow** task into the schema.
3. When prompted, enter the name of the sleep workflow we have created in the recipe *Waiting tasks* in this chapter (06.04.01 Sleep in the example package).
4. Now, edit the **Asynchronous workflow** tasks. The in-parameter is the one from the sleep workflow. Bind it to the sleepTime in-parameter.
5. The out-parameter is a workflowToken. Bind it to the wfToken attribute.
6. Drag one getNow action on each side of the **Asynchronous workflow** tasks.
7. Save the workflow and run it:

Have a look at the execution. The workflow that started the sleep workflow asynchronously has finished (**A** in the previous screenshot) but the sleep workflow is still running (**B**). Also, please note that the sleep workflow doesn't write its logs into the main workflow.

The second example

This example shows how to combine asynchronous workflows with custom events:

1. Duplicate the sleep workflow we created in the recipe *Waiting tasks* in this chapter (06.04.01 in the example package).
2. Edit the workflow and add the following variable:

Name	Type	Section	Use
eventName	String	IN	This transports the custom event name

3. Add **Send custom event** after the **Sleep** task and bind the eventName in-parameter to it.

getNow   Sleep   Send custom event   getNow

4. Save and exit the workflow. Don't run it now.
5. Create a new workflow with the following variables:

Name	Type	Section	Use
sleepTime	Number	IN	Time the asynchronous workflow for when it should sleep.
eventName	String	IN	This is a string that contains an event name.
endDate	Date	IN	This is the date/time until the workflow should wait.
Success	Boolean	Attribute	This is the return value from the wait for a custom event.
wfToken	WorkflowToken	Attribute	This is the return value from an asynchronous task.
isExternalEvent	Boolean	Attribute	Set to false.

6. Drag an **Asynchronous workflow** task onto the schema.
7. When prompted, enter the name of the workflow you have just created (3.15.2 in the example package).

8. Add a **wait for custom event** element to the schema as well as some getNow actions (see the following figure).

9. Bind the variables to the **Asynchronous** task and the **Wait for custom event** element.

10. Save and run the workflow. Watch the execution.

getNow   06.06.02 Sleep and   getNow   Wait for custom eve   getNow

You will see that the main workflow will wait until it has received the custom events, which indicates that the asynchronous workflow has finished.

How it works...

Normally, a workflow executes one element after the other in a serial approach. From time to time, this can mean that your main program has to wait for some other tasks to finish before continuing. Using asynchronous execution, we can make workflows execute in parallel. A typical example is that you clone a VM (which can take a few minutes), and while it clones, you can create a new PortGroup that you can later attach to the cloned VM. To do this, create a new workflow that runs the create VM workflow asynchronously and sends a custom event when it is finished. In the meantime, the main workflow creates the PortGroup and then waits for the custom event to signal that the VM is ready. After the custom event has arrived, you can then map the PortGroup to the VM.

One thing you have to watch out for is a so-called race condition. If you start a workflow asynchronously and in sequence and then wait for the other, you might run into this. If the asynchronous workflow finishes before the sequential does, the event is already sent but nobody is waiting for it, resulting in the fact that the event wait will time out. In this case, you should either use the workflow token (see the recipe *Scripting with workflow tokens* in this chapter) or add a sleep to the asynchronous task to make sure it finishes after the sequential one. As an example for this, check out the example workflow, 06.06.04 wait for asynchronous (Race condition).

See also

See the example workflows:

- 06.06.01 Using Asynchronous Workflows
- 06.06.02 Sleep and send event
- 06.06.03 wait for Asynchronous workflow to finish
- 06.06.04 wait for asynchronous (Race condition)

Scripting with workflow tokens

In this recipe, we have taken a closer look at the workflow token. The workflow token is the execution of a given workflow.

Getting ready

We don't need anything special, just the ability to create a new workflow.

How to do it...

In this example, we start a workflow asynchronously and then wait for it to finish the workflow token:

1. Create a new workflow and create the following variables:

Name	Type	Section	Use
sleepTime	Number	IN	It defines the time the workflow should sleep.
wfToken	WorkflowToken	Attribute	The workflow token of the asynchronous workflow.
waitTaskTime	Number	Attribute	How long to wait between checks.

2. Build the following workflow (`06.07.01 Wait for Workflow Token` in the example package):

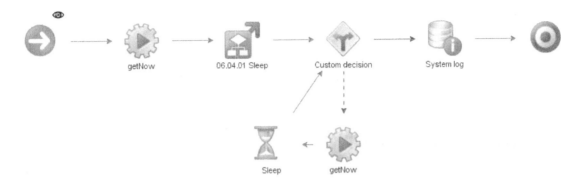

3. The custom decision element should contain the following script:

```
if (wfToken.state =="completed"){
    return true;
} else {
    return false;
}
```

4. Save and run the workflow

How it works...

The **workflow token** is a unique ID that is created with each workflow run. It contains a link to all the content of a workflow run, such as the logs, as well as all the attributes and in- and out parameters. You can access it via JavaScript, the API (see the recipe *Accessing Orchestrator REST API* in `Chapter 7`, *Interacting with Orchestrator*) or the Control Center (see the recipe *Control Center titbits* in `Chapter 2`, *Optimizing Orchestrator Configuration*). When you look at a workflow run (the items underneath a workflow), you see nothing else but the Orchestrator Client accessing the data stored in the workflow token.

In addition to the properties, there are also some methods that allow you to cancel or answer the workflow.

Each workflow token has simple properties and methods, and they are as follows:

Properties and methods	Description
`.id`	Converts the token ID into a string.
`.startDate`	This is the date and time the workflow was started.
`.endDate`	This is the date and time the workflow was finished. `Null` means that it is still running.
`.state`	This is the state the workflow is in. The different states are `waiting`, `failed`, `completed`, `cancelled`, and `running`.
`.name`	This is the name of the workflow.
`.exception`	This is the error message a workflow generated and is `Null` if no error occurs.
`.getAttributes()`	This helps get all the attributes of the workflow; it returns an Orchestrator properties object. The return is a JavaScript object.
`.getInputParameters()`	This helps get all the in-parameters of the workflow; it returns an Orchestrator properties object. The return is a JavaScript object.
`.getOutputParameters()`	This helps get all the out-parameters of the workflow; it returns an Orchestrator properties object. The return is a JavaScript object
`.cancel()`	Cancels the workflow execution.

`.saveSchemaImageToFile(file)`	Saves the image of the workflow schema to a `file`.
`Server.getWorkflowTokenState(String_token_id)`	Gets the state of a given `String_token_id`.

See also

See the example workflow `06.06.04 Wait for Workflow Token`.

Working with user interactions

This recipe will teach us how to create user interactions. User interactions are additional inputs that can be asked of users during the workflow execution.

Getting ready

We need to be able to create a new workflow.

For this recipe, you will need to have more than one AD/LDAP/SSO group configured to access Orchestrator. Remember that you can use the Orchestrator internal LDAP to test this. To facilitate this, please follow the recipe *User management* in `Chapter 7`, *Interacting with Orchestrator*.

For the example, in the *There's more...* section, we will also showcase the interaction with the vSphere Web Client.

How to do it...

We will split this recipe into two parts, the creation of the interaction workflow and the test run that will show how to answer the interaction.

Creating the workflow

1. Create a new workflow with the following variables:

Name	Type	Section	Use
Group	LdapGroup	IN	This contains the group that is enabled to answer the interaction.
userString	String	Attribute	This is defined when the user answers the interaction.
errorCode	String	Attribute	This contains the error code.
Date	Date	IN	This is the date until the customer interactions waits for answers.
inString	String	IN	This is a string value that is defined when the workflow starts.

2. Define for the group attribute an LDAP group that should be allowed to answer the interaction (if you don't have an LDAP/AD/SSO, you can use vcousers from the local Orchestrator LDAP).

3. Drag a **User interaction** element onto the schema and edit it.

4. The **User interaction** element looks different from the elements you have encountered before. The **Attributes** tab contains the security.group and timeout.date attributes, as well as arrays for users and groups. The security.group (or the arrays) attribute defines which users (or groups) are allowed to answer this user interaction. Bind this attribute to the group attribute. The timeout.date attribute defines when this user interaction expires. Bind the date in-parameter to it.

5. The **External inputs** tab defines what variables the user interaction asks for. You

can add workflow attributes or out-parameters here. For our example, we just add the userString attribute:

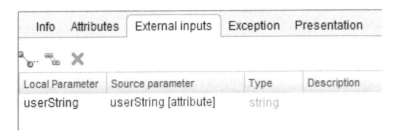

6. The **Presentation** tab works the same way as the normal workflow presentation (see the recipe *Workflow Presentations* in Chapter 5, *Visual Programming*).

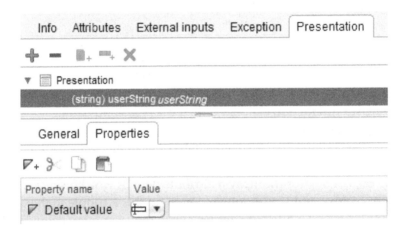

7. We will be building the following structure in the next steps:

8. Drag the **System error** element onto the **User Interaction** element and make sure that the bindings are correct (see the recipe *Error handling in workflows* in `Chapter 5`, *Visual Programming*).

9. To make sure that something happens after the interaction, add **Scriptable task** to the schema (see the previous screenshot) and bind the `inString` and `userString` variables as an in-parameter to it. Also, bind the `outString` out-parameter as an out-parameter. In the scripting section, add `outString=inString+UserString`.

10. We now need to make sure that the group that should answer the interaction actually is able to access the workflow. In the **Permission** tab of the workflow, add the group you have defined as the security group in step 4. The user group needs the **Execute** permission. Check the recipe *User management* in `Chapter 7`, *Interacting with Orchestrator*.

11. Save and close the workflow.

Answering the user interaction

1. Run the workflow you have just created.

2. First, you are presented with the normal input request from the workflow. Enter an expiration date (maybe 15 minutes from now) and some text.

3. If you are an Orchestrator admin, you will now be presented with the user interaction input. If this is the case, click on **Cancel**.

4. Have a look at the workflow; you will notice that it is still running and is now waiting for a user input. Log in to a second Orchestrator Client as a member of the group you defined as the security group in step 10 of the previous section.

5. Select the **Run** mode of the Orchestrator Client and click on the **Waiting for Input** tab. Here, you find all the workflows that are currently waiting for input.

6. Click on the workflow and then on **Answer a user interaction** (the speech bubble icon).
7. The input for the user interaction will now pop up. Enter a value for `userString` and click on **Submit**.
8. Wait till the workflow has finished and then change back to the Orchestrator Client with the administrator login.
9. Take a look at the finished workflow execution.

How it works...

User interactions are created so that a workflow can get additional input when it is already running. You can define variables (**External inputs**) as an input that a user should use, and you can format the input as you have already learned in the recipe *Workflow presentations* in `Chapter 5`, *Visual Programming*.

The `security.assignee` and `security.assignee.groups` fields are new in vRO 7. Please note that you can assign the security group or array input as `NULL`.

The important thing is that you can define a security group that is the recipient of this user request. This makes it possible that one group of Orchestrator users (for example, VM requesters) can start a workflow and have the workflow wait until a different group (VM approvers) has answered the user interaction.

The expiry date is also useful as it lets you define when a user action was not answered in a certain timeframe. If a user interaction was not answered, the **User interaction** element will generate an error with the **Timeout on signal** message. This makes it possible to create a follow-up action, for example, send an e-mail to the VM requester that his request has failed.

A workflow that is in the state of **Waiting** keeps this state, even if the Orchestrator server is powered off, as this information is stored in the Orchestrator database.

A common practice is to put the security group that is used into a configuration (see the recipe *Working with configurations* in `Chapter 8`, *Better Workflows and Optimized Working*).

There's more...

To use the vSphere Web Client to answer a user interaction, follow these steps:

1. Log in to vSphere Web Client as a member of the group you defined as the security group in step 4 in this recipe (or as an Orchestrator admin).
2. Click on **vCenter Orchestrator** and then on **Waiting for interaction**. (You might need to wait a moment for the Web Client to load the information.)
3. You will see all currently waiting workflows. Mark the workflow and select **Answer the workflow run** (the blue person icon). A pop-up window will show you the user interaction:

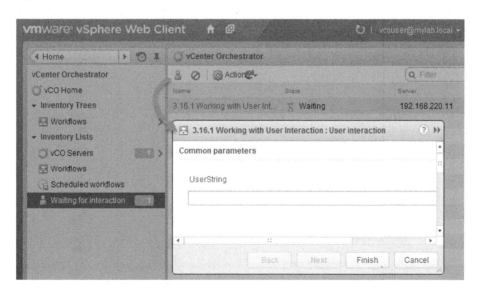

Answering using vRealize Automation

When you start a workflow using **vRealize Automation** (**vRA**) and this workflow contains a user interaction element, the user can answer by navigating to **Inbox** | **Manual User Action**.

See also

See the example workflow `06.08 Working with User Interaction`.

Interacting with Orchestrator

In this chapter, we will have a closer look at how you can interact with Orchestrator. We will be looking at the following recipes:

- User management
- User preferences
- Using Orchestrator through the vSphere Web Client
- Accessing Orchestrator REST API
- Accessing the Control Center via REST plugin
- Running Orchestrator workflows using PowerShell
- Using PHP to access the REST API

Introduction

Orchestrator has a REST-based API that allows you to interact with workflows as well as a lot more. We will be exploring this in this chapter in more detail.

Orchestrator used to have a SOAP API but it was discontinued; however, the VMware document `vrealize-orchestrator-70-develop-web-services-guide.pdf` still contains a chapter on it. So don't be mislead. Orchestrator SOAP is gone.

The REST API, in my opinion, is better and easier to use, especially as we have the fabulous Swagger UI to go and play with it (see the recipe *Accessing Orchestrator REST API* in this chapter).

Orchestrator can be accessed in a lot of ways, but they all come down to using the REST API.

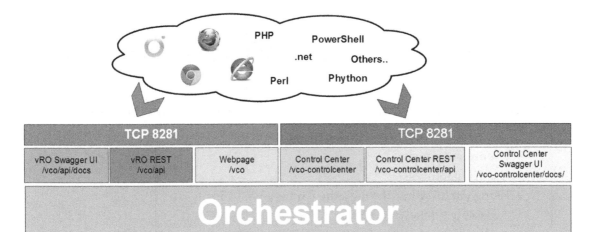

User management

In this recipe, we will see how to control access to Orchestrator. You will learn how to give and control access to users outside the Orchestrator administrator group.

Getting ready

We need a running Orchestrator configured either with vSphere / vRA authentication or AD. Check the recipe *Configuring an external Authentication* in Chapter 1, *Installing and Configuring Orchestrator*.

Also, we need either access to a user management system (LDAP, SSO, or AD) or to have other users and groups on a given user management system. If you are using the Orchestrator appliance without any external authentication you can use the local LDAP user vcoadmin and vrouser which are set out in the recipe *Configuring an external Authentication* in Chapter 1, *Installing and Configuring Orchestrator*.

How to do it...

We have three parts to this recipe, each for different tasks.

Giving non-administrative users access to Orchestrator

Giving restricted access to users is better than just adding everyone to the Orchestrator administrative group. Please note that you can only add LDAP/AD groups. To grant non-administrative access to Orchestrator, follow these steps:

1. Log in to Orchestrator Client as an Orchestrator administrator.
2. The **MyOrchestrator** (the house symbol) page opens up by default. Select the **Run** mode if not already selected.
3. Click on the **Permissions** tab.
4. Click on **Add access right** (the group with a green plus).
5. Select the correct **Domain** from the drop-down menu.
6. In the **Search** field, either just press *Enter* to see all existing groups or enter a string to filter for groups and press *Enter*.
7. Select the group you want to add.
8. Select the rights you want this group to have (**View** is the lowest-needed right).
9. Click on **Select**.

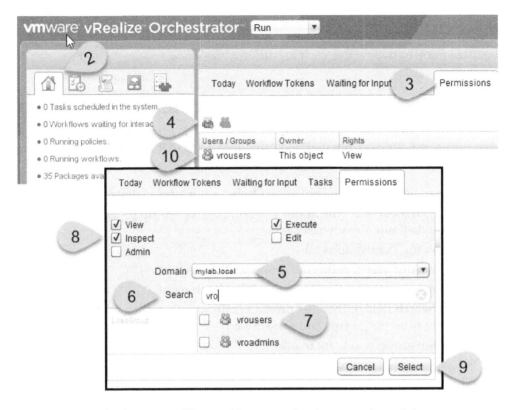

10. Log in to Orchestrator Client with a user that is a member of the user group you added in step 6.
11. You are now logged in as a non-administrative user.

Configuring access to Orchestrator elements

After we are granted non-administrator access to Orchestrator, we can now modify the user rights of other Orchestrator elements:

1. Log in to Orchestrator Client as an Orchestrator administrator.
2. Select an element (for example, a workflow or folder).
3. Click on **Edit** (the pencil symbol).
4. Click on **Permissions** and then on **Add access right** (the group with a green plus).
5. In the **Filter** field, either just press *Enter* to see all existing groups or enter a string to filter for groups and press *Enter*.

6. Select the group you want to add.
7. Select the rights you want this group to have (**View** is the lowest-needed right).
8. Click on **Select**.
9. Click on **Save and Close**.
10. Log in and test.

How it works...

As Orchestrator administrators have access to all Orchestrator elements as well as having all user rights (including delete), you might want to restrict the access that users have.

The best thing is to create a dedicated Orchestrator administrator group in AD and configure this group as the Orchestrator admin group in the **External Authentication** in Control Center. See *Configuring an external Authentication* in `Chapter 1`, *Installing and Configuring Orchestrator*, and add one or more user groups for Orchestrator non-administrative access (such as vRO-test and vRO-production) to your AD and then to Orchestrator. This will result in a user structure you can manage through AD instead of Orchestrator.

The user management in Orchestrator can be a bit tricky. Here are some of the more common problems.

Same user – two groups

If you have a user that is a member of the user group as well as a member of the admin group, then the user will have the rights of the admin group.

The highest right will be used.

Edit user rights

Well...you can't. The only thing you can do is delete the right and then add it again.

Right inheritance

The user rights that are given to one Orchestrator element will automatically be inherited by all its child elements. You cannot break the inheritance. However, you can extend or restrict the rights. Because of this, it is prudent to give only **View** rights to a group on the

My Orchestrator level and extend the rights as needed in the child elements.

To extend or restrict the rights of a user group, just add the same user group to the element again and adjust the rights as required. Have a look at the following screenshot. You find the inherit right (**Parent**) and the current right for this element (**This object**) there. The right of the **This object** element will always overwrite the inheritance. Please note that when you expand or restrict the user rights, all children will again inherit this setting:

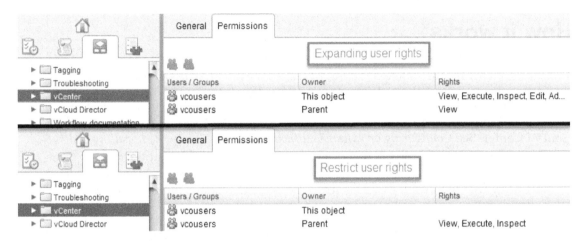

Rights for sub-elements

This is a very typical problem. Let's assume you have a workflow called mainWorkflow that calls the workflow subWorkflow. The user has execute rights for mainWorkflow but not for subWorkflow. The result would be that the mainWorkflow can't be executed by this user.

The only way around that is to use the Switch Credentials workflow element we discussed in the recipe *Changing credentials during runtime* in Chapter 5, *Visual Programming*.

Visibility

Have a look at the following screenshot. You will notice that we have two Administrator groups. One is from `mylab.local` and the other one from `vsphere.local`; however, you can't distinguish between them. The only thing we can do here is to use user/group names that are more descriptive:

Access right

The following are the existing Orchestrator user rights:

User right	Description
View	Base access to Orchestrator Client and view elements but not their schema, presentation, script, and parameter references.
Inspect	View schema, presentation, script, and parameter references in elements.
Execute	Able to run a workflow. If this right is not given, every user can still use the **Run As** feature by right-clicking on it. This right also allows you to answer a user interaction.
Edit	Able to edit elements.
Admin	Able to set permissions on elements.

There's more...

Here are some more notes of interest.

The login format

To log into Orchestrator, you can use one of the following syntaxes:

- `Username` (only if you are using vSphere or vRA setup)
- `username@FQDN-Domain`
- `Domain\username`

Typical error messages

This is a list of the most typical login error messages:

- **Node not Active**: This could mean that Orchestrator isn't fully up yet, or that the connection from Orchestrator to the external Authentication isn't up yet. Waiting or restarting the Orchestrator service helps.
- **[002] User [username] is not authorized**: Here, the user is not a member of the Orchestrator administrator group or doesn't have the **View** right in **My Orchestrator**.
- **Smart client connection is disabled by server security**: Here, non-administrative access to Orchestrator has been disabled.
- **Invalid user/password**: This is one of those error messages that can mean a lot, starting with the obvious typo in the username or password to the fact that the user doesn't exist. A typical problem here is that a user exists and has access rights to Orchestrator. In this case, this message means that the user management system can't find him, indicating that something in the external Authentication is not working correctly.

Disabling non-administrative access to Orchestrator

If you want to turn off the possibility of any non-administrative access to Orchestrator, have a look at the section *System Properties* in the recipe *Control Center Titbits* in Chapter 2, *Optimizing Orchestrator Configuration*.

User preferences

In this recipe, we will have a look at how to configure the behavior of Orchestrator Client. You will learn how to manipulate the coloring of scripts, the start-up behavior, and much more.

Getting ready

We need a running Orchestrator installation as well as an Orchestrator account that we can log into.

How to do it...

1. Log into Orchestrator Client.
2. Click on **Tools** (in the top-right corner of Orchestrator) and select **User preferences...**.

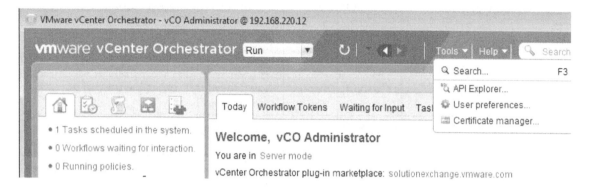

3. The **User Preferences** window will open.
4. Configure the settings as you like.
5. Click on **OK**.

The user preferences have four areas of configuration: **General**, **Workflow**, **Inventory**, and **Script Editor**.

How it works...

The **user preferences** can only be set by Orchestrator administrators, as they determine how Orchestrator Client behaves.

The user preference settings are specific for each user and are stored in the `vmware-vmo.cfg` file that is located in the local Orchestrator Client directory. If you are using Java Web Start (from the Orchestrator home page), the settings are stored in the hidden folder `.vmware` in your local user profile. This means that if you are logging in from the same computer or with the same Windows user account (even when using different Orchestrator users), the settings will be shared.

There are four sections that can be configured: **General**, **Workflow**, **Inventory**, and **Script Editor**.

General

The general section contains the settings for the general behavior of Orchestrator Client. You can set the following items:

Item	Options	Default	Meaning
Auto-edit new inserted	[Yes|NO]	Yes	A new object will open automatically in edit mode
Script compilation delay	[ms]	2000	How often input will be checked by the editor
Show decision scripts	[Yes|NO]	No	Shows the script that is the base of a decision object
Delete non-empty folder permitted	[Yes|NO]	No	Able to delete non-empty folders
Size of run logs	[lines]	300	Amount of lines displayed in the workflow log
Server log fetch limit	[lines]	100	Amount of lines displayed in the **Events** tab of an element
Finder maximum size	[items]	20	Amount of elements returned in a search
Check usage when deleting an element	[Yes|NO]	No	Check whether an element is used by another element before deleting
Check OGNL expression	[Yes|NO]	Yes	Not supported since vCO 5.1

A typical setting you might like to change is **Finder maximum size.** A higher number will return a greater number of search results in a search box, which can be helpful but may also take a bit longer.

Workflow

The workflow settings alter how Orchestrator workflows behave. Changing some of these settings should be considered carefully. Changing them won't damage Orchestrator but can impact the visual presentation of your work. An extremely cool feature is the **Edit workflow items in a pop-up window** option. This will allow you to edit workflow elements directly without clicking on the edit icon. This feature is switched on depending on your screen resolution.

Inventory

There is only one option available, that is, **Use contextual menu in inventory**. The function automatically displays all workflows that can be used with a selected object in the inventory. For example, right-clicking on the cluster in the vCenter Server inventory will display all the workflows that are available for a cluster:

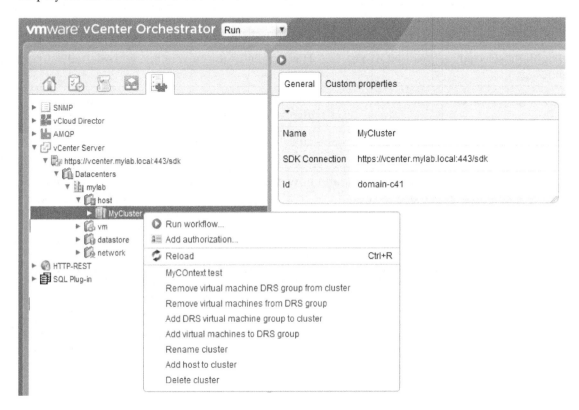

To make this work, you will need to assign the workflow presentation property **Show in Inventory** to an in-parameter of a particular type (for example, VC:ClusterComputeResource). Also see the *Workflow Presentations* recipe in Chapter 5, *Visual Programming*.

Script editor

In the script editor section, you can choose how a script element behaves when you enter the JavaScript code.

Item	Options	Default	Meaning
Enable code assist	[Yes | NO]	Yes	Code assist allows the use of *Ctrl* + spacebar to see the properties or methods of the object.
Highlight selected line	[Yes | NO]	Yes	This highlights the current line you selected.
Highlight brackets	[Yes | NO]	Yes	When the cursor is on a bracket (any type), it will display its corresponding partner.
Display EOL	[Yes | NO]	No	This displays the end of a line of a given line of code.

The rest of the choices are about color and how elements (such as strings and comments) are color coded. You can use the default or create a color scheme that resembles other code editors you use.

Using Orchestrator though the vSphere Web Client

In this recipe, we further explore the Orchestrator integration into vSphere Web Client. You will learn how to run Orchestrator workflows using vSphere Web Client as well as how to configure workflows so that they work with it.

Getting ready

You find the base information on how to integrate Orchestrator into the vSphere Web Client in the recipe *Connecting to vCenter* in `Chapter 1`, *Installing and Configuring Orchestrator*.

For this recipe, we need Orchestrator integrated into vSphere Web Client.

How to do it...

This recipe is made up of two parts, the configuration and the passing along of information between the Web Client and Orchestrator.

Configure workflows for the vSphere Web Client

We now configure workflows for use with the vSphere Web Client:

1. Open the vSphere Web Client in a web browser.
2. Log in to vCenter with a user that is a member of the Orchestrator admin group that you configured in vSphere authentication (see recipe *Configuring an external Authentication* in `Chapter 1`, *Installing and Configuring Orchestrator*).
3. Click on **vRealize Orchestrator** and wait until the Web Client has finished loading all information. You should now see at least one Orchestrator server registered.
4. Click on **Manage** and then on **Context Actions**. You can now see all the workflows that have been configured for use with the right-click menu from vSphere Web Client. If you can't see **Manage**, you need to use a user that is part of the Orchestrator admin group:

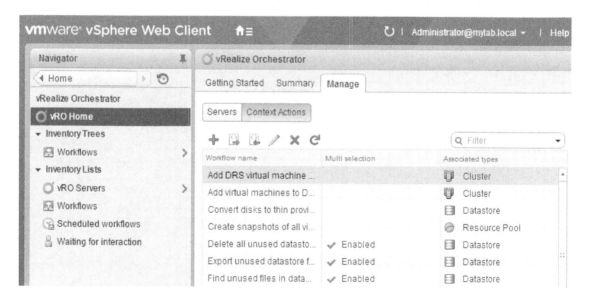

5. To configure a new workflow for use with the vSphere Web Client, click on **Add** (the green plus).

6. Select a workflow from the list of available workflows (choose the workflow **Library | vCenter | Virtual Machine Management | Basic | Rename virtual machine**, as this workflow can be used without extra configuration) and click on **Add**.

7. Select the type of vSphere object this workflow should be available to (such as a VM).

8. **Multi selection** lets you choose not only one but multiple instances of the same vSphere object, for example, not only one VM but multiple VMs. For this to work, you also have to make sure that the workflow has an in-parameter of the `Array of [any vCenterobject]` type.

9. Click on **OK**:

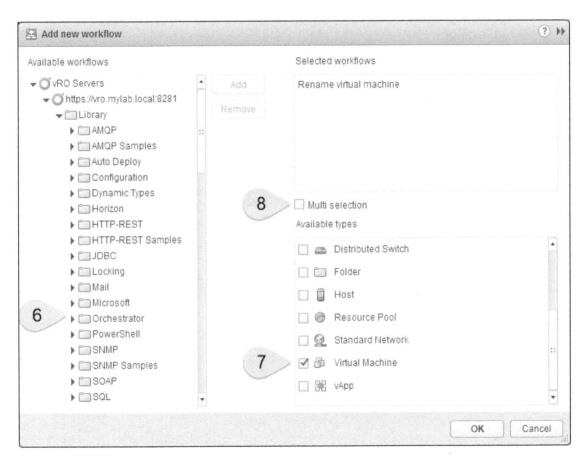

Run workflows

To run workflows, a vCenter user must have at least the `view` and `execute` right in Orchestrator; see recipe *User management* in this chapter.

If you just configured the new workflow you need to re-log in:

1. To run the **Rename Virtual Machine** workflow from our example, navigate in the vSphere Web Client to a VM.
2. Right-click on the VM, and navigate to **All vRealize Orchestrator Actions** | **Rename Virtual Machine**.
3. Enter a new name for the VM and click on **Submit**:

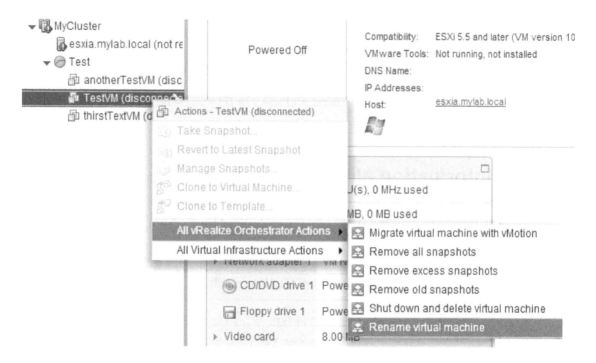

Writing workflows for web integration

When running a workflow from the Web Client, you might want to pass some information to the workflow in Orchestrator, for instance, the vSphere object you are running the workflow on:

1. Open the workflow you want to use with the Orchestrator Client in edit mode.
2. Make sure that you have a workflow in-parameter of the type you want to associate with in the vSphere Web Client, for example, VC:VirtualMachine. If you plan to use the **Multi selection** option, make sure that you use an Array of VC:VirtualMachine.
3. In **Presentation**, assign the **Show in Inventory** property to the workflow in-parameter. If this property is assigned to more than one in-parameter, only one parameter at a time is used. For example, if you have an in-parameter for a VM and for a cluster, both have the **Show in Inventory** property assigned to them. When starting the workflow from a VM, the VM ID will be used and the cluster ID will not be transferred to the workflow. When starting the workflow from a cluster, the cluster ID will be used and the VM ID will be ignored.
4. Save the workflow.

Passing information along

In case you want to use a workflow such as run a SSH command. You will find that you will need to still add a hostname, even if you assign it to a VM. To solve this, follow these steps:

1. Make a copy of the workflow **Library | SSH | Run a SSH Command**
2. Move the input parameter **hostNameOrIP** to attribute (right-click and select **Move as Attribute**)
3. Add an input parameter called VM of type VC:VirtualMachine
4. Add a scriptable task with the input of **VM** and output of **hostNamOrIP**
5. Add the following code:
6. hostNameOrIP=VM.guest.hostName;
7. This little modification will make sure that you can now run the workflow on a VM without entering a hostname.
8. Also, see the example workflow 07.04.5 Run SSH command (Web Client).

How it works...

The vSphere integration of Orchestrator into the vSphere Web Client allows you to easily use workflows that you have created.

You can also start all the workflows from the vSphere Web Client by clicking on **vRealize Orchestrator** | **Inventory Trees** | **Workflows**. The Orchestrator workflow tree you know from Orchestrator Client will appear and you can select and then start the workflow.

It's also possible to schedule workflows; just click on the workflow that you would like to run and then click on the right window onto **Schedule workflow**. This works the same as in Orchestrator Client. You can monitor all scheduled workflows by clicking on **vRealize Orchestrator** | **Inventor List** | **Scheduled workflows**.

The last and most important thing is that you can also interact with workflows that are waiting for interaction. Just click on **vRealize Orchestrator**| **Inventor List** | **Waiting for interaction** to see all workflows that are currently waiting for interaction.

You can see all the workflows that are and have been running on **vRealize Orchestrator** | **vRO Servers** | **[your server]** | **Monitor**. Here, you can also **Cancel** and **Answer** workflows. The workflows you see here are all the Orchestrator workflow runs, not only the ones run via the vSphere Web Client.

Orchestrator presentation properties in vSphere Web Client

The Orchestrator presentation properties that you have set up will be working in vSphere Web Client with an exception; hiding a page.

Check out the example workflow `07.05.01 Presentations test` to test this.

There's more...

As you need to define **Context Actions** (right-click on the menu), it is rather important that you are able to back up or restore these settings.

By clicking on **vCenter Orchestrator** | **Manage** | **Context Actions**, you can use the export action (the white paper icon with the blue right arrow) to export all current settings into an XML file. Using import (the white paper icon with the green left arrow), you can import these settings into Web Client again. Please note that the export contains the workflow ID, so make sure that the workflows on another Orchestrator server have the same ID (see the *Synchronize Orchestrator element between Orchestrator Servers* recipe in Chapter 3, *Distributed Design* and the *Working with packages* recipe in Chapter 4, *Programming Skills*).

See also

- Recipe *Connecting to vCenter* in Chapter 1, *Installing and Configuring Orchestrator*
- Recipe *Working with user interaction* in Chapter 6, *Advanced Programming*
- Recipe *Workflow presentations* in Chapter 5, *Visual Programming*
- Recipe *Language packs (localization)* in Chapter 8, *Better Workflows and Optimized Working*

The example workflows 07.04.5 Run SSH command (Web Client) and 12.05.01 Presentation Test.

Accessing Orchestrator REST API

In this recipe, we are looking at how to access and play with the Orchestrator REST API.

Getting ready

We need a browser, preferably Chrome or Firefox.

To play and explore, we also need access to the Orchestrator Control Center.

We will be using the example workflow 07.02 Access via PowerShell (Input).

How to do it...

The recipe is broken up into multiple parts for easier reading; the best way forward is to work through one after the other.

Accessing the API documentation and enable "play mode"

 Please note that this is a stetting that you shouldn't use in any production environments.

1. Open the Orchestrator Control Center and enter the system property `com.vmware.o11n.sso.basic-authentication.enabled = true` as shown in section *System properties* in the recipe *Control Center titbits* in `Chapter 2`, *Optimizing Orchestrator Configuration*.
2. Open a browser and browse to `https://[Orchestrator]:8281/vco/api/docs/`
3. The SwaggerUI of Orchestrator will open up.

Try it out!

Let's give it a quick go:

1. Navigate to **service-descriptor-controller** and click on it.
2. A lot of functions should show up. Click on **/api/about**:

service-descriptor-service : Service Descriptor Service   Show/Hide   List Operations   Expand Operations   Raw

GET	/api/	Enumerate services
GET	/api/about	Get about info
GET	/api/docs	Redirect docs to docs/index.html
GET	/api/healthstatus	Get health status
GET	/api/schema	Get REST XSD schema file
GET	/api/schema/{name}	Get REST XSD schema file
GET	/api/status	Get vRA registration state
GET	/api/versions	List supported API versions

3. Scroll down a bit and then click on **Try it out!**
4. You should now see the result of your REST request:

Try it out!   Hide Response

Request URL

```
https://192.168.220.12:8281/vco/api/about
```

Response Body

```
{
  "version": "7.0.1.3533702",
  "build-number": "3533702",
  "build-date": "2016-02-09T12:19:45Z",
  "api-version": "5.5.2"
}
```

Response Code

```
200
```

Response Headers

```
{
  "server": "Apache-Coyote/1.1",
  "cache-control": "private",
  "expires": "Thu, 01 Jan 1970 01:00:00 CET",
  "content-type": "application/json; v=5.1.1;charset=UTF-8",
  "transfer-encoding": "chunked",
  "date": "Mon, 23 May 2016 22:14:02 GMT"
}
```

Interactive REST request

We will now request information using some inputs:

1. Go to and expand **workflow-controller**.
2. Select **Post /api/workflows/{workflowId}/executions**.
3. Under **workflowID**, enter **bb7bcb76-515e-4fdb-80e3-63227ad0cfd0**, which is the ID of the example workflow, `07.02 Access via PowerShell (Input)`.
4. Click on the eggshell colored field on the left side. This will fill the basic template into the white right field (number 12).
5. Fill in the values as shown here:

```
{
  "parameters": [
    {
      "value": {"string":{"value":"VMware"}
```

```
            },
        "name": "vmName",
        "type": "string",
        "description": "",
        "scope": "local",
        "updated": false
        }
    ]
}
```

6. Make sure that the **Parameter content type** is set to **application/json**.
7. Scroll down and click on **Try it out!**

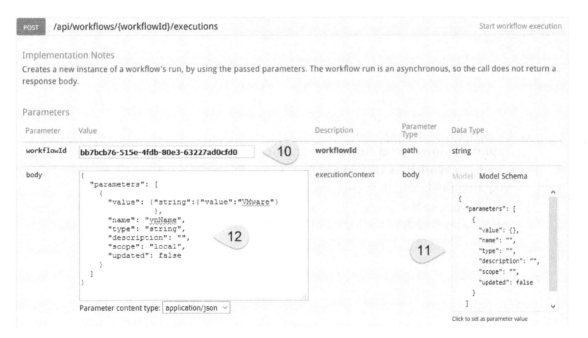

8. If you now check in Orchestrator you see that the workflow was run.
9. Scroll down: you will see that you didn't get an output. For that, you need to look at the workflow execution, the same as you would by using the Orchestrator Client.

10. Have a closer look at the **Response headers**. You'll find a key called **location** and behind it, a URL. This is the response URL to the execution you triggered. It contains the **Workflow ID** and the **Execution ID**:

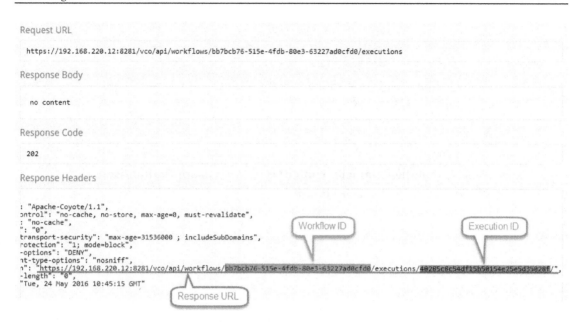

Request URL

```
https://192.168.220.12:8281/vco/api/workflows/bb7bcb76-515e-4fdb-80e3-63227ad0cfd0/executions
```

Response Body

```
no content
```

Response Code

```
202
```

Response Headers

```
: "Apache-Coyote/1.1",
ontrol": "no-cache, no-store, max-age=0, must-revalidate",
: "no-cache",
": "0",
transport-security": "max-age=31536000 ; includeSubDomains",
rotection": "1; mode=block",
-options": "DENY",
nt-type-options": "nosniff",
n": "https://192.168.220.12:8281/vco/api/workflows/bb7bcb76-515e-4fdb-80e3-63227ad0cfd0/executions/40285c8c54df15b50154e25e5d35028f/",
-length": "0",
"Tue, 24 May 2016 10:45:15 GMT"
```

11. Scroll further down to get **/api/workflows/{workflowId}/executions/{executionId}**.

12. Copy the **Workflow ID** and the **Execution ID** from the response URL into the required fields and then click on **Try it out!**.

13. The **Response Body** now shows a JSON object that contains all the links to more information, such as the logs, but it also contains the output parameters that contain the return values of our workflow:

```
"output-parameters": [
  {
    "value": {
      "string": {
        "value": "NSX Manager,4,16  -  vro2,2,4  -  vROCluster-0,1,0.5  -  VMware vRealize Appliance,4,18  -  vro1,2,4
      }
    },
    "type": "string",
    "name": "info",
    "scope": "local"
```

We are finished with the showcase; you might want to reverse the system property you set up in the first section of this recipe.

How it works...

The Orchestrator REST API is the central point of contact for everything Orchestrator. If you understand how to work the API you can use any programming language to connect and run the workflows.

When you run a workflow, you POST the parameters you need in the BODY of the message to the correct URL. If you don't have any parameters, such as in our first example, you POST an empty JSON body { }.

Orchestrator will now run the workflow and store all the parameters (in, out and attributes) as well as the logs with the workflow execution. The return value of the post will contain the current status of the workflow execution (running, completed) as well as the response URL. The response URL consist of the workflow ID and the execution ID:

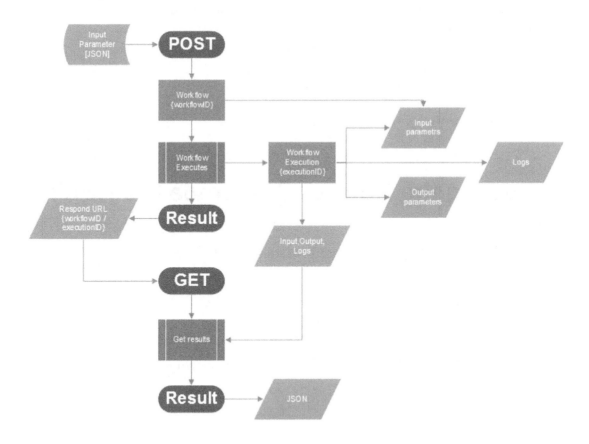

If you now GET the response URL you will receive all the information that the workflow execution contains as JSON.

There's more...

The XSD for the Orchestrator API can be found here:
`https://[Orchestrator]:8281/vco/api/docs/o11n-sdk-rest.xsd`

See also

To further explore the REST API, have a look at the following recipes:

- *Running Orchestrator workflows using PowerShell* in this chapter
- *Working with REST* in `Chapter 9`, *Essential Plugins*
- *Accessing the Orchestrator Control Center API via REST* in this chapter
- *Using PHP to access the REST API* in this chapter
- A collection of examples to connect to REST:

  `http://blog.mashape.com/30-ways-to-make-rest-calls-in-node-js-php-py thon/`

Accessing the Control Center via the REST plugin

In this recipe, we have a closer look at the Orchestrator Control Center.

Getting ready

We need access to the Orchestrator Control Center.

Add the Orchestrator Control Center to the REST plugin as shown in the recipe *Working with REST* in `Chapter 9`, *Essential Plugins*.

How to do it...

The recipe has been broken up into several sections, just work through them.

Explore the Control Center API

We will be having a look at the possibilities of the Control Center API:

1. Open a browser to the URL and authenticate with your Control Center account:
   `https://[Orchestrator]:8283/vco-controlcenter/docs/`
2. You now are connected to the swagger UI, which helps you explore the Control Center API.

vRealize Orchestrator Control Center API

Controls and configures vRealize Orchestrator

authentication-controller : Authentication Controller	Show/Hide	List Operations	Expand Operations	Raw
certificates-controller : Certificates Controller	Show/Hide	List Operations	Expand Operations	Raw
cluster-controller : Cluster Controller	Show/Hide	List Operations	Expand Operations	Raw
database-controller : Database Controller	Show/Hide	List Operations	Expand Operations	Raw
feature-controller : Feature Controller	Show/Hide	List Operations	Expand Operations	Raw
file-system-controller : File System Controller	Show/Hide	List Operations	Expand Operations	Raw
license-controller : License Controller	Show/Hide	List Operations	Expand Operations	Raw
logs-controller : Logs Controller	Show/Hide	List Operations	Expand Operations	Raw
metrics-controller : Metrics Controller	Show/Hide	List Operations	Expand Operations	Raw
password-controller : Password Controller	Show/Hide	List Operations	Expand Operations	Raw
plugin-controller : Plugin Controller	Show/Hide	List Operations	Expand Operations	Raw
properties-controller : Properties Controller	Show/Hide	List Operations	Expand Operations	Raw
server-controller : Server Controller	Show/Hide	List Operations	Expand Operations	Raw
ssl-certificate-controller : Ssl Certificate Controller	Show/Hide	List Operations	Expand Operations	Raw
support-assistant-controller : Support Assistant Controller	Show/Hide	List Operations	Expand Operations	Raw
trust-controller : Trust Controller	Show/Hide	List Operations	Expand Operations	Raw
workflow-tokens-controller : Workflow Tokens Controller	Show/Hide	List Operations	Expand Operations	Raw

3. Expand server-controller and check out GET /api/server/status and POST /api/server/status/start. We used these functions in recipe *Working with REST* in Chapter 9, *Essential Plugins*.

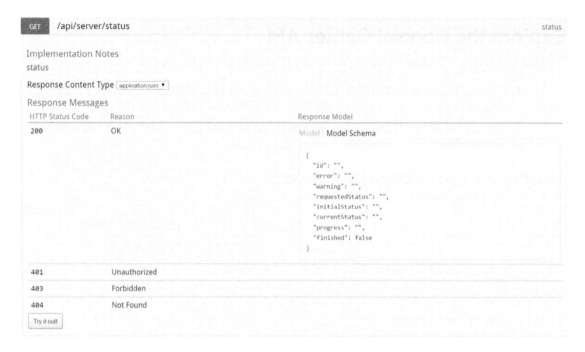

Adding start and stop calls

Create control workflows for your Remote Orchestrators.

1. Check out the swagger UI for the calls /api/server/start, stop, and status calls.

2. Follow the recipe *Working with REST* in Chapter 9, *Essential Plugins*, to add the three functions to the REST host.

3. Create three workflows from the calls

4. Edit the GET workflow to set the correct content type.

5. Edit the POST workflows and move the content input to be an Attribute.

6. Use the recipe *Working with REST* in Chapter 9, *Essential Plugins*, and the *Working with JSON* in Chapter 6, *Advanced Programming*, to understand how to phrase the JSON returns.

Usage

There are several ideas that you can use from here:

- Create a policy that monitors the cluster and restarts VMs or Orchestrator services.
- Auto deploy additional Orchestrators in a server (stop service, import configuration, join cluster, start service)

How it works...

The ability to tie the Orchestrator control into your workflow enables you to use Orchestrator to orchestrate remote Orchestrators much more easily. As there isn't any documentation except the swagger UI at this time, it may be a bit hard, but I wouldn't be surprised to see someone coming up with an Orchestrator Control Center plug-in soon.

You can also attach the Control Center using the swagger specification URL (see recipe *Working with REST* in Chapter 9, *Essential Plugins*). The URL for the swagger spec of Control Center is `https://[FQDN Orchestrator]:8283/vco-controlcenter/api/api-docs`.

See also

There are several examples in the example pack. They won't work, as you need to define the REST host and the REST call (see resource element in Workflows) but these are an example of what they could look like and what could be done with them:

- `07.04.1 Orchestrator Service Status`
- `07.04.2 Start Orchestrator Service`
- `07.04.3 Stop Orchestrator Service`
- `07.04.4 Cluster Status`
- The recipe *Turning Strings into Objects* in Chapter 6, *Advanced Programming*.

Running Orchestrator workflows using PowerShell

In this recipe, we will showcase how to run an Orchestrator workflow using PowerShell.

Getting ready

We need a Windows host that has PowerShell installed (which should be any modern version of Windows). VMware PowerCLI is not needed.

The PowerShell host needs to be able to connect to Orchestrator on TCP port 8281.

If you are new to REST or the Orchestrator REST API, you may like to work through the recipe *Accessing Orchestrator REST API* in this chapter first.

How to do it...

All PowerShell scripts shown here are also stored as a resource with the example package.

Run a workflow

We will start by just running a workflow that doesn't require any input. We will be accessing the example workflow 07.01 Access via PowerShell.

1. Create a new empty PowerShell script. For example, use **Editor**:
2. Write the following code:

```
#some basic variables
$usr = 'vroadmin@mylab.local'
$pwd = 'What4Ever'
$vroServer = '192.168.220.12:8281'
# Example Workflow "07.01 Access via PowerShell"
$wfid = '48e10dcf-998c-4db7-b93d-144678e15368'

# you need this to accept untrusted SSL certs.
add-type @"
    using System.Net;
    using System.Security.Cryptography.X509Certificates;
    public class TrustAllCertsPolicy : ICertificatePolicy {
        public bool CheckValidationResult(
```

```
ServicePointsrvPoint, X509Certificate certificate,
WebRequest request, intcertificateProblem) {
            return true;
        }
    }
"@
 [System.Net.ServicePointManager]::CertificatePolicy = New-Object
 TrustAllCertsPolicy

# you need to add TLS12 for vRO 7, else you cant establish a secure
connection
 [Net.ServicePointManager]::SecurityProtocol =
 [Net.SecurityProtocolType]::Tls12

#we build the BASIC authentication header.
function ConvertTo-Base64($string) {
    $bytes  = [System.Text.Encoding]::UTF8.GetBytes($string);
    $encoded = [System.Convert]::ToBase64String($bytes);

    return $encoded;
}
$token = ConvertTo-Base64($usr+":"+$pwd)
$auth = "Basic $($token)"

# we build the headers we need to call the REST flow
$headers = @{"Authorization"=$auth;"Content-Type"="application/json"}

#build the URL we are connecting to
$URL =
"https://"+$vroServer+"/vco/api/workflows/"+$wfid+"/executions"

#invoke the run of the workflow via REST
$ret = Invoke-WebRequest -Method Post -uri $URL -Headers $headers
-body "
{}"

#Show the raw response of the run
Write-Host $ret.RawContent
```

3. Save and run the script.
4. Check in Orchestrator; a new execution should now exist.

Run a script with input

We will now extend the preceding script to pass along some inputs. We will be accessing the example workflow `07.02 Access via PowerShell (Input)`.

1. Make a copy of the preceding script and edit the copy.
2. Just above the `Invoke-Webrequest` line, enter the following code. Exchange the `$input` content for the name of one of your VMs:

```
#build body
$input="VMware"
$body='{"parameters": [{"name": "vmName","scope": "local","type":
"string","value": {"string": {"value": "'+$input+'"}}}]}'
```

3. Replace the `Invoke-Webrequest` line with the following:

```
#invoke the run of the workflow via REST
$ret = Invoke-WebRequest -Method Post -uri $URL -Headers $headers -
body
$body
```

4. Save and run the workflow.
5. You should now see in Orchestrator that the workflow has been run.

Getting the output of a workflow

We want to get the output of the workflow. We will be accessing the example workflow `07.02 Access via PowerShell (Input)`:

1. Make a copy of the preceding script and edit the copy.
2. Enter the following lines below the `Write-Host` line:

```
#sleep for 20 seconds, to make sure the workflow finished
Start-Sleep -Seconds 20

#get the execution ID from the reply
$URL=$ret.Headers.Location

#ask Orchestrator to give us detail of the workflow
$result = Invoke-WebRequest -Method Get -uri $URL -Headers $headers

#covert and get the output
$outputObj=($result.Content).Replace("output-
parameters","outputparameters")|ConvertFrom-Json
```

```
$output=($outputObj.outputparameters[0]).value.string.value

Write-Host $output
```

3. Save and run the workflow.

How it works...

Using PowerShell to start Orchestrator workflows isn't that difficult as soon as you understand how to build the request lines and the content.

The basics are the same for all REST operations. First, you need to create a POST to start the workflow, which will return an execution ID. With the execution ID, you can go and check the results of the workflow using GET.

Variables

The hard part is the input variables: here you need to be a bit more careful. The JSON object that is the input isn't that easy to get. In the preceding code, I pushed it into one line, in the recipe, *Accessing Orchestrator REST API* in this chapter is the fully expanded code.

Using the `ConvertTo-Json` PowerShell function you can build the JSON body in a more dynamic way from a PSObject.

> The best way to work with Orchestrator input variables is to reduce the input to Strings and numbers; otherwise, the input to them can be quite hard.

JSON return

The return JSON is quite a beast to handle in PowerShell; one reason is that the variables are stored under output-parameter and using `$outputObj.output-parameters` will result in an error, as PowerShell expects a function called `output-parameters`. That's why I'm using a *dirty* trick and renaming the parameter (replace function) before converting from JSON.

There's more…

Here is a nice little addition. The following `do/while` loop will wait until a workflow has finished. You can test it with the workflow `07.03 PowerShell WAIT for it`.

```
#wait until the workflow has finished
$URL=$ret.Headers.Location
do {
    Start-Sleep -Seconds 5
    $result = Invoke-WebRequest -Method Get -uri $URL -Headers $headers
    $status=($result|ConvertFrom-Json).state
} until ($status -eq "completed")
```

See also

- *Accessing Orchestrator REST API* in this chapter
- *Working with Powershell* in `Chapter 10`, *Built-in Plugins*
- *Working with REST* in `Chapter 9`, *Essential Plugins*
- Accessing the Orchestrator Control Center API via REST in this chapter
- Burke Azbill post on how to do the same using Python and Perl: `http://bit.ly/vroClientScripts`

The example workflows `07.01 Access via PowerShell`, `07.02 Access via PowerShell (Input)` and `07.03 PowerShell WAIT for it`.

As well as the PowerShell scripts stored as a Resource

Using PHP to access the REST API

In this recipe, we will quickly look at how you can build an easy webpage using PHP to access the Orchestrator REST API.

Getting ready

We will make our life a bit easier and use a bit of help with PHP and REST. We will use Nate Good's **HTTPFUL**, which you can find at `http://phphttpclient.com/`.

You need to download the following file, `httpful.phar`, from his website and place it in the same directory as your script.

You also need a Webserver that uses PHP and has cURL activated. I used **LAMP stack** from Turnkey `https://www.turnkeylinux.org/lampstack`. See the *There's more* section for a fast how-to.

How to do it...

This is a quick intro only:

1. Edit a file such as `callWorkflow.php`
2. Enter the following code:

```php
<?php
include('./httpful.phar');

$usr = 'vroadmin@mylab.local';
$pwd = 'What4Ever';
$vroServer = '192.168.220.12:8281';
// Example Workflow "07.01 Access via PowerShell"
$wfid = '48e10dcf-998c-4db7-b93d-144678e15368';

// URL for the request
$uri = "https://{$vroServer}/vco/api/workflows/{$wfid}/executions";
$response = \Httpful\Request::post($uri) // use post
    ->sendsJson()            //conent-typ:applicalion/json
    ->basicAuth($usr,$pwd)   //use basic Authentication
    ->body("{}")             //empty jsonboady
    ->withoutStrictSsl()     //ignore SSL certs
    ->send();                //send it off

//get the Associative array out of the response headers
$location=$response->headers;
//get the location for the workflow execution
echo $location[location];
?>
```

3. Save the workflow and access the webpage using `http://[ip]/callWorkflow.php`.
4. You should see a response location.

How it works...

Using PHP mostly employs the same method as using PowerShell or the Swagger UI. You post a request, you get a response, you parse the response.

Using this as a stepping stone, you can now develop your own web services for Orchestrator. The full HTTPFUL document can be found here:
`http://phphttpclient.com/docs/class-Httpful.Request.html`

Please have a look at the recipe *Turning strings into objects* in `Chapter 6`, *Advanced Programming*, to understand how to create an object out of a string.

There's more...

Here is how to get the Turnkey LAMP ready to rumble in some short steps:

1. Download and deploy the ova image from
   `https://www.turnkeylinux.org/lampstack`.
2. Open a console. When asked, define passwords and skip the rest.
3. Connect and log in as root to the web console `https://[ip] :12320`.
4. Run the following commands:

   ```
   apt-get update
   apt-get install curl libcurl3php5-curl
   mv /etc/php5/mods-available/xcache.ini /etc/php5/mods-
   available/xcache.ini.OLD
   ```

5. Reboot the appliance.
6. You can now upload your `.php` script to `/var/www` and call it directly with `http://[ip]/[scipt.php]`. There is also a file manager in the web console, `https://[ip]:12321/filemin/`.

See also

- *Running Orchestrator workflows using PowerShell* in this chapter
- *Working with REST* in `Chapter 9`, *Essential Plugins*
- *Accessing the Control Center API via REST* in this chapter
- *Turning strings into objects* in `Chapter 6`, *Advanced Programming*

8
Better Workflows and Optimized Working

This chapter discusses how you can improve your workflows as well as optimize your work much more. We will be looking at the following recipes:

- Working with resources
- Working with configurations
- Working with Orchestrator tags
- Using the Locking System
- Language packs (localization)
- Working with policies

Introduction

Here, we are going to explore how to optimize your workflows and how to make your workload easier.

Configurations come in handy when you have multiple workflows that need the same inputs. For instance, you have multiple workflows that send e-mails. Instead of having all needed mail settings stored in each workflow, you can put them in a configuration and have them stored centrally. This makes it easier for you when you need to change a setting, such as updating a password.

Another example is that you have one workflow that you use in two environments, like development and production. You design and upkeep one workflow instead of two just by duplicating it, and then storing the different variables in a configuration.

A **resource** is basically a file that is stored in Orchestrator and can be used within a workflow. A typical example is the **language packs**, which are basically text files stored as resources. Another example for resources is to store information in them such as the configurations of connections. The following screenshot shows that when you use the AD plugin, Orchestrator will create a resource element containing all the required information:

The **tags** are not yet very well used; however, they do have some merits. You can use them to tag any element in Orchestrator.

The language packs come in handy when you use Orchestrator workflows with vCenter across multiple language areas; however, if you are using REST or the Orchestrator Client it doesn't help that much.

The **Locking System** can be used for a lot of good work. When you have multiple users or processes that need to use the same resources, such as files or databases, the Locking System can help make sure that only one process is using the resource.

The **policies** will make Orchestrator actively monitor certain things, such as vSphere objects, SNMP, or AMPQ connections. A policy allows Orchestrator to react to events that are monitored. For example, if Orchestrator registers an SNMP trap, a workflow can be executed.

Working with resources

In this recipe, we will work with resources. We will see how we can integrate files with Orchestrator and use them in workflows and for other purposes, such as storing configuration information.

Getting ready

We need a functional Orchestrator. We also need a text file in a directory that Orchestrator can access. To create such a text file, you could use the example workflow `09.02.1 Write a File`. Also see the recipe *File operations* in `Chapter 9`, *Essential Plugins*.

How to do it...

This recipe contains multiple parts, each dealing with different aspects of resources.

Adding resources manually

Let's start by adding a resource to Orchestrator manually:

1. Switch Orchestrator to **Design** mode.
2. Click on **Resources** (the white page with a blue symbol on it).
3. Create a new folder where you can store your resources by right-clicking the root in the tree and selecting **New folder**.
4. Right-click on the new folder and select **Import resources**.
5. Select a file such as an image or text file from your local folder and click on **Open**. The new resource is now available under the folder you created.
6. Click on the resource and browse through the tabs that are presented.
7. Please note that **Description** automatically contains the location from where you imported it. Also, if the file is a picture or text file, you can view it in the **Viewer** tab.

You can also update (re-upload a file) and download (save to a file) resources in Orchestrator.

Using resources in workflows

To add a resource to a workflow, we need to add it as an attribute. This is shown as follows:

1. Create a new workflow and add a new attribute.
2. Rename the attribute `textFile`.
3. Change the type of the attribute to **ResourceElement**.
4. Now click on **Value**. You can now search the existing resources and select one.
5. Add a scriptable task to the schema and edit it.

6. Bind the `textFile` attribute as an input parameter and add the following script:

```
System.log("Name :"+textFile.name);
System.log("MimeType :"+textFile.mimeType);
System.log("Resource Category
:"+textFile.getResourceElementCategory().name);
System.log("Description :"+textFile.description);
System.log("Version :"+textFile.version);
System.log("Size :"+textFile.contentSize);
//get the content as MimeAttachment
Attachment = textFile.getContentAsMimeAttachment();
// get string content from MimeAttachment
content = attachment.content;
System.log("Content: \n"+content);
```

7. Save and run the workflow.

In the logs, we output all the possible properties of `resourceElement`. The most important one is its content.

Creating a new resource element

Instead of manually uploading a resource element, you can dynamically add new resource elements to Orchestrator:

1. Create a new workflow and add the following variables:

Name	Type	Section	Use
name	String	IN	This is the name of the resource
resourceFolder	ResourceElementCategory	IN	This is where the resource should be stored
textContent	String	IN	This is the plain text that the resource should contain

2. Add a scripting task to the schema and bind all variables.
3. Add the following script:

```
//initialize a mime attachment object
var attachment = new MimeAttachment();
//fill it
attachment.name = name;
attachment.mimeType = "text/plain";
```

```
attachment.content = textContent;
//create the resource element from the Mime attachment
Server.createResourceElement(resourceFolder,name,attachment);
```

4. Save and run the workflow.

Create a resource by uploading a file

Instead of using a mime element, you can upload a resource from a file.

1. Create a new workflow and add the following variables:

Name	Type	Section	Use
localfile	path	IN	File that you want to make a resource.

2. Add a scripting task to the schema and bind the variable.
3. Add the following script:

```
//get filename of path
temp=localfile.split("/")
fileName=temp[temp.length-1];
//upload resource
attachment=Server.createResourceElement("vRO Example",
fileName,localfile);
```

4. Save and run the workflow.

After the workflow has finished, check the resource folder vRO Example and its content.

Updating a resource

We can also update existing resources. To do this, perform the following steps:

1. Create a new workflow and add the following variables:

Name	Type	Section	Use
resource	ResourceElement	IN	This is the resource element that should be updated
newTextContent	String	IN	This is the new text content

2. Add a scripting task to the schema and bind all variables.

3. Add the following script:

```
//prepare for update
var attachment = new MimeAttachment() ;
//set new content
attachment.content = newTextContent;
//use old settings
attachment.name = resource.name;
attachment.mimeType = resource.mimeType;
//update
resource.setContentFromMimeAttachment(attachment);
//overwrite the description
resource.description="Updated";
```

4. Save and run the workflow.

When you run the workflow, select a resource to update, preferably one you have created before. After the workflow has finished, check the resource and its content.

How it works...

Resource elements have many uses. First of all, you can use a small picture as an icon for Orchestrator workflows. Secondly, you can use them to send e-mail attachments (see the recipe *Working with mails* in Chapter 9, *Essential Plugins*). There is also a method of storing information as a resource element. Orchestrator uses this method to store the configuration for the SOAP, REST, and multi-node plug-ins. The stored information is the configuration for each SOAP, REST, or Orchestrator server. Go have a look!

Last but not least, you can use the resource elements to store templates. For example, you can store a text template for an e-mail you want to send to customers. You can write variables in the text such as "Dear {name}..." and use the string method replace to substitute the variables before sending the e-mail, for example ResourceContent.replace("{name}", sendToName);. Have a look at the workflows stored under Daniels Toolbox/CoolMail

Any kind of file can be used as a resource element, but typically one uses XML, plain text, or pictures as resource elements.

There's more...

You can do more with resources. Some examples follow.

Accessing resources directly

You don't need to actually add a resource as an attribute to a workflow to access it: you can access them directly.

You can get all existing resource element categories with `Server.getAllResourceElementCategories()`. To get resource elements from a given category, use `ResourceElementCategory.resourceElements`. Use `ResourceElementCategory.subCategories` to get all sub categories from a given category.

The following little script lets you find a resource by its name. It loops through all resource folders and all resource elements:

```
allresource=Server.getAllResourceElementCategories();
for each (category in allresource) {
    for each (resource in category.resourceElements){
        if (resource.name == name ){
            System.log("Found: " + name);
        }
    }
}
```

Deleting a resource

You can delete a resource by using:

```
Server.removeResourceElement(attachment);
```

See also

The following are some example workflows:

- `08.01.1 Use Resources`
- `08.01.2 Create Resources (mime)`
- `08.01.3 Create Resource (file)`
- `08.01.4 Access Resources directly`

- 08.01.5 get resource from name

Working with configurations

In this recipe, we will see how configurations can improve our design. Configurations are like global variables that are centrally defined and can be used by all workflows.

Getting ready

We just need a working Orchestrator, and you will need the rights to create new workflows and run them. We will work with the Orchestrator Client.

We will use the example workflow 05.05 Workflow Presentation to test the configuration.

How to do it…

We will split the recipe in two sections, creating and using a configuration.

Creating a configuration

1. Using the Orchestrator Client in **Design** mode, click on **Configurations** (the white paper with a gear icon).
2. Right-click on the root and create a new folder. Give the folder a name. It's always a good idea to use new folders.
3. Right-click on the new folder and select **New element**. Give the new element a name. The new configuration opens up in edit mode. Click on **Attributes**.
4. Now, we can create new variables as we used to in a normal workflow. Create the following variables:

Name	Type	Value(s)	Use
selectionList	Array of String	First, Second, Third	This represents a selection list
passwordLength	Number	8	This limits the number of letters that can be entered

5. Click on**Save and Close**.

Using a configuration in a workflow

We will now make use of the variables we created in the configuration:

1. Using the Orchestrator Client, either make a duplicate of the example workflow `05.05 Workflow Presentation` or edit it.

2. In the **General** tab, click on the **selection** attribute and click on the two blue arrows right next to value (see the following screenshot).

3. In the window that pops up, you will find all the configurations that Orchestrator knows; click on the one you have created.

4. You now see all the variables that you have defined in this configuration; please note that only the ones that match the current type are black and selectable, all others are grayed out.

5. Select the array of strings and click on **Select**. See how the value of the attribute has changed and that it now points to the configuration.

6. Link the length attribute to the configuration element of the same name.

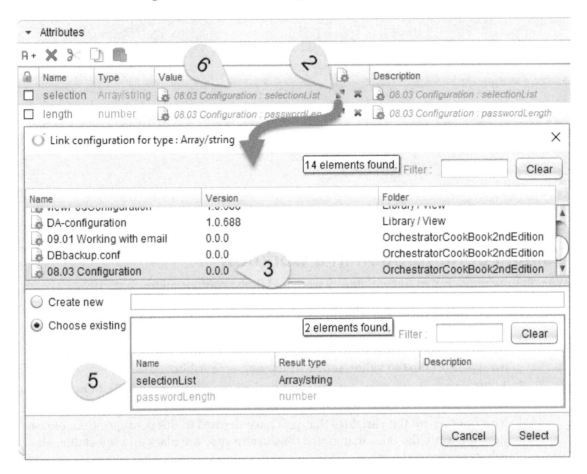

7. You are now able to use the values from the configuration inside the workflow. Give it a go.

How it works...

A configuration is what programmers would call a global variable. A global variable is a centrally-stored variable that is accessible to all workflows. Configurations are commonly used to define global objects, for example, the FQDN and credentials of a mail server or general password policies.

Let's look at a typical example for the use of configurations. You have a Development environment and a Production environment. In each environment, you have different vCenters, mail servers, and so on. You develop your workflows in Development and then use them in Production. Using configurations, you can point the workflow to different configurations that are stored in Development or Production Orchestrator.

Another example is to reduce the number of inputs a workflow requires by pushing the variables to configurations and binding them to attributes. We will explore this in the recipes in `Chapter 12`, *Working with vSphere*. Last but not least, you can use configuration to share the same variables between different workflows, such as mail server configurations.

To integrate a configuration into a workflow you have to link an attribute to the configuration variable. The variables have to be of the same type. After you have integrated the configuration attribute into the workflow, you can use it to not only pass information along (such as credentials or common server names) but also link presentation properties (such as predefined values to reduce the possible selections). We will explore this in the recipe *An approval process for VM provisioning* in `Chapter 12`, *Working with vSphere*.

You can also create new attributes in a configuration from a workflow. You have probably noticed the **Create New** selection in the **Link Configuration** window.

Please note that a configuration also has a history like the workflows do; see the recipe *Version control* in `Chapter 4`, *Programming Skills* for more information.

There's more...

You can use JavaScript to read and write configuration values. The scripting classes are as follows:

- ConfigurationElement
- ConfigurationElementCategory
- Attribute

To read a configuration, you can use this:

```
attrib=configurationElement.getAttributeWithKey(Key);
```

Here, `Key` is a string, which contains the name of the attribute. The return value is of the `Attribute` type.

To set a configuration attribute, use this:

```
configurationElement.setAttributeWithKey(Key, Value);
```

Here, `Key` is a string that contains the name of the attribute and `Value` is the value you would like to set it to.

See also

The example workflows:

- `08.03.1 Using Configuration`
- `08.03.2 read and write configurations`

Working with Orchestrator tags

Let's explore the tagging of workflows. Tagging introduces the same kind of tagging you're familiar with from vCenter server. Tagging allows you to add tags to Orchestrator objects and search for them.

Getting ready

We need some elements such as a workflow or action we can tag.

How to do it...

Tagging involves the following procedures.

Tagging an element (manual)

Let's start by tagging a workflow manually.

1. Open a workflow for editing.
2. Go to the **General** tab and click on the **[Type here to add a tag...]**.
3. Type a tag name such as `glbTest` and then press *Enter*.
4. Next, we are adding a tag with a value. Enter another tag such as `author`, then press *Ctrl + S* and then enter the value for the tag, such as `Daniel`.

5. Click on **Save and close**.

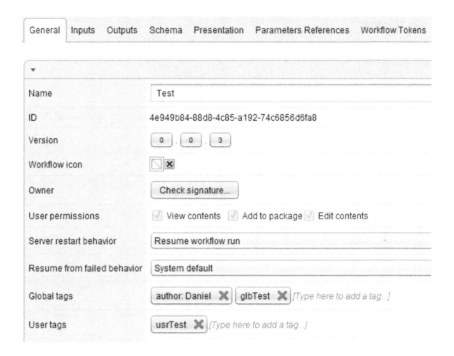

Tagging a workflow (workflow)

You can tag a workflow using a workflow.

1. Start the workflow by navigating to **Library** I **Tagging** I **Tag workflow**.
2. Select the workflow you would like to tag.
3. Enter a tag and a value.

4. Select whether you would like this tag to be global or not. A **Global tag** is visible to all users, whereas non-global (private) tags are only visible to the user who places the tag:

5. Submit the workflow.

Viewing all tags in a workflow

1. Start the workflow by navigating to **Library** | **Tagging** | **List Workflow tags**.
2. Select the workflow for which you would like to see a list of all its tags.
3. After submitting the workflow, check the logs. All tags and their values will be listed:

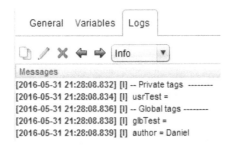

Finding workflows by tag

1. Start the workflow by navigating to **Library** | **Tagging** | **Find objects by tag**.
2. Enter only a tag or a tag and its value.
3. Select whether this tag is global or private and submit the workflow.
4. The output is an array of workflows:

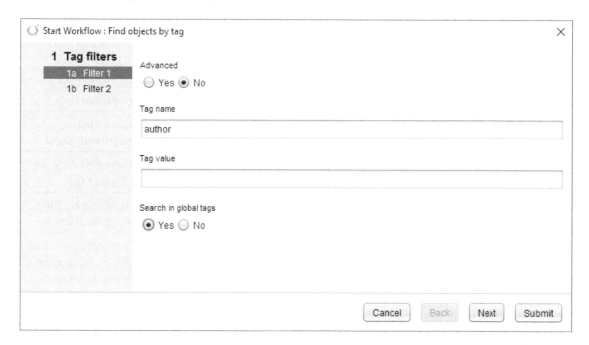

How it works...

Tags have been integrated into Orchestrator since 5.5.1. There are two types of tags: global tags and private tags. A global tag is visible to all users whereas non-global (private) tags are only visible to the user who places the tag.

> Tags can be used on workflows, actions, resources, configurations, packages, policy templates, and you can add them to inventory elements.

Tags are not stored with the workflows. Importing and exporting a workflow to a different Orchestrator will not preserve the tags; however, several websites state that this is the case.

There's more...

The JavaScript behind the tags is straightforward:

JavaScript tags	Function
`Server.tagGlobally(taggedObject,tagName,tagValue );`	This allows tagging an object with a global tag.
`Server.tag(taggedObject,tagName,tagValue);`	This allows tagging an object with a private tag.
`Server.findGlobalTagsForObject(taggedObject);`	This allows listing an object's global tags.
`Server.findTagsForObject(taggedObject);`	This allows listing an object's private tags.
`Server.queryByTags(tagQuery,null);`	This allows finding an object by its tags.
`Server.untagGlobally(taggedObject,tags);`	This allows untagging a global tag from an object.
`Server.untag(taggedObject,tags);`	This allows untagging a private tag from an object.

See also

For using vCenter tags see recipe *Custom Attributes and Tags (vAPI)* in `Chapter 12`, *Working with vSphere*.

Using the Locking System

Here we will have a look at the **Locking System**. We will learn how to lock and unlock objects using locks. Locks are used to make sure objects are only used by one owner.

Getting ready

The Locking System doesn't need anything, as it itself is just virtual.

How to do it...

There are three phases to locking: locking, checking and unlocking.

Create a lock

We will now create a lock:

1. Create a new workflow and add a scriptable task.
2. Add the following variables as input:

Name	Type	Section	Use
object	String	IN	Any string
owner	String	IN	Any string

3. Enter the following script:

```
LockingSystem.lockAndWait(object ,owner);
```

4. Add the workflow **Display all Locks** at the end.
5. Save and run the workflow. Enter as object any string, such as Test and as owner or any other string such as Goofy.
6. Check the logs.

Check for lock

We will now check if an object is locked:

1. Create a new workflow and add a scriptable task.
2. Add the following variables as input:

Name	Type	Section	Use
object	String	IN	Any string

owner	String	IN	Any string
newLock	Boolean	OUT	True if a new lock should be acquired

3. Enter the following script:

```
newLock=LockingSystem.lock(object ,owner);
```

4. Save and run the workflow. Enter as **object** the string from the first workflow and, as owner, any string you like.

5. Check the output, it should be **false** as the workflow is still locked from the first run.

Unlock

We will now unlock a locked object:

1. Create a new workflow and add a scriptable task.

2. Add the following variables as input:

Name	Type	Section	Use
object	String	IN	Any string
owner	String	IN	Any string

3. Enter the following script:

```
LockingSystem.unlock(object ,owner);
```

4. Add the workflow **Display all Locks** before and after the scriptable task.

5. Save and run the workflow. Enter as object the string from the first workflow and the owner from the first workflow.

6. Check the logs.

How it works...

Orchestrator has an internal locking mechanism. It enables you to lock a virtual object, basically, a string. You set a lock with `LockingSystem.lock(object, owner)`. Using the `LockingSystem.lockAndWait(object, owner)` method with the same `object` string will pause the workflow until the `object` is unlocked with `LockingSystem.unlock(object, owner)`.

Please note that the object isn't really locked; only a lock entry is set. The lock is just a flag and nothing else. If you want to use the Locking System, you will need to check for the locking entry. You can check all locking entries with `LockingSystem.retrieveAll()`, which returns an array of strings where each string represents `object,owner`. You can release all locks with `LockingSystem.unlockAll()`. In the example packages, there are three examples of how to use the Locking System.

Have a look at the example workflows `08.02.4 Locktest (RUN ME)` and `08.02.5 secondary locker`, which show how the locking works.

A very important point to note here is that you have to make sure your workflow handles errors (in the workflow) well. You could end up in a situation where you lock a resource and the workflow locking it terminates on error and does not release the log. Have a look at Try-catch-finally in the recipe *JavaScript special statements* in `Chapter 6`, *Advanced Programming*.

See also

For locking elements in the Orchestrator Client, see the recipe *Locking elements* in `Chapter 4`, *Programming Skills*.

The following are some example workflows:

- `08.02.1 Lock`
- `08.02.2 Check for Lock`
- `08.02.3 unlock`
- `08.02.4 Locktest (RUN ME)`
- `08.02.5 secondary locker`

Language packs (localization)

This recipe will look into the possibility of creating localized language packs for workflows. Localization enables users to see workflow presentations in their local language.

Getting ready

We just need an Orchestrator and the ability to edit text files. Additionally, you might want to know a foreign language (or use Google Translate).

How to do it...

We will now create a language pack for the example workflow `00.00 BasicWorkflow`:

1. Navigate to the workflow you want to create localization on.
2. Right-click on the workflow and navigate to **Localization | create localization resources**.
3. Navigate to the Orchestrator resources. You will notice that new `ResourceElementCategory` folders have been created along with `ResourceElements` for English, Japanese, French, German, and Korean:

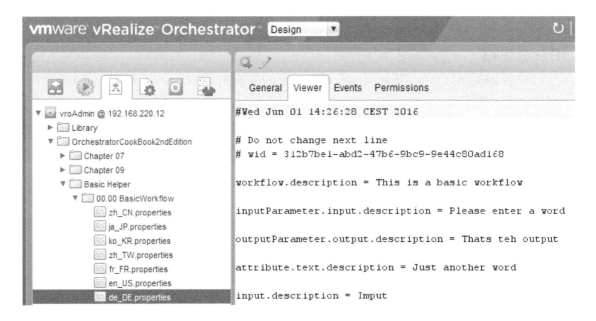

4. Right-click on the workflow again, navigate to **Localization** | **export localization bundle**, and save it onto a local file.

5. Switch to your local filesystem and unzip the localization bundle.

6. Edit one of the language files and replace the text with a local language.

7. Re-zip the file and then upload the bundle by right-clicking on the workflow and navigating to **Localization** | **import localization bundle**.

8. Check ResourceElement to see the updates.

9. To check the result, switch the language of a web browser to the language you have specified, for example, de-DE (not just de). Please note that this is case-sensitive. If you are using a German system, you may want to try English instead.

10. Now start vSphere Web Client and then the workflow (see the recipe *Using Orchestrator through the vSphere Web Client* in Chapter 7, *Interacting with Orchestrator*):

How it works...

Localization works with any application that pulls the REST API using an Accept-Language header to transport the language code, such as de-DE. Orchestrator Client doesn't support this feature.

vRealize Automation (**vRA**) supports localization from version 6.2 onwards.

Working with policies

In this recipe, we will look into policies. We will learn how to create and use policies to react automatically to events that occur outside Orchestrator.

Getting ready

For this recipe, we need something that we can monitor for events. We have a look at policies with the recipes *Working with SNMP* and *Working with AMQP* in `Chapter 10`, *Built-in Plugins*.

In this example, we will monitor objects in the vCenter server.

How to do it...

We will create a simple policy that will monitor a VM by performing the following steps:

1. In the Orchestrator Client, switch to the **Run** mode and click on **Policies**.
2. Click on **Create a new Policy** (the icon that looks like a scroll with a plus sign).
3. After you give the policy a name, you will find a new policy in the policy list. Right-click the policy you have created and select **Edit** (the pencil icon):

4. In the **General** tab under **Startup**, choose whether the policy should be started with the Orchestrator service or not. This is used when Orchestrator is powered down and you want to start the policy with an Orchestrator server start.

5. **Priority** regulates how multiple policies determine priorities about each other.

6. The credentials under **Startup user** are used to run the policy:

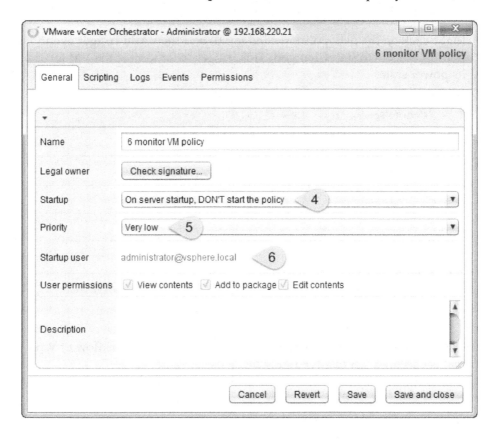

7. Switch to the **Scripting** tab.
8. Click on the top element (scroll icon) and then select **Add policy element** (scroll down; you will see an icon with a plus sign).
9. Select a policy element (choose **VC:VirtualMachine**) and click on **OK**. Then, select a VM that you would like to monitor (I selected a VM called **OrchestratorVM** which is just a plain VM, not the Orchestrator itself).

10. Right-click on the new policy (called tag-0) and then **Add trigger event**. From the pop-up, select **OnStateChanged**. This trigger will monitor the VM for changes in its power state.

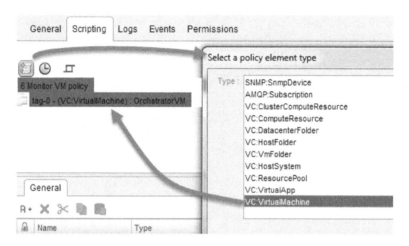

11. Click on the **OnStateChanged** trigger and then select a workflow or write a script that is executed. I wrote the following script:

```
System.log("VM changed state");
```

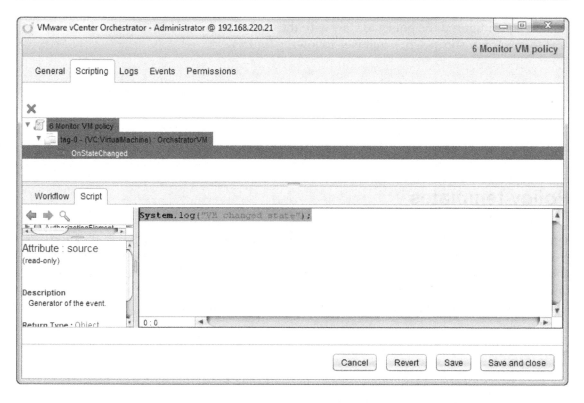

12. Click on **Save and close**.
13. Now start the policy by clicking on the play button. Go to vCenter server and start or stop the VM you are monitoring. If you have used the same script as mine, you should see a message.

How it works...

Policies are constant monitoring programs that check whether a monitored event has been triggered. The VMware documentation about policies is really nonexistent. You will find some more information regarding policies in the upcoming sections.

As a supplement to this recipe, have a look at the recipes *Working with SNMP* and *Working with AMQP* in `Chapter 10`, *Built-in Plugins*. In these recipes, we use policies.

When you configured the policy to start with the Orchestrator server, then the check box next to the policy shows a tick in it (see following figure):

Policy templates

Let's start by defining the difference between polices and policy templates. If you repeat the same recipe as described earlier, under the **Policy Templates** tab you will find that you won't be able to define which VM you would like to monitor. This is what templates are about; you define the raw layout, triggers, and script, and so on. If you then want to apply the template, you can choose **Apply Policy** (scroll down, you will see a green right arrow icon) from either the template in the **Template** tab or the **Policy** tab.

Triggers

Triggers are implemented by plugins and can be used to build policies. There are three basic elements that can be added to policies:

Icon	Name	Function
	Policy Element	This monitors an element such as a VM or SNMP device.
	Periodic Task	This is a workflow or script that will be executed on a given timescale.
	Trigger	This is a trigger that starts a script or workflow.

Each element can have special triggers. A trigger can either start a workflow or run a script, but not both. In the following tables, you will find detailed information on which trigger is available with what element. The OnInit and OnExit triggers can be added to any element. The OnInit and OnExit triggers are actually quite important, for example, when you need to write a script that checks whether all conditions that the policy requires (such as whether an AMQP queue exists or a VM exists) are met:

Element	Trigger element	Threshold
Periodic task	OnExecute	N/A
SNMP:SnmpDevice	OnTrap	N/A
AMQP:Subscription	OnMessage	N/A
VC:ClusterComputerResource	OnOverallStatusChanged	N/A
VC:ComputerResource	OnOverallStatusChanged	N/A
VC:DatacenterFolder	OnOverallStatusChanged	N/A
VC:HostFolder	OnOverallStatusChanged	N/A
VC:VmFolder	OnOverallStatusChanged	N/A
VC:HostSystem	OnOverallStatusChanged OnConnectionStateChanged OnInMaintenanceModeChange	NumMksConnections RealtimeCpuUsage RealtimeMemoryUsage RealtimeDiskUsage RealtimeNetworkUsage
VC:ResourcePool	OnOverallStatusChanged	N/A
VC:VirtualApp	OnOverallStatusChanged	N/A
VC:VirtualMachine	OnOverallStatusChanged OnStateChanged OnConnectionStateChanged	NumMksConnections RealtimeCpuUsage RealtimeMemoryUsage RealtimeDiskUsage RealtimeNetworkUsage

Here is an explanation of all triggers:

Trigger	Meaning
OnInit	This is triggered when the policy is started.
OnExit	This is triggered when a policy is stopped.
OnExecute	This is triggered when a periodic task is triggered.
OnTrap	This is triggered when a new SNMP message is trapped.
OnMessage	This is triggered when a new AMQP message is in the queue.
OnOverallStatusChanged	This is triggered when the health of the object changes.

OnConnectionStateChanged	This is triggered when a VM/host is not available for management; for example, VM is disconnected due to ESXi failure or a host is switched off.
OnInMaintenanceModeChange	This is triggered when a host is entering/exiting the maintenance mode.
OnStateChanged	This is triggered when the power state of a VM changes.
NumMksConnections	This is triggered when the amount of console session towards a VM/host is below or above a set value.
RealtimeXXXUsage	This is triggered when a CPU, memory, disk, or network is below or above a set value; all values are in percentages.

The event variable

The event variable is almost un-documented and any information is hard to find. The following are the known event properties and methods:

Variable	Function
event.when	Gets the date as a number.
event.source	An object that contains the source of the event.
event.getValue("agent")	Receives the SNMP source.
event.getValue("key")	Retrieves the SNMP message.
self.retrieveMessage(event)	Retrieves an AMQP message.

See also

See the recipes *Working with SNMP* and *Working with AMQP* in Chapter 10, *Built-in Plugins*.

9
Essential Plugins

In this recipe, we are looking at essential plugins that are often used. We will be looking at the following plugins:

- Working with e-mail
- File operations
- Working with SSH
- Working with REST

Introduction

These plugins are just normal plugins that are used regularly (well…at least by me). All the plugins shown in this recipe will add a lot of possibilities in your programming kit bag.

Let's have a look at an example: You have a workflow that deploys a VM and after it is finished you would like to send an acknowledgment e-mail to a user and a CSV file to a **CMDB (Content Management Database)**.

Another example would be current or legacy systems that have an SSH interface but no API or plug-in available. The SSH plug-in could be used to SCP files/scripts to and from the target system, automatically backup configurations, or apply approved configurations.

Working with e-mail

In this recipe, we will learn how to interact with e-mails and discuss configuring, sending, and receiving e-mails with Orchestrator. We will discuss both e-mail objects that the API currently has.

Getting ready

Unsurprisingly, we need an e-mail server. If you don't have one handy, you can use **hMailServer** for Windows; refer to the *There's more...* section of this recipe to learn how to install and configure this free, open source e-mail server.

For this recipe, we will use IMAP and SMTP to connect to the e-mail server. In the *How it works...* section, we also take a quick look at POP3 and SSL. We will also need two e-mail addresses. In our example, we will use vcotest@mylab.local and vcotest2@mylab.local.

There are two API objects that can be used when working with e-mail: the MailClient object and the EmailMessage object. We will use EmailMessage to send messages and MailClient to receive e-mail.

How to do it...

We will break this recipe down into configuration and sending/receiving e-mail.

Configuring the e-mail connection

As you probably need e-mail a lot in all your Orchestrator workflows, it's a good idea to store all the necessary e-mail configuration information in a configuration, as shown in the recipe *Working with configurations* in Chapter 8, *Better Workflows and Optimized Working*. Follow these steps to prepare the information you need to interact with a e-mail server:

1. Create a new configuration.
2. Create the following items:

Variable name	Type	Description
mailHost	String	The IP or FQDN of the e-mail server.
mailUser	String	The username that is needed to access the e-mail account (it's the e-mail in the case of hMail).
mailPass	SecureString	The password for the user account.
smtpPort	Number	The TCP port that should be used (the default port is TCP 25).
SmtpFromName	String	A string that identifies the sender, for example, the full name of the user.
smtpFromMail	String	The e-mail address of the sender.
receiveProtocol	String	The protocol used, either POP3 or IMAP.

You can now use this configuration in workflows, as shown in the recipe *Working with configurations* in `Chapter 8`, *Better Workflows and Optimized Working*.

Sending e-mails

To send e-mails, there is a ready-made workflow that we can use by navigating to **Library | Mail | Send notification**. However, we will create a new one to understand the code and API a bit better:

1. Create a new workflow and create the following variables (and if you did the configuration, link the values to your configuration):

Variable name	Section	Type	Description
mailTo	IN	String	The e-mail address the e-mail should go to.
mailCC	IN	String	The e-mail address that should be sent to CC (carbon copy).
mailBCC	IN	String	The e-mail address that should be sent to BCC (blind carbon copy); the BCC e-mail address is not disclosed to other e-mail recipients.
mailSubject	IN	String	The subject of the e-mail.
mailContent	IN	String	The text content you want to send.
mailHost	Attribute	String	The link with the corresponding configuration attribute.

`mailUser`	Attribute	String	The link with the corresponding configuration attribute.
`mailPass`	Attribute	SecureString	The link with the corresponding configuration attribute.
`smtpPort`	Attribute	Number	The link with the corresponding configuration attribute.
`smtpFromName`	Attribute	String	The link with the corresponding configuration attribute.
`smtpFromMail`	Attribute	String	The link with the corresponding configuration attribute.

2. Add a scriptable task to the schema and enter the following code:

```
//Create a message object
    var message = new EmailMessage();
// set connections parameters
    message.smtpHost = mailHost;
    message.smtpPort = smtpPort;
    message.username = mailUser;
    message.password = mailPass;
    message.fromName = smtpFromName;
    message.fromAddress = smtpFromMail;
//Set email specific information
    message.toAddress = mailTo;
    message.ccAddress = mailCC;
    message.bccAddress = mailBCC;
// the subject of the message
    message.subject = mailSubject;
// the mail content, message type and the character
    set
    message.addMimePart(mailContent,"text/html;
       charset=UTF-8");
// send the message
    message.sendMessage();
```

3. Save and run the workflow.

You can now use this workflow to send e-mails.

Receiving e-mails

There are already two workflows to receive e-mails by navigating to **Library** | **Mail**: **Retrieve messages** and **Retrieve messages (via MailClient)**. The problem with them is that they don't have any output that we can use and therefore, they are quite useless to anyone who wants to use e-mails to check for content. In this example, we will use the more powerful `MailClient` object to create a workflow that receives e-mail and outputs the important parts of an e-mail.

1. Create a new workflow and define the following variables; link them to the configuration from the first part, as required:

Variable name	Section	Type	Description
mailHost	Attribute	String	Link with the configuration.
receiveProtocol	Attribute	String	Link with the configuration.
mailUsername	Attribute	String	Link with the configuration.
mailPassword	Attribute	SecureString	Link with the configuration.
deleteMail	IN	Boolean	Should the messages be deleted?
outMail	OUT	Array of properties	The output array for messages.

2. Add a scriptable task and bind all the variables to it.
3. Enter the following script:

```
// initialize array
var outMail = new Array ();
// initialize Property
var mail = new Properties();
//mail constructor
var myMailClient = new MailClient();
//get the default port for the protocol
var mailPort=System.getModule("com.vmware.library.mail").
getDefaultPort(receiveProtocol)
myMailClient.setProtocol(receiveProtocol);
// connect to mail server
myMailClient.connect( mailHost, mailPort, mailUsername,
mailPassword);
//open the inbox
myMailClient.openFolder("Inbox");
// get messages
var messages = myMailClient.getMessages();
//if there are any messages loop thought them
```

```
        if ( messages != null && messages.length > 0 ) {
            for (i = 0; i < messages.length; i++) {
    //get the mail details and write them into a property
                var mail = new Properties();
                mail.put("from",messages[i].from);
                mail.put("date",messages[i].getSentDate());
                mail.put("subject",messages[i].subject);
                mail.put("content",messages[i].getContent());
                // push Properties into array.
                outMail.push(mail);
                //delete messages if this was chosen
                if (deleteMail) {
                    messages[i].delete();
                }
            }
        } else {
            System.warn( "No messages found" );
        }
        // Close mail connection
        myMailClient.closeFolder();
        myMailClient.close();
```

4. Save and run the workflow.

This workflow will output one array, with these property keys: from, date, subject, and content. Refer to the introduction to this chapter to learn how to access the output of this workflow.

Check out the recipe *Working with XML* in Chapter 10, *Built-in Plugins* to change the output of this workflow to XML.

How it works...

E-mail can quickly become a really important addition to Orchestrator. Just think about the possibilities of sending e-mail to users after a task has been successfully finished (or not) or for sending a report of some sort.

In Orchestrator, the Mail.EmailMessage object is responsible for sending e-mails; to receive or work with e-mails, there are actually three objects: Mail.MailClient, Net.POP3Client, and Net.IMAPClient.

Remember that e-mail uses HTML, which can be attractively formatted.

`Mail.MailClient` is the more powerful of the objects for reading e-mails as it comes with a lot of types and methods centered around e-mails that can be useful, such as extracting attachments or using different e-mail folders. The other two objects are more rudimentary and more directed at either POP3 or IMAP. For more information, I would suggest that you check out the API and look for the available attributes and methods that they contain.

The receive workflow that we have created in the recipe isn't very sophisticated, but it lets you build a workflow that extracts all e-mails so that you can check for specific content. Take a look at the example workflow `05.04.3 DoWhile loop` to see how it can be used.

Working with attachments

Sending an attachment is more or less easy; we will showcase it by uploading the attachment as an Orchestrator resource. We covered how to work with resources in the *Working with resources* recipe in `Chapter 8`, *Better Workflows and Optimized Working*.

the following example attaches a picture to e-mail. There is also another example workflow in the example pack that lets you attach any file from the local Orchestrator to an e-mail: `09.01.5 SendAttachment(File)`.

1. You will need to add the following variable to the send the workflow:

Name	Type	Section	Use
attachment	ResourceElement	IN	Contains the Orchestrator resource for the attachment

2. Add the following code to the send script:

```
message.addMimePart(attachment.getContentAsMimeAttachment());
```

In order to fetch an attachment from an e-mail, we need to have a much closer look at how the `MailClient` object works. Each e-mail can have multiple content parts, such as attachments and text. To check whether a message contains more than one part, use the `MailClient.isContentMultiPart()` method; it returns either true or false. To get all the parts, use the following:

```
var multiPartContent = message.getMultiPartContent();
```

This will return an array (`multiPartContent`). Now we need to look into each of the parts by looping through them. We get a single part by using the following :

```
var bodyPart = multiPartContent.getBodyPart(counter);
```

To know whether the body part is an attachment, check `bodyPart.isAttachment()`. To fetch the attachment, use the following :

```
var attachment = bodyPart.getAsMimeAttachment();
```

You now have the attachment as a mime type. Refer to the *Working with resources* recipe in `Chapter 8`, *Better Workflows and Optimized Working*.

To get the mime type of the attachment, use `attachment.mimeType`; to get the name, use `attachment.name`.

There's more...

A fast and pretty easy way to configure the e-mail server is the open source hMailServer, which you can download from `www.hmailserver.com`.

Creating a non-relaying, local-only e-mail server is pretty straightforward. I will not waste too much page space on this, so there are no screenshots. The following steps let you create a e-mail server and e-mail addresses that are configured for SMTP, POP3, and IMAP:

1. In Windows, download hMail and start the installer.
2. Make sure that SMTP (`TCP 25`), POP3 (`TCP 110`), and IMAP (`TCP 143`) can pass through the Windows firewall.
3. Select a folder where you would like to place the program binaries (this is not the place where the e-mails will end up; hMail needs less than 15 MB disk space).
4. Install **Server** and **Administrator tools**.
5. You can now choose to use an external DB (MSSQL, MySQL, or PostgreSQL) or the Microsoft SQL Server Compact Edition (2 MB installation size) shipped with hMail (use the compact edition for the lab).
6. You are now asked whether you would like to create a shortcut (recommended for the lab).
7. Set a password for the admin access of hMail.
8. After the installation is finished, run **Administrator tools**.
9. Connect to the localhost e-mail server and enter the admin password from step 7.
10. After the administrator console opens, click on **Domains** and then click on **Add**.

11. In the **Domain** field under **General**, enter your domain name and click on **Save**.
12. Your domain is now created. Click on your domain, then click on **Accounts**, and then click on **Add**.
13. To create an e-mail address, just fill in the name of the account by navigating to **General | Address** and give it a password. Adjust **Maximum size (MB)** to 10 MB (we will just use some text e-mail). Finally, click on **Save**.

That's it. Now you can play with this recipe.

See also

See the `CoolMail` folder in `Daniels Toolsbox` in the example package a for an example of a way to send HTML e-mail.

The example workflows are:

- `09.01.1 SendMail`
- `09.01.2 getMail`
- `09.01.3 getMail(XML)`
- `09.01.4 SendAttachment(Resource)`
- `09.01.5 SendAttachment(File)`

File operations

Here we will explore how Orchestrator can interact with the filesystem of its operating system. We will also take a look at how to access a network share and execute local files.

Getting ready

Orchestrator needs to be able to access a directory on the local filesystem. To configure this access and set the access rights, take a look at the *Configuring access to the local filesystem* recipe in `Chapter 2`, *Optimizing Orchestrator Configuration*.

In my example, I will simply use the default Orchestrator file location that is set to `rwx` the directory `/var/run/vco/`.

In addition to this, you should have administrative (root) access to Orchestrator's operating system.

How to do it...

We have a bit of ground to cover, so let's start!

Writing a file

This part showcases how to write into a file with, and without, a line feed as well as how to append to an existing file:

1. Create a new workflow and create the following variables:

Name	Type	Section	Use
fileName	String	IN	The name of the file, including its path
fileContent	Sting	IN	Some random content

2. Add a scriptable task to the schema and enter the following script:

```
//FileWriter constructor
var myFileWriter = new FileWriter(fileName);
//open the file for writing
myFileWriter.open();
//Empties existing file. Without it we append
myFileWriter.clean();
//write a line into the file
myFileWriter.writeLine(fileContent);
//write without line feed
myFileWriter.write(fileContent);
myFileWriter.write(" -:- ");
myFileWriter.write(fileContent);
//write line feed
myFileWriter.write("\n");
//Close the file
myFileWriter.close();
```

3. Run the workflow and check the result; you should have a file that contains something like this:

```
Test
Test -:- Test
```

If the `clean` method is not used when opening an existing file, it will be opened for appending. Try it!

Reading a file

This part showcases how to read a file fully and line-by-line.

1. Create a new workflow and create the following variables:

Name	Type	Section	Use
fileName	String	IN	The name of the file, including its path.

2. Add a scriptable task to the schema and enter the following script:

```
//File reader constructor
var myFileReader = new FileReader(fileName);
// check if the file actually exists
if (myFileReader.exists){
//Open the file
    myFileReader.open();
//read everything
    System.log(myFileReader.readAll());
// Close the file (undocumented in API).
    myFileReader.close();
    System.log("---------------------");
//read line by line until the file is empty
    myFileReader.open();
    do{
        temp=myFileReader.readLine();
        System.log(temp);
    } while(temp!=null);
    myFileReader.close();
}
```

3. Run the workflow and check the logs.

Getting information on files

This section showcases how to access information about a directory or file:

1. Create a new workflow and create the following variables:

Name	Type	Section	Use
directory	String	IN	The name of the file, including its path.

2. Add a scriptable task to the schema and enter the following script:

```
//File constructor
var myDir = new File(directory);
//Does the file or directory exist and is it a directory?
if (myDir.exists && myDir.isDir){
    System.log("This is a directory. It Contains:");
//list the content of the directory, returns an array of Strings
    for each (fileInDir in myDir.list()) {
//read file properties. Cause its strings we need to make them files
first
            var temp = new File(fileInDir);
            System.log("FileName: "+ temp.name);
            System.log("Path: "+ temp.path);
            System.log("Directory: "+ temp.directory);
            System.log("FileExtention: "+ temp.extension);
            System.log("Readable: "+ temp.canRead())
            System.log("Writeable: "+ temp.canWrite());
    } //end of Foreach
}//end of ifexists and isdir
```

3. Run the workflow and enter a directory (such as /var/run/vco). Check the logs.

Creating, renaming, and deleting a file or directory

We now showcase how to create an empty file, rename it, and then delete it:

1. Create a new workflow and create the following variables:

Name	Type	Section	Use
directory	String	IN	The name of the file, including its path.

2. Add a scriptable task to the schema and enter the following script:

```
//File Constructor
var myDir = new File(directory);
//is it a Directory
if (myDir.isDir){
    //create a new File Constructor
    var newFile = new File(Directory+"/TempFile");
    //create an empty file
    newFile.createFile();
    //Show directory
    System.log(myDir.list());
    //Rename the file
    newFile.renameTo(Directory+"/RenamedFile")
    //Show directory
    System.log(myDir.list());
    // new constructor as the file name has changed
    var renamedFile = new File(Directory+"/RenamedFile");
    //Delete the File
renamedFile.deleteFile();
//Show directory
    System.log(myDir.list());
}
```

3. Run the workflow and supply a directory. A file will be created, renamed, and deleted.

If you want to create a directory, use the `createDirectory` method. To rename and delete a directory, the `renameTo` and `deleteFile` methods are used, just as we have seen earlier with a file.

How it works...

As you can see, file operations are quite easy and straightforward. They come in handy if you want to save or load XML or CSV content or anything else, for that matter.

Please note that Orchestrator regards a file and a directory the same when it comes to methods.

If you want to use a file to write logs, there is a special scripting class called `LogFileWriter`. However, it is not much different from the `FileWriter` class.

Directory dividers are different in Linux and Windows. Where Windows uses a backslash (\), Linux uses a forward-slash (/). However, when we deal with file paths in Orchestrator, we use only the forward-slash.

Executing scripts

You can execute scripts from the local OS using Orchestrator. To do that, Orchestrator needs access (x) to the folder where the script is located and the Orchestrator user needs to be able to read and execute (rx) it. You also need to allow Orchestrator to execute local files; see the *System properties* section in the *Control Center titbits* recipe in Chapter 2, *Optimizing Orchestrator Configuration*. Here is an example script that will execute the file script.bat:

```
//prepare command
var command = new Command("c:/var/run/vco/script.bat");
//execute the command
command.execute(true);
//get the return code
var returnCode = command.result;
//get the output of the command
var returnOutput = command.output;
```

Please note that the script needs to be in a file location that Orchestrator can access and that Orchestrator will run as user vco with the group vco.

Shared directories

You can use the file writer to write to a shared directory. Check out the *Configuring access to the local filesystem* recipe in Chapter 2, *Optimizing Orchestrator Configuration*.

This is especially important in a clustered Orchestrator environment where storing local files isn't a good solution. You should use NFS or SMB shares; see the *Configuring access to the local filesystem* recipe in Chapter 2, *Optimizing Orchestrator Configuration*.

There's more...

The following points are worth knowing.

CSV files

Comma separated files are quite good for transferring data. For example, you could create a CSV in /var/run/vco and then send it as a e-mail attachment. Here is an example:

```
var myFileWriter = new FileWriter(filename);
myFileWriter.open();
//CSV header
header="VMname,Memory,CPU";
myFileWriter.writeLine(header);
//one line per VM
for each (vm in vms) {
    line=vmName+","+vmMemory+","+vmCPU;
    myFileWriter.writeLine(line);
}
myFileWriter.close();
```

Doing things as root

If you need to execute a command as root, or any other operation that requires you to use root, here are some ideas on how to do it:

- Use SSH with an SSL key to login to 127.0.0.1, as shown in the example workflow 02.01 Tuning the Appliance
- Change /etc/sudoers and add vco ALL=(ALL) NOPASSWD:ALL, which will add vco to the sudoer list and doesn't need a password. You the run commands with sudo [command]
- Add vco to the root group

All of these methods are more or less problematic. With opening SSH and root, you open up a potential attack vector. Using sudoers, you will need to make sure the setting stays after Orchestrator updates. Adding vco to root is the same or worse; it makes it possible for Orchestrator to take over your Linux system, meaning Orchestrator users could alter the local Linux system or even break into other systems.

See also

The example workflows are:

- 09.02.1 Write a File
- 09.02.2 Read a File

- 09.02.3 Getting File information
- 09.02.4 Creating, renaming, and deleting

Working with SSH

This recipe centers on using the SSH plugin. With this plugin, you are able to connect to appliances (think managed routers, switches, and so on…) or a Linux- or Solaris-based system, run programs, or transfer files.

Getting ready

We need to be able to create a new workflow. We also need a Linux or Solaris system that we can access via SSH (for example, as root). If you don't have a Linux system handy, you can use the Orchestrator appliance itself.

For the SCP example, you need to allow Orchestrator access to its local filesystem, or use the default /var/run/vco directory. Refer to the *Configuring access to the local filesystem* recipe in Chapter 2, *Optimizing Orchestrator Configuration*.

If you want to connect to the appliance itself (127.0.0.1) you need to enable SSH access as shown in the *Tuning the appliance* recipe in Chapter 2, *Optimizing Orchestrator Configuration*.

How to do it...

We split this recipe into three parts: SSH access, SSL key access, and SCP usage.

Using SSH

You will find a very good, while rather chatty (logs), SSH workflow in **Library** I **SSH** I **Run SSH command**. However, we will create a new short version to showcase SSH:

1. Create a new workflow and create the following variables:

Name	Type	Place	Usage
Host	String	IN	The IP or FQDN of the host we want to connect to.
User	String	IN	The username to connect to the host.

Password	SecureString	IN	The password of the user to connect to the host.
Command	String	IN	The command we want to run on the host.
Output	String	OUT	The result of the command we run.
exitcode	Number	OUT	The exit code 0 = OK.
Error	String	OUT	The error message encountered.

2. Add a scriptable task to the schema and enter the following script:

```
// Open a new SSH session with password
var mySSHSession = new SSHSession(host , user);
mySSHSession.connectWithPassword(password);
//execute the SSH command
mySSHSession.executeCommand(command , true);
// prepare output
output=mySSHSession.output;
exitcode=mySSHSession.exitCode;
error=mySSHSession.error;
//disconnect the SSH session
mySSHSession.disconnect();
```

3. Save and close the workflow.

When running this workflow, you will have to supply a command string. The string can be a single command or a string of commands the Linux system can utilize. A command you can try is date.

Using SSL key authentication

In the previous example, we used password authentication to log in to the Linux host system. We can use SSL keys to allow automatic login without using a password, which is the method commonly used for automation purposes.

To enable SSL authentication, first we need an SSL key, and we need to store it on the target Linux system. We will use the existing workflows to accomplish this:

1. Start the workflow by navigating to **Library** | **SSH** | **Generate key pair**.

Every time you run this command, a new SSL key pair with the vco_key and vro_key.pub is generated in the /etc/vco/app-server/ directory.

2. Use the default setting and don't enter a password. Basically, just click on **Submit**.

3. Next, we need to register the SSL key on the host with the user we will use for the connection. To do this, we will use the existing workflow by navigating to **Library | SSH | Register vCO public key on host**. This workflow will add `vco-key.pub` onto the file `/root/.ssh/authorized_keys`.

4. Start the workflow, enter the hostname of the target server as well as the credentials of the user, and click on **Submit**.

5. The SSL pairing is now done. Let's try it out. Create a duplicate (or change the original) of the workflow you have created in the first section of this recipe.

6. Replace the `mySSHSession.connectWithPassword(Password);` line with `mySSHSession.connectWithIdentity("../conf/vco_key" , "");`. The shorter path works as Orchestrator's working directory is the `app-server` directory.

7. Remove the password in-parameter from the workflow.

8. Run the workflow. You won't need a password any longer.

Using SCP

SCP stands for Secure CoPy and allows you to transfer files using an SSH encryption tunnel. However, before we can copy anything from or to the Orchestrator server, we need to have a directory that Orchestrator has access to (see the *Configuring access to the local filesystem* recipe in `Chapter 2`, *Optimizing Orchestrator Configuration*. You can also use the default directory, `/var/run/vco`.

1. Make a copy of one of the SSH workflows: either the password or the SSL one.

2. Remove the command in-parameter and add the following in-parameter:

Name	Type	Place	Usage
`filename`	String	IN	The name of the file.
`localDir`	String	IN	The directory on the Orchestrator server.
`remoteDir`	String	IN	The directory on the remote host.

3. Replace the `mySSHSession.executeCommand(Command , true);` line with one of the following, depending on whether you want to send or receive a file:

Upload	`mySSHSession.putFile(localDir+file , remoteDir);`
Download	`mySSHSession.getFile(remoteDir+file , localDir);`

4. Save and run the workflow.

How it works...

Using SSH together with Orchestrator generates a very powerful team. You can use SSH to access an existing Linux system, configure it, or to connect to a Linux-based management system, such as a Red Hat satellite server.

But, even more powerfully, you can connect to the Orchestrator appliance itself. If you generate a SSL key and register it on `127.0.0.1` (Orchestrator itself), you can run commands as root, such as mounting a NFS or SMB directory. Please be aware that opening SSH for Orchestrator may be considered a security risk.

SCP can be used in conjunction with Orchestrator resources to upload and download files or to transfer any other files between Orchestrator and a target system. Please note that you can also transfer files from one remote system to another using Orchestrator as a temporary storage between transfers.

See also

- Refer to the *Configuring access to the local filesystem* recipe in `Chapter 2`, *Optimizing Orchestrator Configuration*.
- Refer to the *File operations* recipe in this chapter.

The example workflows are:

- `09.04.1 SSH (short with password)`
- `09.04.2 SSH (short with SSL Key)`
- `09.04.3 SCPput`
- `09.04.4 SCPget`
- `02.01 Tuning the Appliance`

Working with REST

In this recipe, we will use the REST plugin. We will use it to connect to the Orchestrator Control Center REST API.

Getting ready

We need a REST-capable host you can contact. As every REST host handles things a little differently, we will use the REST interface Orchestrator and the Orchestrator Control Center, to showcase the functionality.

I have also collected some other Orchestrator-REST integration examples in the *See also* section of this recipe.

If you are new to REST, I would like to point you to the *Accessing Orchestrator REST API* recipe in Chapter 7, *Interacting with Orchestrator*.

How to do it...

This recipe is divided into connecting, gathering information, sending information, as well as creating workflows.

Connecting to a REST host

There are two methods (as of vRO7.1) to connect to a host. We will use the normal method here to connect to a REST host, as this showcases a lot of things you should know. The other one (using Swagger) is discussed in the *There's more...* section:

1. Start the workflow by navigating to **Library** | **HTTP-REST** | **Configuration** | **Add a REST host**.
2. Enter the name under which you want to save this connection.
3. Enter **URL** to the REST API of the host.

Orchestrator	`https://[Orchestrator]:8281/vco/`
Orchestrator Control Center	`https://[Orchestrator]:8283/vco-controlcenter/`

4. The default timeouts are OK. Make sure you accept the certificate; click on **Next**.

5. Choose an authentication method (refer to the *How it works...* section) if you're unsure whether basic authentication will work with all clients; however, it isn't safe for production use.

	Orchestrator	Orchestrator Control Center
Authentication	Basic	Basic
Session	Shared or per user	Shared (root)

6. Choose whether you want to share the connection or use the current logged in Orchestrator user. Please remember that the Orchestrator Control Center has only the root user so you have to use shared for that.

7. Choose whether you require a proxy to connect to the REST host. This means that Orchestrator will not connect to the REST host if the hostname you supplied isn't in the SSL certificate. For example, if you add the IP instead of the FQDN (and the IP isn't in the certificate as SAN) then Orchestrator will not connect to this host.

8. The advanced setting can be left at the default for this example.

You have now added the REST host to Orchestrator. However, some REST interfaces (such as vCloud Director) require a certain path for login. To adjust to this behavior, you can have a look at the example workflow: **Library** | **HTTP-REST Samples** | **Set vCloud Director Authentication to a REST host**.

Using GET

We will now demonstrate a GET request to a REST host. GET gets information from a REST host:

1. Start the workflow by navigating to **Library** | **HTTP-REST** | **Configuration** | **Add a REST operation**.

2. Select the REST host to which you want to add the operation.

3. Give the operation a name for the inventory, such as `About` or `Status`.

4. Add the template URL. The template URL is the URL that you will use the method on (in our example here, GET). Use the following examples:

Orchestrator	`/api/about/`	**Displays version information of Orchestrator.**
Control Center	`/api/server/status`	Displays the status of the Orchestrator service.

5. Submit the workflow and wait until it has finished.
6. Start the workflow **Library | HTTP-REST | Invoke a REST operation**.
7. Select the REST operation you created above from the inventory and submit it.

You will see that the GET on Orchestrator will result in a string that contains a JSON object. Have a look at the logs. The Orchestrator will show:

```
Content as string: {"version":"7.0.1.3533702","build-
number":"3533702","build-date":"2016-02-09T12:19:45Z","api-
version":"5.5.2"}
```

Whereas the Control Center shows an error (all in red), which shows:

```
Error in (Workflow:Invoke a REST operation / Check status code (item3)#1)
HTTPError: status code: 415
```

This is due to the way the default content type is used in the request. Check the *How it works...* section of this recipe.

Using POST

While GET gets information, POST will alter, create, or transfer information on the REST host:

1. Start the workflow by navigating to **Library | HTTP-REST | Configuration | Add a REST operation**.
2. Select the REST host to which you want to add the operation.
3. Give the operation a name for the inventory, such as `Info` or `Start`.
4. Add the **Template URL** and **Content type** with the following content:

Host	Template URL	Content type
Orchestrator	`/api/workflows/{id}/executions`	`application/xml`
Orchestrator Control Center	`/api/server/status/start`	`application/json`

The {id} part will be replaced later at execution.

1. Select **POST** and **Submit** the workflow.

   Before we can execute the workflow, we need to get the ID of the workflow. In this example, we will use the example workflow `00.00 BasicsWorkflow`. Using the Orchestrator Client, browse the workflow and copy its ID from the **General** tab (for example, `312b7be1-abd2-47b6-9bc9-9e44c80ad168`):

2. Start the workflow by navigating to **Library | HTTP-REST | Invoke a REST operation**.
3. Select the REST operation from the inventory.
4. For the Orchestrator POST enter the ID of the workflow under **Parameter 1**.
5. For the Orchestrator POST enter the following under **Content**:

```
<execution-context xmlns="http://www.vmware.com/vco">
    <parameters>
        <parameter type="string" name="input" scope="local">
            <string>Entry String</string>
        </parameter>
    </parameters>
</execution-context>
```

6. For the Control Center just leave everything at the defaults.
7. Submit the workflow and use the Orchestrator Client to see the result.

The POST request requires you to enter additional information. The content is in the `string` form; however, it contains XML. The return code should be a **202 status code**, which means that the request was accepted.

The Control Center doesn't need extra information but executes a command that starts the Orchestrator service on the selected host.

Creating a workflow from a REST operation

To create a workflow out of a REST operation, follow these steps:

1. Start the workflow by navigating to **Library | HTTP-REST | Generate a new workflow from a REST operation**.
2. Select the REST operation; if you are using a POST, you will also see the content type you entered.
3. Give the new workflow a name and select a folder for it.

When running the workflow, you will be required to enter the same variables that you entered when using the `Invoke a REST operation` workflow.

Phrasing the return value

For the examples we are looking at, there are only two return types; XML and JSON.

XML parsing is discussed in the *Working with XML* recipe in `Chapter 10`, *Built-in Plugins*.

JSON parsing is shown in the *Introduction* to `Chapter 7`, *Interacting with Orchestrator*.

Using the Swagger spec URL

The other method to connect a host, and probably the best one for Control Center, uses the workflow **Add a REST host by Swagger spec from a URL**.

Swagger is a method describing the operations of a REST host. The interface is pretty common nowadays but not every REST host uses it yet.

To try it out, we will add the Orchestrator Control Center using the following method:

1. Start the workflow by navigating to **Library** | **HTTP-REST** | **Configuration** | **Add a REST host by Swagger spec from a URL**.
2. Enter a name for the connection.
3. As the Swagger spec URL, enter: `https://[FQDN Orchestrator control Center]:8283/vco-controlcenter/api/api-docs`.
4. Choose **HTTPS** and enter `application/json` as the default content type.
5. Accept the certificate silently and click **Next**.
6. Enter the authentication to the Swagger, which can be different to the products authentication. In the case of the Control Center you are connecting with **root**. Click **Next**.
7. Choose **Basic Authentication** and use the credentials that will execute the REST operation. In the case of the Control Center you are connecting with **root**. Click **Next**.
8. Choose weather you want to check the hostname. Just select **No** and **Submit** the workflow.
9. Check your Orchestrator inventory. You should now have all the GETs, PUTs, and so on that are associated with your REST service.

How it works...

REST stands for **Representational State Transfer** and is the way that most applications nowadays use an interface. Even Orchestrator itself switched from a SOAP interface to a REST interface.

Authentications

Orchestrator can use the following authentication methods out-of-the-box:

Method	Description
None	Doesn't use any authentication at all.
OAuth	A token-based authentication. For the difference between v1 and v2, see `https://blog.apigee.com/detail/oauth_differences`.
Basic	Basic authentication, no encryption, and clear text passwords.
Digest	Provides a basic encrypted authentication.
NTLM	**NTLM (NT LAN Manager)** provides encryption using the Window Security Support Provider (SSPI) framework.
Kerberos	Encrypted authentication using tickets. Also see the *Configuring the Kerberos authentication* recipe in `Chapter 2`, *Optimizing Orchestrator Configuration*.

Taking a look at the code behind the workflows, we find that authentications are created by the `RESTAuthenticationManager` object using the `createAuthentication()` method. This method requires the authentication type (Basic, OAuth 1.0, and so on) as well as the authentication parameters (`authParams`). The `authParams` variable can have different content depending on the REST host and login method used. Take a look at this example:

Method	Usage
OAuth 1.0	`var authParams = [consumerKey, consumerSecret, accessToken, accessTokenSecret];`
OAuth 2.0	`var authParams = [oauth2Token];`
Basic	`var authParams = [sessionMode, authUserName, authPassword];`
vCD	`var authParams = [sessionMode, username, password, organization, loginUrl];`

So, if you have trouble connecting to your REST host, you can simply alter `authParams` to the specifications of your REST host.

Working with the results of a REST request

Let's take a look at the results of a request. The results are part of the RESTResponse object. The two important attributes of this object for most users are contentAsString and statusCode. The statusCode attribute contains the status code of the request. You can view the basic response codes at https://[IP or FQDN Orchestrator]:8281/vco/api/docs/rest.html.

The contentAsString attribute returns a string that represents which is returned, which is XML in case of the Orchestrator and JSON in case of the Control Center. You can use the information in the *Working with XML* recipe in Chapter 10, *Built-in Plugins* or the *JavaScript complex variables* recipe in Chapter 6, *Advanced Programming* to phrase the return code.

Default content type

The error we get in the GET of the Control Center is related to the fact that we didn't (or better, couldn't) define a default content type (Header). Other REST servers, such as vCloud Director, might also need some more headers. To fix this you can do the following:

Method A:

1. Generate a new workflow from a (non-working) REST operation and edit it.
2. Edit the scriptable task and find the following section:

```
//Customize the request here
//request.setHeader("headerName", "headerValue");
```

3. Uncomment request.setHeader and replace the header content:

```
request.setHeader("content-type", "application/json");
```

4. Save and run the workflow.

Method B:

1. Duplicate the workflow **Library | HTTP-REST | Configuration | Add a REST operation**.
2. Edit the workflow and remove the **Show parameter input** from the workflow presentation of the defaultContentType variable.
3. Now add the workflow and set the default content type to application/json.

See also

- Orchestrator and VEEAM backup:
    - `http://www.vcoportal.de/2014/02/automating-veeam-with-vco-and-the-restful-api/`

- Orchestrator and Nutanix PrismAPI:
    - `http://philthevirtualizer.com/2014/03/03/connecting-to-the-nutanix-prismapi-with-vcenter-orchestrator/`

- Orchestrator and Avamar:
    - `http://velemental.com/2014/07/18/accessing-avamar-rest-api-from-the-vco-rest-plugin/`

- Orchestrator and vCNS (vShield):
    - `https://v-reality.info/2013/04/provisioning-vds-vxlan-virtual-wires-using-vcenter-orchestrator/`

- Orchestrator and NSX:
    - `http://virtuallygone.wordpress.com/2014/03/27/automating-firewall-rule-creation-in-nsx-with-vco-and-vcac-part-one-rest-host-configuration-in-vco/`

The example workflows are as follows:

- `09.04.1 Copy of Add a REST operation`
- `09.04.2 Invoke 'status: GET /server/status'`
- `09.04.3 Invoke 'start Orchestrator Service: POST server/status/...'`

10
Built-in Plugins

We will now look at all the plugins that come pre-installed in Orchestrator. We will be looking at these recipes:

- Working with XML
- Working with SQL (JDBC)
- Working with SQL (SQL plugin)
- Working with PowerShell
- Working with SOAP
- Working with Active Directory
- Working with SNMP
- Working with AMQP

Introduction

By now you are aware of the importance of plugins and how they expand the capabilities of Orchestrator. The next parts of the book will focus on plugins that were firstly touched upon in Chapter 9, *Essential Plugins*, where we discussed some of the very essential plugins. Here, we will go over all the plugins that are pre-installed in Orchestrator, while future chapters will show additional plugins and then finish on the vCenter plugin, which will round off the possibilities for expansion.

Dealing with return values

We have already had a look at the return values of the REST plugin, but there are also the return values of the SOAP and PowerShell plugin to look at. All of them are a bit more complex than just a string. A lot of the return values are either JSON, XML, or **Arrays of Properties**. In the *JavaScript complex variables* recipe in Chapter 6, *Advanced Programming*, we showcased how to harness them.

The most important thing to figure out is the information you really need for your workflow and whatnot. A request returns a lot of different values that you may or may not really need. What you need is to sort out what values you need and in what format you need them. Then select these values and reformat them into something you can pass back to your workflow.

For example, you may only need to know if an operation you performed worked, so passing back a boolean to your workflow would be enough. On the other hand, you may need several strings, so you could pass on an array of strings back.

If you have to pass on more complex information, it might be a good idea to parse the return values and extract the information you need. Then you could build a brand new JSON or XML string or a property and pass this more complex information back.

Shared or Per User Session

When dealing with REST, PowerShell, SOAP, and SQL, you need to provide credentials. When you need to provide credentials you are mostly asked if you would like to use a **Shared Session** or a **Per User Session**.

It's an important decision that needs to be thought about early on. The differences between methods are as follows.

With a Shared Session you define one user that is used to facilitate all actions that are used. For example, you connected to an SQL server using a user called `srv-dbuser`. The user `srv-dbuser` is a DBO and system administrator on the database. Now a user, for example, James, starts a workflow that uses the SQL connection you have defined, meaning that James will use the user rights of `srv-dbuser` to run the workflow.

Per User Session means that the user credentials of the logged-in (or executing) user are used to facilitate the connection. However, there is a bit of a problem with this. If you are not using LDAP as the external authentication method, then Per User Session will not necessarily work. This is due to the way that SSO/vIDM work. For example, if you are using the vRealize Automation integrated Orchestrator you can't (at the time of writing) use a Per

User Session to connect to vCenter. This is because vRA uses vIDM and vSphere uses SSO, and they are currently not compatible.

I personally prefer using a service account and Shared Session to connect services to Orchestrator. The reason is that I want to keep users out of systems. Instead of adding a ton of users to for example SQL so that they can use the database workflows, I just add one user and make sure that all the other users only use the workflows that they should. This, in my opinion, reduces the amount of administering and reduces the attack vectors.

However, there are cases where a Per User Session is a better fit. For example, when you are using the vRealize Automation plugin (see Chapter 13, *Working with vRealize Automation*), a given user can only interact with the elements that they are entitled to interact with.

Working with XML

In this recipe, we explore how to use the XML plugin to create and phrase XML structures with Orchestrator. XML is a good way to exchange complex information between systems.

Getting ready

We don't need anything special; however, we need to understand the basics of XML. Take a look at http://www.w3schools.com/xml/.

You should be familiar with the JavaScript concept of functions (see the introduction to this chapter).

How to do it...

This recipe is split into two parts; first, we create an XML document, and then phrase an XML document.

Creating an XML document

This is the rather more complex part; however, we will go through it slowly.

We will create a simple XML document that looks like this:

```
<?xml version="1.0" encoding="UTF-8">
<MailMessages>
```

```
<Mail>
  <From>test@test.net</From>
  <Subject>Test message</Subject>
  <Content Date="10/12/12">This is a test message
    </Content>
  </Mail>
</MailMessages>
```

1. Create a new workflow and create the following variables:

Name	Type	Where	Usage
from	String	IN	The sender of the e-mail.
subject	String	IN	The subject of the e-mail.
date	String	IN	The date of the e-mail.
content	String	IN	The content of the e-mail.
XMLout	String	OUT	The XML output in a one-line string.

2. Drag a scriptable task into the schema and enter the following script:

```
//create empty XML document
var document = XMLManager.newDocument();
// add a root element
var mailMessages = document.createElement("MailMessages");
//add the root element to the document
document.appendChild(mailMessages) ;
//Create new node
var mail = document.createElement("Mail");
//add new node under the root element
mailMessages.appendChild(mail) ;
//add a Child node under the mail node
var nodeFrom = document.createElement("From");
mail.appendChild(nodeFrom);
//set a text value for the From node
var txtFrom = document.createTextNode(from);
nodeFrom.appendChild(txtFrom);
//add another node with a value to the mail node
var nodeSubject = document.createElement("Subject");
mail.appendChild(nodeSubject);
var txtSubject = document.createTextNode(subject);
nodeSubject.appendChild(txtSubject);
//add content node
var nodeContent = document.createElement("Content");
mail.appendChild(nodeContent);
var txtContent = document.createTextNode(content);
```

```
nodeContent.appendChild(txtContent);
//Add an attribute to the Content node
nodeContent.setAttribute("Date",date);
//Output the XML Document as string
XMLout=XMLManager.getDocumentContent(document)
```

3. Save and run this workflow. Copy and paste the output into Notepad and check the XML structure you have created.

4. We now improve the program by using the JavaScript `function` command. Use the following script:

```
function createNode(doc,rootNode,NodeName,NodeText,
attribName,attribValue)
{
    var newNode = doc.createElement(NodeName);
    rootNode.appendChild(newNode);
// if there is no NodeText don't add anything
    if (NodeText!= null){
        var newTxt = doc.createTextNode(NodeText);
        newNode.appendChild(newTxt);
    }
// if there is an attribute defined add it
    if (attribName!= null){
        newNode.setAttribute(attribName,attribValue);
    }
// return the new created node
    return newNode;
}

//create empty XML document
var document = XMLManager.newDocument();

mailMessages = createNode(document,document,"MailMessages");
mail = createNode(document,mailMessages,"Mail");
createNode(document,mail,"From",from);
createNode(document,mail,"Subject",subject);
createNode(document,mail,"Content",content,"Date",date);

//Output the XML Document as string
XMLout=XMLManager.getDocumentContent(document);
```

You can see how using the `function` command reduces the number of lines and makes the code more reusable. Alternatively, you can also create an action and put the function content into it.

If you like, you can now go and integrate XML into the workflow that you built in the *Receiving e-mails* section of the *Working with mails* recipe in Chapter 9, *Essential Plugins*, to format the e-mail output.

Parsing XML structures

Taking the XML string we created, we now focus on how to parse the XML structure:

1. Create a new workflow and drag a scriptable task into it.
2. Create the XML in-parameter of type string.
3. In the scriptable task, enter the following script:

```
//convert the string into an XML document
var document = XMLManager.fromString(XMLin);
// get all Child elements of the document (type: XMLNodeList)
var docNodelist = document.getChildNodes();
//as we know from the XML structure there is only mailmessages
var mailmessage = docNodelist.item(0);
//now we get all child elements from mailmessages
var maillist = mailmessage.getChildNodes();
//lets see how many child elements there are
var mails = maillist.length;
//lets walk though each mail (type: XMLNode)
for (i = 0; i < mails; i++) {
    mail = maillist.item(i);
//get the child elements of each mail
    var mailchilds = mail.getChildNodes();
//walk through the mail Childs
    for (j = 0; j < mailchilds.length; j++) {
//get one child
        var child = mailchilds.item(j);
//get child name
        var childName = child.nodeName;
//get child content (type: XMLElement)
        var childText = child.textContent;
//output
        System.log (childName+" : "+childText);
//lets get the childs attributes (type: XMLNamedNodeMap)
        var ChildAttribs=child.getAttributes();
//walk though all attributes
        for (k = 0; k < ChildAttribs.length; k++) {
//get one attribute (type: XMLNode)
            var ChildAttrib = ChildAttribs.item(k);
//get Attribute name
            var ChildAttribName = ChildAttrib.nodeName;
```

```
//get Attribute value
        var ChildAttribValue = ChildAttrib.nodeValue;
//output
        System.log("Attribute : "+ChildAttribName+" :
        "+ChildAttribValue);
    }
  }
}
```

4. Run the workflow. Paste the XML string that was created earlier into the in-parameter, and watch the logs for the output.

Instead of walking through the XML tree, we can take some shortcuts; take a look at the *How it works...* section of this recipe.

How it works...

XML is a very nice way to exchange complex information. As you can see, forming an XML isn't that hard, especially when using a function or action. Parsing an XML is quite straightforward, too; the example we used is very detailed, but it will work for any simple XML. It can be made easier by using some of these XML methods:

- `nodeList = Node.getElementsByTagName(tag)`: This method can be used to create a node list of all nodes that have the same node name
- `attributeValue = Node.getAttribute(attributeName)`: This is an undocumented method that is quite useful, as you can directly access the value of the attribute by supplying the attribute's name
- `XMLDoc = XMLManager.loadDocument(file, validate);` `XMLManager.saveDocument(XMLDoc, file)`: Using these methods, you can load and save XML documents onto the local Orchestrator filesystem

There's more...

In addition to the XML plugin that we looked at in this recipe, Orchestrator also supports the JavaScript built-in XML (E4X). Please note that most browsers no longer support E4X and therefore it is doubtful how long its shelf life in JavaScript will be. On the other hand, the JavaScript implementation of Orchestrator isn't a new one either, so for that purpose it doesn't matter.

Here is a short introduction to E4X XML:

- Define a new XML doc:

  ```
  var doc = new XML(XMLin);
  ```

- Output the amount of children:

  ```
  doc.Mail.length()
  ```

- Output all From tags:

  ```
  doc.Mail.From
  doc..From
  ```

- Output only the From tag from the first child:

  ```
  doc.Mail[1].From
  ```

- Get the Date attribute from the From tag:

  ```
  doc.Mail[1].Content.@Date
  ```

- Output the Mail record for the From tag that has the Username text in it:

  ```
  doc.Mail.(From=='Username')
  ```

- Change the text of the tag:

  ```
  doc.Mail[1].Subject = "Test";
  ```

- Change the attribute of the tag:

  ```
  doc.Mail[1].Content.@Date = "04.09.14";
  ```

- Loop throughout the children of the element:

  ```
  for each (mail in doc)
  ```

See also

To learn more about E4X, take a look at the following URLs:

- http://wso2.com/project/mashup/0.2/docs/e4xquickstart.html
- http://www.xml.com/pub/a/2007/11/28/introducing-e4x.html

The example workflows are as follows:

- 10.01.1 CreateXML
- 10.01.2 CreateXML(Function)
- 10.01.3 phraseXML(General)

Working with SQL (JDBC)

This recipe focuses on the interaction between Orchestrator and an SQL database using the **Java database connector** (**JDBC**). You will learn how to send SQL queries as well as commands to a database.

Getting ready

Obviously, we need a database. This database can be PostgreSQL, MS SQL, Oracle, or MySQL. For testing, you can use the PostgreSQL database that is implemented in the appliance (refer to the *Tuning the appliance* recipe in Chapter 2, *Optimizing Orchestrator Configuration*). Also, take a look at the *There's more...* section of this recipe.

We will use a Microsoft SQL 2008 R2 database in this example; however, the steps are the same for all databases. The database we will be using is called testDB.

You will need an existing database and a user who is able to create/drop tables as well as insert/delete information, for example, the DBO role.

How to do it...

This recipe has multiple parts that will cover all aspects of working with a database.

Creating a JDBC connection URL

To connect to an SQL database, Orchestrator uses **JDBC**. Therefore, first, we need to create a JDBC URL:

1. Log in to the Orchestrator Client and start the workflow by navigating to **Library | JDBC | JDBC URL generator**.
2. Select the type of database you would like to connect to.

3. Enter the database's IP or FQDN, the database name, as well as the authentication details.

4. For a Microsoft SQL server, you may need to provide additional information, such as the SQL instance and the DB's domain name:

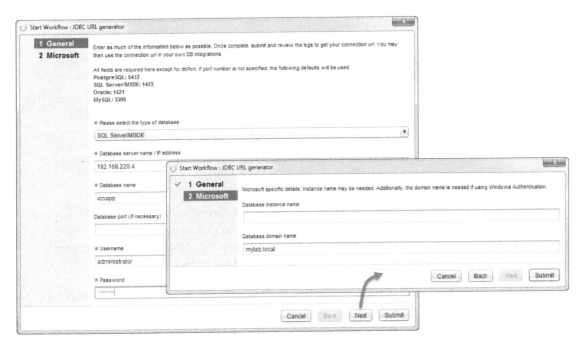

5. After the workflow has finished successfully, it's easy to copy the connection string from the logs. The string for my SQL server looks like the following:

```
jdbc:jtds:sqlserver://192.168.220.4:1433/vcoapp;domain=mylab.local
```

This workflow not only creates the URL, it also tests it, which is quite handy. Keep the URL, as we will need it for all the other parts of the recipe. A good idea is to store the URL in a configuration.

Connecting to and disconnecting from a database using JDBC

We are now going to open and close the JDBC connection to a database:

1. Create a new workflow and the following variables:

Name	Type	Place	Usage
jdbcURL	String	Attribute	The JDBC URL from the first part of this recipe.
user	String	Attribute	The username for the DB connection.
password	SecureString	Attribute	The password for DB connection.

2. Search for or browse the SDK module, SQL. This module contains all the methods we will use in this recipe.

3. Drag a scriptable task onto the schema and enter the following script:

```
// constructors for JDBC DB and connection
var myDB = new JDBCConnection();
var myConnect;
// connect to DB
myConnect = myDB.getConnection(jdbcURL, user , password);

//further scripting

// if the connection is open, close it.
if (myConnect) {
    // disconnect from DB
    myConnect.close();
}
```

Executing an SQL statement using JDBC

Next, we pass an SQL statement to the SQL server to be executed. Note that this executes an SQL statement, not an SQL query; we will address SQL queries in the next section of this recipe. The difference is that queries return values, whereas the execution of an SQL statement is either successful or unsuccessful:

1. Duplicate (or add to) the workflow from the first part of this recipe.

2. Create the following variables and bind them to the scriptable task:

Name	Type	Place	Usage
`sqlStatement`	`String`	IN	The string with the complete SQL command.
`result`	`Number`	OUT	The result of the SQL command. 0 = OK.

3. Enter the following script after `//further scripting`:

```
// Open SQL statement
var mySQL = myConnect.createStatement();
// Open SQL results
var result = mySQL.executeUpdate(sqlStatement);
//close SQL statement
mySQL.close();
```

4. Run the workflow. The following SQL statement will create a table called `testtbl` that contains the ID, `LastName`, and `FirstName` columns:

```
CREATE TABLE testtbl (ID int, LastName varchar(255),FirstName
varchar(255));
```

5. Run the workflow again and use the following statement. It will create an entry in the table:

```
INSERT INTO testtbl VALUES (1,'Langenhan','Daniel');
```

In the *How it works...* section of this recipe, we will discuss the difference between the `createStatement` and `prepareStatement` methods.

SQL queries using JDBC

In this part, we will look at how to deal with the results from a query. We will create a CSV of the results of the query:

1. Duplicate the workflow from the first part of this recipe.
2. Create the following variables and bind them to the scriptable task:

Name	Type	Place	Usage
`sqlQuery`	`String`	IN	The string with the SQL query.
`output`	`String`	OUT	The output in a CSV format.

3. Enter the following script after `//further scripting`:

```
// constructors for JDBC DB and connection
var myDB = new JDBCConnection();
var myConnect;
// connect to DB
myConnect = myDB.getConnection(jdbcURL, user , password);
//initialize output
output="";
//open SQL statement
var mySQL = myConnect.createStatement();
// open query
var results = mySQL.executeQuery(sqlQuery);
// get number of columns in a table from results metadata
var resultMetaDate = results.getMetaData();
var colCount = resultMetaDate.getColumnCount();
//walk thought all rows
while ( results.next() )   {
    //Walk thought all columns
    for (i = 1; i < colCount+1; i++) {
        // Past row together
        output = output+","+results.getStringAt(i);
    }
    //new line after end of row
    output = output+"\n";
}
// close query
results.close();
// close SQL statement
mySQL.close();
```

4. Try the workflow with a SQL query such as `select * from testtbl`.

Also, take a closer look at the `ResultSet` and `ResultSetMetaData` objects for more possibilities on how to deal with the output of an SQL query.

How it works...

Orchestrator's ability to use an external database and queries and execute statements on them makes it possible for Orchestrator not only to integrate with other systems, but also to store and process data. A typical system that Orchestrator will integrate with is a **configuration management database (CMDB)**.

The difference between the prepare and create statements

Looking into the methods of the Connection object, we find the createStatement() method that we used earlier as well as the prepareStatement() method. The difference between these is that you can use variables in the prepareStatement method; these are defined during runtime, whereas in createStatement, we can use only fixed queries. Let's work through an example. We want to delete an entry from the database. The SQL delete statement is the following:

```
DELETE FROM testtbl where (FirstName = "Daniel" and LastName = "Langenhan")
```

If we wanted to delete something else, we would have to rewrite the whole statement every time. Using prepareStatement, we don't have to do that. We use the following SQL statement:

```
DELETE FROM testtbl where (FirstName = ? and LastName = ?)
```

To make this work, we have to not only change the code of the script, but also add two new in-parameters (lastName and firstName). The new code looks like this:

```
var stat = mySQL.prepareStatement( sqlStatement );
// exchange the first ? for the content from the in-parameters
stat.setString( 1, firstName );
// exchange the second ? for the content from the in-parameters
stat.setString( 2, lastName );
//run the altered statement
var result = stat.executeUpdate();
//close the statement
stat.close ;
```

Basically, we just substituted ? with the values of in-parameters while the workflow is running.

Creating a new database in the appliance's PostgreSQL

The appliance comes with a preinstalled PostgreSQL database that can (but should not) be used. The appliance is configured to allow local access, so you just need to create a new database. To do this, follows these steps:

1. Log into the appliance with root access.
2. Run the following commands one after another:

```
su postgres
```

```
psql
CREATE USER testuser with PASSWORD 'testpass';
CREATE DATABASE testdb;
GRANT ALL PRIVILEGES on DATABASE testdb to testuser;
\q
exit
```

This will create a database called `testdb` and give `testuser` all rights using the password `testpass`.

See also

You can learn more about SQL at `http://www.w3schools.com/sql/default.asp`.

The example workflows are as follows:

- `10.02.1 Connecting to a DB`
- `10.02.2 Execute SQL statement`
- `10.02.3 Execute SQL Query`
- `10.02.4 Execute SQL statement (with prepareStatement)`

And the configuration item is `10.02 DB Config`.

Working with SQL (SQL plugin)

In this recipe, we will explore the SQL plugin to work with SQL. This is a bit different from the JDBC recipe.

Getting ready

Obviously, we need a database. This database can be PostgreSQL, MS SQL, Oracle, or MySQL. For testing, you can use the PostgreSQL database that is implemented in the appliance (refer to the *Tuning the appliance* recipe in `Chapter 2`, *Optimizing Orchestrator Configuration*). Also, take a look at the *There's more...* section of this recipe.

We will use a Microsoft SQL 2008 R2 database in this example; however, the steps are the same for all databases. The database we will be using is called `testDB`.

You will need an existing database and a user who is able to create/drop tables as well as insert/delete information, for example, the DBO role.

How to do it...

See the following sections.

Add an SQL DB to Orchestrator

In this section, we will connect an SQL server to Orchestrator:

1. Start the **Library** I **SQL** I **Configuration** I **Add a database** workflow.
2. Enter a name for the connection.
3. Select the kind of database you like.
4. Enter the JDBC connection string to your database. You can use the **Library** I **JDBC** I **JDBC URL generator** workflow to create and test the string:

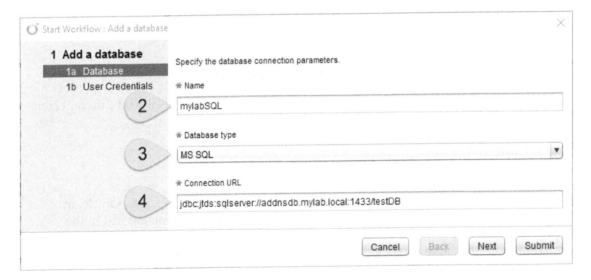

5. When the workflow has finished, go and check the inventory:

Run SQL statement

We will now run a SQL statement:

1. Start the **Library | SQL | Execute a custom query on a database** workflow.
2. Select the database.
3. Enter the following as a statement: `INSERT INTO testtbl VALUES (2,'some lastname','some firstname');`.
4. Run the workflow and check the database table.

Run an SQL query

We will now run an SQL query:

1. Create a new workflow.
2. Add the workflow and create the inputs as in-parameters. Assign the output variable (array of `SQL:ActiveRecord`) as an attribute.
3. Add a scriptable task and assign the attribute as in-parameter.
4. Enter the following script:

```
for each (result in resultRecords){
    columns=(result.getFieldNames());
    for each (column in columns){
          System.log("Column :"+column+"
content:"+result.getProperty(column));
    }
}
```

5. Save and run the script with a SQL query such as `select * from testtbl`.

How it works...

The SQL plugin is a bit different than the JDBC connector as it uses Orchestrator objects. There are the following Orchestrator scripting classes:

- SQLActiveRecord
- SQLColumn
- SQLDatabase
- SQLDatabaseManager
- SQLTable

Also extremely valuable are the Generate CRUD workflows for a table. **CRUD** stands for **Create**, **Read**, **Update** and **Delete** and will create these four workflows a given table.

See also

The example workflow 10.03.1 Execute SQL query (SQL plugin).

Working with PowerShell

In this recipe, we will enable Orchestrator to execute PowerShell scripts on a Windows host and deal with the results.

Getting ready

We need a Windows host where the PowerShell scripts are stored and can be executed from. This can be any Windows host; however, a Windows 2008 R2 (or better) server contains all the programs required to allow Orchestrator to connect to the Windows host.

To configure the Windows host, we need to use **Windows Remote Management (WinRM)**, which is already installed and integrated into Windows.

Installing the VMware PowerCLI add-on to PowerShell on the Windows host is optional.

You may also add a Linux PowerShell host to vRO. Check this:
http://kaloferov.com/blog/how-to-add-a-linux-machine-as-powershell-host-in-vro-skkb1030/

How to do it…

This recipe is split into preparation, adding the host, executing a PowerShell script, and generating a workflow.

Preparing the Windows host with WinRM

In this part, we will configure WinRM with basic authentication, HTTP, and unencrypted transfer. To configure WinRM for HTTPS, please refer to the PowerShell plugin documentation:

1. Log in to the Windows OS with administrator rights.
2. Create a local user who is part of the local administrator group.
3. Start a Windows command line with elevated rights.
4. Run the following command to configure the listener:

   ```
   winrm quickconfig
   ```

5. Enable basic authentication and unencrypted transfer for the service by running the following commands:

   ```
   winrm set winrm/config/service/auth @{Basic="true"}
   winrm set winrm/config/service @{AllowUnencrypted="true"}
   ```

6. Last but not least, we need to increase the package size that can be received:

   ```
   winrm set winrm/config/winrs @{MaxMemoryPerShellMB="2048"}
   ```

7. Make sure that TCP 5985 is accessible from Orchestrator to the PowerShell host.

This is a fast and easy configuration that leaves security wanting; however, it enables you to connect Orchestrator to a PowerShell host and run PowerShell scripts without facing any obstacles. If this connection works, you might want to shift to the more secure Kerberos connections (discussed later).

Adding a PowerShell host

Now that have we configured the Windows host, we need to connect Orchestrator to the Windows host. As this is a one-off operation, we will use the existing workflow to do this:

1. Start the workflow by navigating to **Library** I **PowerShell** I **Configuration** I **Add a PowerShell host**.

2. Enter a name for the connection to the PowerShell host. We will use this name later to establish connections to this host. Also, add the FQDN of the Windows host as well as port 5985

3. Choose **WinRM**, **HTTP** (HTTP:5985, HTTPS:5986) as the transport protocol and **Basic** for the authentication.

4. If your Orchestrator is configured for SSO, you have to choose **Shared Session**. Otherwise, you are welcome to use **Session per User**. If you choose **Shared Session**, you will need to provide a username and password.

5. Click on **Submit** and wait until the workflow is completed successfully. If that is not the case, check out the WinRM configuration:

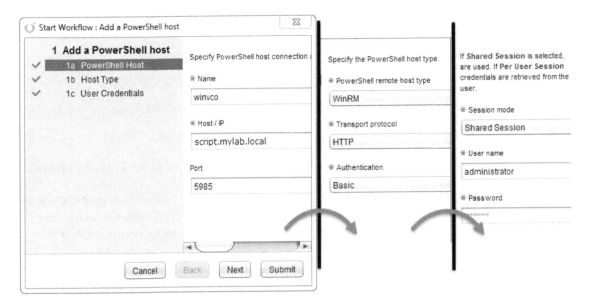

6. In the Orchestrator Client, click on **Inventory** (the paper symbol with a blue puzzle piece) and explore the tree under **PowerShell**. You will find all available PowerShell SnapIns as well as their Cmdlets:

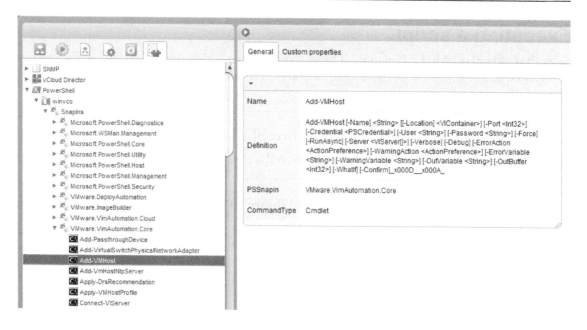

Using Kerberos authentication

In this section, we are configuring Orchestrator to connect to the PowerShell host using Kerberos authentication:

1. In Windows host, make sure Kerberos is enabled:

```
winrm set winrm/config/service/auth @{Kerberos="true"}
```

2. The AD user that should be used needs to be part of the `Administrator` group.
3. Use the *Configuring the Kerberos authentication* recipe in `Chapter 2`, *Optimizing Orchestrator Configuration,* to configure Orchestrator to use Kerberos authentication (even if you are using the Windows version).
4. Rerun the `Add a PowerShell host` workflow but, this time, use **Kerberos** as the authentication type.

This should work in most cases; however, Windows can be a bit tricky. If you experience problems, take a look at Spas Kaloferov's awesome article (see the *See also* section of this recipe for the link).

Executing a script

Now that we have added a PowerShell host, we can run a script. There are two workflows that can be used for this by navigating to **Library | PowerShell**; they are discussed in upcoming sections.

Calling a script that is stored on the PowerShell host

For this to work, you need a PowerShell script on the PowerShell host, preferably one that requires some arguments, such as `get-PSDrive -name c:`

1. Start the workflow by navigating to **Library | PowerShell | Invoke an external script**.
2. Select the PowerShell host that you have added to Orchestrator.
3. Enter the complete path to the script.
4. In **Arguments**, enter all the arguments that you want to transfer, like this:

   ```
   -Argument1 value1 -Argument2 value2
   ```

5. Click on **Submit** and wait until the script is executed.
6. Take a look at the logs to see the results.

Sending a script to be executed to the PowerShell host

1. Start the workflow by navigating to **Library | PowerShell | Invoke a PowerShell script**.
2. Select the PowerShell host that you have added to Orchestrator.
3. For the script, enter `Get-PSDrive -name c`.
4. Click on **Submit** and wait until the script is executed.
5. Take a look at the logs to see the results.

Generating an action and workflow from a script

The PowerShell plugin brings with it the ability to automatically create an action and a workflow from a PowerShell script. This allows you to integrate PowerShell permanently into your automation:

1. Start the workflow by navigating to **Library | PowerShell | Generate | Generate an Action from a PowerShell script**.

2. Enter the script you would like to run in the script. Replace all argument values with the `{#ParamName#}` placeholder. Here's an example:

Original	Get-PSDrive -Name C
Enter	Get-PSDrive -Name {#DriveName#}

3. Select a name for the action you would like to create as well as the module where you want to create it.
4. Choose whether you would like to create a workflow and also choose the folder you would like to create it in.
5. Click on **Submit** and wait until the process has finished.
6. Check out the created workflow, called `Invoke Script [Action Name]`:

openSession   Drive   closeSession   checkErrorsAction

7. See how `{#Parameter#}` has been changed into an in-parameter in the action you created:

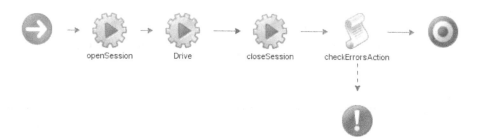

General Scripting Events Permissions

Return type : PowerShell:PowerShellRemotePSObject

#	Name	Type	Description
⇨	host	PowerShell:PowerShellHost	
⇨	sessionId	string	
⇨	Drive	String	

PowerShell:PowerShellRemotePSObject Drive(*PowerShell:PowerShellHost* host,*string* sessionId,*String* Drive)

```
var psScript = ''
psScript +='Get-PSDrive -Name ' + Drive + '\n';
return System.getModule("com.vmware.library.powershell").invokeScript( host,psScript,sessionId) ;
```

8. Run the new workflow and take a look at the logs.

How it works...

Adding PowerShell to Orchestrator will give you a far greater perspective on what Orchestrator can be used for. In the last few years, PowerShell has become a broadly used tool to write automation scripts. Microsoft uses PowerShell for a lot of management functions, such as **System Center Configuration Manager (SCCM)**, **System Center Virtual Machine Manager (SCVMM)**, and **System Center Operations Manager (SCOM)**.

Using PowerShell with Orchestrator, we are basically able to execute PowerShell scripts with a right-click in the vSphere Web Client and even transport VMware objects to PowerShell scripts.

Workflow TLC

A workflow or action that has been generated by Orchestrator will require some TLC (tender loving care), for instance, changing a password entry from `string` to `SecureString`, reworking the naming structure, rearranging the variables in the workflow call, and so on.

Another typical and vital task is escaping variables. When you run a command that requires entering a string that contains special characters such as spaces, backslashes \ or quotation marks ", you need to escape them using an additional \ or use single quotation marks '. In the following example, we will show you both methods:

Original	`psScript +='Get-PSDrive -Name ' + DriveName + '\n';` Output: `Get-PSDrive -Name c:`
Using "	`psScript +='Get-PSDrive -Name "' + DriveName + '" \n';` Output: `Get-PSDrive -Name "c:"`
Escaping '	`psScript +='Get-PSDrive -Name '' + DriveName + '' \n';` Output: `Get-PSDrive -Name 'c:'`

The difference between " and ' is that PowerShell will look inside " " for $ and assumes that what follows is a variable, whereas it will take all content between the ' as it is.

Entry	`"Test $date"`	`'Test $date'`
Output	`Test 12.01.12`	`Test $date`

Basic versus Kerberos authentication

In this recipe, we used the basic connection to connect Orchestrator to the PowerShell host. As mentioned, this is the easiest way to build the connection, and therefore it is good for a beginner. As a professional, you want to use Kerberos as the authentication; however, you should first try to connect via the basic method to make sure that you don't have any Firewall or other basic connection problems before going for the secure connect.

One of the differences between basic and Kerberos authentication is that basic authentication can only use local users, whereas Kerberos uses AD users. Secondly, Kerberos uses encryption when communicating, whereas basic doesn't. This is quite a big difference, especially in a business environment where local users should really not be used and encryption is a must.

As already mentioned, if you use Orchestrator with SSO, you can *only* use **Shared Session**, as Orchestrator is not able to forward the session. You can use **Session per User** only with an LDAP-connected Orchestrator.

PowerShell output to XML

To convert the PowerShell output into XML, run the following lines:

```
psXML = PowerShellOutput.getXml();
```

The XML output of PowerShell can be quite messy. The first thing that one needs to realize is that the PowerShell XML output adds a large amount of spaces between tags. To clean this up, run the following regular expression:

```
xmlClean = psXML.replace(/>\s+</g, "><");
```

The following is an example of the `Get-Culture` PowerShell command. You can clearly see how the diminished command-line output (the blue PowerShell window) looks in PowerShell XML:

```xml
<?xml version="1.0"?>
- <Objs xmlns="http://schemas.microsoft.com/powershell/2004/04" Version="1.1.0.1">
  - <Obj RefId="0">
    - <TN RefId="0">
        <T>System.Globalization.CultureInfo</T>
        <T>System.Object</T>
      </TN>
      <ToString>en-AU</ToString>
    - <Props>
        <I32 N="LCID">3081</I32>
        <S N="Name">en-AU</S>
        <S N="DisplayName">English (Australia)</S>
        <S N="IetfLanguageTag">en-AU</S>
        <S N="ThreeLetterISOLanguageName">eng</S>
        <S N="ThreeLetterWindowsLanguageName">ENA</S>
        <S N="TwoLetterISOLanguageName">en</S>
      </Props>
    </Obj>
  </Objs>
```

```
PS C:\Users\Daniel> Get-Culture

LCID            Name            DisplayName
----            ----            -----------
3081            en-AU           English (Australia)
```

As you can see, PowerShell creates tag names along with the variable names (`Obj`=Object, `S`=String, and `I32`=32-bit Integer) and sets the name of the output as an attribute with the `N` key. It's not easy to phrase these constructs; however, it's doable.

See also

- This blog about using PowerShell and Orchestrator:
    - http://blogs.vmware.com/management/2015/05/optimizing-powe
      rshell-workflows-vrealize-orchestrator.html

- Learn PowerShell:
    - http://technet.microsoft.com/en-us/scriptcenter/powershell
      .aspx

- Learn PowerCLI:
    - https://www.packtpub.com/virtualization-and-cloud/learning
      -powercli

- Refer to the *Working with XML* recipe in this chapter to learn more about phasing XML with Orchestrator

- Connecting Orchestrator to PowerShell using Kerberos:
    - http://blogs.vmware.com/orchestrator/2012/06/vco-powershel
      l-plugin-how-to-set-up-and-use-kerberos-
      authentication.html

- http://kaloferov.com/blog/adding-vco-powershell-host-with-account-other-than-the-default-domain-administrator-account/

- The example workflows are as follows:
  - 10.04.1 Invoke Script psExample and the psExample action in the com.packtpub.Orchestrator-Cookbook module
  - 10.04.2 Cleanup PS XML

Working with SOAP

This recipe focuses on the interaction between Orchestrator and a SOAP-based server. We will learn how to add a SOAP host to Orchestrator and execute SOAP operations.

Getting ready

We need a host that can present SOAP operations for Orchestrator to use. If you don't have a SOAP host that you can access, you can follow our example.

Orchestrator's SOAP API has been retired and is not available anymore.

To add a SOAP-based service to the Orchestrator host, we need its WSDL address.

For our example, we will use http://www.webservicex.net to test our SOAP plugin. The WSDL we will use is http://www.webservicex.net/globalweather.asmx?WSDL.

How to do it...

Again, this recipe is split into different parts.

Adding a new SOAP client

Before we can execute any SOAP operations, we need to add the SOAP interface of a host to Orchestrator:

1. Open the Orchestrator Client and switch to **Design** mode.
2. Make sure that you have imported the SSL certificate of the SOAP host (refer to the *Important Orchestrator settings* recipe in Chapter 1, *Installing and Configuring Orchestrator*).

3. Start the workflow by navigating to **Library** | **SOAP** | **Configuration** | **Add a SOAP host**.

4. Choose the name you want to save this SOAP host under.

5. Enter the WSDL address, click **Next**.

6. If you need to use a proxy to connect to the internet then fill it in now, or else click on **Next**.

7. Choose **None** for **Authentication type** and click **Next**. The authentication method depends on the type of server and can be very different.

8. For the **Session** mode, you won't have to choose anything as we choose no authentication. If you choose another SOAP service, you need to decide between using a **Shared Session** or **Per User Session**.

9. Click on **Submit** to finalize.

Now we have access to all SOAP operations that are exposed:

Invoking a SOAP request

We will now test out a SOAP request:

1. Open the Orchestrator Client and run the workflow by navigating to **Library |
   SOAP | Invoke a SOAP operation**.
2. Click on **Operation** and then select from the inventory an operation, such as
   GetCitiesByCountry.
3. Click on **Next** and then replace the parameter1 with a state, such as Germany.
4. Click on **Submit**. When the workflow has finished, check out the logs:

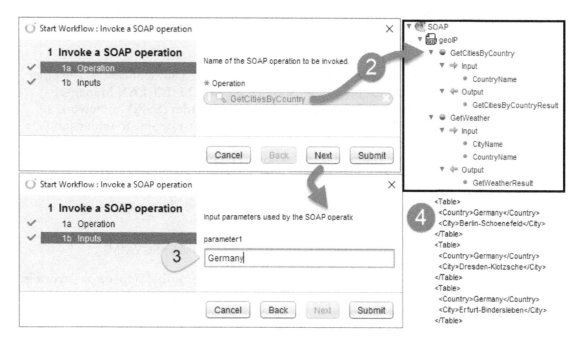

Generating a new SOAP workflow

To invoke a SOAP operation, we will create a new workflow:

1. Open the Orchestrator Client and run the workflow by navigating to **Library |
   SOAP | Generate a new workflow from a SOAP operation**.
2. Click on **Operation** and select a workflow, such as GetWeather. Click on **Next**.
3. Choose a name for the new workflow as well as a folder where the new workflow
   should be located.

4. As the format, you can just use the default.

5. After clicking on **Submit**, a new workflow will be created in the folder you specified. The in-parameters and out-parameters for the workflow are aligned to the inputs and outputs of the SOAP operation.

6. You can now run this workflow. The workflow will invoke the SOAP operation on the SOAP host. The return values will be returned in properties.

How it works...

SOAP (Simple Object Access Protocol) is a common way to access automation or scripting services via a network. A SOAP service advertises what scripts can be run on the SOAP host and what variables are needed to run it on its WSDL interface.

We used the **Digest** authentication, which provides an encrypted authentication. The other authentication types are basic (no encryption) and NTLM. **NTLM (NT LAN Manager)** provides encryption using the Window **Security Support Provider (SSPI)** framework. If you want to use NTLM, the SOAP host you're connecting to must be able to understand and use it (this is not the case with Orchestrator). Additionally, you also need to provide additional information in the configuration workflow. You need to specify the NTLM domain and, additionally, maybe a NTLM workstation.

If your Orchestrator is SSO-configured, we have to use shared sessions, as we already discussed in the *Working with PowerShell* recipe.

A typical SOAP-Orchestrator integration is with Microsoft SCOM or SCVMM.

Most generated workflows require a bit of aftercare. A typical example is that a password is handled as a `string` not a `SecureString`. Refer to the *How it works...* section in the *Working with PowerShell* recipe.

See also

A full workout of this can be found in `http://blogs.vmware.com/orchestrator/2011/06/example-of-high-level-workflow-with-the-soap-plug-in.html`.

Working with Active Directory

In this recipe, we will look at how Orchestrator uses the **Active Directory** (**AD**) plugin.

Getting ready

We need an AD server for this recipe as well as access to the AD server OS itself.

How to do it...

We split this recipe into multiple parts.

Preparing AD for SSL

You can add AD to Orchestrator without using SSL; however, you will not be able to create users, change passwords, or use any other more secure options. If you decide not to use SSL, skip this step.

First, we will install Active Directory Certificate Services.

 Microsoft does not recommend that you run a CA server on a domain controller; however, for a lab, it is totally okay.

To activate SSL for AD, follow these steps:

1. Log in to the Windows server that will host the CA. In my case, this is my domain controller, `central.mylab.local`, with domain administrator rights.
2. Add the **Active Directory Certificate Services** server role.

3. Just click on **Next** and accept all the default settings. In the following screenshot, you'll find all the settings I used (the default ones for my domain):

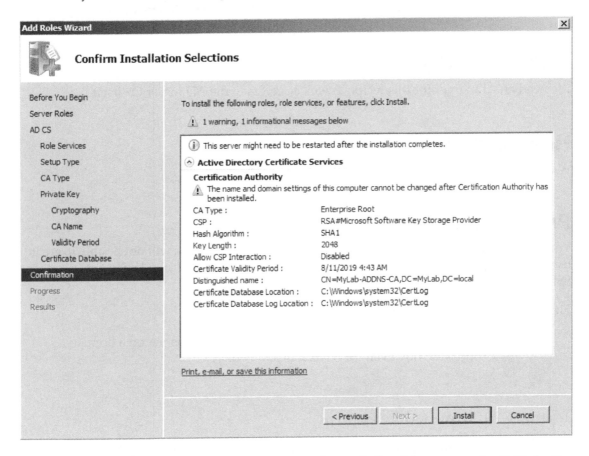

4. After the wizard has finished, open up **Group Policy Manager** and edit **Default Domain Controller Policy**.

5. Navigate to **Computer Configuration** | **Policies** | **Windows Settings** | **Security Settings** | **Public Key Policies** | **Automatic Certificate Request Settings** and then go to **New** | **Automatic Certificate Request Setup**.

6. Finish this wizard again by just clicking on **Next**, which forces the creation of a certificate for your domain controllers.

7. Wait a few minutes or force a policy update on the domain controller using the `gpupdate/force` command.

8. Start the **Certification Authority** tool and check in **Issued Certificates** whether the domain controller was issued with a certificate.

9. To test the SSL configuration connection, we will use Microsoft's **ldp** tool (`C:\Windows\System32\ldp.exe`). Start **ldp** and connect to the domain controller using SSL (port `636`). If this test is successful, continue. If not, check out `http://technet.microsoft.com/en-us/library/cc875810.aspx`.

10. Last but not least, make sure that the Windows firewall allows `TCP 389` (with `SSL TCP 636`) to pass.

Registering AD with Orchestrator

Now, we add AD to Orchestrator:

1. Start the workflow by navigating to **Library | Microsoft | Active Directory | Configuration | Add an Active Directory server**.

2. Give the connection a name.

3. Enter the FQDN of your AD server.

4. Enter the port you are using: `389` without SSL and `636` with SSL.

5. The root is written in the LDAP format, for example, `DC=mylab,DC=local`.

6. Choose whether to use SSL or not. If you are using SSL, you can choose to be asked when importing the certificate.

7. The default domain is written in the `@[FQDN Domain name]` format, for example, `@mylab.local`.

8. If you have configured Orchestrator with SSO, you have to choose a **Shared Session**. Enter domain-administrator credentials.

9. In **Options** you can choose to follow referrals, meaning that if the AD doesn't have a given object in its own tree it might know the right domain controller. You can also specify a timeout to reduce the amount of time you spend waiting for an object in a large AD structure.

There is an additional workflow that lets you define some additional settings for AD. The workflow is **Library** | **Microsoft** | **Active Directory** | **Configuration** | **Configure Active Directory Plug-in options**. Here, you can define a default AD server (if you are using multiple) as well as a maximum number of returned items:

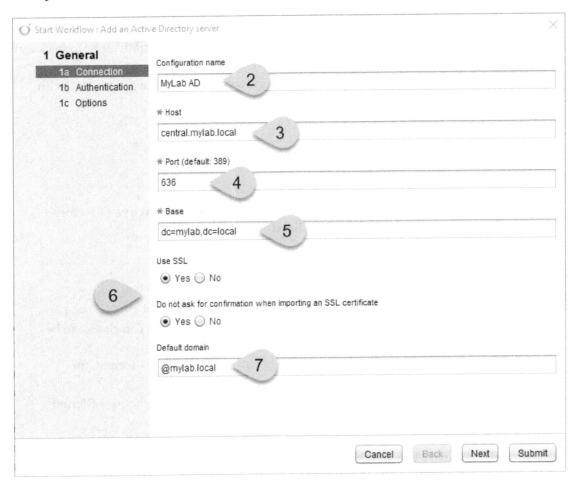

Working with AD

The AD plugin comes with a lot of great workflows that work without a problem. The following table shows you which workflows exist:

Workflow	Use
Computer	Create, destroy, disable, and enable a computer.
Organizational unit	Create and destroy.
User	Create, destroy, disable, enable, change password, add, and remove from groups.
User groups	Create and destroy groups and add and remove users, computers, and groups to/from groups.

As long as you have added the domain controller to your Orchestrator, you can run and integrate all these scripts into your own workflows.

How it works...

The Microsoft plugin is quite easy to use; however, as you may have noticed, setting it up isn't as straightforward. The main issue is using SSL with the domain controller; as soon as this is working, you're home free.

The drawback of an SSO-configured Orchestrator should now be apparent, making it necessary to use a shared session. Some clients have argued that it would make more sense to use an LDAP integration rather than an SSO one, so they can use a **Session per User**. My argument is that SSO integration is the way forward with VMware and that the same customers are happy to use vCloud Director or VMware View with a dedicated user.

Microsoft integration allows a range of possibilities, user management being the prime target. There are more possibilities that the plugin offers; explore the AD API object.

When you are using a large AD directory you might like to consider using a different base for your AD connection. You could, for instance, use an OU such as the following:

```
OU=acme,DC=mylab,DC=local
```

See also

Refer to the *Managing AD users with vRA* recipe in `Chapter 13`, *Working with vRealize Automation*.

Working with SNMP

This recipe centers on SNMP. Here, you will learn how to use Orchestrator to receive SNMP traps from vCenter/ESXi and use them to trigger workflows.

Getting ready

For this recipe, we need an SNMP source. We will use vCenter and ESXi hosts as SNMP sources.

To prepare vCenter and ESXi servers to send or receive SNMP messages, refer to the *There's more...* section of this recipe.

How to do it...

We will split this recipe into configuring and using SNMP with Orchestrator.

Configuring SNMP devices

To configure Orchestrator to send or receive SNMP messages from SNMP devices, follow these steps for each SNMP device:

1. In **Device address**, enter the IP or FQDN of the device you want to send or receive SNMP messages to/from.
2. In the Orchestrator Client, start the workflow by navigating to **Library** | **SNMP** | **Device Management** | **Register an SNMP device**.
   - **Name** is just a string to identify the SNMP device in the inventory.
3. The **Advanced** function is the configuration that is used to send SNMP messages. Here, you can configure the port, the protocol function, as well as the community string for sending.

 Please remember that for vCenter, you just need to configure the hostname, as vCenter won't answer SNMP requests.

Sending a GET query to an ESXi host

Having configured ESXi to send and receive SNMP messages, let's try one out:

1. In the Orchestrator Client, start the workflow by navigating to **Library | SNMP | Query Management | Add a query to an SNMP device**.
2. In **Device**, select the ESXi server and select **GET** in **Type**.
3. In **OID**, enter `1.3.6.1.2.1.1.5.0` (this gets the hostname of the device).
4. In **Name**, enter `Hostname`.
5. Next, run the query by running the workflow; navigate to **Library | SNMP | Query Management | Run an SNMP query**.
6. Select the query underneath the ESXi SNMP device and click on **Submit**. Check the logs for the results.

Refer to the *How it works...* section for more information about OIDs.

Configuring a vCenter alarm to send an SNMP message

vCenter can only send an SNMP message using an alarm configured to send SNMP messages. We will configure an alarm that goes off when a new resource pool is created:

1. Open your vSphere Web Client.
2. Navigate to the object the alarm should be added to, such as a cluster.
3. Click on the **Manage** tab and then click on **Alarm Definitions**.
4. Click on **Add** (the green plus icon).
5. Give the new alarm a name such as `SNMP Example`, opt to monitor **Clusters**, and select **specific event occurring on this object**.
6. Use add (the green plus icon) to add a trigger. Use the selector to choose **Resource Pool created** and set the status to **Warning**. Click on **Next**.
7. Use add (the green plus icon) to add an action. Use the selector to choose **Send a notification trap** and click on **Finish**.

> To learn more about vCenter alarms, please take a look at the vSphere documentation, or check out this article:
> `http://www.pearsonitcertification.com/articles/article.aspx?p=19 28231&seqNum=6`

Receiving an SNMP message from vCenter

After you have configured vCenter to send an SNMP alarm, we now use Orchestrator to receive the SNMP message:

1. In Orchestrator, start the workflow by navigating to **Library** | **SNMP** | **Wait for a trap on an SNMP device**.
2. Select the SNMP device you want to listen to. The OID is optional.
3. The workflow will pause until it receives an SNMP message from the selected device.
4. In vCenter, create a new resource pool. This should trigger the configured alarm and send an SNMP message to Orchestrator.
5. Check the logs of the workflow after it has received the SNMP message.

Refer to the *How it works...* section for more information about OID.

Using policies to trap SNMP messages

To use Orchestrator to continually monitor a device for new SNMP messages, follow these steps:

1. Switch Orchestrator to the **Administer** mode.
2. Click on **Policy Templates** (the yellow page with a green border icon).
3. Navigate to **Library** | **SNMP** | **SNMP Trap** and select **Apply policy**.
4. Give the new policy a name and description.
5. Select the SNMP device you would like to use and click on **Submit**.
6. Orchestrator automatically switches to the **Run** mode, into the **Policies** section, and onto the policy you have just created. Select **Edit** (the pencil icon).
7. In **Scripting**, expand the subscription and click on **OnTrap**.
8. In the **Script** tab, you will find that there is already a script that will output the SNMP message to the logs.
9. Save and close.

Instead of the existing script, you can create a script or workflow to phrase the SNMP messages. To get to the SNMP message data from the policy event as an array of properties, follow this script:

```
//get the SNMP data out of the Policy
var key = event.getValue("key");
var snmpResult = SnmpService.retrievePolicyData(key);
// convert the SNMPSnmpResult into Array of Property
var data =
System.getModule("com.vmware.library.snmp").processSnmpResult(snmpResult);
```

You can then use the OID number to fork to different workflows to address the issues raised by the SNMP message. A very good example of this can be found at
http://blogs.vmware.com/orchestrator/2013/04/vcenter-operations-integration-wit h-vcenter-orchestrator-in-5-minutes-or-less.html.

How it works...

SNMP stands for **Simple Network Management Protocol** and is used to manage and monitor systems by sending or receiving SNMP messages. A system can be monitored or managed by either making it send SNMP messages, or by responding to requests for information.

Each SNMP message can be accompanied by a community string. When an SNMP message is received, the receiver checks the community string against the one defined in the SNMP trap. If the string matches the message, it is accepted. The community string acts as a security measure. The default community string is `public`.

The important thing to understand about vCenter is that vCenter can only send SNMP messages when it starts up or when a triggered alarm is configured to send an SNMP message; it doesn't respond to SNMP requests.

ESXi hosts, however, can not only send messages, but can also react to SNMP requests.

OID and MIB

A **Management Information Base (MIB)** is a file that contains descriptions of **Object Identifiers (OIDs)**. Each vendor defines its own OIDs that are then distributed in MIBs. The VMware MIBs can be downloaded from `kb.vmware.com/kb/1013445`.

A text file that can be downloaded from `kb.vmware.com/kb/2054359` contains all the VMware OIDs in a more readable version.

Working with SNMP return data

The return data of the default SNMP workflows is an array of properties. Each of the array elements contains one OID. Each property contains the following keys:

Key	Meaning	Example key content
oid	The OID identifier	1.3.6.1.4.1.6876.4.3.306.0
type	The Orchestrator variable type	String
snmpType	The SNMP variable type	Octet String
value	The content of the message	Alarm ResourcePool - Event: Resource pool created (6656) Summary: Created resource pool asdsadfsad in compute-resource MyCluster in mylab Date: 16/11/2014 3:07:01 PM User name: VSPHERE.LOCAL\Administrator Resource pool: MyCluster Data center: mylab Arguments: parent.name = Resources

However, this is produced by the processSnmpResult action in the com.vmware.library.snmp module. The real SNMP results are stored in a bit more complex variable type, which is SNMPSnmpResult. In Orchestrator, it is easier to work with the array of properties, but check out the action and the variable type yourself.

SNMP – port 162 versus port 4000

The default port to send SNMP messages on is TCP 162; however, due to the fact that Linux systems have security restrictions for listening on ports below 1024, the Orchestrator SNMP listener is set to listen on port 4000. This is true for the Orchestrator appliance as well as for the Windows installation.

If you have a device that is not able to send SNMP messages on any port other than 162, here is a way around it (at least with the appliance):

1. Log in to your Orchestrator appliance with the root.
2. Run the following command:

```
iptables -t nat -A PREROUTING -p udp --dport 162 -j REDIRECT --to
4000
```

3. To make this change stick, run the following command:

```
iptables-save
```

There's more...

In this section, we take a look at how to configure SNMP on vCenter and on ESXi.

Configuring SNMP for vCenter

For vCenter to be able to send SNMP messages using alarms, we need to configure it first:

1. You can add up to four different SNMP receivers that vCenter can send messages to. For each one you need to specify the following:
2. Click on **SNMP receivers**.
3. Click on **Settings** and then click on **Edit**.
4. Navigate to your vCenter and then click on the **Manage** tab.
5. Open your vSphere Web Client.
    - The IP or FQDN of the SNMP receiver.
    - The port. The default is TCP 162; however, the listener on the Orchestrator appliance is set to TCP 4000.
    - The community string (if you're unsure, use the default, public).
6. When finished, click on **OK**.
7. Don't forget to configure your firewall to allow TCP 4000 out.

Configuring ESXi servers for SNMP

There are quite a lot of ways to configure SNMP on ESXi hosts. However, they all come down to the same basic method: set SNMP locally for every ESXi, and then open the ESXi firewall. You can use PowerCLI or any other method to interact with the API or use host profiles. In the following steps, we will use the esxcli command directly on the ESXi host to configure SNMP v1 and v2. Please note that the default port of the Orchestrator SNMP listener is TCP 4000 not TCP 162:

1. Configure the SNMP target(s):

   ```
   esxcli system snmp set --targets target_address@port/community
   ```

2. Set a different GET port for SNMP (if required):

   ```
   esxcli system snmp set --port port
   ```

3. Enable SNMP:

   ```
   esxcli system snmp set --enable true
   ```

4. Allow SNMP on the ESXi firewall:

   ```
   esxcli network firewall ruleset set --ruleset-id snmp --allowed-all
   true --
   enabled true
   esxcli network firewall refresh
   ```

We have used the local esxcli commands in this example simply because you could write an SSH workflow to patch all your ESXi hosts based on this example.

To configure SNMP v3 (using authentication and encryption), take a look at the vSphere Monitoring and Performance Guide, which is part of the VMware vSphere documentation set.

By default, ESXi SNMP is configured to send SNMP messages for CIM hardware monitoring. This means that you will receive SNMP messages if a hardware component of your ESXi server is alerted.

See also

Check out the SNMP example that comes with vRO7.

An example of automating hardening for new VMs is here:
http://blogs.vmware.com/vsphere/2012/07/automatically-securing-virtual-machines
-using-vcenter-orchestrator.html

Here's an example showing you how to integrate vCOPs into Orchestrator:
http://blogs.vmware.com/orchestrator/2013/04/vcenter-operations-integration-wit
h-vcenter-orchestrator-in-5-minutes-or-less.html

Working with AMQP

This recipe demonstrates how to use Orchestrator as a producer and consumer of AMQP message queues, how to create a subscription, and how to use Orchestrator policies to react to messages in the queues.

Getting ready

If you are totally new to AMQP, I suggest you start reading the *How it works...* section first.

An AMQP broker such as RabbitMQ is required. You can download it from
http://www.rabbitmq.com. You can find a fast and easy Windows installation and configuration for RabbitMQ in the *There's more...* section.

How to do it...

As with SOAP, REST, and a lot of other modules, we can actually use the provided workflows. So in the following sections, we will make use of them.

Adding an AMQP host

To start with AMQP, we first need to add an AMQP broker to Orchestrator:

1. Start the workflow by navigating to **Library** | **AMQP** | **Configuration** | **Add a broker**.
2. Give the connection a name.
3. Add the broker IP or FQDN; the default port is `TCP 5672`.
4. **Virtual host** (vhost) is always in a freshly installed AMQP broker.
5. You can use SSL (and probably should) and then enter the username and password that are granted access to the virtual host.
6. After you have submitted the workflow, check out the inventory. Your host should now be visible:

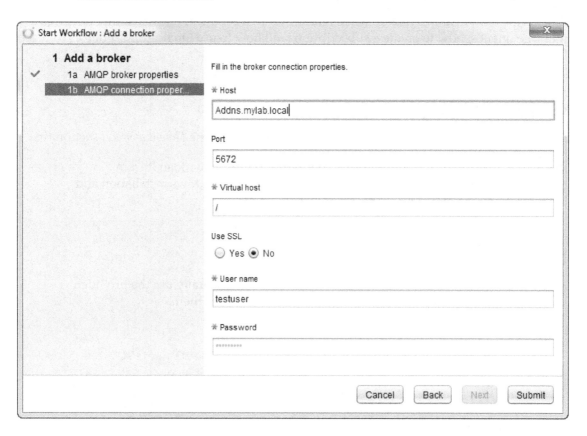

Defining exchanges, queues, and binds

To work with AMQP, we need exchanges and queues, so we will define them now:

1. Run the workflow by navigating to **Library | AMQP | Declare an exchange**.
2. Select the broker for which you want to add the exchange.
3. Give the exchange a name such as `systemExchange` (this is used by vCloud Director).
4. Select a type of exchange (refer to the *How it works...* section).
5. **Durable** means that messages will be kept in the broker even if it restarts.
6. **AutoDelete** will delete the exchange as soon as there are no more queues bound to it.

Now we will create a queue:

1. Run the workflow by navigating to **Library | AMQP | Declare a queue**.
2. Select the broker.
3. Name the queue, such as `vco`.
4. Select **Durable**.
5. **Exclusive** means that only one client is allowed for this queue.
6. **Auto Delete** in a queue means that the queue itself will be deleted as soon as there are no more subscribers to it.

Now we will bind the queue to an exchange:

1. Run the workflow by navigating to **Library | AMQP | Bind**.
2. Select the broker.
3. Select the queue name and the exchange you want to bind it to.
4. Enter a routing key (# is a wildcard for everything).

Sending messages

We will now send a message to the exchange:

1. Run the workflow by navigating to **Library | AMQP | Send a text message**.
2. Select the broker.
3. Enter the exchange as well as the routing key (at this stage, anything will do).
4. Enter a text message.
5. The message is now stored in the queue until it is read.

Receiving messages

We will now read the message we sent to the queue:

1. Run the workflow by navigating to **Library** | **AMQP** | **Send a text message**.
2. Select the broker.
3. Enter the queue you would like to receive the message from.
4. The message body is in the out-parameter body.

If you are new to AMQP, then I would suggest that you read the *How it works...* section at this stage, where an example of the value of all this is provided.

Subscribing to a queue

Subscribing to a queue means that Orchestrator can use a policy to monitor this queue continually for new messages:

1. Run the workflow by navigating to **Library** | **AMQP** | **Configuration** | **Subscribe to queues**.
2. Enter a name for the subscription by which you can later identify it in the policy.
3. Select the broker.
4. Select the queue(s) you would like to subscribe to, such as vco.
5. Your subscription is now visible under the AMQP infrastructure.

Using a policy as trigger

You should be aware of how Orchestrator policies work; refer to the *Working with policies* section in Chapter 8, *Better Workflows and Optimized Working*.

1. Switch Orchestrator to the **Administer** mode.
2. Click on policy templates (the yellow page with the green border icon).
3. Navigate to **Library** | **AMQP** | **Subscription** and select **Apply policy**.
4. Give the new policy a name and description.
5. Select the **AMQP** subscription you would like to use and click on **Submit**.
6. Orchestrator automatically switches to the **Run** mode, and you are automatically presented with the policy you have just created in the **Policies** section. Select **Edit** (the pencil icon).
7. In the **Scripting** tab, expand the subscription and click on **OnMessage**.

8. In the **Workflow** tab, click on **Choose a workflow** (the magnifying glass icon) and select the workflow to execute when a new message arrives. You can choose the example workflow `10.06.1 AMQP Worker`.

9. Save and close.

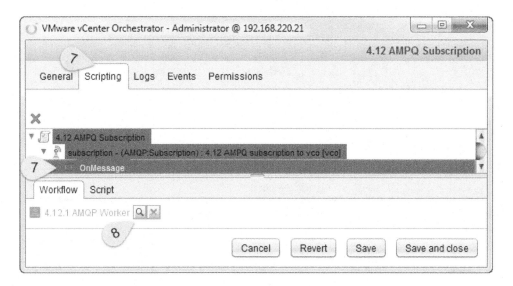

10. Now, start the policy (the green play button).

11. You can use the example workflow, `10.6.3 Fill`, to fill up the queue with messages. Watch the logs in the policy to see the execution happening.

How it works...

A message bus such as RabbitMQ can be compared to a mail server that stores e-mails until they are taken off the server. The **Advanced Message Queuing Protocol** (**AMQP**) defines a publisher/producer as someone sending messages, a broker (server) as the storage and process host, and a client/consumer as someone who receives messages.

Any message that is sent to the broker will be put in an exchange. The exchange will use the routing key to route the message into a queue. A consumer will read messages from a queue.

AMQP uses a virtual host or vHost (nothing to do with virtualization), which defines authentications, which means that you can have different vHosts that provide access to different users, as you cannot give access rights to exchanges or queues.

Here is a simple example using Orchestrator (example workflows `10.06.1 AMQP Worker` and `10.6.2 Fill up and work`):

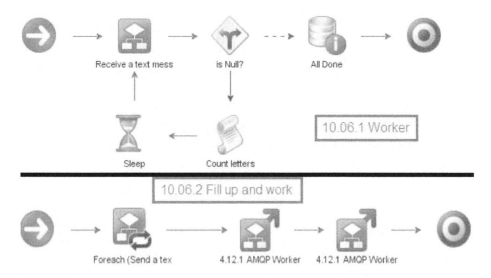

The example workflow `10.6.2 Fill up and work` will fill up the `systemExchange` exchange from an attribute (an array of strings) using the # routing key. The # routing key will just forward everything into the `vco` queue. It will then start the workflow example `10.06.1 AMQP Worker` twice asynchronously. Each of the *Worker* workflows will go and get a message from the queue, check whether the body is defined (not `Null`), and then sleep one second for each letter in the message.

When you run the workflow, you will see how the two worker workflows grab the next message in the queue and work on it until the queue is empty.

To understand routing and exchanges, we need to explain the four different kinds of exchange:

Exchange type	Description
Direct	This exchange routes messages, depending on their routing key, to a specific queue that is specified by the routing key in the exchange-queue binding.
Fanout	All messages sent to this exchange will be forwarded into all queues that are bound to it.
Headers	This ignores the routing key. It routes messages depending on the sender (as in, mail headers).
Topics	Routing is done using wildcards. There are two wildcards that AMQP understands: * means exactly one word and # means none to many words.

There's more...

Let's take a quick look at how to install and get AMQP going using RabbitMQ.

Installing RabbitMQ

The following steps will install RabbitMQ on a Windows host and configure a user to connect from the outside. Please note that this is a quick-and-dirty installation and configuration that is only okay for labs; however, it gets beginners going:

1. Download RabbitMQ from `http://www.rabbitmq.com` (in this example, we will use the Windows installation).
2. Download OTP from `http://www.erlang.org/download.html`, as RabbitMQ for Windows, requires this package.

> Perform all the following steps on the same host. This is important, as RabbitMQ is configured to only accept localhost connections by default.

3. Make sure `TCP 5672` and `15672` are open in and outgoing.
4. Install **OTP** with the defaults.
5. Install RabbitMq with the defaults.
6. Run the program by navigating to **Start | RabbitMQ Server | Command Prompt (sbin dir)**.

7. In the console that opens, type `rabbitmq-plugins enable rabbitmq_management`.
8. Open a browser and browse `http://localhost:15672`.
9. The default user is `guest` and the password is `guest`.
10. In the RabbitMQ management, click on **Admin**.
11. Enter a new username (for example, `testuser`) as well as a password. Add the tag **Admin** and click on **Add user**.
12. The user is created. Now, click on the user, as shown in the following screenshot.
13. The details of the user are displayed. Click on **Set permission**.

You are now able to connect from the outside to **RabbitMQ** and use it:

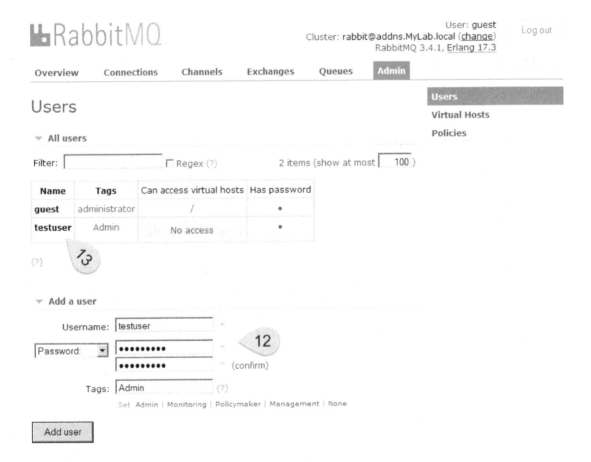

See also

Check out the AMQP example that comes with vRO7.

AMQP basics:

- `https://www.rabbitmq.com/tutorials/amqp-concepts.html`
- `http://www.rabbitmq.com/tutorials/tutorial-one-java.html`

There's a worthwhile article on how to use AMQP, vCloud Director, and Orchestrator together at:

`http://www.vcoteam.info/articles/learn-vco/179-configure-the-amqp-plug-in.html`.

The example workflows are as follows:

- `10.06.1 AMQP Worker`
- `10.06.2 Fill up and work`
- `10.06.3 Fill`

11
Additional Plugins

This chapter is dedicated to some of the more commonly used plugins for Orchestrator. All these plugins require that you download them. We will be looking at the following plugins:

- NSX integration
- Horizon Integration
- vSphere Replication
- SRM (Site Recovery Manager) integration
- vROps (vRealize Operations Manager) integration

Introduction

In the last two chapters, we took quite an intense look at all the plugins that come with Orchestrator. Now we will look at plugins you can add to it. The selection is based on using them with clients and discussions with other consultants.

There are many different plugins, such as VMware-based plugins for a lot of VMware products, as well as plugins from EMC, NetApp, Cisco UCS, Infoblox, F5, and more.

Installing plugins

Installing plugins is pretty simple; please see recipe *Installing Plugins* in `Chapter 1, Installing and Configuring Orchestrator`.

Please note that when you download a plugin, your download should contain either a `.vmoapp` or `.dar` file. If the download is a ZIP file, it needs to be unzipped first.

Obtaining plugins

There are three main ways (in my opinion) to get plugins: from the VMware site, from the vCO/vRO team website, and from VMware Solution Exchange.

VMware core plugins

The VMware page (`https://www.vmware.com/support/pubs/vco_plugins_pubs.html`) contains download links, as well as release notes and any additional documentation for the following plugins:

- vRealize Automation
- Amazon Web Services
- AMPQ
- Auto Deploy
- Elastic Services
- HTTP-REST
- Multi-node
- PowerShell
- SNMP
- SOAP
- SQL
- UCS Manager
- vCenter Chargeback Manager
- vCenter Service
- vCenter Site Recovery Manager
- vCloud Director
- vSphere Replication

vRO/vCO Team

The **vCOTeam** web page is run by Christopher Decanini and Burke Azbill, who not only reviewed this book but are also considered global experts on Orchestrator within VMware.

The site contains a very good collection of available plugins and also a great deal of information and tutorials on Orchestrator. For more information, refer to:

`http://www.vcoteam.info/links/plug-ins.html`

VMware Solution Exchange

The VMware Solution Exchange is a platform run by VMware featuring extra material for vRealize Operations, vRealize Log insight, vRealize Orchestrator, vRealize Automation, and vSphere Web Client and is a source of really useful documentation.

You may be required to create a free account to access some of the downloads or some additional licensing from vendors. For more information, refer to `https://solutionexchange.vmware.com/store`.

NSX integration

In this recipe, we take a look at automating NSX with Orchestrator.

Getting ready

You need NSX installed and connected to your vCenter. There are some good YouTube videos that show the essential setup. For more information, refer to `https://www.youtube.com/watch?v=CATcY254pP8`.

You will need the latest version of the NSX plugin (as of writing, version 1.0.4) and to install it in your Orchestrator. You can find it here by logging into `www.vmware.com` and then selecting **NSX** and then under **Drivers & Tools**.

To understand NSX, there is a wonderful **Hands-on Labs** from VMware that you may like to work through: `http://www.vmware.com/products/nsx/nsx-hol.html`.

How to do it...

This recipe is broken up into two sections: configuring and an example.

Configuring an endpoint

1. Run the workflow**Library | NSX | Configuration | Create NSX endpoint**.
2. Enter a name for the endpoint.
3. The user must be defined as an NSX user (you can also use the **admin** user you defined when installing the NSX appliance).

4. The URL is `https://[FQDN NSX appliance]`.

5. The default settings are fine for the time being. They define how often and how long Orchestrator should try with an NSX operation.

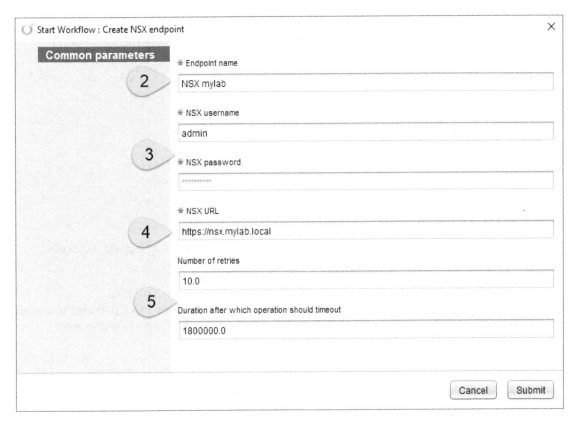

6. We need to check if everything has worked. In the Orchestrator Client, click on **Inventory** and then expand the NSX entry. You should see some items, as shown in the following screenshot:

Creating a new logical switch

We will now create a new logical switch in NSX with default settings (unicast and IP discovery). You need an existing Transport Zone for this to work.

1. First we need to get the **MoRef** of the Transport Zone (for MoRefs, see the *Introduction* to `Chapter 12`, *Working with Vsphere*). In Orchestrator Client, click on NSX and browse to the Transport Zone you need.

2. The **objectId** is what you're looking for:

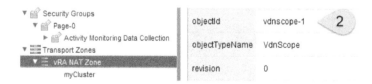

3. You can mark and copy this using *Ctrl + C*.
4. Run the workflow **Library | NSX | NSX workflows | Create logical switch**.
5. Select the NSX endpoint you have defined.
6. Paste (*Ctrl + V*) the Transport Zone MoRef.
7. Give the network a name and description.
8. The **Tenant id** can be left empty; this is a value that vRealize Automation uses:

9. After submitting the workflow, check your NSX in vCenter.

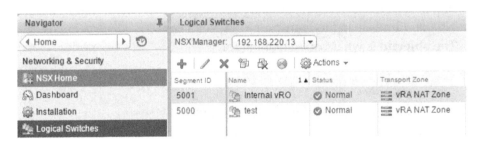

How it works...

The NSX plugin is a useful tool for automating; however, the workflows that come with the plugin are mostly designed for vRealize Automation. It's important to understand that they return mostly an NSX object, meaning that they need to be modified before they can be used in vSphere or vRA XaaS:

- Add IP pools to DHCP
- Add load balancer to edge
- Add NAT rules
- Add secondary IP addresses to edge vNic
- Add static routes
- Add VMs and IpSet to security group
- Add VMs to existing load balancer pools
- Add VMs to security group
- Apply security policy on security group
- Apply security tags on VM
- Configure firewall rules between interfaces
- Connect logical switch to router
- Create edge
- Create logical switch
- Create security group
- Delete edge
- Delete logical switch
- Delete NAT rules
- Delete security group
- Delete static routes from edge
- Disconnect router interface
- Remove secondary IP addresses assigned to edge vNic
- Remove VMs from load balancer pools
- Set default route

If you want to use the workflows for some kind of automation, you need to use some extra programming. As we saw earlier, you need to provide all the MoRefs of each object. Here is an example of how to do this:

To get all the scopes (Transport Zones) use the following code:

```
scopes=NSXVdnScopeManager.getVdnScopes(connection);
```

To show-case this, I have provided an example workflow `11.01 Create logical switch` and its two actions: `getAllScopes` and `getScopeIDFromName`.

vRealize Automation integration

NSX is directly integrated into vRA and is configured and used through the vCenter Endpoint.

To integrate NSX, you need to configure the vCenter Endpoint to allow for NSX integration as well as create a vRO Infrastructure Endpoint, follow these instructions:

1. In the vCenter Endpoint, click on the box **Specify manager for network and security platform**.
2. Enter the address of your NSX manager in the form of `https://[FQDN NSX]`.
3. The credentials should be a user who has the rights to manage your NSX.
4. Follow the recipe *Adding Orchestrator as an Infrastructure Endpoint* in `Chapter 13`, *Working with vRealize Automation* to add Orchestrator as an Infrastructure endpoint.

For vRA to be able to use the NSX, we need to have at least one transport zone as well as one **Distributed Logical Router (DLR)**.

Please note that you could attach the DLR directly onto the external network if this network would have a VLAN ID other than 0. In my example, I used an extra Edge.

The following is an example of the setup that allows me to create NSX networks that can connect to **iNet** (see the following figure):

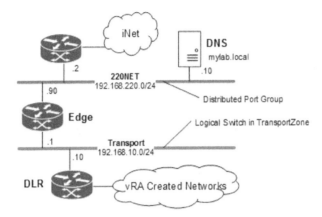

1. You need to create a **Unicast Transport Zone**.
2. Create a **Unicast Logical Switch** on this **Transport Zone** with the default settings.
3. Create an **Edge Service Gateway** with two interfaces:
    - An **Uplink** to an external network on a Distributed Port Group (220Net). Use an IP from your external network (192.168.220.90).
    - An **Internal** to the Logical Switch you created (Transport), use the IP that will be the gateway for the Logical Network (192.168.10.1)

    As the Gateway, you select the **Uplink** and enter the IP of your external Network Gateway (192.168.220.2).

4. Create a **Distributed Logical Router (DLR)** with one interface:
    - Connect the **HA interface** to the Logical Network (Transport)
    - Create an **Uplink** to the Logical Network (Transport), and use an IP from the Logical Network (192.168.10.10)
5. In vRA, go to **Infrastructure | Reservation | Network Profiles**.
6. Create an **External Network Profile** that matches your External network settings.

7. Create an **External Network Profile** for your Logical network (`Transport`) with the DNS setting of your External Network (`220Net - Mylab.local`). Set the IP of your Edge (`192.168.10.1`) as the Gateway.

8. Make sure that you update your data collection so that vRA sees the new DLR you created.

9. Assign in the reservation the Transport Zone as well as the DLR with its **Logical Network** and the **External Network Profile**.

10. You can now create **Routed** and **NAT**ed Network profiles, which you can connect directly to the External Network (`220Net`) using its Gateway.

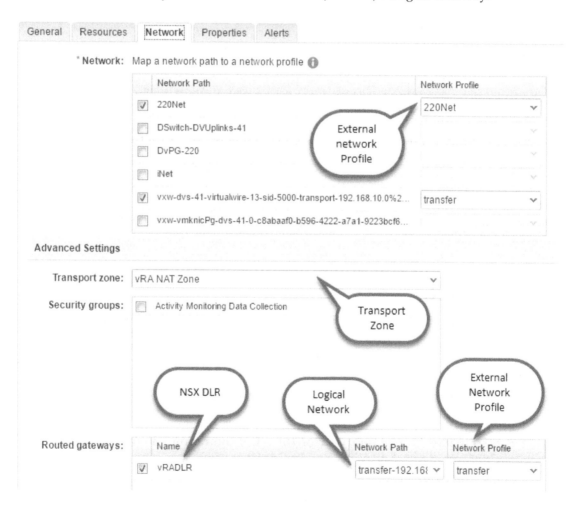

See also

Example workflow `11.01 Create logical switch`.

Horizon integration

In this recipe, we will look into integrating VMware Horizon View into Orchestrator.

Getting ready

You need the Horizon 7 plugin and you need to load it into Orchestrator. The plugin can be found at .

There is a known issue (plugin version 1.3 at the time of writing). Follow `kb.vmware.com/kb/2144316` in order to switch on **TLSv1.1** and 1.2 for Orchestrator.

> Always fully read the release notes of any plugin or update. There are five known issues that you need to be aware of: `https://pubs.vmware.com/Release_Notes/en/hvro-plugin/horizon-vro-plugin-13-release-notes.html`.

You also need the Horizon infrastructure. The minimum would be a Connection Server with one pool and one VM.

How to do it…

The following shows the basic setup, an example, and access point automation.

Basic setup

We will now connect Orchestrator to Horizon. This basic setup will allow a chosen user to do everything:

1. Start the workflow **Library | Horizon | Configuration | View Pod Configuration | Add View Pod In Configuration**.
2. Give the POD an alias.
3. Enter the FQDN of the connection server. The IP doesn't work most of the times.
4. Enter a Horizon user with administrator rights.

5. Click on **Submit** and wait until the workflow has finished.

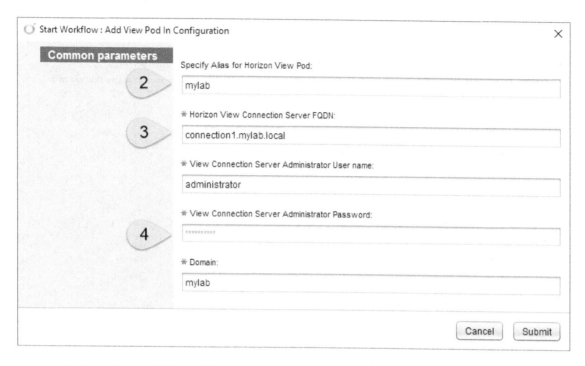

6. Start the workflow **Library | Horizon | Configuration | Delegated Admin Configuration | Add delegated Administrator Configuration**.

7. If the Horizon View Pod isn't a drop-down menu, the last workflow hasn't worked, even if it has showed no error. Check kb.vmware.com/kb/2144316 to fix this issue.

8. Choose **Yes** on all questions in order to make the user you choose in step 9 an admin who is able to perform all the actions on all pools.

9. Choose a user or group that is allowed to administer Horizon through Orchestrator:

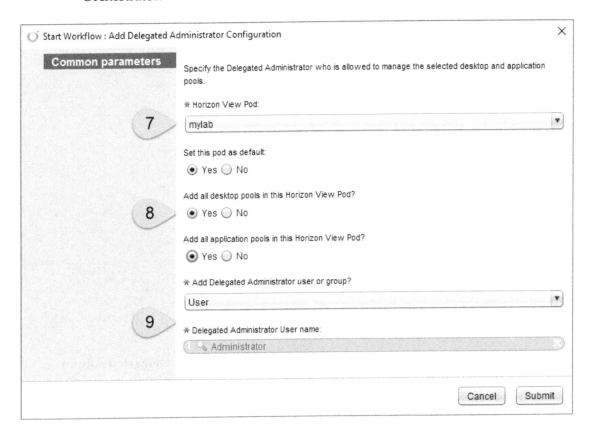

10. Click on **Submit** and wait until the workflow has finished.
11. Run the workflow **Library** | **Horizon** | **Configuration** | **Manage Self Service Pool Configuration**.

12. Set all to **Yes** to make sure that the user from step 9 is allowed everything.

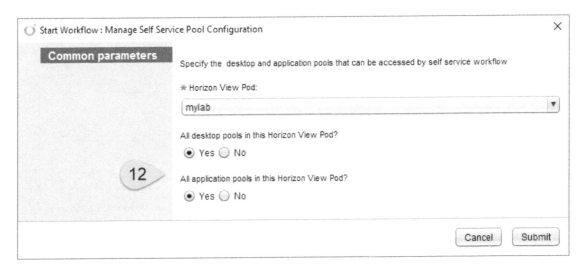

13. Click on **Submit** and wait until the workflow has finished.

Examples

Let's run an example by adding a user to a pool.

1. Run the workflow **Library | Horizon | Configuration | Workflow delegation | Add User(s) to Desktop Pool**.
2. Select the delegated administrator you defined earlier.
3. Select the pool you would like to add a user to.

4. Enter a user (or users) to be added.

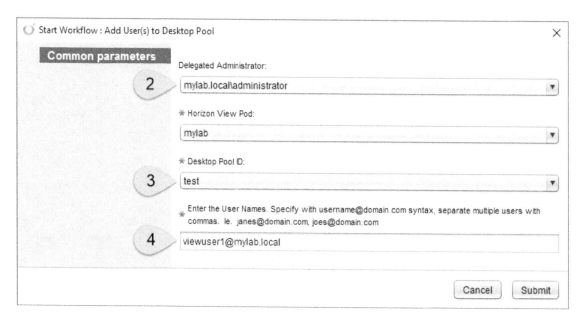

5. Click on **Submit** and wait until the workflow has finished.
6. Check your pool in Horizon.

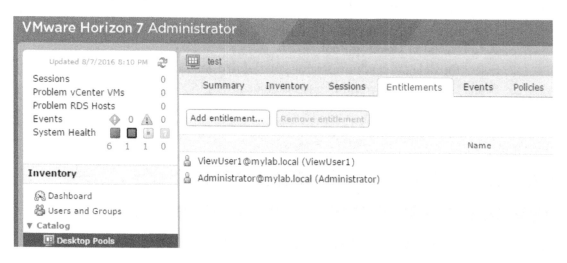

Access point configuration

Access points can be configured during deployment but also via REST. So let's do that. Please have a look at the following recipes: *Working with REST* in Chapter 9, *Essential Plugins* and *Working with JSON* in Chapter 6, *Advanced Programming* and *Accessing the Control Center via REST plugin* in Chapter 7, *Interacting with Orchestrator*, before starting.

The swagger UI URL for the access point configuration is as follows:

```
https://[FQDN accesspoint]:9443/swagger-ui/index.html
```

1. Add the Access point as a REST host. The URL is `https://access1.mylab.local:9443/rest/` with basic authentication using the admin user you defined during deployment.
2. Add the following REST operation with `Content-Type=application/json` and create workflows for it: PUT `/v1/config/certs/ssl`.
3. Update the workflows with the header:

   ```
   request.setHeader("Content-Type", "application/json");
   ```

4. Edit the PUT `/v1/config/certs/ssl` workflow.
5. Move content to attributes and add `privateKey` and `chain` as the `string` input-parameter.
6. Add a scriptable task with the following code:

   ```
   var propList=new Properties();
   propList.put("privateKeyPem",privateKey);
   propList.put("certChainPem",chain);
   var jsonObj = new Object();
   for each (key in propList.keys){
       jsonObj[key]=propList.get(key);
   }
   content= JSON.stringify(jsonObj);
   ```

7. This will now enable you to directly put a new SSL certificated onto the access point.

You could now create a workflow that updates the configuration just by using these operations:

- GET `/v1/config/edgeservice`
- PUT `/v1/config/edgeservice/view`

How it works...

The Horizon plugin is written to be used with the vSphere Web Client or with vRealize Orchestrator. If you explore the workflows that come with the plugin, you will see that there are vCAC (for vRA) and vSphere Web Client specific versions of all the basic workflows shown in workflow delegation.

From here it's just a small step to build the plugin into vRealize Automation or the vSphere Web Client.

Once you run the configuration workflows, the configuration is stored as an Orchestrator configuration (also see the recipe *Working with configurations* in Chapter 8, *Better Workflows and Optimized Working*) in a folder called View.

The Horizon plugin also comes with a lot of Orchestrator resource elements (see *Working with resources* in Chapter 8, *Better Workflows and Optimized Working*), which contain Icons as well as configured localizations (see recipe *Language packs (localization)* in Chapter 8, *Better Workflows and Optimized Working*) for the vSphere Web Client and vCAC (vRA) workflows.

There's more...

Let's look at the integration of the Horizon Client into vSphere and vRealize Automation.

Integration into vSphere Web Client

The Horizon plugin comes with preconfigured workflows aimed at being used in the vSphere Web Client. You find them in the folder **Library | Horizon | Workflows | vSphere Web Client**.

Add Managed Machines to Pool	Desktop Allocation for Users	Remove Users From Application Pool
Add Unmanaged Machines to Pool	Desktop Assignment	Remove Users From Desktop Pool
Add User(s) to App Pool	Desktop Entitlement	Session Management
Add User(s) to App Pools	Desktop Recycle	Set Maintenance Mode
Add User(s) to Desktop Pool	Desktop Refresh	Unassign User
Advanced Desktop Allocation	Global Entitlement Management	Update App Pool Display Name
Application Entitlement	Recompose Pool	Update Desktop Pool Display Name
Assign User	Recompose Pools	Update Desktop Pool Min Size
Desktop Allocation	Register Machines to Pool	Update Desktop Pool Spare Size

You can use them directly in the vSphere Web Client. However, you can also customize the workflows; for example, you could restrict the workflows to only one view pool (or a couple of pools). To do so, follow these instructions:

1. Take one of the workflows, such as **Desktop Allocation for Users**, and create a copy of it.
2. Edit the copy.
3. Move the input-parameter **poolID** as an attribute by right-clicking on the **poolID** and selecting **Move as attribute**.
4. Click on **General** and then put in the name of the pool. The value is case-sensitive.
5. Do the same with the **PodAlias**.
6. In the Presentation section, click on **Presentation** (the top element) and then on **General**, and enter the following text:

   ```
   This will add a user to the pool: <b>${poolId}</b> in the Pod:
   <b>${podAlias}</b>
   ```

7. Running the workflow now will only ask for the user.

An even better method is using configurations (also see the recipe *Working with configurations* in `Chapter 8`, *Better Workflows and Optimized Working*) to manage the settings centrally.

Also, see the example workflow: `11.03 Desktop Allocation for Users`.

VRA integration

The Horizon plugin comes with a lot of preconfigured workflows that are ready to be XaaS blueprints and actions.

The process to create a vRA Horizon Integration is a pretty lengthy one and will not fit into this book. However, the Horizon plugin comes with a not so bad PDF that describes the process. Go to the plugin download page or search for `using-horizon-vro-plugin-13-guide.pdf`.

Some things that are not discussed in this PDF but are essential are as follows:

- Configure a new Tenant with AD connection and external Orchestrator using basic authentication
- Install and configure an Orchestrator with vSphere authentication that uses the same AD as Horizon
- Your Horizon should be connected to the same AD as the Tenant and the Orchestrator (using vSphere Authentication)
- The users/groups you use in vRA should also have permissions in Horizon
- The vRA VDI admins should also be delegated admins in the Horizon plugin

The Horizon plugin also contains a collection of icons (Configuration, **Library** | **Horizon** | **Icon**). You can export these to a local disk and then import them into vRA when you import the workflow or action.

See also

Configure Access points via REST:
`https://communities.vmware.com/people/Windspirit/blog/2016/08/08/configuring-an-horizon-accesspoint-the-easy-way.`

VMware documentation for Horizon plugin:
`https://pubs.vmware.com/horizon-7-view/topic/com.vmware.ICbase/PDF/using-horizon-vro-plugin-13-guide.pdf.`

vSphere Replication

In this recipe, we explore the vSphere Replication plugin.

Getting ready

You need the vSphere Replication deployed. You also need a second vCenter (not really required but it makes things more interesting) or a Cloud service such as VMware vCloud Air. If you want to use vCloud Air, check `kb.vmware.com/kb/2083867`.

If you are new to vSphere Replication, check out the video at:

`https://www.youtube.com/watch?v=EWRs36nS5F0`

You need to have at least one replication site configured.

Last but not least, you need the vSphere Replication plugin (see the introduction to this chapter).

How to do it...

This recipe is split into several sections.

Registering sites

The first thing we need to do is register the sites for Orchestrator to use. This requires that you have already registered a site with vSphere Replication in the vSphere Web Client.

1. Check out the Orchestrator inventory for the sites that the Replication can see. In my example, Replication can see my two vCenters.

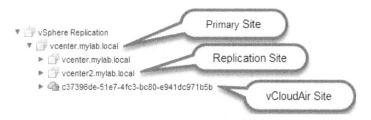

2. Run the workflow**Library | vSphere Replication | Remote Site Management|
Register VC Site**, which registers the credentials for the connection to a site with
Orchestrator; these workflows do not register sites in Replication.

Setting up a replication

We will now quickly set up a replication of a new VM.

1. Start the workflow **Library | vSphere Replication | Configure Replication |
Configure Replication**.
2. For **Site**, select from your the Orchestrator inventory in **Replication** your **Primary
Site** (see first figure of the section *Registering Sites*).
3. For **Source VM**, select from the Orchestrator inventory in **vCenter Server** a VM
you would like to replicate.
4. For the **Target Site**, select your replication site from the Orchestrator inventory in
Replication. Then select a target datastore.
5. Last but not least, you can select replication options (if you're not sure, select the
default values).
6. The VM should now be replicated.

Recovery

Well … there is no API exposed way to do a vCenter Replication recovery. Only to/from
vCenter Replications in the cloud are exposed and can be used.

How it works...

vSphere Replication is a really useful tool that is included in vSphere licensing (from Standard onward). The tool allows you to replicate VMs between sites. Please note that the recovery site doesn't have to be a separate vCenter. I have customers who have multiple sites (as in distance from each other) in the same vCenter using one Replication appliance to replicate VMs between Sites. However, two vCenters are more fun for this example.

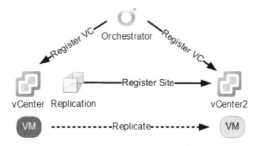

It is a great oversight that there is no vCenter – vCenter Recovery function exposed on the API and I sincerely hope that it will be back filled at some stage.

The following vSphere Replication workflows exist:

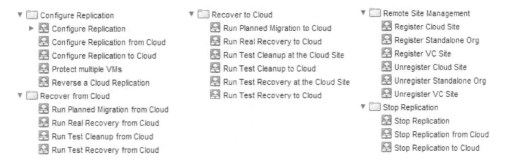

There's more...

There are a couple of things to explore.

Using vCloud Air for recovery

To use vCloud Air for recovery you require a vCloud Air subscription with service credits for **Disaster Recovery to the Cloud**. The Replication doesn't work with service credits for **Virtual Private Cloud OnDemand**.

If you don't have a vCloud account, you can still test it. Just use this **Hands-on Labs** at `https://www.vmware.com/vca-dr-hol-labs.html`.

To configure a vCloud Air target, follow these steps:

1. Log in to your vCloud Air .
2. Click on **Disaster Recovery to the Cloud** and select your source datacenter (in this example **UK Slough 1 6**).
3. Click on the **Connection** icon on the left side.
4. Copy the **URL** and the **Organization Name** into a notepad.
5. Log in to your vCenter.
6. Go to vSphere Replication and then click on **Manage**.
7. Go to target sites and click on ⬛.
8. Copy the **URL** into **Cloud provider** address and the **Organization Name** in the field with the same name.
9. The login credentials are those you use to sign into vCloud Air.
10. Click on **Next** and select **Virtual Data Center** (in this example VDC1).
11. After you have finished the **Connect to a Cloud Provider** Wizard, you need to map the networks between vCenter and vCloud Air. Right-click on the vCloud Air connection and select **Configure target networks**.
12. In Orchestrator, run the workflow **Library | vSphere Replication | Remote Site Management | Register Cloud Site**.

You are now ready to use Replication with vCloud Air.

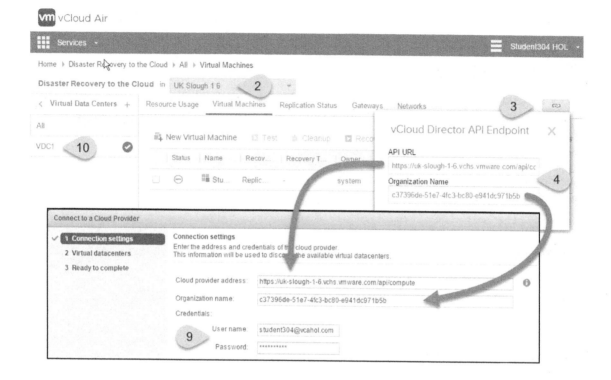

Integration into vSphere Web Client

Integration into vSphere Web Client isn't really needed as vSphere Replication already is a plugin. However, you could create some workflows that create a VM replication with your typical values. The value in this would be to use the Orchestrator user management to allow a user to run a workflow that configures replication with preset values.

See also

Recipe *SRM (Site Recovery Manager) integration* in this chapter.

The example workflow: `11.04 Protect`.

SRM (Site Recovery Manager) integration

In this recipe, we will look into how to automate **SRM (Site Recovery Manager)**.

Getting ready

You will need SRM installed and base configured. Meaning that SRM should be configured either with vSphere Replication or an **SRA (Storage Replication Adapter)** that connects to your storage. If you are new to SRM, have a look at the video at
`https://www.youtube.com/watch?v=drOdnRaDZ4Q`.

Last but not least, you need the vSphere Replication plugin (see the introduction to this chapter).

How to do it…

This recipe is broken up into several sections.

Preparation

You need to make sure that the following things are set:

- Orchestrator is *authenticating* to the PSC (vSphere authentications)
- Orchestrator is configured to use *both* the protected and the recovery vCenter
- The protected and the recovery vCenter *must* be in the same SSO domain
- The user that is used in the vCenter connection should have *SRM rights* on both the protected and the recovery vCenter

Configuration

The following steps are needed to connect to SRM:

1. Run the workflow **Library | SRM | Configuration | Configure Local Site**.
2. Just accept the certificates; nothing much to do here.
3. Run the workflow **Library | SRM | Configuration | Configure Remote Site**.
4. Click on **Local Site** and expand the SRM tab in the inventory. If the tab is empty, then you need to check the rights of the vCenter user. Select the protected vCenter and accept the certificates.

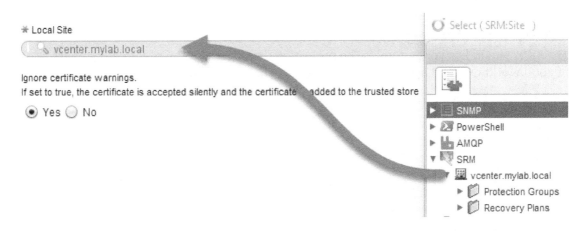

5. Run the workflow **Library I SRM I Configuration I Login Remote Site**.
6. Select the local site and enter a user that has SRM administrator rights.
7. Check the Orchestrator inventory; it should now show the protected and the recovery sites.

Working with the plugin

Now that it is all configured, let's try something. For this we will use vSphere Replication. You need a defined protection group and a recovery plan.

1. Make sure you have protected a VM using vSphere Recovery. You could use the vSphere Replication plugin as discussed in recipe *vSphere Replication* in this chapter.
2. Run the workflow **Library I SRM I Protection Group I Add Replicated VM to vSphere Replication Protection Group**.
3. Select the **Protection Group** and the VM you have replicated.
4. Wait until the workflow is finished. The VM added to the protection plan, however, is not configured.
5. Run the workflow **Library I SRM I Protection Group I Protect All Unprotected Virtual Machines Associated with Protection group**.
6. The VM is now protected with the recovery plan in the protection group.

How it works...

The SRM plugin lets you automate the protection of your VMs. The plugin comes with a lot of good workflows and actions that fulfill almost all your automation needs.

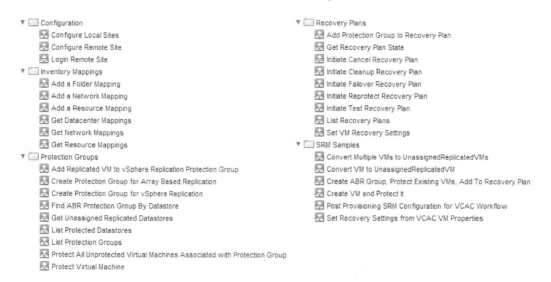

The only negative is that you can only use the plugin on vCenters that are in the same SSO domain, therefore limiting its use.

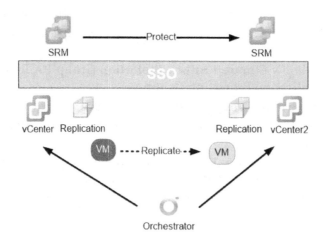

There's more…

Let's talk about the integration possibilities for the plugin.

vSphere Web Client integration

Integration into vSphere Web Client is pretty straightforward. You can either implement the existing workflows or modify them using configurations to create fixed settings.

Another choice is to create a workflow that will replicate a VM, add it to a recovery plan, and configure its protection in one go. What would be good in addition to that is to assign tags to the VMs that show the protection group and the recovery plan (see *Custom Attributes and Tags (vAPI)* in `Chapter 12`, *Working with vSphere*).

Also, see the example workflow: `11.04 Protect`.

vRealize Automation integration

The integration of SRM into vRealize Automation 7.x is described very nicely in the following PDF from VMware (you need to Google for it): `vrealize-suite-70-disaster-recovery-SRM-61.pdf`.

See also

See the recipe *vSphere Replication* in this chapter.

Also see the example workflow: `11.04 Protect`.

vROps (vRealize Operations Manager) integration

In this recipe, we explore how to use Orchestrator to expand the capabilities of **vRealize Operations Manager (vROps)**.

Getting ready

You will need a vROps installation collecting data from vCenter. You also need to have Orchestrator connected to the same vCenter.

You need to download the vROps plugin from **Solution Exchange** (see the introduction to this chapter). You may need to create a free account to access the download.

If you are new to vROps, check out the video at:
`https://www.youtube.com/watch?v=aN85uCtPtJ4`.

How to do it...

This recipe is split into multiple sections. To reduce confusion about what plugin is which, I will talk about the vROps plugin, meaning the plugin that goes into vROps and the vROps package that went into Orchestrator.

Deploy

After you have downloaded the ZIP folder from Solution Exchange, you need to unzip it. It contains the `.package` file from Orchestrator and the `.pak` file for vROps. We will now deploy them:

1. Import the `.package` file into Orchestrator (see recipe *Working with packages* in `Chapter 4`, *Programming skills*). This will create a new folder that contains the workflows that vROPS will call.
2. Log in to vROps as an vROps administrator (for example, using the local admin account you created on install).
3. Go to **Administration** and then to **Solutions**.
4. Click on the green **+** sign to add a solution. Choose the `.pak` file that comes with the plugin and click on **Upload**.
5. Wait until the package is uploaded. Click on **Next** and accept the warning about the signature.
6. **Accept** the EULA and click **Next**.
7. Wait until the installation is done and then click on **Finish**.
8. Now click on **Support** and then on **Redescribe**; then run **Redescribe**. Wait until you read **Describe operation completed successfully**.

9. Go back to **Solutions**, select **vRealize Orchestrator Action Adapter**, and click on **Configure** (the gear icon on top).
10. Enter a name for the configuration.
11. Enter the IP or FQDN of your Orchestrator.
12. Click on the green plus sign to create new credentials. The user should have permissions to execute workflow in Orchestrator depending on your vCenter Orchestrator connection (shared or not) rights in vCenter.
13. Click on **Test Connection** and accept the Orchestrator certificate.
14. If the test was successful, click on **Save Settings** and then on **Close**.

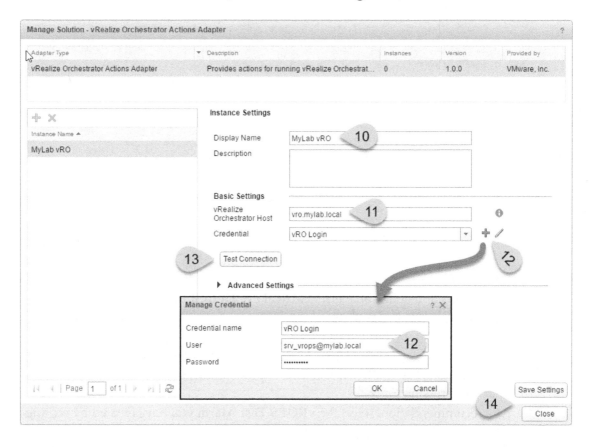

Working with the plugin

We will now use one action in vROps. We will configure an alarm and then trigger it.

1. First we have to assign an action to a recommendation. Click on **Content** and then on **Recommendations**.

2. Click on the green plus sign to create a new recommendation. Select an action and enter text such as vROPS Test Alarm.

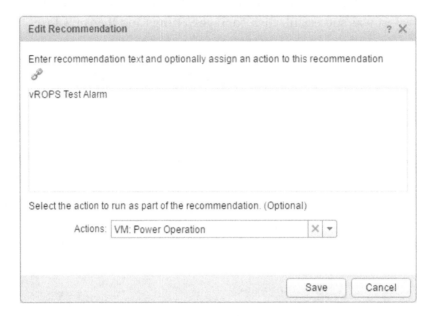

3. Next we need to define an alarm. Go to alarm **Definitions** and click on the green plus sign to create a new alarm.

4. Name the alarm vROPS test.

5. Select **Base Object Type**: **Virtual Machine** from **vCenter Adapter**.

6. As a symptom, select **Virtual machine is powered off** by writing power into the filter and pressing *Enter*.

7. As a recommendation, select the **vROPS Test Alarm** you have created by writing vrops into the filter and pressing *Enter*.

8. **Save** the alarm and wait for five minutes.

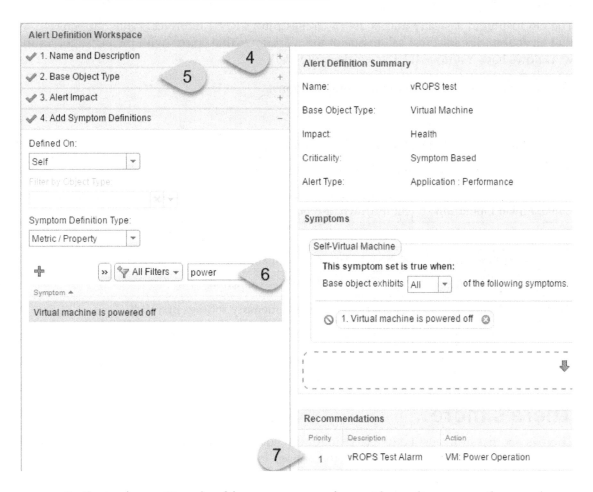

9. Go to alarms. You should see now some alarms (depending on weather you have a powered off VM or not). Click on one of them and you can execute the action.

How it works...

The vROpsplugin basically makes use of Orchestrator's REST interface. What happens is that an action triggers a rest call to one of the workflows that comes with the package. As all workflows have a unique ID, this works quite well.

The package contains the following vROps actions:

vROps actions	Description
Host: Maintenance Mode	Puts a host in or out of maintenance mode.
Host: Decommission Host	Puts a host in maintenance mode and then removes it from vCenter.
Host: Power Operation	Shuts down or reboots a host.
VM: Migrate	Moves a VM to a different host and datastore.
VM: Power Operation	Reboots, shuts down, or starts a VM.
VM: Manage Snapshots	Takes, reverts, or deletes snapshots.
VM: Reconfigure	Changes the CPU and memory settings of a VM.
VM: Upgrade Tools	Runs the automated VMware Tool upgrade.

All these action are not assigned to any vROps recommendation.

There's more...

There is another little post I'd like to point out to you. It's highly unsupported but still a cool way to do it. In this post, a REST outbound is used to start an Orchestrator workflow. For information, refer to:

`http://pierrelx.com/new-vrops6-outbound-plugin-alarms-vro-workflows/`.

12
Working with vSphere

This chapter is dedicated to working with vSphere—or, to put it bluntly, the vCenter itself. We will be looking at the following recipes:

- Working with the vCenter API (to change a VM's HA settings)
- Standard vSwitch and Distributed Switch ports
- Getting started with vAPI
- Custom Attributes and Tags (vAPI)
- Executing a program inside a VM
- An approval process for VM provisioning

Introduction

Here we will have a look into the vSphere plugin and what we can do with it.

vSphere automation

The interaction between **Orchestrator** and vCenter is done using the vCenter API. Let's have a closer look at the interaction, and how it works, in more detail.

A user starts an Orchestrator workflow (**1**) either in an interactive way through the **vSphere Web Client** or the **Orchestrator Client**, or through the API. The workflow in Orchestrator will then send a job (**2**) to vCenter and receive a task ID back (type VC:Task). vCenter will then start enacting the job (**3**). Using the `vim3WaitTaskEnd` action (**4**), Orchestrator pauses until the task has been completed. If we do not use the wait task, we can't be certain whether the task has ended, was successful, or has failed. It is extremely important to use the `vim3WaitTaskEnd` action whenever we send a job to vCenter. When the wait task reports that the job has finished, the workflow will be marked as finished, as shown in the following diagram:

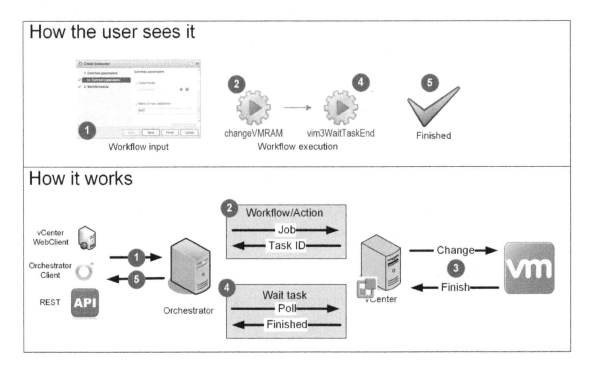

The vCenter MoRef

The **Managed Object Reference (MoRef)** is a unique ID inside vCenter for every object. MoRefs are basically strings. The following table shows some examples of different MoRefs:

VM	Network	Datastore	ESXi host	Data center	Cluster
vm-301	network-312 dvportgroup-242	datastore-101	host-44	datacenter-21	domain-c41

The MoRefs are typically stored in the attribute `.id` or `.key` of the Orchestrator API object. For example, the MoRef of a vSwitch network is `VC:Network.id`. We will make use of them in the *Standard vSwitch and Distributed Switch Ports* recipe of this chapter.

The MoRefs that are defined in vCenter are shown as ID in Orchestrator. This can either be in the Orchestrator inventory or as an attribute of an API class such as `VM.id`. To browse for MoRefs, you can use the **Managed Object Browser (MOB)**, documented at `http://pubs.vmware.com/vsphere-60/index.jsp#com.vmware.wssdk.pg.doc/PG_Appx_Using_MOB.20.1.html`, or the Orchestrator inventory and looking for the field ID.

The vim3WaitTaskEnd action

As previously mentioned, `vim3WaitTaskEnd` is one of the most central actions while interacting with vCenter. The action has the following variables:

Category	Name	Type	Usage
IN	`vcTask`	VC:Task	This will carry the reconfiguration task from the script to the wait task.
IN	`progress`	Boolean	Write the progress of a task to the logs as a percentage.
IN	`pollRate`	Number	How often the action should be checked for task completion in vCenter.
OUT	`ActionResult`	Any	Returns the task's result.

The waiting task will check (`pollRate`) the status of a task that has been submitted to vCenter at regular intervals. The task can have the following states:

State	Meaning
Queued	The task is queued and will be executed as soon as possible.
Running	The task is currently running. If the progress is set to `true`, the progress will be displayed in the logs as a percentage.
Success	The task has finished successfully.
Error	The task has failed and an error will be thrown.

The function behind this is the scripting class Task based on type VC:Task, which has quite a lot of functions:

Other vCenter wait actions

There are actually five waiting tasks that come with the vCenter server plugin. The following table gives an overview of the other four:

Task	Description
vim3WaitToolsStarted	This task waits until the VMware tools are started on a VM or until a timeout is reached.
Vim3WaitForPrincipalIP	This task waits until the VMware tools report the primary IP of a VM or until a timeout is reached. This typically indicates that the operating system is ready to receive network traffic. The action will return the primary IP.
Vim3WaitDnsNameInTools	This task waits until the VMware tools report a given DNS name of a VM or until a timeout is reached. The in-parameter addNumberToName is not used and can be set to Null.
WaitTaskEndOrVMQuestion	This task waits until a task is finished or a VM develops a question. A vCenter question is related to user interactions.

Things to try...

With the release of vSphere 6, a few new features have been added for Orchestrator to consume.

vAPI

From vSphere 6, the vAPI is a new way to automate vCenter. Have a look at the *Getting started with vAPI* and *Custom Attributes and Tags(vAPI)* recipes in this chapter for more details.

Linked Cloning

Linked Cloning allows you to create new VMs quickly and with minimal storage use. All the workflows you could ask for exist and I would highly recommend giving it a try, especially as this vCenter function is only available (at this stage) through the API. This feature has been available since vCO 5.5:

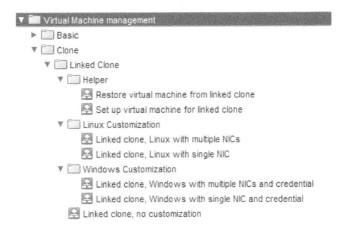

vSAN

Several new workflows for vSAN have been added since vRO 6.

The workflow **Library** | **vCenter** | **Host management** | **Basic** | **Enter Maintenance mode** has a vSAN option.

There is also the new workflow **Library** | **vCenter** | **Networking** | **VSAN**, which allows for VSAN network settings.

In **Library** | **vCenter** | **VSAN** you will find a new workflow to manage day-to-day operations.

Working with the vCenter API (to change a VM's HA settings)

This recipe will showcase how to derive a function for a more complicated feature. We will be configuring the HA setting for a single VM. Here, we will primarily be focusing on how to work with the vCenter API.

Getting ready

For this recipe, we will need a vCenter cluster that is configured for VMware **High Availability (HA)**, as well as a VM which has an HA restart priority that we can change.

To do this, you should have an understanding of the introduction to Chapter 6, *Advanced Programming*, as well as the recipes *Working with the API* and *JavaScript complex variables* in the same chapter.

How to do it…

We will use the API and find out how to set VM's HA restart priority. This recipe requires you to take a close look at each of the objects that we will visit and read its properties and external documentation.

It is best to follow this step by step using the API browser:

1. Create a new workflow and create the following variables:

Name	Type	Section	Use
priority	String	IN	This variable denotes the HA priority. It can have the values `clusterRestartPriority`, `disabled`, `high`, `medium`, and `low`. It can also use the presentation property `Predefined answers`.
VM	VC:VirtualMachine	IN	This is the VM we will be working with.
cluster	VC:ClusterComputeResource	IN	This is the cluster the VM is in.
vcTask	VC:Task	Attribute	This variable will carry the reconfiguration task from the script to the wait task.
progress	Boolean	Attribute	The default value is `false`. It shows the progress of a task.
pollRate	Number	Attribute	The default value is 5 (seconds). It shows how often it should be checked for task completion.

2. Add a scriptable task to the schema and edit it.
3. Use the API browser to search for the word **restart**.
4. Check the results. You should find `VcClusterDasVmConfigInfo.restartPriority` and `VcClusterDasVmSettings.restartPriority`. Click on the first one and open it in the API browser.
5. Then, click on **External documentation**. Your web browser will open and bring you to the vCenter API documentation. Take a look; the things we need are marked as **Deprecated**, meaning they are of no use to us. They still work, but it's not a good idea to use functions that are about to be removed:

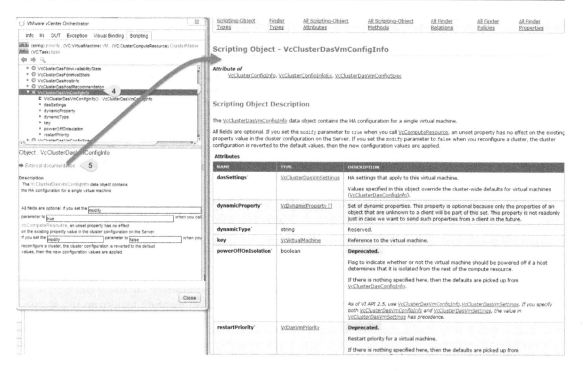

6. Repeat Step 5 with the second choice. You will find that there are no deprecated functions, meaning we can use them. Let's start adding some lines to our script. First, we need the constructor. We will copy and paste `VcClusterDasVmSettings`, which results in the following:

```
var myVcClusterDasVmSettings = new VcClusterDasVmSettings();
```

7. Then, we need to add the `restartPriority` attribute to it. Clicking on the `restartPriority` attribute tells us that it is of the type `VcClusterDasVmSettingsRestartPriority`, so take a look at that. We will use the value directly, as shown in the following line:

```
myVcClusterDasVmSettings.restartPriority=
VcClusterDasVmSettingsRestartPriority.fromString(priority);
```

8. Next, we need to think about changing the configuration. The external documentation also tells us that `VcClusterDasVmSettings` is a property of `VcClusterDasVmConfigInfo`. Taking a look at this object, we find that the attribute `.key` is a VM object, and that the `.dasSettings` attribute will take our `myVcClusterDasVmSettings`.

9. Now we will add the constructor of `VcClusterDasVmConfigInfo` to our script, as well as the rest of the lines:

```
var myVcClusterDasVmConfigInfo = new VcClusterDasVmConfigInfo();
myVcClusterDasVmConfigInfo.key=VM;
myVcClusterDasVmConfigInfo.dasSettings=myVcClusterDasVmSettings;
```

10. Again, we need to go higher in the API tree. Looking at the parent of `VcClusterDasVmConfigInfo` we find `VcClusterDasVmConfigSpec`. This has a `.info` attribute, which will take a value of `VcClusterDasVmConfigInfo`. However, a closer look at the external documentation shows us that we need to define the `.operation` attribute. We know this because all the other attributes come with a * saying that they do not need to be present, meaning the operation has to be there. So, we will add that as well:

```
var myVcClusterDasVmConfigSpec = new VcClusterDasVmConfigSpec();
myVcClusterDasVmConfigSpec.operation = VcArrayUpdateOperation.add;
myVcClusterDasVmConfigSpec.info = myVcClusterDasVmConfigInfo;
```

11. We will still need to go higher. The parent of `myVcClusterDasVmConfigSpec` is `vcClusterConfigSpecEX`. It has a `.dasVmConfigSpec` attribute, which will take a value of `VcClusterDasVmConfigSpec`, but further inspection reveals that it needs an array of `VcClusterDasVmConfigSpec`. So let's do that:

```
var myVcClusterDasVmConfigSpecArray = new Array() ;
myVcClusterDasVmConfigSpecArray.push( myVcClusterDasVmConfigSpec );
var myVcClusterConfigSpecEx = new VcClusterConfigSpecEx() ;
myVcClusterConfigSpecEx.dasVmConfigSpec =
myVcClusterDasVmConfigSpecArray;
```

12. The next part isn't documented, but results from trial and error. We need to define the `.dasConfig` attribute. Try the finished script and comment the next two lines out, and you will get an error message telling you that you need `VcClusterDasConfigInfo`:

```
var myVcClusterDasConfigInfo = new VcClusterDasConfigInfo() ;
myVcClusterConfigSpecEx.dasConfig = myVcClusterDasConfigInfo;
```

13. We are almost there; one more step and we are done. Check out the `VcClusterConfigSpecEx` object, which tells us that it can be used with a cluster, so let's look the other way around. Search for **Cluster** and take a closer look at `ClusterComputeResource`. It has a method called `reconfigureCluster_Task()`, which will take our `VcClusterConfigSpecEx`. So, let's use the following:

```
vcTask=cluster.reconfigureComputeResource_Task
( myVcClusterConfigSpecEx, true );
```

14. The return value of this attribute is a vCenter task. We will define the Boolean of the method as `true`, as only the changes to the cluster are needed. If we set it to `false`, it will apply all the changes defined in `VcClusterDasConfigInfo`.

15. Our little script is finished and looks like the following:

```
var myVcClusterDasVmSettings = new VcClusterDasVmSettings();
myVcClusterDasVmSettings.restartPriority=
VcClusterDasVmSettingsRestartPriority.fromString(priority);

var myVcClusterDasVmConfigInfo = new VcClusterDasVmConfigInfo();
myVcClusterDasVmConfigInfo.key=VM;
myVcClusterDasVmConfigInfo.dasSettings=myVcClusterDasVmSettings;

var myVcClusterDasVmConfigSpec = new VcClusterDasVmConfigSpec() ;
myVcClusterDasVmConfigSpec.operation = VcArrayUpdateOperation.add;
myVcClusterDasVmConfigSpec.info = myVcClusterDasVmConfigInfo;

var myVcClusterDasVmConfigSpecArray = new Array() ;
myVcClusterDasVmConfigSpecArray.push( myVcClusterDasVmConfigSpec );
var myVcClusterConfigSpecEx = new VcClusterConfigSpecEx() ;
myVcClusterConfigSpecEx.dasVmConfigSpec =
myVcClusterDasVmConfigSpecArray;
var myVcClusterDasConfigInfo = new VcClusterDasConfigInfo() ;
myVcClusterConfigSpecEx.dasConfig = myVcClusterDasConfigInfo;

vcTask=cluster.reconfigureComputeResource_Task
( myVcClusterConfigSpecEx, true );
```

16. As the final step, we will add the action `vim3WaitTaskEnd` to the workflow:

Scriptable task   vim3WaitTaskEnd

How it works...

This recipe has probably caused you a bit of a headache, but it is also extremely important to understand how to create workflows that use properties that are not implemented in the existing library. Working through the API, finding the items, and putting them together is a vital part of advanced programming skills in Orchestrator.

The method shown here is a difficult one, but, if you already know to which object a setting belongs, you can also move from the top down. In this case, you will have to drill down from `ClusterComputeResource`. If you like, give it a try. Have a go at the DRS setting for a VM. It basically follows the same route.

There is another way to generate this kind of script. Check out the Onyx project at `labs.vmware.com/flings/onyx`.

Onyx integrates itself between vSphere Client and vCenter Server and translates the actions in a script. However, it is always better to understand what actually happens and how to search and find it.

There's more...

To make the workflow work better, we will apply a few presentation properties to it. We looked at these in the *Workflow presentations* and *Linking actions in presentations* recipes in `Chapter 5`, *Visual Programming*:

1. Add the **Predefined answers** property to the presentation of the in-parameter **priority**. The correct answers are found in the `VcClusterDasVmSettingsRestartPriority` object. This will only show the correct values that should be entered.

2. Add the **Predefined list of elements** property to the presentation of the in-parameter VM.

3. Click on the purple puzzle piece (it helps us to create an action call), and in the pop-up, search for **Cluster**; select the only return action called `getAllVMsOfCluster` and assign it to the input of the cluster:

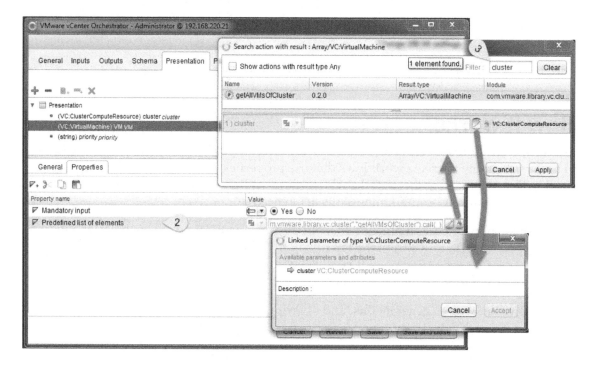

See also

Refer to the example workflows, `12.02.1 Change VM HA settings` and `12.02.2 Change VM DRS settings`.

Standard vSwitch and Distributed Switch ports

Here, we will discuss the problems that arise in vCenter from the difference between vSwitch and Distributed Switch ports in vCenter. We will learn how to bypass these problems, and create a workflow that will connect a VM to a Standard vSwitch or Distributed Switch port.

Getting ready

We need a vSphere environment that has at least one vSwitch and at least one Distributed Switch configured, each with at least one VM Network port group. For this recipe, it is not necessary for the switches to be actually connected to any NICs; they can be implemented as blind switches.

To understand the creation of the action, you should understand how to use the vCenter API, as showcased in the recipe *Working with the vCenter API (to change a VM's HA settings)*.

We also need a VM with a virtual network card.

How to do it…

We will split this recipe into three parts: building an action, building a workflow that uses the action, and the final piece, to make it work the way we want it to.

Creating an action

We will create a new action that will connect a VM to any network. I derived the code for this action from the existing vCenter server plugin actions `connectVmNicNumberToVirtualDistributedPortgroup` and `createVirtualEthernetCardNetworkConfigSpec`. Take a look at their source code. To create an action, complete the following steps:

1. Create a new action and name it `connectVmToNetwork`.
2. Define the following variables:

Name	Type	Section	Use
vm	VC:VirtualMachine	IN	This variable contains the VM that should be changed
network	VC:Network	IN	This variable defines the new network you will connect to
startConnected	Boolean	IN	This variable denotes whether or not the network should be connected at the start of the VM
connected	Boolean	IN	This variable denotes whether or not the network should be connected

	VC:Task	Return	The return value of the action that contains the vCenter task ID

3. Enter the following script:

```
//connection settings
var connectInfo = new VcVirtualDeviceConnectInfo();
connectInfo.allowGuestControl = false;
connectInfo.connected = connected;
connectInfo.startConnected = startConnected;
//check if this is a distributed switch?
if (network.id.indexOf("dvport")>=0){
    //backing for distributed switch
    var netBackingInfo = new
    VcVirtualEthernetCardDistributedVirtualPortBackingInfo();
    var port = new VcDistributedVirtualSwitchPortConnection();
    var dvSwitch = VcPlugin.convertToVimManagedObject(network,
    network.config.distributedVirtualSwitch);
    port.switchUuid = dvSwitch.uuid;
    port.portgroupKey = network.key;
    netBackingInfo.port = port;
} else {
    //backing for vSwitch
    var netBackingInfo =
    new VcVirtualEthernetCardNetworkBackingInfo();
    netBackingInfo.deviceName = network.name;
}
//Devicespecs are arrays
var nicArray = new Array();
//constructor for VM configuration
var vmspec = new VcVirtualMachineConfigSpec();
//constructor for the device configuration
var devicespec = new VcVirtualDeviceConfigSpec();
//get existing configuration
var devices = vm.config.hardware.device;
//go through all devices to find NIC
for( var i in devices){
// is it a NIC?
    if (System.getModule("com.vmware.library.vc.vm.network")
    .isSupportedNic(devices[i])) {
        devicespec.device = devices[i];
        //edit the exiting configuration
        devicespec.operation =
        VcVirtualDeviceConfigSpecOperation.edit;
        //attach new backing
        devicespec.device.backing = netBackingInfo;
        //attach new connection setting
```

```
            devicespec.device.connectable = connectInfo;
            //make array
            nicArray.push(devicespec);
    }
}
//build config
vmspec.deviceChange = nicArray;
//enact change on VM
return vm.reconfigVM_Task(vmspec);
```

4. Save and close the action.

 Please note that this is a simplified version that will connect all virtual network cards of a VM to the new network. Please refer to the original action, `connectVmNicNumberToVirtualDistributedPortgroup`, for pointers on how to select a single network card.

Creating the workflow

Now we will create the workflow:

1. Create a new workflow and define the following variables:

Name	Type	Section	Use
vm	VC:VirtualMachine	IN	This contains the VM that should be changed
network	VC:Network	IN	This is the new network which you connect to
task	VC:Task	Attribute	This transports the vCenter Task ID
progress	Boolean	Attribute	Value False. Show progress in percent
pollRate	Number	Attribute	Value 5. Interval for task check

2. Add the following actions to the schema:

- connectVmToNetwork
- vim3WaitTaskEnd

connectVmToNetwork   vim3WaitTaskEnd

3. Bind all the parameters.

4. Run the workflow. You will see that at the moment, you can only select vSwitch ports. Distributed Switch ports cannot be selected.

Making it work with presentation

Now, we will make the workflow function for distributed port groups:

1. Edit the workflow and go to presentation.

2. Add the following properties to the network in-parameter:

Property	Value
Predefined list of elements	`GetAction("com.vmware.library.vc.network","getNetworkForResourcePoolHostVm").call( null , null , #vm )`
Select value as	`list`

3. Save and run the workflow.

Now when you select the network, you will be presented with a list of all the existing networks (vSwitch and Distributed Switch).

How it works...

There isn't much magic here; what we have used is a deeper understanding of the API. VMware introduced the Distributed Switch back in vSphere 4, and before that, only normal switches (vSwitch) existed. So, VMware has added new types for the Distributed Switch. A vSwitch port group is of the `VC:Networks` type, while a distributed port group is of the `VC:DistributedVirtualPortGroup` type. If you take a look at each of these types in the API browser, you will find that they have the same structure. Both types are more or less interchangeable.

Let's discuss how this workflow functions in more detail:

- We will use the property in the presentation to display all the available vSwitch and Distributed Switch ports.
- We will then push either `VC:Network` or `VC:DistributedVirtualPortGroup` in a `VC:Network` in-parameter. As both are the same, this works. We will use `VC:Network` because of the existing action we used in the presentation.
- In the action, we will check the ID of the network object. The ID is the MoRef (Managed Object Reference-refer to the *Introduction* section of this chapter) string that each object in vCenter has. The MoRef of `VC:Network` begins with **network**, and that of `VC:DistributedVirtualPortGroup` starts with **dvport**.
- We will then use the method for either vSwitches or Distributed Switches to define `VcVirtualEthernetCardNetworkBackingInfo`.
- The rest is more or less a straightforward copy of the action, `connectVmNicNumberToVirtualDistributedPortgroup`.

If you take a closer look at the script, you will see the difference in how the vSwitch and the Distributed Switch ports are connected. Both use the `BackingInfo` type to build the connection. Please note that although they are interchangeable, they are actually different types.

The vSwitch port uses a `netBackingInfo` instance, `var netBackingInfo = new VcVirtualEthernetCard` **Network** `BackingInfo();`, and then simply connects the network name to it, as follows:

```
netBackingInfo.deviceName = network.name;
```

For the Distributed Switch, we will also use a `netBackingInfo` instance; however, we will use a slightly different one:

```
var netBackingInfo = new
VcVirtualEthernetCardDistributedVirtualPortBackingInfo();
```

We need to define a port connection:

```
var port = new VcDistributedVirtualSwitchPortConnection();
```

The port connection requires the UUID of the Distributed Switch:

```
var dvSwitch = VcPlugin.convertToVimManagedObject(network,
network.config.distributedVirtualSwitch);
port.switchUuid = dvSwitch.uuid;
```

Instead of the name, we will connect the network using its key (MoRef):

```
port.portgroupKey = network.key;
```

Now we can build the connection:

```
netBackingInfo.port = port;
```

Independent of the vSwitch or Distributed Switch, we will use the `backinginfo` variable to alter the device settings of the VM:

```
devicespec.device.backing = netBackingInfo;
```

See also

Refer to the example workflow `12.05 Connect VM to Network` and the `connectVmToNetwork` action.

Getting started with vAPI

In this recipe, we will look at the vAPI plugin that comes with vSphere 6.

Getting ready

You will need the vAPI plugin (which is already integrated into vRO 7.x).

How to do it…

This recipe is broken up into two parts just work though them in sequence.

Configuring vCenter endpoint and metadata

We will now create a vCenter vAPI endpoint and import the metadata:

1. Run the workflow **Library | VAPI | Add vAPI Endpoint**.
2. The vAPI endpoint is the `https://[FDQN vCenter]/api`.
3. Using SSL is always a good idea.
4. If you are using self-signed certificates you can import them without warnings.

5. Use a user that will be the connection between Orchestrator and vCenter:

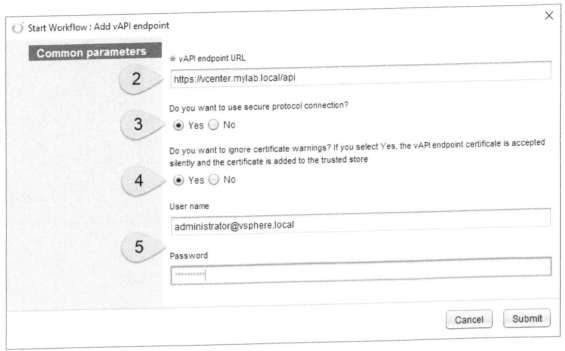

6. We now need to import the metamodel of the vAPI endpoint. Run the workflow **Library | VAPI | import vAPI metamodel**.
7. The inputs are the same as with adding the endpoint.

Exploring the content

Now we have created an endpoint and imported the metamodel, let's have a look what we get.

1. Select **Tools | API Explorer** from the upper right-hand corner of the Orchestrator Client.

2. Scroll down to the VAPI plugin and expand it:

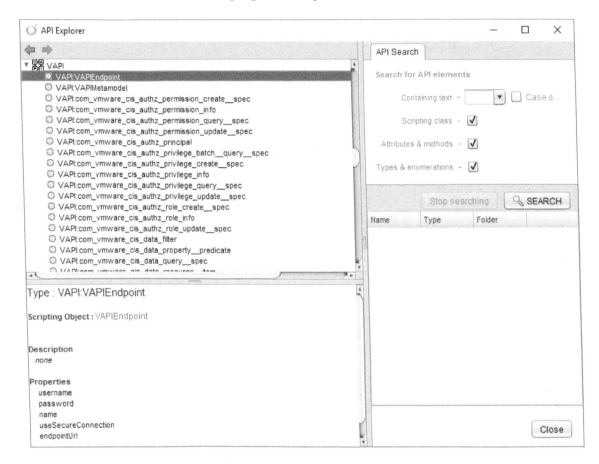

What you see here is the metamodel that has been imported, showing all objects and properties that are available for this endpoint. Have a look and scroll.

We will be giving the vAPI a go in the *Custom Attributes and Tags (vAPI)* recipe of this chapter.

How it works...

With vSphere 6, VMware also released the vAPI. The vAPI is a REST-based package that is actually called VMware vCloud Suite SDK. At this stage it has some limited functionality such as tagging, transfer services, and access to the content library; however, VMware has announced that functionality will be increased in the future.

As VMware (and lots of other vendors) are moving towards a REST-based API, the common old SOAP API of vCenter will be replaced more and more with the vAPI. However, never fear: too much money and effort has been sunk into vCenter API programming for it to vanish overnight.

The most interesting thing about the vAPI is the way that the API content is delivered. Traditionally, the API content is included in the plugin, but with the vAPI, you import the content and the metamodel (see the *Working with the vCenter API* recipe in this chapter). This makes it possible to have one plugin to handle multiple API contents. It is reminiscent of the SOAP model, where the API documentation is contained in the interface.

See also

Christophe Decanini's blog on the vAPI at `https://cto.vmware.com/vmwares-solution-to-api-challenges/`.

Using REST to talk to the vAPI at `http://www.vcoteam.info/articles/learn-vco/307-leveraging-vcenter-6-vapi-rest-endpoint.html`.

Custom Attributes and Tags (vAPI)

In this recipe, we will see how to create and use custom attributes and tags. We are talking about vCenter tags and not about Orchestrator tags, which have no common ground. This recipe will also use the vAPI plugin.

Getting ready

You need to have a VM to which you can tag or assign a custom attribute.

For tagging, you need to have a vAPI vCenter Endpoint. See the *Getting started with vAPI* recipe in this chapter.

How to do it...

We will split this recipe into two parts. The first part concerns Custom Attributes, while the second concerns Tags.

Custom Attributes

Please note that Custom Attributes are only visible in the vSphere Client (also called Fat client or c-Client).

We will now work through the lifecycle of a Custom Attribute:

1. Create a new workflow.
2. Drag the `setOrCreateCustomField` action onto the schema. This action will create a definition and set a value to an object.
3. Drag the `getCustomField` action onto the schema. This action will read a Custom Attribute from an object.
4. Now assign all the variables as input parameters.
5. Change the type of `managedEntity` from **Any** to **VC:VirtualMachine**.
6. Drag a scriptable task onto the schema. The following script will create the *delete* custom attribute:

```
var vimHost = managedEntity.vimHost;
var key;
  var customFieldDefs = vimHost.customFieldsManager.field;
  for (var i = 0; i < customFieldDefs.length; i++) {
    if (customFieldDefs[i].name == customFieldName) {
    key = customFieldDefs[i].key;
      break;
    }
  }
  vimHost.customFieldsManager.setField(managedEntity, key, "");
```

7. Drag a scriptable task onto the schema. The following script will delete the custom attribute definition:

```
var vimHost = managedEntity.vimHost;
var customFieldDefs = vimHost.customFieldsManager.field;
  for (var i = 0; i < customFieldDefs.length; i++) {
    if (customFieldDefs[i].name == customFieldName) {
      key = customFieldDefs[i].key;
      break;
    }
  }
  vimHost.customFieldsManager.removeCustomFieldDef(key);
```

8. Now assign all the variables as input parameters.
9. Change the type of `managedEntity` from **Any** to **VC:VirtualMachine**.
10. Save and run the workflow.

See also the example workflow `12.02.1 Custom Attribute Lifecycle`.

vSphere Tags

We will now work with Tags using the vAPI:

1. Create a new workflow with the following variables:

Name	Type	Section	Use
endpoint	VAPI:VAPIENDPOINT	IN	The endpoint we want to use
tagCatName	String	IN	Name of the tag category
tagName	String	IN	Name of the tag
tagValue	String	IN	Value of the tag
VM	VC:VirtualMachine	IN	VM to tag
tagCatID	String	Attribute	ID of the tag category
tagID	String	Attribute	ID of the tag

2. Drag a scriptable task onto the schema. The following script will create a new tag category. Define `tagCatID` as OUT:

```
var client = endpoint.client();
var tagging = new com_vmware_cis_tagging_category(client);
var spec = new com_vmware_cis_tagging_category_create__spec();
spec.name = tagCatName;
spec.description = tagDesciption;
spec.cardinality = "MULTIPLE";
spec.associable_types = ["VirtualMachine"];
var tagCatID = tagging.create(spec);
```

3. Drag a scriptable task onto the schema. The following script will create a new tag using the created tag category. Define `tagID` as OUT:

```
var client = endpoint.client();
var tagging = new com_vmware_cis_tagging_tag(client);
var spec = new com_vmware_cis_tagging_tag_create__spec();
spec.category_id = tagCatID;
spec.description = tagDesciption;
spec.name = tagName;
var tagID = tagging.create(spec);
```

4. Drag a scriptable task onto the schema. The following script will associate a tag with a VM:

```
var client = endpoint.client();
var tagging = new com_vmware_cis_tagging_tag__association(client);
var objectId = new com_vmware_vapi_std_dynamic__ID() ;
objectId.id = VM.id;
objectId.type = VM.vimType;
tagging.attach(tagID, objectId);
```

5. Drag a scriptable task onto the schema. The following script will read all tag and tag category information:

```
var client = endpoint.client();
var tagging = new com_vmware_cis_tagging_tag(client);
var tag = tagging.get(tagId);
System.log("Name :"+tag.name+"\nCategory
:"+tag.category_id+"\nDeciption :"+tag.description);

tagCatID=tag.category_id;
var tagging = new com_vmware_cis_tagging_category(client);
var tagCat = tagging.get(tagCatID);
System.log("Name :"+tagCat.name+"\nCategory
:"+tagCat.cardinality+"\nDeciption :"+tagCat.description+"\nTypes
:"+tagCat.associable_types);
```

6. Drag a scriptable task onto the schema. The following script will delete a tag from a VM:

```
var client = endpoint.client();
var tagging = new com_vmware_cis_tagging_tag(client);
tagging.delete(tagID);
```

7. Drag a scriptable task onto the schema. The following script will delete a tag category:

```
var client = endpoint.client();
var tagging = new com_vmware_cis_tagging_category(client);
tagging.delete(tagCatID);
```

8. Assign all the parameters and then run the workflow. For testing purposes, you may want to comment the delete instructions from Steps 6 and 7 out.

The Notes field

The only field that is the same in vSphere Client and vSphere Web Client is the Notes field. Here is how to read it:

```
content=vm.config.annotation;
```

Here is how to set it:

```
var spec = new VcVirtualMachineConfigSpec();
spec.annotation = "test";
vm.reconfigVM_Task(spec);
```

How it works...

This recipe is actually more about the changes in vSphere in the last couple of years. Until vSphere 5.5 and the first real workable vSphere Web Client, the vSphere Client using Custom Attributes have been the way to handle things. With vSphere 6, vAPI and a higher value in vSphere Web Client tagging is the way to go.

With the instructions in this recipe, you could create a workflow that transports your Custom Attributes into Tags:

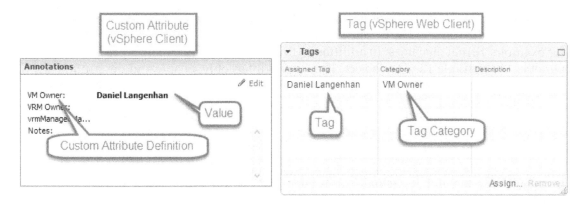

Custom Attributes

Custom attributes are actually two things. First, we have the custom attribute definition and then we have the custom attribute value. The definition is set once and is then available for all (or almost all) objects inside vCenter. A value is specifically assigned to one object. For instance, you set a Definition called *Manager*. This field is now available to all objects in vCenter. Then you define a value of *Mickey Mouse* to one (or more) VM(s).

There are basically only three methods of `customFieldsManager` that we are using:

Method	Description
`addCustomFieldDef()`	Adds a definition to vCenter.
`removeCustomFieldDef()`	Removes a definition from vCenter.
`setField()`	Sets a value to an object.

vAPI tagging

Tagging is one of those things that has been missing from Orchestrator since their introduction. The only way around that was to use PowerShell. With the vAPI, things are easier.

Tags in vSphere are a combination of a tag category and the Tag itself. Both items are available for all vCenter objects. The tag category can be limited to specific types of Objects, for example, virtual machines. In addition to this, a tag category can be set to either one Tag per object or multiple Tags per object. The Tag itself has only a name and description, however, it's the item that gets assigned to an object.

To get some more information about the vAPI documentation, here is what I used:

```
https://pubs.vmware.com/vsphere-60/index.jsp#com.vmware.dcli.cmdref.doc/com/
vmware/cis/tagging/Category.html
```

If you get the hang of it, it's actually quite easy, and I'm looking forward to more possibilities.

See also

See also the following example workflows:

- 12.03.1 Custom Attribute Lifecycle
- 12.3.2 Tag Lifecycle
- 12.3.3 assignTag2VM

Executing a program inside a VM

In this recipe, we will take a look at how to use **Guest Operations** (formerly called **VIX**) with Orchestrator. Guest Operations is a method by which vCenter can transfer files and execute programs inside a VM using VMware Tools. This method is of interest in DMZs, where security reduces the amount of automation possible.

Getting ready

We will need a running VM of any OS flavor you are happy with. This VM also needs to have VMware Tools installed. In this example, we will use a Windows VM.

We also need a program to install in the operating system. In this example, we will use Java for Windows. The silent install instructions can be found at
https://www.java.com/en/download/help/silent_install.xml.

You will need to upload this file to Orchestrator in a directory that is accessible to Orchestrator. Refer to the *Configuring access to the local filesystem* recipe in Chapter 2, *Optimizing Orchestrator Configuration*. In this example, we will upload the file to the Orchestrator appliance in the /var/run/vco/ directory.

You need a user that has local administrator rights on the VM's operating system.

How to do it...

We will divide this recipe into two steps: first, building the two necessary workflows, and second, conducting a test run.

Creating a waiting workflow

When we want to run a program on a VM, we need to know when it has finished. So, let's build a waiting workflow first:

1. Create a new workflow and name it `waitUntilProgramInstalled`.
2. Define the following variables:

Name	Type	Section	Use
vmUsername	String	IN	This variable denotes the local VM user.
vmPassword	SecureString	IN	This variable denotes the local VM user password.
vm	VC:VirtualMachine	IN	This variable denotes the VM to run on.
processID	Number	IN	This variable denotes the process ID of the program that is running.
sleepTime	Number	IN	This variable denotes the time to wait between polls, in seconds.
counter	Number	Attribute	The default value of this variable is 0.
errorCode	String	Attribute	This variable denotes the error code.

3. Create the workflow shown in the following figure by adding the following elements:
   - **Sleep**
   - **Get process from guest**
   - **Custom decision**
   - **Decision**
   - **Increase counter**
   - **Scriptable task**
   - **Throw exception**

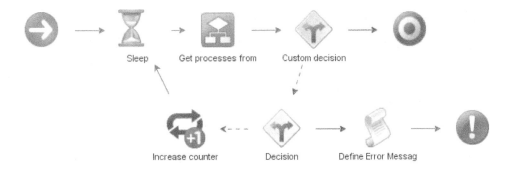

4. Edit the **Get process from guest** element and bind the **result** out-parameter as an attribute. We will do this because **result** is a composite type and is too complicated to create manually.

5. In the **Custom decision** element, select **processID** and **result** (defined in the previous step) as in-parameters. Add the following script:

```
var finished=true;
for each (value in result) {
    if (value.pid == processID) {
        finished=false;
        System.log(processID+" still running");
    }
}
return finished;
```

6. In the **Decision** element, set `counter` as equal to, or greater than, 9.

7. In the **Increase counter** element, set `counter` as `in-parameter` and `out-parameter`.

8. In the **Scriptable task** element, add the following parameters:

In-parameters	`vm`, `sleepTime`, `counter`, **and** `processID`
Out-parameters	`errorCode`

Script	`time=sleepTime*counter;`
	`errorCode="PID:"+processID+" on VM "+vm.name+" still`
	`running after "+time;`

9. Bind `errorCode` to **Throw exception**.

10. Save and close the workflow. Proceed to the next section.

Creating an installation workflow

We will now build a workflow that will copy a file to the VM, install a program, and perform clean up:

    1. Create a new workflow and define the following variables:

Name	Type	Section	Use
vmUsername	String	IN	This variable denotes the local VM user password.
vmPassword	SecureString	IN	This variable denotes the local VM user password.
vm	VC:VirtualMachine	IN	This variable denotes the VM to run on.
programFileName	String	IN	This variable denotes the name of the file to run.
arguments	String	IN	This variable denotes the install arguments.
dirPath	String	Attribute	This variable denotes the path directory on VM.
createParents	Boolean	Attribute	This variable denotes whether or not to create parent folders.
result	Boolean	Attribute	This variable is set to true if the directory is created successfully.
vcoPath	String	Attribute	This variable denotes the path on the vCO server.
guestFilePath	String	Attribute	This variable denotes the path on the VM.
overwrite	Boolean	Attribute	This variable allows you to overwrite a file if it exists.
interactiveSession	Boolean	Attribute	This variable enables an interactive session for the program running on the VM.
ProcessID	Number	Attribute	This variable denotes the process ID of the running program.

recursive	Boolean	Attribute	This variable allows deletion of the directory content recursively.
sleepTime	Number	Attribute	This variable denotes the time between the polls.
errorCode	String	Attribute	This variable denotes the error code.

2. Now we need to assign some values to all the attributes. The attributes that are not mentioned in the following table do not require a start value:

dirPath	c:\OrchestratorInstall
createParents	False
vcoPath	/var/run/vco
overwrite	True
interactiveSession	False
recursive	True
sleepTime	90
errorCode	nothing

3. Create the workflow shown in the following figure by adding the following elements:

- **Scriptable task**
- **Create directory in guest**
- **Copy file from vCO to guest**
- **Run program in guest**
- **waitUntilProgramInstalled**
- **Kill process in guest**
- **Delete directory in guest**
- **Decision**
- **Throw exception**

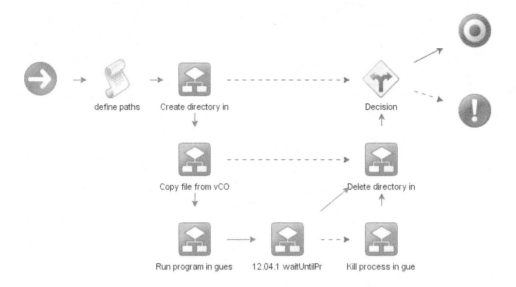

4. In the **Scriptable task** element, add the following parameters:

In-parameters	programFileName, vcoPath, **and** dirPath
Out-parameters	vcoPath **and** guestFilePath
Script	vcoPath=vcoPath+"/"+programFileName; guestFilePath=dirPath+""+programFileName;

Please note the double backslashes \\. We need to escape the \ for Windows.

5. In the **Decision** element, set errorCode, equal, and nothing.
6. Bind all the other parameters to all the other workflow elements.

An example run

Now, let's play through an example run of the workflows:

1. Copy the Java installation file (`jre-8u25-windows-i586.exe`) to the Orchestrator appliance in the `/var/run/vco` directory. You may need to change the access rights with `chmod 555 jre-8u25-windows-i586.exe`.
2. Make sure that your test VM is ready, has VMware Tools installed, and that you have access to it as a local administrator. Creating a snapshot at this stage isn't a bad idea either.
3. Run the workflow, **Install program on VM** (the second workflow you created).
4. Select the VM on which you want to execute the program and enter the credentials for the local administrator.
5. The value of `programFileName` is `jre-8u25-windows-i586.exe`.
6. The input for **Arguments** is `/s` (refer to Java's silent install options).
7. Submit the workflow.
8. The workflow will now create a directory, `C:\OrchestratorInstall`, in the VM and copy the Java install file from the Orchestrator to the VM through VMware Tools. If any of these actions fail, the program will clean up and exit with an error.

The program will now be executed and the process ID is piped to the waiting workflow (the first workflow you built).

1. In the waiting workflow, we will first wait a bit before we get all the processes that run on the VM. We will check whether the process ID exists, and if so, we will go back to waiting. To make sure that we can break out of this loop, we will only run the loop 10 times.
2. If the wait task finishes with an error, we will kill the install process on the VM, clean up, and exit with an error.
3. If the installation finishes, we will delete the directory we created.
4. If no error has occurred, `errorCode` will still contain the start value `"nothing"`; so, we will check whether this is the case, and if so, we will exit successfully. Otherwise, if an error exists, `errorCode` will throw an error.

How it works...

In this recipe, we used the Guest Operations system, which is implemented with VMware Tools in the VMs. This allows us to work directly inside the Guest OS, without the need for network connectivity between the VM and Orchestrator. Guest Operations is useful for a lot of functions:

- VMs that are in a DMZ and can't be accessed through a network by Orchestrator.
- VMs that have no network connection. Typically, you do this when you want to configure the VM first before connecting it to a network. A good example is to reconfigure an SQL server you have just cloned.
- You can also configure VMs that are hardened and do not allow a network to log in to the OS.

There's more...

One way to optimize this workflow is as follows:

- Creating a configuration element to store the central configuration elements
- Adding decisions to choose between Linux and Windows VMs and to adjust the guestPath accordingly
- Copying the file to be installed from a central shared directory onto Orchestrator first
- Checking whether the program has installed correctly

See also

Refer to the example workflows, 12.04.1 waitUntilProgramInstalled and 12.04.2 Install program on VM.

An approval process for VM provisioning

This recipe looks at how to build an **approval** process. If you don't happen to have vRealize Automation this could be an easy way forward.

Getting ready

Depending on how you want to build it, you may either need an e-mail server or a web server.

How to do it...

The approval process we are discussing is not a finished program but more of an architecture on how to construct one.

Using User interaction

This would be a program that uses User interaction for approval:

1. Create a workflow that will provision a VM.
2. Before the VM is actually provisioned, add a **User interaction**.
3. Make sure the user interaction's `timeout.date` is somewhat in the future.
4. Make sure that the `security.group` or the `security.assignees` have the users that are allowed to approve this VM assigned.
5. Add a Boolean into the external inputs that approves or disapproves a VM.
6. After the **User interaction**, add a base decision that works on the Boolean:

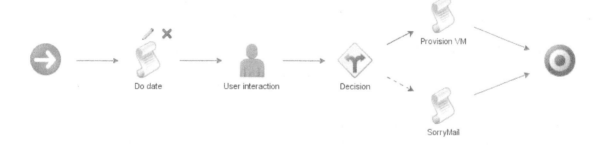

Using e-mail

This would be a program that uses email for approval:

1. Develop a workflow that sends e-mail.
2. Develop a workflow that checks an e-mail account for a given body text.
3. Create a workflow that will provision a VM.
4. Before the VM is actually provisioned, add a workflow that does the following:
   - Sends an e-mail to an approver
   - Checks the e-mail for a given sentence or word
   - Depending on the e-mail, either provisions or sends a "Sorry" e-mail to the user

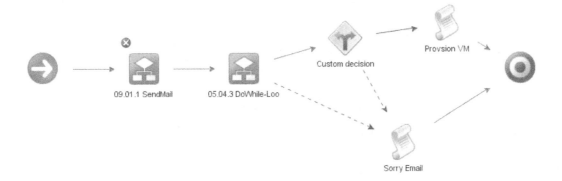

Using a web page

This would be a program that uses a web page for approval:

1. Develop a workflow that sends a custom event.
2. Create a workflow that will provision a VM.
3. Before the VM is actually provisioned, add a workflow that does the following:
   - Checks if the Custom Event has happened
   - Depending on that, deploys the VM

How it works...

There are lots of ways to create an approval process. The ones given here are the easiest. More complicated ones could involve a database where a user stores the information about the VM he wants. Another policy would check the DB each day and provisions the VMs where a certain flag is set. The flag can be altered through a workflow that uses either e-mail or a web interface.

You already have all the tools you need to create such a workflow or the ones given here. The recipes you need are as follows:

- *Sending and waiting for custom events* in Chapter 6, *Advanced Programming*
- *Using PHP to access the REST API* in Chapter 7, *Interacting with Orchestrator*
- *Working with policies* in Chapter 8, *Better Workflows and Optimized Working*
- *Working with e-mails* in Chapter 9, *Essential Plugins*
- *Working with SQL (JDBC)* and *Working with SQL (SQL plugin)* in Chapter 10, *Built-in Plugins*

13
Working with vRealize Automation

This chapter is dedicated to the interaction between Orchestrator and **vRealize Automation** (**vRA**). In this chapter, we will cover the following topics:

- Working with the vRA-integrated Orchestrator
- Automating a vRA instance in Orchestrator
- Configuring an external Orchestrator in vRA
- Adding Orchestrator as an Infrastructure endpoint
- Adding an Orchestrator endpoint
- Integrating Orchestrator workflows as XaaS Blueprints
- Managing AD users with vRA
- Using the Event Manager to start workflows

Introduction

Automation has changed since the arrival of Orchestrator. Before tools such as vCloud Director or vRA, Orchestrator was the main tool for automating vCenter resources. In fact you may remember **VMware Life Cycle Manager** (**LCM**) which was the first such product based on Orchestrator.

With version 6.2 of **vCloud Automation Center** (**vCAC**), the product has been renamed to vRealize Automation.
However, you will find the name vCAC all across the API.

Now, vRA is the central cornerstone in the VMware automation effort. **vRealize Orchestrator (vRO)** is used by vRA to interact with and automate VMware and non-VMware products and infrastructure elements.

Throughout the various vRA interactions, the role of Orchestrator has changed substantially. Orchestrator started off as an extension to vCAC and became a central part of vRA. The following list only focuses on the changes that influence Orchestrator:

- In vCAC 5.x, Orchestrator was only an extension of the IaaS life cycle. Orchestrator was tied in using Stubs.
- vCAC 6.0 integrated Orchestrator as an **XaaS (Everything as a Service)** using the **Advanced Service Designer (ASD)**.
- In vCAC 6.1, Orchestrator is used to perform all VMware NSX operations (VMware's new network virtualization and automation), meaning that it became even more of a central part of the IaaS services.
- With vCAC 6.2, the ASD was enhanced to allow more complex formula designs, allowing a better leverage of Orchestrator workflows.
- With vRA 7, an automated IaaS install was added making the initial deployment much easier. The Event Manager was introduced as well as other new features.
- With vRA 7.1, a lot of small but important things changed. The ASD has gone and is now called XaaS. It has been announced that Stubs are now deprecated and Event Manager should be used.

How the integration of vRA and Orchestrator works

As you can see in the following diagram, vRA connects to the vCenter Server using an infrastructure endpoint, which allows vRA to conduct basic infrastructure actions, such as power operations, cloning, and so on. It doesn't allow any complex interactions with the vSphere infrastructure such as HA configurations. Using the XaaS endpoint, vRA integrates the Orchestrator (vRO) plugins as additional services. This allows vRA to offer the entire plugin infrastructure as services to vRA. The vCenter Server, AD, and PowerShell plugins are typical of integrations used with vRA.

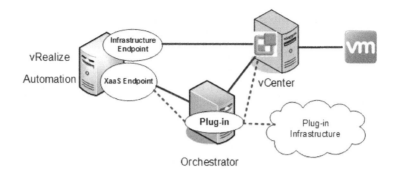

Using XaaS, you can create integrations that use Orchestrator workflows. XaaS allows you to offer Orchestrator workflows as vRA catalog items, making it possible for tenants to access any IT service that can be configured with Orchestrator via its plugins. The following diagram shows an example using the Active Directory plugin. The Orchestrator Plugin provides access to the AD services. By creating a custom resource using the exposed AD infrastructure, we can create a service Blueprint and resource actions, both of which are based on Orchestrator workflows that use the AD plugin. In the *Managing AD users with vRA* recipe in this chapter, we will showcase all of these features.

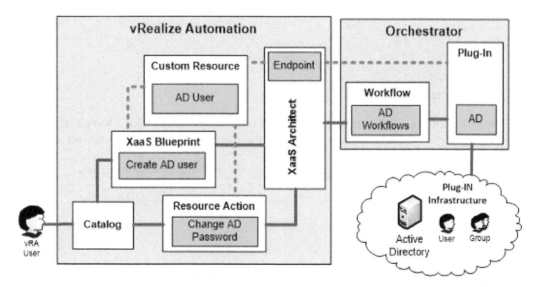

Prior to vRA 7, the only way to integrate additional functions into the life cycle was using Stubs. Stubs were predominately used in vCAC 5.x and allowed you to attach a workflow at certain points (Stubs) in the IaaS workflow, such as pre-provisioning, post-provisioning, and so on. Such actions could be taken to change the VMs HA or DRS configuration or to use the guest integration to install or configure a program on a VM. From vRA7.1 onward, Stubs are deprecated and will soon be removed.

With vRA7, the Event Manager was introduced, allowing for a much higher integration into the life cycle. Where the Stubs offered only 6 entry points for integration, the Event Manager offers 33. We will show how to integrate Orchestrator into the Event Manager in the *Using the Event Manager to start Workflows* recipe in this chapter.

Installation

How to install and configure vRA is out of the scope of this book, but take a look at:

```
https://www.youtube.com/watch?v=RM-X5TGuKJo.
```

If you don't have the hardware or the time to install vRA yourself, you can use the **VMware Hands-on Labs**, which can be accessed after clicking on **Try for Free** at:

```
http://hol.vmware.com.
```

Read more...

To read more about the Orchestrator integration with vRA, please take a look at the official VMware documentation. At the time of writing the documentation can be found at:

```
https://www.vmware.com/support/pubs/vrealize-automation-pubs.html.
```

The document called `vrealize-automation-71-extensibility` discusses customization using Stubs.

Working with the vRA-integrated Orchestrator

In this recipe, we explore the vRA-integrated Orchestrator. We will have a closer look at what is integrated and how it is working.

Getting ready

You need Java installed to start the Orchestrator Client and access the vRA shell (root access).

How to do it...

I have split this recipe into several small independent sections.

Accessing the vRA-integrated Orchestrator Client

To start the Orchestrator Client, follow these steps:

1. Open a web browser and enter the IP or FQDN of the vRA appliance.
2. Click on the **vRealize Orchestrator Client** link.
3. Enter [IP or FQDN of the vRA appliance]:8281 as **Host name** and administrator@vsphere.local as **User name** with the corresponding password and click on **Login**.

Starting the vRA-integrated Orchestrator Control Center

The Orchestrator Control Center is by default switched off to conserve resources since it is only needed during configuration and to install plugins. To switch it on, you need to login to the vRA and execute the following command:

```
Service vco-configurator start
```

Also see the example workflows 13.01.1 Start vRA vRO Control Center and 13.01.2 Stop vRA vRO Control Center.

Tuning vRA

If we decide to use an external Orchestrator, we can give the vRA appliance some resources back by disabling the startup of the Orchestrator Services:

1. Log in to the vRA appliance as root.
2. Run the following script, line by line:

```
chkconfig vco-server off
```

```
service vco-server stop
chkconfig vco-configurator off
service vco-configurator stop
```

This will stop and disable the services for Orchestrator and the Orchestrator Configurator.

How it works...

The vRA appliance comes with an installed and configured vRO instance. The integrated instance is pretty well balanced and does everything you need. With vRA7.1, when you add vRA nodes to a cluster, the integrated Orchestrator will also be added as nodes.

The direction for vRA/vRO clusters is definitely towards using the embedded version.

Please also check the *Configuring an external Orchestrator in vRA* recipe in this chapter for more information on external Orchestrator installations.

Users

The registered Orchestrator administrator group is vcoadmins, which contains the following user: administrator@vsphere.local.

Database

The database that Orchestrator uses is the one vRA uses.

Database	vcac
User	vcac
Port	5433

vRA 7.x and above dynamically generates and encrypts the vcac user password upon installation. The following steps will show how to obtain that password, allowing you to connect things such as PGAdmin to the DB:

1. Login to vRA as root.
2. In the /etc/vcac/server.xml file, look for password, for example:

    password="s2enc~3g5DjU8zn4/0akhnM0uSUheiZZyGagt0dEdjg="

3. Run the following command:

```
vcac-config prop-util -d --p
"s2enc~3g5DjU8zn4/0akhnM0uSUheiZZyGagt0dEdjg="
```

4. The result will be the password for the connection to the database, which you can access by the following command:

```
psql -U vcac -p 5433 -h localhost -d vcac
```

Automating a vRA instance in Orchestrator

Not only can vRA use Orchestrator to access vCenter or other plugins, but you can also automate your vRA instance using Orchestrator. In this recipe, we will show you how to do the initial steps.

Getting ready

Please make sure that you read the introduction to vRA at the beginning of this chapter. We need a functional and configured vRA. We also need the vRA plugin for Orchestrator installed.

The vRA plugin is integrated into Orchestrator from version 7.1 onward.

However, you should be aware that even the plugin (7.1 at the time of writing) still shows vCAC and vCACCafe in Control Center, and it shows up in the Library as vRealize Automation.

How to do it...

This recipe is split into Preparation and Example.

Preparation

To configure the vRA plugin, perform the following steps:

1. Log in to the Orchestrator Client.
2. Run the workflow **Library** | **vRealize Automation** | **Configuration** | **Add a vRA host**.

3. Add a name for the vRA host.

4. Enter the HTTPS URL of the vRA installation, as `https://vra.mylab.local`.

5. Agree to install the SSL certificates.

6. Leave the connection variables at their defaults and click **Next**.

7. Choose **Shared session** and enter the name of the **Tenant** as `vSphere.local`.

8. Enter a vRA **Infrastructure Admin** account.

9. Click on **Submit** and wait till the workflow has finished.

10. Run the workflow **Library | vRealize Automation | Configuration | Add the IaaS host of a vRA host**.

11. Select the vRA host from the Inventory.

12. Accept the defaults, but don't forget to add the Administrator password for the Windows IaaS host.

13. Check out your Orchestrator Inventory.

Example

Let's run an example by creating a new Machine Prefix:

1. Log in to the Orchestrator Client.

2. Run the workflow **Library | vRealize Automation | Infrastructure Administration | Extensibility | Machine Prefix | Create a Machine Prefix**.

3. Set the IaaS host from **vRealize Automation Infrastructure**, as shown in the following screenshot:

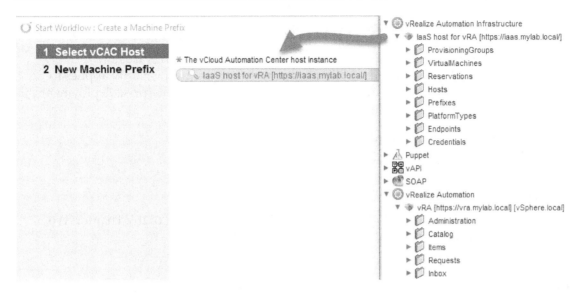

4. Enter the **New Machine Prefix**, such as `Test`, as well as the number of digits and the next number.

5. Check on vRA for the new Machine Prefix.

How it works...

You have hooked up Orchestrator to vRA and are able to do a lot of things. You can now use vRO to configure vRA.

With this plugin, you can create and configure vRA tenants automatically. It becomes even more handy when you are using the Event Broker and want to retrieve some additional information from vRA.

The difference between the vRA Host (VCAC:VcacCafeHost) and the IaaS Host (VCAC:VcacHost) is that things such as requests and catalog items are stored in the vRA Host and objects such as VMs in the IaaS host.

For any automation of vRA you need to configure this plugin.

Configuring an external Orchestrator in vRA

vRA comes with an installed and configured Orchestrator. While VMware now recommends using the embedded vRO in production systems, this primarily applies to small-/medium-sized infrastructure deployments. In much larger enterprise deployments, it may be beneficial to use an external vRO cluster.

Another example is if you require a different vRO for a given tenant.

Getting ready

Please make sure you read the introduction to vRA at the beginning of this chapter. We need a functional and configured vRA.

How to do it...

This recipe has three parts. First, we will configure the Orchestrator, bind it to vRA, and then we will clean up the vRA appliance.

 Changing between Orchestrators will result in losing all your endpoints that you have configured with Orchestrator.

Building and configuring an external Orchestrator

To attach an external Orchestrator, we first need an Orchestrator that we can connect to:

1. Install the Orchestrator appliance (refer to the *Deploying the Orchestrator appliance* recipe in `Chapter 1`, *Installing and Configuring Orchestrator*).
2. You may want to configure Orchestrator with an external DB (refer to the *Configuring an external database* recipe in `Chapter 1`, *Installing and Configuring Orchestrator*).
3. Configure the appliance for vRealize Automation authentication (or vSphere, see the *How it works...* section); refer to the *Configuring an external Authentication* recipe in `Chapter 1`, *Installing and Configuring Orchestrator*.
4. Tune the appliance by disabling LDAP and the local DB (refer to the *Tuning the appliance* recipe in `Chapter 2`, *Optimizing Orchestrator Configuration*).

If you want to build an Orchestrator cluster, you should check out `Chapter 3`, *Distributed Design*.

Configuring a general default external Orchestrator

To configure an external Orchestrator as a default for all tenants, follow these steps:

1. Log in to the vRA default Tenant as a **System Administrator**, such as `Administrator@vspehre.local`.
2. Click on **Administration** | **Advanced Service** | **Server Configuration** and select **Use an external Orchestrator server**.
3. Continue with section *Connecting the external Orchestrator*.

Configuring an external Orchestrator for each Tenant

If you want to connect one specific Orchestrator for each Tenant, follow these steps:

1. Log in to vRA Tenant as an **Infrastructure** or **Tenant** admin.
2. Click on **Administration** | **vRO Configuration** | **Server Configuration** and select **Use an external Orchestrator server**.
3. Continue with section *Connecting the external Orchestrator*.

Connecting the external Orchestrator

In this section, we will discuss the connection settings:

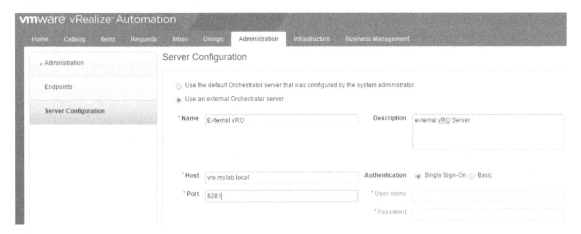

Perform the following steps:

1. Select a name under which you would like to store this configuration and description.
2. In the **Host** field, enter the FQDN or IP of the Orchestrator or the Orchestrator cluster.
3. The default port is 8281.
4. Choose either **Single Sign-On** or **Basic** authentication (see this section's *How it works...* for more details).
5. Test the connection, and when successful, click on **OK**.
6. After you click on **OK**, you can be notified that the existing endpoints will be deleted. These are the existing Orchestrator endpoints. Accept and then add new endpoints. Follow recipe *Adding an Orchestrator endpoint* in this chapter.

How it works...

The vRA appliance has Orchestrator installed in it, the same way as in the Orchestrator appliance. The initial configuration of vRA is done to use the internal Orchestrator. VMware no longer recommends using Orchestrator as an external server or using an external DB. In fact, VMware now recommends using an embedded DB and an embedded vRO for production use.

Authentication

The two different methods of authentication are quite important:

- **Single Sign-on**: This requires Orchestrator and vRA to be in the same SSO domain, meaning the external Orchestrator should use vRealize Automation authentication configured with the vRA. Starting with vRA, 7.0 vIDM is used; however, vCenter still (as of 6.0 U2) uses SSO (also see the recipe *Configuring an external Authentication* in Chapter 1, *Installing and Configuring Orchestrator*). This can currently lead to some problems. This functions the same way as the shared connection in Orchestrator that we have discussed several times previously.
- **Basic**: This uses one account to connect and execute workflows. The account used must be a member of the Orchestrator administrator group. You could configure the external orchestrator with any kind of authentication; this may especially make sense for some plugins that depend on vCenter SSO, such as Horizon Replication and SRM.

This is a problem for the time being as vCenter and vRA do not use the same authentication base (vIDM versus SSO).

There's more...

You can define a workflow folder per-tenant. This enables you to expose different workflows to different tenants. The default value is the base folder.

1. Log in to the vRA default Tenant as a **System Administrator**, such as `Administrator@vspehre.local`.
2. Navigate to the **Administration** | **Advanced Services** | **Default vRO** folder.
3. Select the Tenant you want to assign a base folder to and click on **Edit**.
4. Browse to the Orchestrator workflow folder and then click on **Add**.

Adding Orchestrator as an infrastructure endpoint

This will add Orchestrator as an additional endpoint into the vRA infrastructure. This will allow you access to plugins that are not part of the endpoints we can configure in the *Adding an Orchestrator endpoint* recipe in this chapter.

Getting ready

You need an external or internal Orchestrator as well as a user account that has Administrator rights in Orchestrator.

How to do it...

We are now adding Orchestrator as a vRA Infrastructure endpoint:

1. Log in to vRA with an Infrastructure Admin account.
2. Go to **Infrastructure** | **Endpoints** | **Endpoints**.
3. Click on **New** and select **Orchestration** | **vRealize Orchestrator**.
4. Give the Orchestrator a name.

5. The Address for the internal Orchestrator is `https://[vra FQDN]/vco`, and for an external Orchestrator it is `https://[vRO FQDN]/vco`. As vRA uses a proxy, you don't have to specify the port number anymore.

6. Create **Credentials** with a user who is a member of the vRO Administrator group.

7. Add a new property by clicking on **New**. Enter `VMware.VCenterOrchestrator.Priority` and set **Value** to 1. Click on The green tick button to save this setting.

8. Click on **OK** to save the endpoint.

Edit Endpoint - vRealize Orchestrator

Manage a specific endpoint.

General

* Name:	vROEndpoint	4
Description:		
* Address:	https://vra.mylab.local/vco	5
* Credentials:	admin@vsphere	... 6

Custom properties: ⊕ New   ✎ Edit   ✖ Delete

	* Name	▲	Value	Encrypted
7 ⊘ ⊖	VMware.VCenterOrchestrator.Priority		1	☐

To avoid conflict with vRealize Automation properties, use a prefix such as a company or feature name followed by a dot for all custom property names.

OK   Cancel

How it works...

An Orchestrator endpoint lets you create additional customization and lets you use plugins that are not part of the endpoints we configured in the *Adding an Orchestrator endpoint* recipe in this chapter.

For some features, such as NSX, you may require an Orchestrator Infrastructure endpoint. Also see the recipe *NSX integration* in `Chapter 11`, *Additional Plugins*.

There's more...

You can associate a Blueprint with a given Orchestrator Infrastructure endpoint by adding to the Blueprint the Custom Property `VMware.VCenterOrchestrator.EndpointName` and, as a value, the endpoint name you specified.

Adding an Orchestrator endpoint

Before you can use any Orchestrator plugins in vRA, you need to define them as endpoints. In this recipe, we will show you how to do this. This is not how to add an Orchestrator as an Infrastructure endpoint (for this see the *Adding Orchestrator as an Infrastructure Endpoint* recipe in this chapter).

Getting ready

For this recipe, you will need a working and configured vRealize Automation installation. Please refer to the introduction to this chapter.

You can either use the vRA-integrated Orchestrator or an external Orchestrator.

In this example, we will add an Active Directory endpoint. Please note that, if you want to add users or change passwords, you will need to enable SSL for AD (refer to the recipe *Working with Active Directory* in `Chapter 10`, *Built-in Plugins*).

How to do it...

There are some plugins that can be added directly in vRA. See *How it works...* for more details:

1. Log in to vRA as an **Infrastructure** admin.
2. Navigate to **Administration** | **Advanced Services** | **Endpoints**.
3. Click on **Add** (the green plus sign) and select the plugin that you would like to configure as an endpoint, such as the Active Directory plugin.
4. Give the endpoint a name, such as `ActiveDirectory`.

5. Follow the recipe *Working with Active Directory* in `Chapter 10`, *Built-in Plugins*, to configure this endpoint. What you are basically doing is running the configuration workflow.

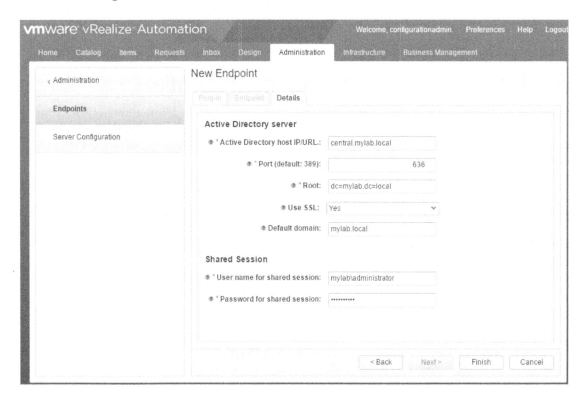

6. Click on **Finish** to add the endpoint.

How it works...

As discussed in the introduction to this chapter, endpoints are essentially the connection points between vRA and plugin-driven infrastructures.

Using the vRA-integrated Orchestrator, you can add the following endpoints out-of-the-box. The following table contains the recipes in which the plugin is discussed and a quick overview of the prerequisites for using the plugin:

Plugin	Recipe/chapter	Prerequisite
Active Directory	*Working with Active Directory* in `Chapter 10`, *Built-In Plugins*	AD SSL Certs, SSL Cert import
HTTP-REST	*Working with REST* in `Chapter 9`, *Essential Plugins*	SSL Cert import
PowerShell	*Working with PowerShell* in `Chapter 10`, *Built-In Plugins*	WinRM and Kerberos configurations
SOAP	*Working with SOAP* in `Chapter 10`, *Built-In Plugins*	SSL Cert import
vCenter Server	*Connecting to vCenter* in `Chapter 1`, *Installing and Configuring Orchestrator*	SSL Cert import

Integrating Orchestrator workflows as XaaS Blueprints

We will now showcase how to integrate Orchestrator workflows in vRealize Automation. We will learn how to create a vRA Catalog item that will run a workflow when requested.

Getting ready

In order to use an Orchestrator workflow as a vRA Catalog item, you should have the following vRA items configured:

- Entitlements
- Services
- Business groups

To configure these items, please refer to the link shown in the introduction to this chapter or take a look at the official VMware documentation for vRA.

We will use the example workflow `00.00 BasicWorkflow` to add to the vRA catalog.

How to do it...

This recipe is divided into three parts.

Activating the XaaS tab

By default, the **Xaas** tab is not visible, so the first step is to make it appear:

1. Log in to vRA as an **Infrastructure** admin.
2. Navigate to **Administration** | **Users & Groups** | **Custom Groups**.
3. Click on **Finish**.
4. Give the group a name and then assign it the role of **XaaS Architect**.
5. Click on **Next** and select a group or user to assign to this group.
6. Log out and log in with the user that you specified in step 5.

The **XaaS** tab should now be visible.

Adding a XaaS Blueprint

We will now add a simple Orchestrator workflow as a vRA Catalog item. We will add the example workflow `00.00 BasicWorkflow`.

1. Log in to vRA with a user who is a service architect.
2. Navigate to **Design** | **XaaS** | **XaaS Blueprint** and click on **New**.
3. Select the workflow `00.00 BasicWorkflow`. On the left-hand side, you will see all in- and out-parameters of the workflow. Click on **Next**.

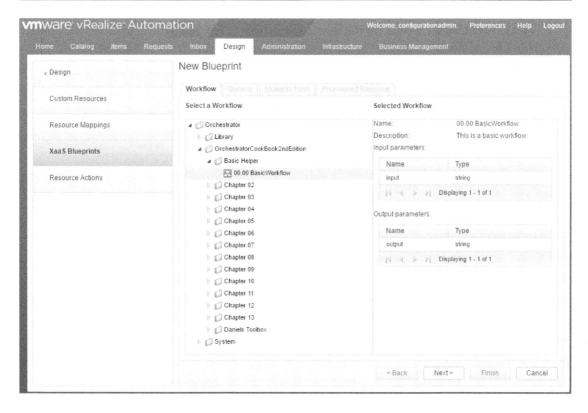

4. You can now change the display name of the workflow as well as modify the **Description** and the **Version** fields. Click on **Next**.

5. The Blueprint form allows you to modify the presentation screen. A detailed discussion is beyond the scope of this book, so see section *How it works...* for more details. For now, just click on **Next**.

6. You are now asked what you would like to provision. As we did not define any custom resources, you can only choose **No provisioning**. Click on **Finish**.

Publishing and adding the workflow to the catalog

We will now publish this workflow and then add it to the catalog:

1. Navigate to **Design** I **XaaS** I **XaaS Blueprint**, click on the service Blueprint that you created in the last section, and then select **Publish** (the green-colored tick).

2. Now, navigate to **Administration** I **Catalog Management** I **Catalog Items**. The service Blueprint can now be seen. Click on it and select **Configure** (a gray gear icon).

3. You can now change the icon that will be displayed with the Catalog item. This icon will always be an Orchestrator Item, and it has no connection to the workflow item in the Orchestrator Client.

4. Select the **Status** as **Active** to make it usable in the catalog.

5. Select a **Service** to attach (not **<None>**) and then click on **OK**:

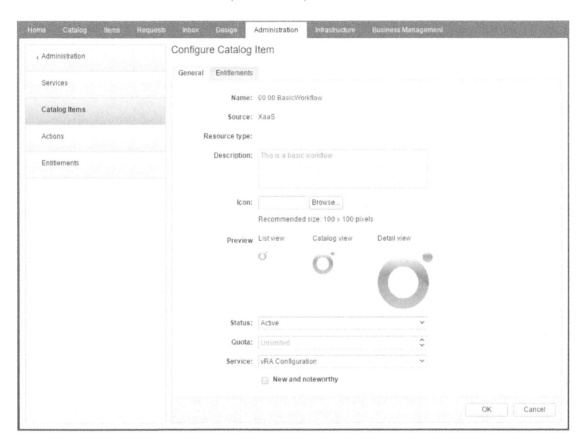

6. Now, go to the **Catalog** tab and take a look at the result:

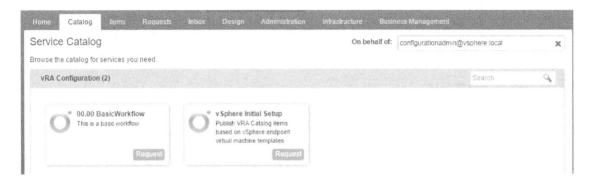

You can now **Request** this Catalog item, which results in the workflow being executed. Check the Orchestrator Client for the result.

How it works…

This is a very simple integration of a workflow with vRA, but it shows the power of the whole concept and the possibilities.

In this example, we have just used a simple workflow that doesn't interact with any infrastructure. In the *Managing AD users with vRA* recipe in this chapter, we will use a more elaborate setup; however, the principle is the same for all workflow interactions.

If the workflow you are executing uses a customer interaction, you can find and start the interaction by clicking on your inbox.

Orchestrator presentation properties in vRA

The Orchestrator presentation properties that you have set up will be working in vRA with the following exception:

- Hide a page
- Show root element

Check out the example workflow 07.05.01 Presentation Test to test this.

Managing AD users with vRA

In this recipe, we will explore the full spectrum of the Orchestrator/vRA integration. You will learn how to create custom resources and actions and how to integrate and use them.

Getting ready

In order to add an Orchestrator workflow as a vRA Catalog item, you should have the following vRA items configured:

- Entitlements
- Services
- Business groups

To configure these items, please refer to the link shown in the introduction of this chapter or take a look at the official VMware documentation for vRA.

The **Design** tab must be activated as shown in the *Integrating Orchestrator workflows as XaaS Blueprints* recipe in this chapter.

You also have to add the AD endpoint as shown in the *Adding an Orchestrator endpoint* recipe in this chapter, and the AD endpoint needs to be configured with SSL for this recipe to work.

How to do it...

We have split this recipe into multiple sections. Work though them one after another.

Creating a custom resource

We will first need to create a custom resource, which makes it possible for vRA users to manage their resources:

1. Log in to vRA with a user that is a **XaaS Architect**.
2. Navigate to **Design** | **XaaS** | **Custom Resources** and click on **New**.
3. Start typing `AD:User` in the **Orchestrator Type** field. You will see how the field's selection is reduced. Click on **AD:User**. This is the Orchestrator variable type we will add to vRA.

4. Give this resource a name under which it will be shown in vRA, such as **AD User**, and then click on **Next**.

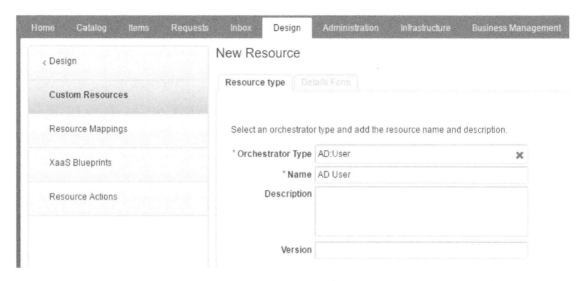

5. The **Details Form** shows all attributes of the variable type we just defined. We need to delete the **Category name** attribute as it can't be used in vRA. Hover the mouse to the right on the **Category Name** field and click on the red X sign.
6. Finish the setup by clicking on **Finish**.

Creating the service Blueprint

Next, we will create the service Blueprint to create a new AD user:

1. Follow the *Integrating Orchestrator workflows as XaaS Blueprints* recipe in this chapter to add a service Blueprint with the following changes.
2. Use the workflow by navigating to **Library** | **Microsoft** | **Active Directory** | **User** | **Create a user with a password in a group**.

3. In the **Provisioned Resource** tab, select the custom resource (**AD User**) that you have created.

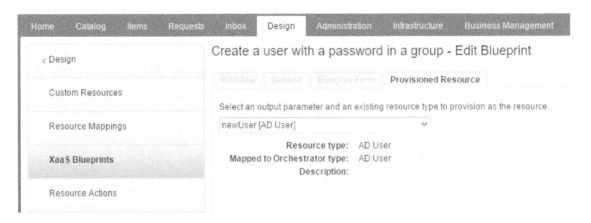

Don't forget to add the Blueprint to the catalog.

Creating a resource action

We will now create a resource action and bind it to an entitlement:

1. Navigate to **Design** | **XaaS** | **Resource Actions** and click on **New**.
2. Select the workflow by navigating to **Library** | **Microsoft** | **Active Directory** | **User** | **Change a user password** and click on **Next**.
3. As **Resource type**, select the custom resource that you created, as **Input parameter**, select **user**.
4. In the **Details** screen, you can just accept the default settings by clicking on **Next**.
5. You can now change the form with which a user will interact. Click on **Add** and finish creating this action.
6. Now, publish this action by clicking on **Publish**.
7. Navigate to **Administration** | **Catalog Management** | **Entitlements**.
8. Click on your entitlement and edit it.
9. Under **Items & Approvals** in **Entitled Actions**, add the custom action you have just created. Click on **Finish**.

Conducting a test run

We will now start a test run to see what we have achieved and how it works:

1. Go to your vRA catalog and request the service Blueprint that you have created.
2. Wait a minute until it is finished.
3. Click on **Items** and you will find a new item: the user you have just created.
4. Click on the user and select **Actions**. You will find the custom action you created here:

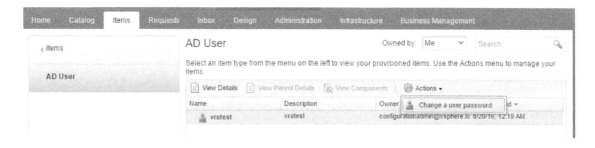

How it works...

This example shows how powerful the Orchestrator integration in vRealize Automation has become.

A custom resource is simply an Orchestrator plugin type that you reuse as a resource and that can be managed and worked with using custom actions. Please note that the request and approval mechanism of vRA can also be used to regulate the use of custom actions and Blueprints.

You can leverage any Orchestrator plugin type to manage its life cycle from vRA or you can create your own type using the Orchestrator Dynamic Types.

Using the Event Manager to start workflows

With vRA7.1, Stubs are deprecated and will be soon gone. The Event Broker is the new way of interacting with the vRA life cycle.

Getting ready

We need a connection to vRA as an Infrastructure Admin.

We also need an Orchestrator client open and ready.

To fully try this recipe out, you will need a working Blueprint that deploys a VM.

How to do it...

This recipe is split into several sections. In this recipe, we will only activate the event subscription for the event when a VM is provisioned.

Create a workflow

We now need a workflow we can trigger when the VM is deployed. (You can also use the example workflow `13.03 EventBrokerTest`):

1. Go to the Orchestrator Client and create a new workflow.
2. Add an input called **payload** of type **Properties**.
3. Add a scriptable task with the following code:

```
for each (key in payload.keys) {
   System.log(key + " : " + payload.get(key));
}
var lifecycleState = payload.get("lifecycleState");
for each (key in lifecycleState.keys) {
   System.log("Life "+key + " : " + lifecycleState.get(key));
}
var machine = payload.get("machine") ;
for each (key in machine.keys) {
   System.log("Machine "+key + " : " + machine.get(key));
}
var properties = machine.get("properties") ;
for each (key in properties.keys) {
   System.log("Props "+key + " : " + properties.get(key));
}
```

4. Save and close the workflow.

Seting up the Blueprint

We need to add some custom properties to the Blueprint so that we get a lot more data to play with.

1. Log in to vRA as an Infrastructure Admin.
2. Go to **Design | Blueprints** and edit your existing Blueprint.
3. Click on your VM and add a **Custom Property** as follows with the **Value** of * (star):

`Extensibility.Lifecycle.Properties.VMPSMasterWorkflow32.MachineProvisioned`

4. Now add a second **Custom Property** `proptest` with the **Value** `false`.

5. Click on **Finish** to save the changes to your Blueprint.

Subscribing to an event

We now link the workflow to the event. To do so, follow these steps:

1. Go to **Administration** | **Events** | **Subscriptions**.
2. Click on **New** to generate a new event subscription.
3. Select **Machine provisioning**.
4. Select **Run based on conditions**.
5. Expand **Data** and then the **Lifecycle** state, and then choose **LifecycleState Name**.
6. Choose **Equals** and then select
   `VMPSMasterWorkflow32.MachineProvisioned`.
7. Click on **Next** and then select the workflow you created.
8. Click on **Finish**.
9. Now select the Subscription you created and click on **Publish**.

Try it out

1. Request the Catalog item from the Blueprint you altered.
2. Watch what's happening in Orchestrator.
3. Check the variables and try to find the property `protest`.

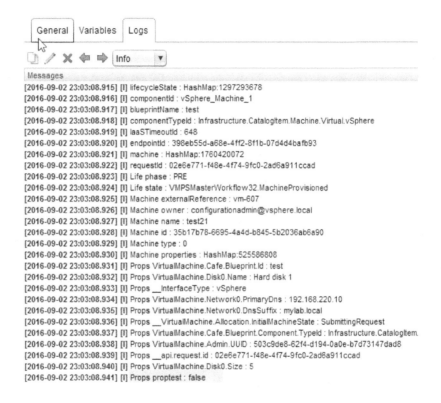

How it works...

The Event broker is a powerful tool that lets you really explore the full possibilities of vRA.

Adding properties to a Blueprint or other areas makes it possible for you to steer your programming. For instance, you can now check if the `proptest` property is `true`, and if it is, you could run a workflow on it.

There are a lot more, 33 in total, different events you can subscribe to; here are some of the ones that you will properly use a lot:

- `VMPSMasterWorkflow32.Requested`
- `VMPSMasterWorkflow32.WaitingToBuild`
- `VMPSMasterWorkflow32.BuildingMachine`
- `CloneWorkflow.CloneMachine`
- `CloneWorkflow.CustomizeMachine`
- `CloneWorkflow.InitialPowerOn`
- `CloneWorkflow.CustomizeOS`
- `CloneWorkflow.BuildComplete`
- `VMPSMasterWorkflow32.BuildingMachine`
- `VMPSMasterWorkflow32.MachineProvisioned`
- `VMPSMasterWorkflow32.MachineActivated`
- `VMPSMasterWorkflow32.DeactivateMachine`
- `VMPSMasterWorkflow32.UnprovisionMachine`
- `VMPSMasterWorkflow32.Disposing`

There's more...

If you want to see all events and properties, follow these steps:

1. Create a workflow with the following code:

```
function getSubproperties(subject,prop){
   for each (subkey in prop.keys) {
     subcontent=prop.get(subkey);
     if ((typeof subcontent) == "object"){
       getSubproperties((subject+"/"+subkey),subcontent);
     } else {
       System.log((subject+"/"+subkey) + " : "
       + subcontent);
     }
   }
}

for each (key in payload.keys) {
   content=payload.get(key);
   if ((typeof content) == "object"){
     getSubproperties(("/"+key),content);
   } else {
     System.log("/"+key + " : " + content);
   }
}
```

2. Add the custom property
   `Extensibility.Lifecycle.Properties.VMPSMasterWorkflow32` to your
   Blueprint.

3. Subscribe the workflow you created to all events.

Index

4

4K display scaling
  working 58

A

Access points configuration, via REST
  reference 428
access, to local filesystem
  configuring 68
  fast and easy 68
actions
  creating 245, 246, 455
  implementing, into workflow 247
  linking, in presentations 216
  undeleting 170
  working 248
Active Directory (AD)
  preparing, for SSL 389, 390, 391
  registering, with Orchestrator 391, 392
  working with 389, 393
AD users, managing
  custom resource, creating 502
  resource action, creating 504
  service Blueprint, creating 503
  test run, conducting 505
  with vRA 502, 506
Advanced Service Designer (ASD) 482
AMQP host
  adding 402
AMQP
  messages, receiving 404
  policy, using as trigger 404
  queue subscription 404
  references 409
  working with 401, 405, 406
appliance's PostgreSQL

database, creating in 372
approval process, VM provisioning
  building 476
  building, with email 478
  building, with user interaction 477
  building, with we 478
array methods 230
array of properties 231
arrays 204, 227
asynchronous workflows
  example 255, 257
  using 255
  working 258
attachments
  working with 337
attributes 179, 180
authentication methods
  Basic 355
  Digest 355
  Kerberos 355
  None 355
  NTLM 355
  OAuth 355

B

backup, Orchestrator
  Cron job 91
  external databases 91
  internal database, backing up 89
  Orchestrator configuration, backing up 88
  vRO Control Center API 92
  vRO policy 91
basic authentication
  versus Kerberos authentication 383
Basic decision 189, 192
binds
  defining 403

Blueprint
  setting up 507
breakpoints 169

C

camelCase convention 180
central management 105
Certificate Authority (CA) 70
certificates
  creating 75
  generating, with alternative names (SAN
    certificate) 76
  importing 76
  signing 76
cluster design 102
cluster upgrade
  about 127
  major upgrades 127
  minor upgrades 127
CMDB (Content Management Database) 331
command
  executing, as root 345
configuration management database (CMDB) 371
configurations
  creating 310, 311
  reading 313
  using, in workflows 311, 312
  working with 310, 312, 313
Control Center API
  about 98
  accessing 293, 294
  system properties 98
Control Center titbits
  about 92
  Control Center user name, changing 95
  File System Browser 96
  system properties 94, 95
  workflows, inspecting 92, 94
Control Center
  working 97
control workflows
  creating, for Remote Orchestrator 294
create statement
  versus prepare statement 372
credentials

changing, during runtime 218
CRUD 376
CSV files 345
Custom Attributes
  about 468
  creating 463, 464, 467
Custom decision 190, 193
custom events
  receiving 252
  sending 252, 253
  waiting for 252
  working 254
custom validation
  creating 215

D

database
  creating, in appliance's PostgreSQL 372
date tasks 250
Decision activity 191, 193
decision loop
  about 200
  do-while 204
  example 203
  for 204
  while-do 204
decision
  Basic decision 189
  Custom decision 190
  scripting with 188
  Switch element 192
  working 192
default certificates
  backing up 75
default error handler 197
directory
  creating 342, 343
  deleting 342, 343
  renaming 342, 343
distributed design
  about 103
  geographically distributed 104
  logically distributed 104
  scaling out 105
Distributed Logical Router (DLR) 418

distributed port groups
  workflow functions, creating 458
domain manager 102
dynamic binding 211

E

e-mails
  sending 333
  working with 332, 336
E4X XML 366
E4X
  reference 366
element
  tagging, manually 314
embedded workflows
  presentation settings, reusing 175, 176
error handling
  about 198
  in workflows 195, 196
errors
  ignoring, in workflows 198
ESXi host
  GET query, sending to 395
ESXi servers
  configuring, for SNMP 400
Event Manager
  used, for starting workflows 506
event variable 330
exception 198
exchange type
  direct 407
  fanout 407
  headers 407
  topics 407
exchanges
  defining 403
external authentication
  configuring 31, 32
  internal LDAP 38
  LDAP 35, 36
  SSO (legacy) 33
  test login 38
  vRealize Automation (vRA) 32
  vSphere (PSC), setting 32
  working 37

external database
  configuring 26, 27, 28
  database roles 29
  exporting 29
  importing 29
  purging 30
  sizing 29
external events 254
external Orchestrator
  authentication, basic method 492
  authentication, single sign-on method 492
  building 490
  configuring 491
  configuring, for each Tenant 491
  configuring, in vRA 490
  connecting 491
  general Orchestrator, configuring 491
  working 492

F

failed workflows
  resuming 164
features, vSphere 6
  Linked Cloning 447
  vAPI 447
  vSAN 447, 448
file operations 339
file
  creating 342, 343
  creating, by uploading resource 307
  deleting 342
  information, obtaining on 342
  reading 341
  renaming 342, 343
  writing 340
Foreach element 204
Foreach loop 202

G

GET query
  sending, to ESXi host 395
GET request
  using 351
global tag 317
Guest Operations

about 469
example run 475
installation workflow, creating 472
using 469
waiting workflow, creating 470
working 476

H

handle error element 199
Hands-on-Labs, VMware
reference 413
help task
creating 249
High Availability (HA) 448
hMailServer 332
reference 338
Horizon 7 plugin
reference 420
Horizon Client
integrating, into vSphere Web Client 426, 427
Horizon integration
about 420
access point configuration 425
basic setup 420, 422, 423
example, running 423, 424
Horizon plugin
VRA integration 427
working 426
HTTPFUL
reference 300, 302

I

in-parameter 180
iNet 418
input variables 299
interaction workflow
creating 263
internal PostgreSQL 31
items
searching, in Orchestrator API 240

J

Java Database Connector (JDBC) 367
Java, tuning
about 64, 65

JVM metrics, in Control Center 65
JavaScript complex variables
about 227
arrays 227
objects 229
properties 228
JavaScript style guide
reference 248
JavaScript tags 318
JavaScript
basics 223
if and else 194
loops 205
reference 223
special statements 235
Switch statement 195
tricks and tips 223, 225, 226
JDBC connection URL
creating 367
JDBC connection
closing 369
opening 369
JDBC
used, for creating SQL queries 371
used, for executing SQL statement 369, 370
JSON object
creating 233, 234, 235
modifying 234
reference 233
JSON REST returns
parsing 233
JSON return 299
JSON, elements
number 234
string 234
value 234
JSON
working with 232

K

Kerberos 67
Kerberos authentication
configuring 66, 67
using 379
versus basic authentication 383

Key Distribution Center (KDC) 67

L

LAMP stack, from Turnkey
  reference 301
language packs
  about 304
  creating 322, 323
licensing, Orchestrator 12
Linked Cloning 447
load-balanced Orchestrator cluster
  with vCenter web client 125
load-balancing Orchestrator
  about 116, 117
  health checks 120
  load-balancer, configuring 119
  new NSX Edge, creating 117, 118
  pools, configuring 121
  SSL certificates 124
  SSL certificates, dealing with 119
  virtual server 121, 122
  working 123
localization 322
lock
  checking for 319
  creating 319
locked object
  unlocking 320
Locking System
  about 304
  using 318
  working 321
locking, phases
  checking 319
  locking 319
  unlocking 320
log elements
  altering 187
log event
  categories 186
log files
  checking 185
log location file 187
logs
  creating 184

scripting with 183
working 186
loops, JavaScript
  for 205
  for each 205
  while 205
loops
  decision loop 200
  Foreach loop 202
  scripting with 200
  working 203

M

mail connection
  configuring 332
Managed Object Browser (MOB)
  reference 445
Managed Object Reference (MoRef) 444
Management Information Base (MIB) 397
Microsoft SQL 30
Microsoft System Center Virtual Machine Manager
  (SCVMM) 46

N

non-administrative access
  disabling, to Orchestrator 276
Notes field 467
NSX integration
  about 413
  endpoint, configuring 413
  logical switch, creating 415, 416
NSX plugin
  reference 413
  vRealize Automation integration 417
  working 417
NTLM (NT LAN Manager) 388

O

Object Identifiers (OIDs) 397
objects
  about 229
  strings, turning into 238, 239
ONGL (Object-Graph Navigation Language) 212
Onyx project
  reference 453

Oracle 31
Orchestrator API
  items, searching in 240
  programming help 241, 243, 244
  working with 240, 244
Orchestrator appliance, tuning
  about 60
  IP and hostname, changing 61
  root account expires setting 63
  SSH access, turning on and off 62
  time (NTP), setting 61
  unneeded services, switching off 62
  Virtual Hardware 61
Orchestrator appliance
  basics 13, 14
  Control Center, logging in 19
  deploying 15, 16, 18, 21
  downloading 15
  Orchestrator Client, logging in 18
  working 20
Orchestrator certificates
  CA-signed certificate 73
  default SSL certificate 73
  PEM encoded files 74
  self-signed certificate 73
  VMCA 74
Orchestrator Client
  4K display scaling 57
  about 137
  auto-setup parameters 140
  General section 278
  gotchas 139, 140
  icons 138
  Inventory 279
  script editor section 280
  workflow settings 278
Orchestrator cluster
  building 106
  configuring, in vSphere 110
  content, changing 114
  example workflow 116
  failover, simulating 111
  first node, configuring 107
  load-balancing method 115
  node, joining 109, 110

node, removing 115
  Orchestrator Client, using 114
  preparation work 107
  prerequisites 106
  push configuration 112
  settings, changing 115
  settings, configuring 108
  SSL Certificates, in vRO7.1.0 114
  working 113
Orchestrator Control Center
  accessing, via REST plugin 292
Orchestrator elements
  exporting, steps 149
  importing 149, 150
  importing, steps 149
  object, exporting 149
  synchronizing, between Orchestrator servers
    134, 136
  working 151
Orchestrator endpoint
  adding 495, 496
Orchestrator log files
  about 77
  accessing, via SSH 79
  log file behavior, changing 80
  server log, configuring with Control Center 78
  server log, in Control Center 77
Orchestrator Log Insight Agent
  configuring 86
Orchestrator logs, redirecting to external server
  about 82
  Log Insight agent 84
  Syslog, with Log4J 83
  vRealize Log Insight 82
Orchestrator presentation properties
  in vSphere Web Client 285
Orchestrator REST API
  accessing 286
  accessing, PHP used 300
  documentation, accessing 287
  interactive REST request 288
  play mode, enabling 287
  working 291
Orchestrator service SSL certificate
  CA-signed certificate 72

configuring 70
self-signed certificates 71
VMCA generated certificates, using 71, 72
Orchestrator settings
about 22
force plugins reinstall 25
licensing 23
Orchestrator service, restarting 22
Orchestrator service, starting 22
Orchestrator service, stopping 22
Packaging Signing Certificate 24
trusted SSL certificates 25
working 25
Orchestrator version control
about 141
reverting, to older versions 144
using 142
version differences, comparing with 143
working 144
Orchestrator workflows integration
Advanced Services tab, activating 498
prerequisites 497
XaaS Blueprint, adding 498
Orchestrator workflows
adding, to catalog 499, 501
integrating, as XaaS Blueprints 497
Orchestrator workflows, integrating as 497
output, obtaining 298
publishing 499, 501
running, PowerShell used 296
Orchestrator, and Avamar
reference 357
Orchestrator, and NSX
reference 357
Orchestrator, and Nutanix PrismAPI
reference 357
Orchestrator, and vCNS (vShield)
reference 357
Orchestrator, and VEEAM backup
reference 357
Orchestrator
about 269, 270
Active Directory (AD), registering with 391, 392
adding, as infrastructure endpoint 493, 494
and vRA 14

backup 87
connecting, to vCenter 40
licensing 12
login format 275
moving from Windows, to appliance 51
non-administrative access, disabling to 276
reference 384
restore 89
restore process 87
SQL DB, adding to 374
typical error messages 276
updating 48
using, through vSphere Web Client 280
vRA instance, automating 487
OTP
download link 407
out-parameter 181

P

packages
deleting 156, 157
export options 159
exporting 153
import options 159
importing 154, 155
importing, from remote 157, 158
new package, creating 153
working 158, 159, 160
working with 151, 152
Per User Session 360
PHP
used, for accessing Orchestrator REST API 300,
301
plugin-specific properties, workflow presentations
authorized only 215
root object, specifying in chooser 214
select value as 214
show in inventory 214
plugins
disabling 47
installing 44, 45, 46, 411
obtaining 412
plugin log level 46
uninstalling 47
updating 47

VMware core plugins 412
policies
  about 304
  used, for trapping SNMP messages 396, 397
  working with 323, 324, 325, 326, 327
policy templates 328
POST request
  using 352, 353
PowerCLI
  reference 384
PowerShell host
  adding 378
  script, calling 380
  script, executing 380
  script, sending 380
PowerShell output
  converting, into XML 383, 384
PowerShell script
  action, generating from 380
  running, with input 298
  workflow, generating from 380
PowerShell
  about 66
  reference 384
  used, for running Orchestrator workflows 296
  using 382
  working with 376
prepare statement
  versus create statement 372
presentations
  about 183
  actions, linking in 216
private tag 317
program installation
  reference 469
properties
  within properties 231
property 228
PSC (Platform Controller Service) 71

Q

queues
  defining 403

R

RabbitMQ
  download link 407
  installing 407
  reference 401
recovery
  vCloud Air, using for 432
regular expressions
  reference 215
remote Orchestrators
  managing 128
  Orchestrator server, adding 129, 130
  packets, managing 131
  proxy workflows, creating 130
  working 132
resource element
  creating 306
Resource Tuner
  URL 57
resources
  about 304
  accessing, directly 309
  adding, manually 305
  deleting 309
  updating 307
  using, in workflows 305
  working with 304, 305, 308
REST host
  connecting to 350, 351
REST operation
  workflow, creating from 353
REST outbound, for Orchestrator workflow
  reference 442
REST plugin
  Control Center, accessing via 292
REST request
  results, viewing 356
REST
  working with 350, 355
restore, Orchestrator 89, 90
return values
  dealing with 360
  phrasing 354
root

command, executing as 345

S

SAN (Subject Alternative Name) 124
schema
  working with 182
SCP (Secure CoPy)
  using 348
scripting tasks
  A - show all objects 222
  B - find stuff 222
  C - line and character 222
scripts
  executing 344
Security Support Provider (SSPI) 388
self-signed certificate 71
shared directories 344
Shared Session 360
Sleep task
  using 250
SNMP devices
  configuring 394
SNMP messages
  policies, used for trapping 396, 397
  receiving, from vCenter 396
SNMP return data
  working with 398
SNMP
  configuring, for vCenter 399
  ESXi servers, configuring for 400
  port 162, versus port 4000 398, 399
  references 401
  working with 394, 397
SOAP client
  adding 385
SOAP request
  invoking 387
SOAP workflow
  generating 387
SOAP
  reference 385
  working 388
  working with 385
special statements, JavaScript
  function statement 237

try, catch, and finally statement 235
SQL (JDBC)
  working with 367
SQL DB
  adding, to Orchestrator 374
SQL plugin
  working with 373, 374, 376
SQL query
  creating, JDBC used 370
  running 375
SQL statement
  executing, JDBC used 369, 370
  running 375
SQL
  reference 373
SRA (Storage Replication Adapter) 434
SRM (Site Recovery Manager) integration
  preparation 434
SRM (Site Recovery Manager)
  about 434
  configuration 434
  reference 434
  vRealize Automation integration 437
  vSphere Web Client integration 437
  working with 435, 436
SSH
  using 346
  working with 346, 349
SSL certificates, and load-balancing
  about 124
  SSL offload 124
  SSL passthrough 124
  SSL SAN (SSL passthrough) 124
SSL key authentication
  using 347
SSL store password
  obtaining 75
SSL
  Active Directory (AD), preparing for 389, 390, 391
standard vSwitch ports
  and Distributed Switch port differences, issues 454
static binding 211
strings

turning, into objects 238, 239
Swagger spec URL
  using 354
Switch element 193
System Center Configuration Manager (SCCM)
  382
System Center Operations Manager (SCOM) 382
System Center Virtual Machine Manager (SCVMM)
  382

T

tagging 314
tags
  about 304
  viewing, in workflow 316
  workflows, finding by 317
  working with 314, 317
triggers 328
Turnkey LAMP
  obtaining 302

U

update process, Orchestrator
  about 48
  applying 49
  ISO file, using 48
  VMware repository, using 49
  working 50
user interactions
  answering 265, 266
  answering, vRealize Automation (vRA) used 268
  answering, vSphere Web Client used 267
  creating 262
  working with 266, 267
user management
  about 270
  access right 275
  access, configuring to Orchestrator elements
    272
  non-administrative users access, giving to
    Orchestrator 271
  right inheritance 273
  rights for sub-elements 274
  same user - two groups 273
  user rights, editing 273

  visibility 274
user preferences 276, 277

V

vAPI plugin
  content, exporting 461
  metadata, importing 460
  reference 463, 468
  using 460
  vCenter endpoint, configuring 460
  working 462
vAPI tagging 468
variable types
  any 181
  boolean 181
  credential 181
  date 181
  encrypted string 181
  NULL 181
  number 181
  secure string 181
  string 181
variables
  about 179
  in general section 180
  in input section 180
  in output section 181
vCenter alarms
  reference 395
vCenter API
  working with 448, 449, 452, 453, 454
vCenter automation
  wait actions 446
vCenter connection
  access 43
  configuring 40, 41, 42
  logging 43
  rights 43
  technical user 43
vCenter tags
  creating 463
vCenter wait action
  Vim3WaitDnsNameInTools 446
  Vim3WaitForPrincipalIP 446
  vim3WaitToolsStarted 446

WaitTaskEndOrVMQuestion 446
vCenter
  configuring, for sending SNMP message 395
  SNMP message, receiving from 396
  SNMP, configuring for 399
vCloud Air target
  configuring 432
vCloud Air
  reference 428
  using, for recovery 432
vCloud Automation Center (vCAC) 481
vCO Team
  reference 412
VIX 469
VM provisioning
  approval process, building 476, 479
VMCA (VMware Certificate Authority) 71
VMware core plugins
  about 412
  reference 412
VMware documentation, for Horizon plugin
  reference 428
VMware Hands-on Labs
  reference 484
VMware MIBs
  download link 397
VMware Solution Exchange
  about 413
  reference 413
vRA instance
  automating, in Orchestrator 487
  configuring 487
  example, running 488
  working 489
vRA-integrated Orchestrator Client
  accessing 485
vRA-integrated Orchestrator Control center
  starting 485
vRA-integrated Orchestrator
  database 486, 487
  users 486
  working 486
  working with 484
vRealize Automation (vRA)
  about 11, 37, 481

and Orchestrator, working 482
external Orchestrator, configuring 490
installation 484
installation link 488
Orchestrator presentation properties 501
tuning 485
used, for answering user interactions 268
used, for managing AD users 502
used, for starting Event Manager 510, 511
vRealize Operations Manager (vROPS) integration
  about 437
  files, deploying 438, 439
vRealize Operations Manager (vROPS)
  actions 442
  reference 438
  working 442
  working with 440, 441
vRealize Orchestrator 7
  changes 12
vRO/vCO Team 412
vRO7 11
vSphere Authentication 37
vSphere automation
  about 444
  vCenter MoRef 444, 445
  vim3WaitTaskEnd action 445, 446
vSphere Replication
  exploring 428
  recovery 430
  reference 429
  replication, setting up 430
  sites, registering 429, 430
  vSphere Web client integration 433
  working 431
vSphere Standard license 12
vSphere tags
  creating 465, 467
vSphere Web Client
  Horizon Client, integrating into 426, 427
  used, for answering user interactions 267
  workflows, configuring for 281, 282
vSphere
  about 443
  automation 443, 444
vSwitch port 458

W

waiting tasks 249, 251
web integration
  workflows, writing for 284
Windows host
  preparing, with WinRM 377
Windows Orchestrator installation, moving to
    appliance
  about 51
  external database 53
  migration tool 52
  package transfer 54
Windows Remote Management (WinRM)
  about 376
  Windows host, preparing with 377
workflow debugging function
  using 167, 168
workflow functions 459, 460
workflow presentations
  about 206
  basic linking 211
  description 208
  general properties 212
  groups 209
  in-parameter properties 208
  input values, hiding 210
  plugin-specific properties 213
  preparation 207
  steps 209
  working 211
workflow TLC 382, 383
workflow tokens
  scripting with 259, 260
workflow
  about 179
  actions, implementing into 247
  actions, modifying 145, 146
  actions, moving 146, 147

actions, renaming 146, 147
auto documentation 162, 163, 167
configurations, using in 311, 312
configuring, for vSphere Web Client 281, 282
creating 457, 507
creating, from REST operation 353
elements, modifying 145
error handling 195, 196
errors, ignoring in 198
finding, by tag 317
linking, to event 508
parameters, modifying 145, 146
receiving 335
related elements, finding 147, 148
resources, using in 305
running 283
scheduling 171, 173, 174
tagging 315, 316
tags, viewing in 316
undeleting 170
working 148
writing, for web integration 284
WYSIWYG 212

X

XaaS (Everything as a Service) 482
XML document
  creating 361, 364
XML methods 365
XML structures
  parsing 364
XML
  PowerShell output, converting into 383, 384
  reference 361
  working 365
  working with 361
XSD, for Orchestrator API
  reference 292

46677811R00309